**ARCHITECTURE AND DEVELOPMENT**

# ARCHITECTURE AND DEVELOPMENT

AYALA LEVIN

Israeli Construction in Sub-Saharan Africa
and the Settler Colonial Imagination, 1958–1973

DUKE UNIVERSITY PRESS   DURHAM & LONDON   2022

© 2022 Ayala Levin

This work is licensed under a Creative Commons Attribution-NonCommercial-NoDerivatives 4.0 International License, available at https://creativecommons.org/licenses/by-nc-nd/4.0/.

Designed by Aimee C. Harrison
Typeset in Warnock Pro and Univers LT Std by BW&A Books

Library of Congress Cataloging-in-Publication Data
Names: Levin, Ayala, [date] author.
Title: Architecture and development : Israeli construction in Sub-Saharan Africa and the settler colonial imagination, 1958–1973 / Ayala Levin.
Description: Durham : Duke University Press, 2022. | Includes bibliographical references and index.
Identifiers: LCCN 2021020438 (print)
LCCN 2021020439 (ebook)
ISBN 9781478015260 (hardcover)
ISBN 9781478017882 (paperback)
ISBN 9781478022503 (ebook)
ISBN 9781478091820 (ebook other)
Subjects: LCSH: Architecture—Africa, Sub-Saharan—History.
| Jewish architects—Africa, Sub-Saharan—History—20th century.
| Technical assistance, Israeli—Africa, Sub-Saharan. | Urbanization—Africa, Sub-Saharan. | Architecture—Political aspects—Israel.
| Israel—Foreign relations—Africa, Sub-Saharan. | Africa, Sub-Saharan—Foreign relations—Israel. | BISAC: HISTORY / Africa / General
| HISTORY / Middle East / Israel & Palestine
Classification: LCC NA1591.65 .L485 2022 (print) | LCC NA1591.65 (ebook)
| DDC 720.95694—dc23
LC record available at https://lccn.loc.gov/2021020438
LC ebook record available at https://lccn.loc.gov/2021020439

Cover art: Photograph of University of Ife, early 1970s. Photographer unknown. Source: Amos Spitz collection.

Duke University Press gratefully acknowledges UCLA, Architecture and Urban Design, which provided funds toward the publication of this book.

This book is freely available in an open access edition thanks to TOME (Toward an Open Monograph Ecosystem)—a collaboration of the Association of American Universities, the Association of University Presses, and the Association of Research Libraries—and the generous support of Arcadia, a charitable fund of Lisbet Rausing and Peter Baldwin, and the UCLA Library. Learn more at the TOME website, available at: openmonographs.org.

TO NIV AND NOLA

## contents

ACKNOWLEDGMENTS ix

1  **introduction**  Settler Colonial Expertise in the Theater of Development

25  **chapter one**  Fast-Tracking the Nation-State: The Design and Construction of the Sierra Leone Parliament

68  **chapter two**  Rootedness and Open-Ended Planning: The Sierra Leone National Urbanization Plan

97  **chapter three**  Planning a Postcolonial University Campus: The University of Ife, Nigeria

125  **chapter four**  Designing the University of Ife: Climate, Regeneration, and Ornament

165  **chapter five**  Israeli Aid, Private Entrepreneurship, and Architectural Education in Addis Ababa

195  **postscript**  Ghosts of Modernity

NOTES 219
BIBLIOGRAPHY 269
INDEX 295

# acknowledgments

COMPOSING THESE NOTES during the COVID-19 pandemic deepens my appreciation of the intellectual community that sustains prolonged efforts such as writing a book—and renders them worthwhile. From its beginning as a seminar paper, *Architecture and Development* has owed its formation at every step to an always converging and diverging circle of friends and family, mentors and colleagues, institutions and fellow travelers.

Originating during my doctoral studies at Columbia University's Graduate School of Architecture, Planning and Preservation, this book was born out of the camaraderie of mentors—most notably Felicity D. Scott, Reinhold Martin, and Gwendolyn Wright—and peers, among them Ginger Nolan, María Gonzáles Pendás, Marta Caldeira, and Peter Minosh, whose brilliance, rigor, and constant challenging of architectural history's boundaries and stakes shaped the intellectual environment that fostered this project. Conversations with Hannan Hever on the study of Zionist ideology have had a major impact on this work. Impassioned debates with Neta Feniger and Anat Mooreville, both of whom worked on closely related subjects, helped refine my arguments.

Other mentors, colleagues, and friends have graciously read parts of the manuscript in various stages of its development and offered their keen observations and unique forms of expertise. Among them are Daniel Monk, Suzanne Preston Blier, Louise Bethlehem, Eitan Bar-Yosef, Michael Osman, Arindam Dutta, Eszter Polonyi, Gabriella Szalay, Ran Zwigenenberg, Martin Hershenzon, Abraham Rubin, Shirly Bahar, Abou B. Bamba, and Bronwen Everill. Bruno Carvalho, Alison Isenberg, Lucia Allais, Cyrus Schayegh, Aaron Shkuda, Sarah Lopez, Megan Eardley, Susanne Schindler and Helene Nguyen provided helpful feedback during a fellowship at the Princeton-Mellon Initiative in Architecture, Urbanism and the Humanities. My former colleagues in the art history department at Northwestern University, especially Hannah Feldman, Jesús Escobar, Christina Normore, and Holly Clayson, provided a supportive environment and shrewd advice when I was in the final stages of writing this book.

I tested out many of the ideas in this book at various conferences and talks, and the conversations these occasions prompted have helped shape and nuance them. These gatherings included meetings of the Society of Architectural Historians, the European Architectural History Network, the Association for Jewish Studies, and the Urban History Association, as well as the conferences "Crossing Boundaries: Rethinking European Architecture beyond Europe" in Palermo, "Theoretical Currents: Architecture, Design and the Nation" at Nottingham Trent University, "Zionism as a Cultural Movement" at Brown University, "Whose Interests? Exploring Middle East Involvement in Africa" at the Afro-Middle East Center, Pretoria, and "What Is the Urban? Registers of a World Interior" at Iowa State University. Provocative and useful discussions also took place following talks I gave at the Graduate School of Architecture, Planning and Preservation and the Department of Middle Eastern, South Asian, and African Studies at Columbia University, Princeton University's School of Architecture, the University of South Africa, the Technion, the Hebrew University of Jerusalem, and the Department of Politics and Government at Ben-Gurion University. Among the many scholars who convened these productive exchanges or provided important feedback are Mark Crinson, Charles L. Davis II, Alona Nitzan-Shiftan, Andrew Herscher, Haim Yacobi, Ross Exo Adams, Keller Easterling, Łukasz Stanek, Rachel Kallus, Kim de Raedt, and Tom Avermaete. Conversations with members of the Aggregate Architectural History Collaborative, and specifically Meredith TenHoor, Zeynep Çelik-Alexander, Daniel Abramson, and Ijlal Muzaffar, have pushed the conceptual boundaries of this work.

Research for this book was funded by the Social Science Research Council International Dissertation Research Fellowship, the Temple Hoyne Buell Center for the Study of American Architecture, and the Institute for Religion, Culture and Public Life at Columbia University. I am grateful for the assistance of archivists at the Israel State Archives, the Lavon Institute for Labour Research, the National Archive of Nigeria in Ibadan, the National Archives of Sierra Leone, the Institute of Ethiopian Studies, and the Planning Department Archive at Obafemi Awolowo University. Of special note is Anat Drenger of the Azrieli Architectural Archive Collection, who most generously and enthusiastically made the papers and drawings of the Arieh Sharon estate accessible to me even before the archive opened to the public. I also appreciate the tips and advice Haggai Erlich and Fasil Giorgis shared with me about research in Ethiopia, and Lynn Schler about research in Nigeria. Cordelia Osasona, Nnamdi Elleh, Amos Spitz, and Otitoola Olufikayo provided tremendous help and opportunities that facilitated my research in Nigeria, and the same is true for Shraga Israel and Rama Musa in Sierra Leone. My research assistants Tiwaloluwa Oluwamuse Osasona and Joseph Ayodokun Titowa helped me navigate the institutional complexity of archives in Nigeria with determination and ease.

I am grateful to the many people whom I interviewed for this project and their families, including: Zalman Enav, the late Michael Tedros, the late Zvi Meltzer, the late Ram Karmi, the late Harold Rubin, Tommy Leitersdorf, Habte G. Indrias, Jack Shelemay, Miriam Keini, Peter J. Kulagbanda, Joseph Mouna, Christopher Bankole Ndubisi Ogbogbo, Michael A. O. Johnson, Olu Wright, Zvi Szkolnik, the late Tamar Golan, Rivka Feldhai, and Yoram Feldhai. It has been an especially heartwarming experience to have Pe'era Goldman, Naomi Halachmi, and Nili Schreiber-Vernick open their homes to me and trust me with the family archives of their uncle and father, Eliezer Schreiber.

The publication of this book has been supported by the UCLA School of the Arts and Architecture. Parts of chapter 1 have been published in "Prefabricating Nativism: The Design of the Israeli Knesset (1956–1966) and the Sierra Leone Parliament (1960–1964)," in *Israel as a Modern Architectural Lab, 1948–1978*, edited by Anat Geva and Inbal Ben-Asher Gitler (Bristol, UK: Intellect Books, 2019), and parts of chapter 5 appeared in "Haile Selassie's Imperial Modernity: Expatriate Architects and the Shaping of Addis Ababa," *Journal of the Society of Architectural Historians* 75, no. 4 (December 2016): 447–468. The book has enjoyed the careful stewardship of Elizabeth Ault at Duke University Press, and Michelle Niemann's perceptive language editing. Raia Levin, my mom, always the nurturer, and Nathan Eden provided much-needed space for a writing retreat at a crucial moment in the book's production. Finally, this book is dedicated to Niv Klainer, whose critical outlook and unrelenting love sustained this journey, and to Nola, whose coming into this world set me the harshest and most joyful deadline.

# introduction

Settler Colonial Expertise in the Theater of Development

FIGURE I.1
Queen Elizabeth II, accompanied by Prince Philip, discussing the Sierra Leone parliament building model with architect Zvi Meltzer, November 1961. The wig of an unknown member of Sierra Leone's new parliament is visible to Meltzer's right. Courtesy of Zvi Meltzer.

IN A PHOTOGRAPH depicting the Israeli architect Zvi Meltzer presenting a model of the Sierra Leone parliament building to the queen of England, another figure standing between the two is barely visible and recognizable only by his British-style wig: a member of Sierra Leone's newly founded parliament (fig. I.1). What can we make of this strange triangular constellation that comprised the queen of England, the Israeli architect, and the anonymous Sierra Leonean parliament member? On the face of it, this triangulation might seem to represent the smooth transition from colonial to neocolonial forces in Africa, with new actors like Israel gaining a foothold in the postcolonial development market via technical aid.[1] But such an analysis only further obscures the Sierra Leonean member of parliament and what he represents—the key role that African elites played in the development of their countries after independence, as initiators of projects such as the Sierra Leone parliament building. These African elites often chose to commission, when they could, not English or French construction companies but instead companies from Israel and other countries that presented an alternative to the colonial powers in the region.

While both the Israeli architect and Sierra Leone's member of parliament still sought the warmth of the queen's approving gaze, their partnership in fact transgressed old colonial hierarchies. Sometimes over British objections, Israeli officials established relations with Britain's West African colonies even prior to independence by offering them the services of the Israeli construction company Solel Boneh, as well as those of other governmental companies. Solel Boneh, whose name means "Paves-Builds," was owned by the Histadrut, the General Federation of Laborers, a cooperative organization established in 1920 that laid the foundations for the Israeli state's institutional infrastructure and political leadership in its first decades of statehood.[2] Solel Boneh established local partnerships with African governments and executed these governments' most prestigious projects, often commissioning Israel's best-known architects for them. In Sierra Leone, the Israeli company had won its bid for the parliament project over the much better financed and locally experienced general contractor, the British firm Taylor Woodrow. Behind the smiles posed for the camera was a queen who had to step over the rubble that the Israeli managers had left on the site, perhaps slowly reckoning with her diminishing authority in a postimperial age.

Challenging the prevailing understanding of development discourse as homogenous and of the development expert as disembodied technocrat, this book calls attention to what has been long overlooked in development scholarship, just as it is obscured in the photo.³ That is, in the competition over development aid in Africa, incited by decolonization and shaped largely by the politics of the global Cold War, new centers of knowledge production emerged and, with them, the opportunity for African governments to negotiate with various aid donors and choose the forms of aid—and by extension the forms of modernity—that they desired. Though these choices were shaped by Cold War politics, they were not completely determined by them, as the competition over aid allowed room for sophisticated maneuvering even between countries associated with the same bloc.⁴

The "golden age" of Israeli-African relationships from 1958 to 1973, whereby Israel sought to gain support at the United Nations against the Arab League's pressures, coincided with optimistic development plans that African governments carried out with the support of foreign aid.⁵ "The Development Decade," as the Kennedy administration named the 1960s, marked the transition of British, French, and Belgian colonies in Africa to independence, and abundant faith—domestic and international—in the new nations' economic and social development, perceived as the interdependent and inevitable product of modernization. During that short but intense period, many international players, old and new, competed over this newly opened development market that had previously been monopolized by colonial powers. Whether acting as proxies for the new superpowers or assuming an independent position such as that offered by the Non-Aligned Movement, these new players included, besides Israel, West Germany and the German Democratic Republic, North and South Korea, Poland, Hungary, Bulgaria, Romania, the Scandinavian countries, Yugoslavia, Egypt, India, Cuba, and China.⁶ This multiplicity of exchanges presses us to consider aid relationship beyond an assumed binary by which donor countries represent the Western "developed world," and recipients the non-Western "developing world." By focusing on exchanges between African states and Israel—which was itself a "developing country" during this period—this book introduces a third category between the global North and the global South that complicates existing narratives of development and directs attention to the diverse social and political stakes that undergirded north-south exchanges.⁷

Architecture offers a unique lens for examining this complex history. While it was by no means the only field in which Israel offered development aid, its hypervisibility and its confluence of aesthetics and governing politics provides a rich archive for deciphering the material and discursive practices that informed the Israeli-African exchange. This book presents an in-depth analysis of prestigious governmental projects in Sierra Leone, Nigeria, and Ethiopia, demonstrating how architectural aid operated at interlocking scales, mediating both between international institutions and governing elites and between governing elites and domestic stakeholders, and how it connected individual buildings to broader transformations of cities and regions. By focusing on Sierra Leone's parliament building and national urbanization plan, the University of Ife (today Obafemi Awolowo University) in Nigeria, and the Ethiopian Ministry of Foreign Affairs and the Filwoha Baths in Addis Ababa, Ethiopia, this book offers both an architectural history of development aid and a development aid history of architecture.

This introduction lays the groundwork for the book's analysis by examining how Israel self-fashioned its geopolitical position with respect to African governments and how the state structured its aid as "cooperation." This analysis pertains mainly to the early years in the formation of these relations up to the mid-1960s, the period in which most of the projects discussed in this book were completed. Since my focus is on how Israel staged itself as a new center of knowledge production that could circumvent international professional hierarchies, I then proceed to how it turned its settler colonial experience into development expertise that could be exported to other developing countries. I situate this turn in the crisis of "pioneering" that Israeli society faced during its transition from voluntary society to statehood. Before concluding with an overview of the chapters that describes how Israeli architects performed this expertise in the context of the conditions they encountered in African countries, I develop the conceptual framework of "development theater" to account for the complex dramaturgy of aid among donors and recipients, and the role architectural modernism assumed in it.

Israel and Africa: "Cooperation," Not Aid

After a visit to Israel in 1957, John Tettegah, the secretary general of Ghana's trade union movement, declared, "Israel has given me more in eight days than I could obtain from two years in a British university." Similarly, Tom Mboya, the Kenyan trade unionist, commented, "Any African who tours Israel cannot fail to be impressed by the achievements made in such a short time from poor soil and with so few natural resources. We all tended to come away most excited and eager to return to our countries and repeat all those experiments."[8] As these two quotes demonstrate, Israel's appeal to African leaders was rooted in speed—both how quickly Israel had developed and how quickly African countries could do so following its model. Tettegah's and Mboya's emphasis on the temporality of development attests to a fundamental turn in postcolonial development thinking. Encompassing industry, agriculture, infrastructure, health, and education, African postcolonial development plans often continued late colonial development plans. Yet in their unprecedented comprehensiveness, scale, and funding, they marked a decisive shift from the "not yet" approach that characterized colonial rule. Measuring the colonies with a universal yardstick of development, this approach served to justify colonial presence even during later stages of decolonization.[9] With the emergence of "development" as an object of modernization theory following World War II, inherent causes, whether environmental or racial, could no longer explain "backwardness" and legitimize the perpetuation of external rule. The new developmental narrative postulated latecomers' ability "to catch up," and thereby align themselves with "universal history" as recorded and narrated by the West, via the omnipotence of science and technology, rational economic planning, and social engineering.[10] As Michael Adas explains, this narrative involved compressing the time required for development from centuries to decades, and transferring agency from the Western powers whose civilizing, paternalistic approaches had characterized colonial rule to Africans and Asians themselves.[11] While the United States was the main exponent of this modernization theory, which was based on its historical experience in the late nineteenth century, Israel presented African states with a more tangible example of such a "leap"—a contemporaneous test case that proved the theory. To be sure, Israel's model of development, as well as that of most of the African countries it aided, adhered to the same universal history yardstick and enjoyed Western patronage. But while European and American histories rested on centuries or decades of such historical progress, Israel's emergence on the world stage in 1948 presented a moving picture of development in the making—an acceleration of history that could be emulated and repeated elsewhere.

For African leaders, aid did not mean showering gifts on passive recipients. Nor, as Frederick Cooper has argued, did independence turn late colonial political and economic entitlement into supplication.[12] In 1964, G. Odartey Lamptey, Ghana's representative in Washington, explained that in order to maintain its independence Ghana preferred to accept loans rather than gifts:

> Loans with interest payable, and technicians loaned to a developing country with the receiving country paying much of their upkeep are not aid in the restrictive sense. As far as the Government of Ghana is concerned only a very insignificant amount of the cooperative assistance it had received from other countries could be considered outright gifts with no chance of gain of the giving country . . . we are appreciative of the technical skills that we have acquired with the cooperation of other peoples but most of these things are joint projects and the gain goes both ways.[13]

As Lamptey made clear, Ghana wished to be perceived as a partner worth investing in, not a charity case. African recipients did not expect or desire development aid prompted by disinterested philanthropy, but rather wanted aid to derive from business and diplomatic interests that would prove mutually beneficial. From these relationships, Israel hoped to gain not only support at the UN, where the anticipated decolonization of African states presented a lucrative field of diplomatic opportunity, but also access to raw materials, a large market for its trade in arms and other goods, and the chance to gather intelligence on the Arab League via its African activities.[14] Moreover, Israel used its influence in Africa to assert its own significance to Western countries, particularly the United States, while the African countries hoped to have influence in Washington via Israeli channels.[15] If anything, these relations were based on mutually agreed upon "contractual dependency."[16] This contractual dependency, in the case of the joint companies Solel Boneh established with African governments, was limited to specified periods of management and skill transfer, which relieved African governments of the fear of prolonged interventions. Attentive to these anxieties, Golda Meir, then the Israeli foreign minister, explained, "We'll look for the most professional people available, but development of Ghana can be carried out only by the Ghanaians themselves."[17] Similarly, the foreign ministry's Department of International Aid and Cooperation, which grew out of the Section for Technical Cooperation that Meir had established in 1958, was renamed the Department of International Cooperation (Mashav) in 1961 to avoid the patronizing connotations of the word "aid" itself.[18] This strategy proved successful. By the end of 1962, Israel had twenty-two embassies in Africa, and by 1973, over three thousand Israeli experts had worked in the continent.[19]

While Israel's extensive efforts to establish relations with African countries are often attributed to Meir's term as foreign minister from 1956 to 1966, it was David Hacohen's experience in Burma in 1953–54 under Moshe Sharett, Meir's predecessor, that consolidated Israel's unique approach to aid in practice. A leading figure in the Jewish settlement in Palestine, Hacohen was nominated to serve as Israel's first envoy in a Third World country—"a guinea pig in the Jungle," as he put it—where he devised the basic principles of Israeli aid.[20] Recognizing that the development market, once freed from colonial monopolies, would have significant economic and diplomatic potential, Hacohen emphasized the urgency of entering it before other major players did. He also stressed the need to involve Israeli public or semipublic companies, specifically Solel Boneh and the Israel Military Industries (Ta'asia Tzvait), rather than private firms. Hacohen's final principle, designed for speed, was that local workers from the country in question should be brought to Israel for training, while Israeli personnel set up the companies that would employ those workers in the recipient country.[21]

Before becoming a parliament member and diplomatic envoy in Burma, Hacohen laid the foundations for Israel's architectural role in Africa as managing director of Solel Boneh. Established in 1924 as a subsidiary of the Histadrut, Solel Boneh played an instrumental role in demarcating the territory of the Jewish settlement and facilitating the New Jew's occupational shift from commerce to manual labor.[22] In addition to projects initiated by Zionist organizations, Solel Boneh carried out public works for the British mandate government. In this dual capacity, it collaborated with the British Empire in Syria, Lebanon, Egypt, Iraq, Iran, Bahrain, and Cyprus, even while defying the British in clandestine operations toward Zionist ends, as in the case of the Tower and Stockade operation (1936–39).[23] As such, Solel Boneh exemplifies the complex positionality of the Jewish settlement in Palestine, which benefited from and collaborated with the British Empire but also undermined its authority when Britain acted against Zionist interests. A cartoon about Solel Boneh's work under the British in Abadan, Iran, portraying a Jewish worker crouching as an army of British officers looms over him, demonstrates the Jewish settlers' understanding of themselves as anticolonial (fig. I.2). With the establishment of Israel, Solel Boneh's power multiplied, as it reasserted its national role in industrialization by creating jobs, training thousands of immigrants, building New Towns for a growing population, and offering services such as financing, credit, marketing, and transportation. Within a decade, however, it became clear to the Histadrut—backed by the Labor government, which sought to encourage private investment—that they needed to contain the company's expansionist but often economically risky logic.[24] In 1958, Solel Boneh was subdivided into three functional units: Building and Public Works, Koor Industries and Crafts, and Overseas and Harbour Works.[25] This move, I propose, was meant to contain Solel Boneh domestically while relegating its expansionist logic to Third World countries, where its ability to mobilize manpower and execute complex tasks under strenuous conditions could be put in service of Israeli diplomacy.

To gain a competitive edge over other donor countries, most of which could afford to provide considerably more financial assistance and well-established know-how, Israel positioned itself as a fellow postcolonial developing country—a feat perhaps made more difficult by its association with former colonial powers through its role in the 1956 Suez Crisis. Israel's foreign ministry capitalized on the narrative of racial oppression,

FIGURE I.2  A Solel Boneh cartoon of the work it did for the British Army in Abadan in 1943–45, depicting British supervision as an army of taskmasters dwarfing the Hebrew laborer. Courtesy of the Labour Movement Archives, Lavon Institute for Labour Research, Tel Aviv, IV 320-6.

Diaspora, and national-cultural rejuvenation that Pan-African intellectuals such as Edward Blyden and Marcus Garvey shared with Zionist thinkers in the late nineteenth and early twentieth centuries. Like the latter, they conceived of repatriation as a condition for African racial, political, and spiritual regeneration.[26] This intellectual connection not only ensured that the educated African elite accepted the Israeli foreign ministry's rhetoric but also attracted the advocacy and concrete help of contemporary intellectuals such as George Padmore, a leftist journalist and Ghanaian prime minister Kwame Nkrumah's advisor, who assisted Golda Meir in her initial diplomatic steps in Africa.[27] This intellectual connection may also explain why the first country to host an Israeli military-diplomatic display on the continent was Liberia, itself a repatriate settler colonial state. On April 18, 1955, the exact date that the first Afro-Asian conference opened in Bandung, Indonesia, the Liberian honorary guard welcomed an Israeli warship to Monrovia's shores.[28] This was a highly symbolic gesture for both parties: Israel's attempts to participate in the first Afro-Asian conference had been thwarted, and while Momolu Dukuly, the Liberian foreign minister, attended the Bandung conference, his country affirmed relations with Israel despite its exclusion. Moreover, in the wake of the Holocaust, Israel's narrative of how the Jewish people's racial oppression led to national sovereignty differentiated it from most European countries and the United States, whose own contemporaneous social and political struggles over race were being exploited by the Soviet Union to frustrate American diplomatic efforts in Africa. To secure its own independent postcolonial image, Israel distanced its aid from American institutions such as the Ford and Rockefeller Foundations.[29] While it is suspected that Israel's aid was at times secretly funded by the United States and at least once by Germany, and while Israel was willing to coordinate its aid with the British Commonwealth or France, it did not abide their dictates when they were against Israeli interests.[30] In practice, Israeli architects, planners, and companies sometimes collaborated with consultants from the US Agency of International Development (USAID), as in the planning of the University of Ife in West Nigeria, or established partnerships with American private investors, as did Solel Boneh's Reynolds company, which worked extensively in Ethiopia.

While associated with the Western bloc, Israel's official stance in relation to the Cold War was neutral. Israel's neutrality and the labor movement's hegemony in the country offered African leaders a "third way" between communism and capitalism, without the strings that the superpowers attached to their aid. In addition, Labor Zionism's "constructive socialism," which married class interests with national causes, appealed to African governments, many of which had grown from the ranks of trade unions, as the Israeli ruling party Mapai had in the years before Israel's statehood. Labor Zionism's subsumption of trade union loyalty to state-building tasks presented a seemingly viable model for countering Africans' entrenched distrust of governmental authority due to generations of colonial rule.[31] In addition to the social cause of labor solidarity that was sometimes compared to African communitarianism, Israel's experience in forging a coherent—albeit exclusively Jewish—national identity despite the varied origins of its immigrants, and in relation to the broad Jewish Diaspora, also resonated with African governments facing similar challenges.[32]

Certainly, these concerns were not shared equally among the leadership of all African countries. The three African countries discussed in this book—Sierra Leone, Nigeria, and Ethiopia—presented various governance challenges rooted in their divergent histories. Sierra Leone gained independence from Britain in 1961, and its newly elected government used Israeli architectural aid to help unite a country divided culturally and economically by its history of African settler colonialism and the consequent British colonial divide between direct and indirect rule. In the nineteenth century, Sierra Leone played an important role in West Africa: it was home to liberated African slaves and boasted the first university in the region. By the mid-twentieth century, however, its glory as the "Athens of Africa" had completely waned, as its inland population gained political dominance over the Krio descendants of liberated slaves, thus reversing the former settler colonial power balance. Israeli architectural aid attempted to provide both the symbols to support this new cultural hegemony, as well as the means to achieve it through labor mobilization and the territorial distribution of the population.

Much larger in size and diplomatic importance, Nigeria consisted of three self-governing regions that corresponded to its major ethnic groups when it gained independence from Britain in 1960. Nigeria's regions used Israeli aid in their competition over the allocation of resources in the country's federal system. The Muslim-dominated north refused direct Israeli aid. The eastern region—whose secession in 1967 led to the Nigerian Civil War, also known as the Biafran War—evoked the Holocaust in its pleas for military and humanitarian aid, pressing Israel to act on its stated ideology at an inconvenient time, as Israel had diplomatic relations with Nigeria's federal government.[33] The western region, which is the focus of this book, used Israeli architectural aid to advance higher education in direct defiance of the federal government's recommendations.

Unlike the two West African countries, Ethiopia was occupied only briefly by Italy in the mid-1930s, followed by British occupation during World War II. With the wave of decolonization in the continent, imperial Ethiopia capitalized on its long history as a Christian monarchy to become a symbol of African independence, in a regional competition with Egyptian president Gamal Abdel Nasser, who had growing influence in the continent. In Ethiopia, as in other East African states, Israel's explicit strategic goal was to secure regional alliances with non-Arab states, such as Turkey and prerevolutionary Iran, which resulted in a periphery pact all countries signed in 1958. Ethiopia used extensive Israeli military and intelligence aid, as well as aid in civilian fields, to bolster its own territorial ambitions in neighboring Muslim countries Eritrea and Somalia, as well as to curb civilian unrest within its growing educated class. As these snapshots show, in these three cases neither were the goals of development aid unified nor were its political ideologies consistent. To explain how Israeli experts could promote African imperialism in Ethiopia on the one hand, while defending a nativist hegemony in Sierra Leone on the other, we now turn to the settler colonial roots of Israel's development aid expertise.

Settler Colonialism as Development Expertise

Israeli development aid emerged in conjunction with the crisis of "pioneering" in Labor Zionism, as Israel transitioned from voluntary society to statehood. With the era of voluntary settlement coming to an end, Israel's first prime minister, David Ben-Gurion, attempted to institutionalize "pioneering" as part of his new doctrine of *mamlakhtiut*.[34] Among its various characteristics, mamlakhtiut sought to preserve the pioneering zeal that had characterized the heretofore voluntary society by transforming it into a mobilizing force that would unite veteran and new immigrants around a national sense of purpose. Perhaps surprisingly, international development aid was one of these national causes. In 1959, Ben-Gurion announced that the peoples of Asia and Africa "desire rapprochement not because we are rich in possessions that enable us to influence them, but because they view the spiritual values enshrined in Israeli *halutziut* [pioneering] as worth learning."[35] Coupling aid with pioneering, Ben-Gurion and others in the labor movement constructed Israeli aid in the Third World as a continuation of Zionist prestate pioneering tasks. Imbuing aid with such spiritual and moral values can be interpreted as a means of alleviating the fear that once Zionism had achieved its teleological aim—that is, national sovereignty—Israel would become "a nation like all nations" and Zionism would be divested of its moral purpose.

As a settler colonial project that aimed to extinguish its colonial character, Zionism successfully naturalized itself as a sovereign nation.[36] Yet it was precisely the success of the Zionist colonial project in establishing Israel's boundaries as a sovereign nation that was at the heart of the country's postindependence crisis. As Adriana Kemp has shown, until 1967 Israeli borders operated both as an icon that unified the nation within and as a porous frontier for military border crossing.[37] If Jews who had recently emigrated from North Africa were forced to serve the settler project as a civilian shield in the country's periphery, then military operations served as an outlet for a desire to transgress the border, which was construed not as a fixed entity but as one that needed to be perpetually sealed against Palestinian return. Since these borders seemed temporary and ambiguous, citizenship could not be defined only by rights, but had to be undergirded by a sacrificial settler voluntarism. If border crossing served to hone the military and intelligence expertise that Israel also deployed in its military aid in some African countries, then nonmilitary aid presented a civilian form of border crossing. The restructuring of Solel Boneh and relegation of its prestate colonial expertise to postcolonial governments can be considered one manifestation of this crisis, as it served to contain the company's unruly behavior within Israel while unleashing its expansionist drive overseas. This civilian border crossing allowed Israeli professionals to continue refining their settler colonial expertise in development, while providing an outlet for the country's surplus of "development experts."[38]

The idea that Jewish settlement in Palestine might be beneficial to Africans stretches back to a seminal text in the birth of Zionism, Theodor Herzl's 1902 utopian novel *Altneuland*. While others have pointed to this work in connection with Israeli diplomacy in Africa, they have not attended to the assumptions embedded in the novel's imagined forms of knowledge production or examined how it envisions the forms of knowledge produced by Jewish colonization as benefitting Africans.[39] In the key passage on the subject, one of the protagonists, a bacteriologist named Professor Steineck, declares that once the Jewish problem is resolved, it will be time to attend to the "Negro problem."[40] Steineck, who set up a research institute in Palestine modeled after the Pasteur Institute in Paris, hoped to find a cure for malaria to allow for mass repatriation of diasporic Africans, while also promoting this as a measure to relieve unemployment in Europe by facilitating white settler colonialism in Africa.[41] In this succinct example, Herzl, the visionary of Political Zionism, shifted the center of colonial knowledge production from European metropoles to the Jewish settlement in Palestine, where the experimental medicine was to be tested locally before being exported elsewhere in the Southern Hemisphere.

Unlike the form of imperial science Herzl advocated, however, Labor Zionism privileged the laborer-pioneer over the scientist, and concrete action in the harsh conditions of the field over experimentation in a sterile lab.[42] Although the two were in fact complementary, as the history of malaria eradication demonstrates—the scientists needed the pioneers just as the pioneers needed the scientists[43]—this ideological position helped Labor Zionist settlers disavow the colonial character of their project. Fields that require an unmediated familiarity with conditions on the ground, such as construction, made this disavowal possible. Contemporaneous publications on knowledge transfer from Israel often emphasized Israeli experts' personal and social qualities—such as unpretentiousness and a "hands-on" approach, the ideal characteristics of the Zionist settler-pioneer—as much as their technical knowledge.[44] Such qualities did not simply complement technical expertise, but rather conditioned it, since experts produced knowledge by facing unprecedented challenges, such as a difficult climate, lack of natural resources, and the conditions of warfare. At the same time, these qualities conveyed the informal, down-to-earth, and nonhierarchical character of Israeli experts in the social sphere of labor relations with African workers.[45] Inflected by a minority consciousness and a sense of a corrective historical mission, Labor Zionist settlers rationalized practices that reimagined the diaspora Jew as a new man, while dispossessing the Palestinians of their lands.[46] Development aid was one of the conduits through which the Israeli Labor government sought to sustain this disavowal, despite the fact that it had turned about 800,000 Palestinians into refugees following the 1948 Arab-Israeli War, and had subjected many of the 160,000 who remained within Israeli borders to military rule, which lasted until late 1966, just a few months before the Israeli occupation of the West Bank and the Gaza Strip began.[47]

In conceptualizing settler colonialism as a repressed imaginary that informed practices of foreign aid, this book draws from Megan Black, who argues that the US Department of the Interior's "institutional memory rooted in conquest" undergirded not only its technocracy for managing Indigenous Americans and domestic natural resources but also its involvement in the Point Four aid program.⁴⁸ International relations historian Odd Arne Westad similarly argues that the Cold War superpowers extended the "deep structures" of their ideologies to the global arena as an extraterritorial continuation of their civil wars.⁴⁹ Like Black and Westad, I argue that Labor Zionist settler-pioneer ideology was the deep structure undergirding Israel's foreign policy. However, rather than interpreting this continuity as ideologically consistent, as both Black's and Westad's arguments might imply, I interpret it as an anachronistic attempt, in the face of domestic and international crises, to restore Israel's imagined prestate past as a pioneering and just society, however selective this vision of "justice" was. As we shall see in various examples throughout this book, the labor invested in holding on to prestate practices and values reveals the contradictions embedded in this anachronism.

Considering Israeli development thinking in African countries in terms of settler colonial expertise sets this book apart from the growing critical literature on Israeli-African aid relationships, as well as from scholarship on Israel's contemporaneous export of architecture and urban planning models to the Middle East.⁵⁰ While scholars such as Haim Yacobi, Eitan Bar-Yosef, and Rivi Gillis have identified "pioneering" as a central trope in Israeli aid to Africa, and Bar-Yosef has tied the latter to the Israeli crisis in pioneering, they have not considered "pioneering" a settler colonial mode of professional expertise.⁵¹ The most extensive study of the spatial imaginary of Israel's relations with Africa to date, of which two chapters are dedicated to the export of Israeli architectural and planning expertise to Africa, is Haim Yacobi's *Israel and Africa: A Genealogy of Moral Geography* (2016). Focusing on the state period, this study does not take into account the decades of prestate settler colonialism that provided the state with its institutional and physical infrastructure. Beginning with the state as point zero runs the risk of reifying the very myth of exceptionalism Israel tried to promote—that of becoming a "development miracle" in just a decade. *Architecture and Development* demonstrates that Israeli architecture, as a profession, cannot be separated from the settler colonial experience that shaped it into a crucial instrument in the projects of "the conquest of labor" (*kibush ha'avoda*) and "the conquest of wasteland" (*kibush hashmama*), the founding myths of Zionist settler colonialism.⁵² This historical consideration of the architectural profession in Israel helps refine our understanding of architects' perceptions of the conditions they encountered in Africa beyond the generalized colonial imaginary of terra nullius that Yacobi invokes.⁵³ Moreover, while Yacobi acknowledges Israel's unique geopolitical positioning, his analysis predetermines Israeli-African relations by arguing that by joining the Western "donor club," Israel could perpetuate its self-image as "a Western, modern, white state."[54] This explanation might be overdetermined by Israel's current unequivocal association with the United States—an alliance that was fully consolidated only in 1967. Even if plausible, this account does not explain how Israeli architects differentiated their expertise from that of former colonial powers, and does not attend to the multiplicity of actors who made up this so-called donors' club in the context of a new geopolitics in which modernity was no longer exclusively the purview of the West. Lastly, as the title of Yacobi's book in Hebrew, *Kan lo Africa* (It Is Not Africa Here), suggests, it is primarily concerned with the effects of these relations on the Israeli imaginary. In contrast, my work aims to situate these relations in the concrete conditions Israeli architects encountered in the African countries where they worked.

While Israeli architects did export Zionist settler colonial practices to African countries, their interventions did not assume the extension of Israeli settler colonialism to African territories, nor did they prefigure post-1967 colonial relations. By asking what African elites were interested in emulating, how Israeli architects translated their experience to conditions in Africa and responded to other aid donors' complementary or competing models, and how the architectural results differed from both their Israeli precedents and African elites' expectations, this work complicates scholarly understanding of Israel's export of its settler colonial model, which can explain only part of the multifaceted exchange. The "theater of development," the concept I introduce next, helps us analyze the role of architecture and architectural expertise in this exchange in the specific context of the Cold War development race, and against the backdrop or active influence of competing actors and stakeholders.

Theater of Development and Architectural Modernism

Within the complex geopolitical dramaturgy of the competition over aid, Israeli actors' portrayal of themselves as anticolonial was a performative stance that had real effects regardless of their sincerity.[55] This applies as much to actors from other competing donor countries as to those from recipient African countries who solicited their aid. Just as the authenticity of Israel's position is beside the point, so it is reasonable to assume that African leaders' warm statements about Israel were equally performative. As Jean-François Bayart has argued poignantly, Africans "have been active agents in the *mise en dépendance* of their societies."⁵⁶ Rejecting a dichotomy between collaboration with or resistance to international forces, Bayart explains that African dependency is a strategy of extraversion "astutely fabricated as much as predetermined," designed to exploit the resources of (in)dependence.⁵⁷ The issue at stake is not the extent of these states' autonomy in relation to international forces, but rather how they took hold of and mobilized resources to accommodate local interests.⁵⁸

I use the term "development theater," on the one hand, to underscore the geopolitical stakes of aid exchanges through an intentional echo of the military expression "theater of war," and, on the other, to highlight the complex mise-en-scène produced by the performances of human and inanimate actors. While development was performed by an international network of governments, institutions, and professionals both within and beyond its African locales, I use the theater metaphor, with its suggestion of a bound space, in order to examine these architectural objects in relation to their local effects and the forms of modernity that they aimed to produce. The theater metaphor also describes the nexus of human and inanimate actors more accurately than the term "development industry" coined by James Ferguson, since it acknowledges the active engagement of both producers and consumers of architecture as signs of modernity as well as the performative capacities of the objects produced.⁵⁹ Furthermore, the self-conscious positionality of the participants in this performance of development, whether as donors or recipients, distinguishes it from "spectacle," a term others have used to characterize African postcolonial modernization.⁶⁰ Calling development a "spectacle" risks reducing African desire for modernity to mere commodity fetishism—a manifestation of false consciousness inflected by the "colonization of the mind." This book instead emphasizes the capacity of subjects to set into motion architectural projects, showing how the role of African commissioners extended beyond passive consumption. Likewise, as "plot motivators," the objects themselves played an active role far beyond that of evoking fetishistic desire. As harbingers of long processes to come, they addressed both domestic and international audiences. Internationally, they represented the donor country's aid relationships—which one Israeli diplomat called "a dam against diplomatic crises"⁶¹—and acted as a catalyst for further foreign investment. Domestically, they represented an independent state's institutions to its own citizens as evidence of the government's ability to fulfill its promises, giving concrete form to the abstract economic and social processes described in dry technical terms in national development plans.

Because of their scale and aesthetic qualities, architectural objects played a significant role in making aid visible. In terms of form, these projects were conceived in relation to an existing repertoire of images of modernist architecture and planning that circulated in the media, and that members of the African elite also saw in person during their education abroad or on professional and political tours. These projects aimed to connect African locales—usually, but not always, capitals—to the international system through an aesthetic language that, for the most part, was based on similarity and virtuosic repetition, not iconic difference.[62] For this reason, there was no contradiction between national aspirations and an international modernist outlook, and no particular insistence on the employment of local architects—in countries where they were available, such as Nigeria—for prestigious governmental projects.[63]

Even if the buildings and development projects were produced not by creative African individuals but by a group of foreign and local stakeholders, they constituted an "ontology of not-yet-being" in the societies in which they were staged. According to Ernst Bloch, the Frankfurt school theorist who coined this term, cultural products such as architecture can carry a utopian imaginary. Even the false promises and false needs produced by advertisements, he argued, can express wishes that subvert the logic of capitalism.[64] Or, as Arjun Appadurai put it, "Where there is consumption there is pleasure, and where there is pleasure there is agency."[65] The temporal disjuncture expressed in Bloch's politics of hope, by which he means the germination of the future in the present, is useful for conceptualizing the tantalizing gap between modernity and modernization in postcolonial societies.[66] From this perspective, even if these architectural objects did not directly express African wishes and desires because they were produced by an international Western-dominated market, they could still function as objects of desire that articulate "a complex configuration of unmet needs" that transgressed material consumption.[67]

To understand how architectural objects translated development into practice, we need to complement and substantiate the analysis of forms with reflection on architectural objects as agents and instruments in the mobilization of resources. Like props in a play—think of Chekhov's gun that must fire in one of the following acts if it appears in the first—architectural objects not only served as a backdrop for the main action of development but also prompted it through the mobilization of workers, international funds, lands, infrastructure, and policy making. While Bayart interprets the African "politics of the belly" as primarily oriented toward access to resources, the architectural objects produced in the first decade of independence served as active agents not only in securing resources but also in mobilizing and distributing them.[68] Rather than focusing solely on form, this study asks how these architectural objects were envisioned to mobilize resources and how these attempts are reflected in their design.

Understanding form in relation to resource mobilization is crucial for articulating the work that the architecture of independence did beyond representation. This is especially significant given the crisis of representation that independence entailed in African countries. According to Mamadou Diouf, if the emblems of colonialism were roads, commerce, and sanitation, then the emblems of independence were schools, community clinics, and electricity.[69] Social welfare and mobility were to be improved by intensifying the focus on infrastructure and government services that had begun during the colonial era, not by discontinuing it. Okwui Enwezor reflected on the elusive character of this transformation: "The distance between colonial modernity and postcolonial modernity is one of degrees, for each incorporates and contradicts the other. Each is a mirror of the other."[70] The modern emblems of African independence thus call for a more subtle reading, one that locates the crisis of representation in the historical impossibility of a radical break from the colonial past.

Even if postindependence projects did not differ in style from the modernism of late colonial ones—and even if the International Style, the lingua franca of architectural modernism, traversed alliances beyond the divide between capitalism and communism—differences among architectural modernism's various enunciations can be found in practice, especially in the choice of materials, labor relations, and the structure of know-how transfer. As Cole Roskam has demonstrated, in the 1960s, Guinea and Ghana employed Chinese construction companies that emphasized process over the finished object and the reuse of materials, conveying these values aesthetically through the material and structural thrift of the buildings.[71] Similarly, Łukasz Stanek has shown how the Ghanaian National Construction Company, which was originally established by Solel Boneh, hired Eastern European architects who provided expertise comparable to that of their Western colleagues but offered a crucial difference at the level of work relations by having them work under Ghanaian administration.[72] Importantly, this focus on practice directs attention to the previously unacknowledged role of construction companies in the mediation between diplomacy and architecture, ideology and development. It also emphasizes how expertise was performed, the final subject to which we turn here.

Performing Expertise

One of the main questions this book asks is how Israeli architects performed and staged their development expertise as adaptable from one context to another, and how this act of translation made Israel's experience particularly relevant to that of other countries. This focus on expertise was perhaps more common when the donor country emphasized the export of personnel over monetary aid, as in the case of Israel. Unlike "professional knowledge," which is codified by technical language and international standards, "expertise," which etymologically derives from experience, can explain how personal biographies affected professional ones and highlight the effects of sociocorporeal experiences on the construction of professional knowledge. Examining professional knowledge and practices in this framework sheds light on aspects of embodied expertise that otherwise cannot be accounted for in purely professional terms.

To attend to how a localized expertise in architectural modernism was made adaptable and relevant to other locations, it is not enough to postulate that architectural modernism has always been cosmopolitan and situated, as Vikramaditya Prakash has compellingly argued; one needs to account for modernism's routes and the various subject positions that architects could assume in its travel.[73] The case of Israeli aid in Africa demonstrates how interstitial colonial positions were used to make claims on expertise in the postcolonial world. Just as in the diplomatic realm, where alternative forms of aid were nuanced versions rather than outright rejections of dominant models, this professional competition did not upset hegemonic frames of reference. The fact that Israeli architects belonged to the first wave of modernism via their education in Central and Western Europe, including in prestigious institutions such as the Bauhaus, gave them a privileged position with regard to firsthand access to knowledge, connections, and early experiences of adaptation.[74] In the postwar period, it also gave them a privileged position in the expanding but racialized and uneven global market for architectural production. Having made one translation from Europe to the Middle East, where they put modern architecture in service of Zionist settler colonialism, Israeli architects were exporting to Africa not an "Israeli architecture" but rather their experience adapting modernism to non-Western locales. The fact that their locally derived expertise could be translated from one location to another demonstrates that situated knowledge not only *can* travel but also,[75] by virtue of its inherent adaptability, can be remade and *re*situated through that travel.

SETTLER COLONIAL EXPERTISE

The chapters that follow trace the adaptation of architectural practices from Israel to Sierra Leone, Nigeria, and Ethiopia, and situate these adaptations against lingering British colonial models or complementary ones from other donor states. Chapter 1 examines the design of the Sierra Leone parliament (1960–61) by acclaimed Israeli architects Dov Karmi (1905–62) and Ram Karmi (1931–2013), a father-and-son team who were concurrently revising the contested design for the Israeli parliament, the Knesset. At the heart of Israel's public debate about the aesthetics of the Knesset was a conflict over how to express Jewish national belonging in the territory, whether through a timeless classicism drawn from British colonialism, or through a dynamic modernism that expressed the Labor Zionist movement. The result was a compromise between the two. This chapter analyzes how the architects translated their Knesset design to the Sierra Leone context by using on-site prefabrication techniques to convey rapid technical development on the one hand, and deep-rooted historical belonging on the other. The chapter then analyzes how local Sierra Leonean media documented the parliament's rapid construction and staged it as a national event that subjugated class interests and ethnic divisions to national causes. As I argue in this chapter, this emphasis on the visibility and performance of labor—something that opening the parliament building before its completion also underscored—articulates a conceptual shift from the colonial sublime, which focused on the completed object as a technological feat and a tantalizing promise for participation in modernity, to a new emphasis on process and the agency of the citizenry in achieving that goal.

Chapter 2 analyzes the national urbanization plan that Israeli urban planner Aryeh Doudai (1911–1982) devised for Sierra Leone in 1965. Unlike the Karmis and Arieh Sharon (1900–1984), the protagonists of chapters 3 and 4, who are famous for designing Israel's foremost governmental, cultural, and educational institutions, Doudai is much less known in Israeli architectural history.[76] Yet he was influential as the chief planner of the Settlement Department of the Jewish Agency in the 1950s and as head of the governmental Institute for Planning and Development, in which capacity he worked in Sierra Leone. Originally conceived as a survey in an attempt to solicit funds from the UN, Doudai's national urbanization plan redefined the entire territory of the country by identifying potential future urban centers in its interior. This plan followed recent planning trends in Israel that directed its legions of immigrants from the urban coasts to newly built towns and villages distributed inland to secure Jewish control over the contested territories following the 1948 war. This chapter shows how Doudai fashioned the plan as decisively postcolonial, despite drawing from British New Towns and German and Italian internal colonization models, which had been adapted in Israel. Unlike its Israeli precedent, however, the Sierra Leone plan did not entail the creation of new settlements in a fixed master plan. Instead, it emphasized open-ended and reciprocal relations between town and country, using the plan as a tool to enhance the Sierra Leone government's administrative power by reinforcing the customary rule of paramount chiefs, who were its main powerbrokers. This chapter shows that the central objectives of the plan, despite its title, were to contain rural-urban migration and secure a rural workforce in the chiefdoms.

Chapter 3 turns to Arieh Sharon's campus plan for the West Nigerian University of Ife (1962–76) as part of a regional competition over the allocation of higher education in the federal state. In an attempt to address the growing needs of the region, the university was to present a semirural democratic alternative to the neighboring federal University College Ibadan, which was established under the British rule in 1948 and followed the Oxbridge model. Devised in conjunction with the production of a postcolonial university curriculum, and in cooperation with USAID consultants, the resulting plan combined the American Land Grant University campus with the planning principles of *kibbutzim* (Zionist agricultural collectives), which Sharon knew well, first as a kibbutz founder and later as a prominent kibbutz planner. As I demonstrate in this chapter, the coupling of kibbutz planning with American rural-suburban landscaping presented a new rural-suburban typology that refashioned the countryside as a modern alternative to the lure of the city, so that it could draw faculty to the semirural area as well as keep students from relocating to major urban centers upon graduation.

Chapter 4 focuses on how Arieh Sharon's team designed the monumental core of the University of Ife campus. While the campus design has received much attention, due in part to Sharon's education in the famed Bauhaus school, the scholarship has mainly focused on the formal aspects of campus buildings.[77] Understanding Sharon's work in relation to his experience as a Zionist settler colonial pioneer allows me to redirect the conversation to the racial thinking that undergirds discourse on climate in the tropics via a comparison with British colonial architecture. As this chapter demonstrates, Sharon emphatically rejected the then-prevailing British colonial tropical architecture approach, epitomized in prominent

British architects E. Maxwell Fry and Jane Drew's design for the University College Ibadan, which focused on the building's envelope as a climatic barrier. To counter this approach, which was originally developed to protect the British military and administration from the tropical climate, Sharon instead proposed a volumetric solution in the form of an inverted pyramid. I argue that this inverted pyramid embodied his Zionist ideal of unmediated relationship with the environment as a condition of the settler becoming a productive New Man, in contrast with the image of the effeminate, degenerate Jew of the diaspora. By linking Zionist discourse on national regeneration to architectural discourse on degeneration in fin de siècle Vienna, this chapter shows how Sharon employed modernist architectural principles to cast the British approach as inhibiting Nigeria's national development.

The first four chapters represent the hegemony of Labor Zionism and its institutions, with which the Karmis, Sharon, and Doudai were associated. Chapter 5, in contrast, considers the entanglement of private interests with those of the state, turning to the prolific design and educational work of Zalman Enav (b. 1928) and his Ethiopian partner, Michael Tedros (1921–2012), in Addis Ababa (1959–66). A generation younger than Dov Karmi, Sharon, and Doudai, Enav established his professional career in Addis Ababa, where he lived for a number of years, in contrast with most of the Israeli architects working in sub-Saharan Africa at that time. Enav designed multiple buildings in addition to teaching in Ethiopia's first architecture department. Unlike the projects described in earlier chapters, which were mediated via state institutions, Enav's practice in Addis Ababa was a private initiative and consequently differed in scope and variety in terms of his effect on the local architectural scene and the development of the city. This chapter narrates how Enav gained access to Addis Ababa's building market via his connections with a Jewish trader's family from Aden in Yemen as well as with the royal family, the Ethiopian government, and Israeli aid personnel.

This chapter demonstrates that although Enav was free from institutional ties to the Israeli government, he took advantage of and promoted strong Israeli trade, military, and diplomatic connections in Ethiopia. Unlike in Sierra Leone and Nigeria, where Solel Boneh established local partnerships with governments and subcontracted prominent Israeli architects for its prestigious jobs, in Ethiopia, where it failed to establish a local partnership, Enav was instrumental in recommending Solel Boneh for jobs he was commissioned for. This chapter considers Enav and Tedros's designs for the Ministry of Foreign Affairs and Filwoha Baths in the context of Haile Selassie's attempts to curb social reform while advancing modernization. I discuss this design activity in relation to the department of architecture in the Israeli-run College of Engineering at Haile Selassie I University, where Enav taught, and which played a role in the competition over higher education aid among Israel, West Germany, and Sweden. The entanglement of private and state interests is further examined in the book's postscript. The liberalization of the Israeli economy in the 1960s shaped the Mayer brothers' entrepreneurial touristic projects in Monrovia, Liberia, and Abidjan in the Ivory Coast, as well as practices of architecture and construction post-1973, in which Labor Zionist modernist aesthetics still continue to reverberate despite their neoliberal context.

As this book emphatically demonstrates, these architectural projects belong to histories of African modernity, even though they were primarily the vision of a Western-educated elite and were designed and implemented by Israeli professionals. Thus *Architecture and Development* challenges the common perception of such objects as foreign intrusions in the African urban landscape. Though materializing an African modernism refracted through a Zionist settler colonial imaginary, the projects discussed in the following chapters articulate a qualified departure from preceding local colonial experiences. Because they operated within a Western epistemology and the international economic system, these projects could not manifest a truly decolonial alternative. And still, as we shall see next, these are not primarily stories of failure but of the hopes and challenges African governments faced in their precarious transition to independence.

# fast-tracking the nation-state

The Design and Construction of the Sierra Leone Parliament

IN A SERIES OF DESIGNS for public buildings in Africa, Asia, and the Middle East, published in 1963 in the *Journal of the Association of Architects, Engineers, and Town Planning* in India, one could find the Israel National Museum in Jerusalem alongside the Fine Arts Building in Baghdad, Iraq, Gandhi's Memorial Museum in Ahmedabad, India, and the Palace of Justice in Mohammedia, Morocco.[1] Israel's inclusion in this new geography of postcolonial nationalism did not end with the showcasing of architecture at home. Among the list of projects was the parliament of Sierra Leone, which was designed by the Israeli architects Dov and Ram Karmi, a father-and-son team, and their partner, Zvi Meltzer (fig. 1.1). As the list of projects demonstrates, Israel inhabited a dual position in the building of the decolonizing world, acting both as a member nation and as an exporter of design and construction to other postcolonial countries.

The ability to perform this dual role only a decade after gaining sovereignty reflects Israel's inherent ambiguity as a settler colonial nationalist project, or a "postcolonial colony," to use Joseph Massad's apt phrase.[2] While the Jewish settlement's efforts to forge solidarities with anticolonial movements, particularly that of Mahatma Gandhi, preceded the formation

FIGURE 1.1 Sierra Leone parliament building (undated). Courtesy of Amos Spitz.

of the state, these were formalized into a foreign policy by the mid-1950s, first in failed attempts in Asia, and then in Africa, following Israel's exclusion from the Bandung Conference in 1955. Israeli politicians and diplomats purported that racial oppression and state building were challenges that Israel shared with African states; they proposed Israel as a neutral ally that could offer African states a developmental path midway between socialism and capitalism without the strings attached by the superpowers. To architects, engineers, and construction managers fell the task of translating these claims into a sociotechnical reality, leading to an aesthetic program that manifested this distinct relationship between social, economic, and nationalist agendas. This chapter brings together the design and construction of the Sierra Leone parliament to reflect on the role of architectural conception in managing the local workforce. While the subjects of design and labor management are typically considered separately, I examine them together here to emphasize how they were interrelated in the practices of Labor Zionist settler colonialism and how both were translated into the conditions of Sierra Leone in its first year of independence.

Dov and Ram Karmi's design for the Sierra Leone parliament was based on their revision of the Israeli parliament, the Knesset, after architect Joseph Klarwein won the competition for its design in 1956. The stripped neoclassical structure in Klarwein's vision generated a heated public debate in the modernist-inclined Israeli architectural community. Under the hegemony of the labor movement, modernist architecture's emphasis on functionalism lent itself to an aesthetics of austerity that not only offered a practical solution to the country's economic conditions but also projected the ethos of self-sacrifice associated with socialist "pioneering." Dov Karmi, who had just won the first Israel Prize in Architecture (the state's highest award), was hired in the late 1950s to help Klarwein rework his design. His son Ram Karmi, who had recently returned from his studies at the prestigious Architectural Association in London, joined the project. Soon after, Solel Boneh, the Israeli construction company involved in the construction of the Knesset, commissioned the Karmi-Meltzer-Karmi office to design the parliament building that the Sierra Leone government slated Solel Boneh to construct.

This chapter asks how the contemporaneous design of the Israeli Knesset informed the design of the Sierra Leone parliament. In other words, it poses the question how the buildings' design by the same architects brought the modernist representation of national belonging in Israel to bear on the Sierra Leonean context. As this chapter demonstrates, it was the tension between two temporalities—the rapid technical development that was the basis for the Zionist economic claim to territory, on one hand, and the deep-rooted historical belonging that served to legitimate Zionism and to set it apart from other colonial enterprises, on the other—that was at the heart of the debate in Israel. This temporal division, and Ram Karmi's settler-nativist solution for it, I argue, was in turn projected onto the design of the Sierra Leone parliament. Significantly, it was not only design but also construction—particularly the managerial ideology that directed it and the staging of it as a national event in the local press—that articulated the program of national development as it was imported from Israel and appropriated in Sierra Leone. While the design of the Sierra Leone parliament projected an image of timeless autochthony, it also presented the building as a symbol for an incomplete project of national becoming. This symbolism, which was mainly expressed in the materiality of the building's facade, was further articulated in the phased construction process and the performance of its labor, as this chapter will show.

From Enlightenment Colony to Nation-State

Although born out of the debate on national representation in Israel, the design for the Sierra Leone parliament reflected a wider postwar international debate over the question of representation in the modernist idiom. Early in the twentieth century, modernism for the most part had been heralded as adhering only to functional perquisites, and therefore free of symbolic content. In the years leading up to World War II, but more forcefully in its aftermath, members of the Congrès Internationaux d'Architecture Moderne (International Congress of Modern Architecture), the leading organization of the modernist movement, reconsidered the role of representation in architecture in light of the rise of fascist and totalitarian regimes, whose preferred style was neoclassicism. The failure to provide modernist symbols around which democratic societies could unite motivated leading architects in the United States and Europe to search for a "new monumentality" that would give residents of New Towns and urban renewal projects a sense of belonging. However contentious it was, the most representative building of this period—the United Nations Headquarters in New York—embodied this language of new monumentality and gave a new public image to the postwar international order.[3]

Outside of Europe and the United States, the postwar state-building context presented the added task of national representation, which was a challenge given the prewar conception of the modernist movement as cosmopolitan and international. For the new nation-states that joined as members with decolonization, or were established like Israel following the war, the challenge was to shore up the language of the modern movement in the service of national representation. The new nations faced the predicament of how to assert their belonging in the family of nations while also articulating a national difference that did not lapse into chauvinism. In Israel, the question revolved around how to create a physical manifestation of as well as a concrete image for Jewish nationalism that would express both territorial belonging and modernity, while overcoming the inherent contradictions of an ethnocratic democracy.

Sierra Leone shared some of these challenges with Israel, since both nations' histories involved settler societies that marginalized the indigenous population. With Sierra Leone having been founded as an "Enlightenment colony" in 1787 by British abolitionist Granville Sharp, its history, like that of Israel, was shaped by Enlightenment ideas that put in motion a series of partitions and displacements.[4] What came to be known as Sierra Leone started out as a radical experiment in resettling liberated slaves in Africa. In the late eighteenth century, as the problem of the Jews' assimilation exposed the internal inconsistencies of European liberalism, the unresolved status of freed slaves, who found themselves with neither legal rights nor employment opportunities, presented an acute challenge to British liberalism. Geographic displacement was adopted as an ostensibly neat solution that would ensure equal rights through separation. Sharp conceived his "Province of Freedom" as a model society based on self-governance and private land ownership. The experiment in self-rule lasted only three years before the Sierra Leone Company took over the management of the colony. However, the company continued Sharp's philanthropic heritage, establishing Freetown according to an orthogonal street layout and absorbing repatriated settlers from Nova Scotia, Jamaican Maroons, and, following the abolition of the slave trade, recaptured slaves (African slaves seized by the British naval blockade from 1807 through the 1860s).[5]

As in the case of Jewish settlement in Palestine, this "return" triggered a chain reaction of displacement and set up a cultural hierarchy between the repatriated slaves and the local population. Freetown's population, who were of varied ethnic backgrounds, identified themselves as Creole or Krio and distinguished themselves economically, culturally, and religiously from the indigenous population.[6] This distinction was legally formalized in 1808, when Britain declared Freetown a Crown colony, and was made even more dramatic when Britain annexed the hinterland in 1896.[7] This annexation created what Mahmood Mamdani has characterized as the colonial bifurcated state, consisting of a legal and administrative division between the direct rule of the colony, encompassing the Freetown peninsula, which signified a form of "urban civil power," and the indirect rule of the protectorate, which signified a "rural tribal authority" and encompassed the hinterland provinces.[8] The Krio enjoyed the language of rights and civil society that they had developed in Freetown, which in its heyday in the nineteenth century became known as the "Athens of Africa." The settlers were ardent proponents of Christianity and the European powers' "civilizing mission" in Africa.[9] With the establishment of the Fourah Bay College in Freetown by the Church Missionary Society in 1827, Freetown became an intellectual center for British West Africa. The historical affinity with Zionism was not lost on Edward Blyden, a leading pan-Africanist intellectual who was born in the West Indies and immigrated to Liberia, which, like Freetown, was established by liberated slaves in 1850. Blyden, who lived the last years of his life in Freetown, recognized in Zionism a comparable model for African racial and cultural regeneration.[10] Like Zionist thinkers who imagined Jerusalem as a spiritual center for the world Jewry on the one hand, and as a vehicle to "awaken" the Orient from its deep slumber on the other, Edward Blyden imagined Sierra Leone as a similar center for the African race, from which "western civilization and culture could spread and illuminate the surrounding areas."[11]

The Krios' cultural hegemony presents a case of settler national revivalism under colonial patronage comparable to that of the Jewish settlement in Palestine in the following century.[12] By the time of independence, however, much of the glory of the "Athens of Africa" had waned, and so had Blyden's hope for national unity based on race rather than ethnicity. The annexation of the provinces entailed a British policy of strengthening the protectorate at the expense of the Krios. By the time of decolonization, the Krios' continuing minoritization throughout the twentieth century, coupled with their bourgeois individualism, resulted in a fragmented society. When the process of decolonization was set into motion in the 1950s, their loss of political power and the imminent threat of being governed by the provinces even led the Krios to demand that Freetown alone become independent, leaving the provinces under colonial rule. This cry for separatism was a desperate attempt to revive the hegemony that they had enjoyed before they became a political minority. With the successful consolidation of the provinces' coalition party, the Sierra Leone People's Party led by Sir Milton Margai, the Krios' cultural identity and political interests faded to the background of the new nation, and were marginalized in Parliament.[13]

With the shift of hegemony from the colony to the provinces, the question of creating national symbols that would unite the four administrative regions—the northern, eastern, and southern provinces and the former colony in the west peninsula—presented a challenge to the nascent democracy. If in Israel it was the Jewish settlers' ambition to prove belonging in the territory, in Sierra Leone, the settler society largely identified with the British colonizers and the attributes of Western culture, namely European attire and architecture.[14] In contrast, the provinces' "natives," as the British administration named them, affirmed their unquestioned territorial belonging by turning to symbols of earthiness, such as the palm tree that has stood for the Sierra Leone People's Party since its foundation in 1951.[15] At the same time, blunt assertions of tradition and ethnic identity could not

FIGURE 1.2 Ram Karmi, Sierra Leone parliament, perspective, Freetown, 1960. A reproduction of this image appeared in the *Daily Mail*. Courtesy of the Azrieli Architectural Archive; Dov and Ram Karmi collection, DRK-1-037_8267379999026_01_001_160.

serve as national symbols. The public media—specifically the government-owned *Daily Mail*, which played an active role in educating the public in the transition from colonial subjects to sovereign citizens—took the lead in negotiating matters such as composing a national hymn and designing a flag and a national costume, and opened these questions to public debate. When the editor announced that the search for a national costume had been entrusted to the Sierra Leone Federation of Women's Organizations, he added that the public was invited to contribute by sending photographs of their own costume designs.[16] Building on the civic pride of Freetown residents, the *Daily Mail* also declared a competition for the best-looking house facade as part of the city's face-lift in preparation for the independence celebrations.[17] The public discourse that the media facilitated helped to alleviate the association of tradition with ethnic specificity; opening the search for national costume to the public married Freetown's urban civility with ethnic traditionalism.

Incidentally, the call for the public to participate in the search for a national costume was printed just below a perspective rendering of the Israeli-designed parliament building (fig. 1.2). That the design of the House of Representatives, the single most important national public building, was presented as a fact rather than a subject for public debate or competition demonstrates the extent to which references for its desired architectural image were wanting. The *Daily Mail* attempted to create a public discussion by informing its readers about similar efforts at national representation in their neighboring countries, specifically the other former Crown colonies Nigeria and Ghana (formerly the Gold Coast). However, because there was no tradition of African public buildings suitable for modern institutions, and without a specific program, the search for an architectural language that would diverge from the predominantly neoclassical precedents of the British was left in the hands of the Israeli architects.

### A Building That Grows from the Ground

Since Israel had already constituted diplomatic relations with its West African neighbors Liberia, Guinea, Ghana, and Nigeria, its entry into Sierra Leone seemed like a natural development to both parties.[18] With its independence imminent, Sierra Leone took a conciliatory stance toward England and the Western powers, since, as Dr. Richard Kelfa-Caulker, the commissioner for Sierra Leone, explained, citing a "Sherbro proverb . . . 'the shrub you know in the bush is the one from which you take your medicine.'"[19] Along with the United States, West Germany, and France, Sierra Leone's government included Israel as "a possible maybe" in the list of non-African countries in which it planned to open commissioners' offices in 1960.[20] This inclusion was no doubt thanks to the Israeli minister of foreign affairs Golda Meir's visit to Freetown earlier that year.[21] This visit proved crucial in other respects as well, as it set in motion the establishment of a joint Israeli-Sierra Leonean water and construction company by Solel Boneh and the Sierra Leone government. Moreover, in Jerusalem a Sierra Leone delegation secured a loan that covered half of the parliament's projected costs.[22] This model of joint Solel Boneh–government operations, albeit for specific projects, was also proposed in Israel as a way to manage risk in Solel Boneh's 1958 reorganization—and probably in order to prioritize Solel Boneh in the government's allocation of development funds. Similarly, the loan that the Israeli government offered to Sierra Leone echoed Solel Boneh's mode of operating in the 1950s, when it offered credit to incentivize development in local municipalities. Such credit gave Solel Boneh an edge over its competition in bids for contracts.[23] Seen by the Israeli Foreign Ministry as an instrument for technical cooperation that preceded formal diplomatic agreements, the establishment of these joint ventures ensured Israel a visible presence as an aid donor immediately upon independence.

Father and son architects Dov and Ram Karmi arrived in Freetown accompanied by Mordechai Spitz, Solel Boneh's chief construction engineer, in August 1960. Solel Boneh commissioned the Karmis for the job because, along with Dov Karmi's established relationship with the company, the father-and-son team reworked the design of the Knesset.[24] Immediately upon their arrival, the architects began the design work, and submitted preliminary plans within two weeks, while Spitz surveyed the land chosen for the site (fig. 1.3).[25] Although this was their first commission outside of Israel (which also led to the design of the Cape Sierra Hotel in Freetown), the Karmis set aside questions of cultural difference and historical context, recognizing in Tower Hill, the former location of the British barracks, a site comparable to that of the Knesset on Givat Ram (Ram Hill) in Jerusalem.[26] The Tower Hill site had just become available the previous month, when the British handed over the land to the Sierra Leone government as part of the withdrawing colonial power's concessions.[27]

Tower Hill was not the first location considered for the parliament. Following colonial city planning, the Sierra Leone government had initially positioned the future parliament in the gridded historical nucleus that

FIGURE 1.3 The Israeli team surveying the Tower Hill site (Dov Karmi is third from the left), Freetown, 1960. Courtesy of the Azrieli Architectural Archive; Dov and Ram Karmi collection, 8267357058013.

served as the city's administrative and market center.[28] This choice of site stirred an outcry from the market's saleswomen, whose businesses were concentrated in this central location.[29] Perhaps in response to this outcry, but more likely following the advice of the Israeli consultants, the Tower Hill site was chosen instead. A remarkably similar decision had been made in Israel in 1949, when the Knesset was moved from its provisional location in the commercial center of Jerusalem to the more prominent hill of Givat Ram.[30]

That Tower Hill was not the first choice of site may have had to do with the colonial administration's urban planning recommendations, made by eminent British architect E. Maxwell Fry, who acted as the town planning advisor to the resident minister in West Africa. In a report accompanying the draft planning scheme for Freetown that he submitted on December 14, 1944, Fry deplored the state of the governmental and municipal buildings and the lack of a civic center.[31] Yet although he observed that, from a military point of view, Tower Hill's functions had become obsolete, he did not recommend it as the desired civic center. While he described Tower Hill as not central enough for administrative functions, inaccessible in its height, and cumbersome in its walling, Fry nonetheless cited these negative qualities as fortuitous for "European housing."[32]

When he recommended Tower Hill for European housing, Fry must have considered the hill's elevation a natural barrier that would provide sufficient isolation for a salubrious European quarter, according to the "topography of health" that justified the racial segregation of British colonial hill stations.[33] Since the report was made as part of late colonial development plans, Fry's racially based zoning was condemned by an interim town planning committee appointed a year later, which suggested referring to class distinctions alone.[34] In lieu of the segregated neighborhood Fry proposed, the committee suggested that Tower Hill be kept as a large open space reserved for recreation, thereby transforming the site into a green lung with minimal capital expenditure.

As with Tower Hill, Givat Ram became accessible to Israel's new government following recent military operations. When the site was chosen for the government precinct, Givat Ram was comprised mainly of land expropriated from the Palestinian Arab suburb Sheikh Badr.[35] The appropriation of this area for the country's most important national institutions—the National Museum and the Hebrew University in addition to the Knesset—continued a prestate practice of building civilian institutions in contested zones to alleviate their military connotations and preempt their future reclamation.³⁶ As the British barracks had been on Tower Hill, the Israelis may have assumed that the Sierra Leoneans would appreciate the appropriation of a site that used to buttress colonial military power and its transformation into a symbol of national independence. However, as the preservation of the Martello tower (water tank) on the site the year after indicates, prominent Krio figures—such as Dr. Macormack Charles Farrell Easmon, who presided over the Monuments and Relics Commission—considered the colonial symbols part of their national history.³⁷ As was the case in most decolonizing African countries, Sierra Leone's history could not be easily constructed as independent of its colonial past. This challenge was particularly grave in Sierra Leone, since its very symbols of independence, such as the Cotton Tree and the name Freetown, allude to a history of entanglement with, and dependence on, British institutions.

If the erection of civic buildings served to domesticate contested territories in Palestine during the early years of Israel's foundation, their architectural articulations often betrayed an uneasy relationship with these sites. Joseph Klarwein's stripped neoclassic design for the Knesset is a case in point. In one interview, he traced his inspiration to Jerusalem's Old City walls, built by the Ottomans in the sixteenth century, as well as to archeological sites in the area. When confronted with the question of the influence of Greek temples, he situated Greek architecture within the *longue durée* of Oriental traditions.³⁸ In another interview he stated that while he was not seeking a particular Oriental style, he may have been inspired by ancient Egyptian temples. Yet the style he came up with for the Knesset, he stressed, "does not belong to any period—it belongs to all periods."³⁹ Similarly, he said of the Jerusalem Wall, "It is built with simple straight lines. Simple and arid stones like the rocky ground around it. It is always beautiful. Modern and beautiful."⁴⁰ The reference to simple lines that, whether Egyptian, Greek, or Ottoman, embody eternal beauty and are therefore "modern" is reminiscent of the synthetic approach of British colonial architects such as Sir Edwin Landseer Lutyens in New Delhi and Austen St. Barbe Harrison in Mandatory Palestine. While the first used classicism as a way to offer a universal (i.e., Western-mediated) vision for India by abstracting its local vocabularies, the latter employed "stripped Orientalism" in order to preserve tradition against the Jewish settlement's rapid modernization.⁴¹ Similarly, Klarwein identified in the simplicity of stripped classicism a key to an ostensible universal language of forms and turned to a wide range of "regional" sources for inspiration. In the name of universalism and the search for a timeless modernity, he actively divested these forms of their history and politics.

While the prevalent modernist idiom asserted Zionism's revolutionary intervention in the area, Klarwein situated the State of Israel in a colonial Western lineage, as part of an imagined *longue durée* of the Orient. The temporality of Klarwein's vision in part prompted the Israeli architectural community's ardent response to his winning entry. Arguing that the building did not embody the spirit of the time, the modernist architects deemed it unfit to represent a dynamic young state.[42] To appease the angry architectural community, in early 1960 modernist Dov Karmi was invited to rework the Knesset design in collaboration with Klarwein.[43] His son Ram, who had joined his office in 1956 after graduating from the Architectural Association in London, also helped with the project. The Karmis introduced significant modifications, including changing the building's rectangular shape into a square, removing the courtyards, placing the assembly hall off center, and adding terraces for offices on the south slope rather than locating the offices along the perimeter of the assembly hall, as in Klarwein's original design. The result—a stone-coated building resting on glass-faced terraces—represented a compromise between Klarwein's design and that of the Karmis (fig. 1.4). Against Klarwein's original insistence on a unitary image that he hoped to achieve by referring to the Old City wall, the addition of the glass terraces presented a competing logic of structural flexibility for further extension of the offices.[44] Reaching this compromise, faulty as it was, had not been without friction, as the notoriously temperamental young Karmi objected vociferously to the columns in Klarwein's design.[45]

Although Klarwein's and the Karmis' approaches may seem structurally and visually incompatible, both derive from a similar settler colonial desire to connect the structure to the ground as a form of autochthonic belonging. If Klarwein did this via the material but timeless connotations of the local stone and the firmness projected by the colonnade, the Karmis, and specifically the young Ram Karmi, in contrast rendered the connection to the ground through the technological possibilities expressed in the modernist image of concrete and glass. As contemporary critics observed, this resulted in a tectonic incongruity between the stone-coated structure and the glass-faced terraces underneath, and the building failed to give a sense of structural unity or continuity between the two parts.[46]

Ram Karmi's persistent objections to Klarwein's columns resulted in a severe clash that led his father to remove him from the project and relegate him to the design of the Sierra Leone parliament. While Tower Hill presented a perfect location for the design of a modern acropolis, one that would recall Freetown's nineteenth-century status as the "Athens of Africa," this option was out of the question for Ram Karmi, who saw in Sierra Leone a chance to diverge completely from the classical model and design a "Knesset without columns."[47]

Sierra Leone provided Ram Karmi an early opportunity to experiment with a settler-nativist, nationalist aesthetic he would later develop in Israel, as part of what Alona Nitzan-Shiftan has called the "turn to locality" in Israeli architecture. Excited by the building possibilities on the other side of the Green Line following the 1967 Arab-Israeli War, a generation of Israeli architects influenced by the European architectural group Team X,

FIGURE 1.4 The Knesset under construction, Jerusalem, early 1960s.
Photograph: Moshe Fridan, Israel Government Press Archive.

which dominated the Architectural Association where Karmi had studied from 1951 to 1956, turned to vernacular forms in their revision of modernist architecture. Seeking to create a sense of belonging in the territory, this generation of "Sabra" architects, the first "natives" of the Israeli state—Ram Karmi becoming by the late 1960s their most eloquent representative—looked to the Palestinian vernacular, and particularly to the figure of the Arab *fellah,* as inspiration for asserting a more authentic relationship with the Israeli territory than that of their modernist émigré predecessors.[48] While the appropriation of Arab vernacular as a form of European primitivism among Jewish artists and architects dates back to the 1920s and 1930s, only in the 1950s and 1960s did the Arab village emerge as a full-fledged object of study.[49] According to Gil Eyal, this emergence is linked with military rule and the academic practices to which it gave rise. The latter solidified the Arab village into a discursive object bound to tradition—a distinct spatial and social entity comparable to the chiefdoms whose traditions were fixated when they became administrative units in the British colonial system of indirect rule.[50] Only through its removal from Israeli public space (purifying the hybrid, in the Latourian terminology Eyal employs) and isolation as an object of study and governance was the Arab village made into an aestheticized and politically neutral image to emulate. As Israeli architects observed the Arab village from a secure distance that conflates geographic separation with temporal distance, their interest in Palestinian vernacular is akin to the contemporaneous phenomenon of "settler primitivism" in Australia, New Zealand, and South Africa.[51]

This turn to the Palestinian vernacular, however, did not mean completely abandoning these architects' modernist creed. While borrowing from the Palestinian vernacular, this generation of architects also sought to differentiate themselves by asserting a radical beginning—a modernity that denied its own historicity.[52] In a retrospective theorization of his oeuvre, Karmi juxtaposes the "corporeal expansiveness" of the Arab fellah's confident relationship with the territory and an image of a transparent and thin muscular tissue supported by a skeletal infrastructure:

> The modern building ceased to be a stable mass that sits on the ground in the corporeal expansiveness of a fellah sitting confidently on his land. The building becomes transparent, thin, and muscular: its skeleton is like a tree trunk that is not laid on the ground but planted in it, sinking its roots deep. And the deeper the roots, the vaster the foliage, since the leaves do not depend on the tree's weight but on its strength, on its

dynamic muscularity that reaches its long lean arms to the sides, as if hanging by a thread.[53]

Karmi locates the source of strength of his imagined "muscular" yet airy structure in its dynamic motion downward and upward, vertically and horizontally, so that the passive confidence he associates with the fellah is replaced by tension, "as if hanging by a thread." In this context, Karmi also refers to Fallingwater, the famous house that American architect Frank Lloyd Wright designed for the Kaufmann family in Pennsylvania, and whose reinforced concrete cantilevers effortlessly project over a creek while the structure is grounded to a rock at its center.

Like Fallingwater, the stone-faced concrete structure of the Knesset assembly hall does not "sit confidently on the land" but instead rests on Karmi's seemingly fragile glass-faced terraces, creating a visual tension between the two. While the terraces may be an homage to the vernacular form of agriculture practiced by Arab fellahin in the environs of Jerusalem, the material chosen for them resembles that of the industrially produced greenhouses that heralded modern architecture in their use of iron and glass. The dynamic relationship between building and territory at the Knesset is thus achieved not only by the material juxtaposition of stone and glass and the tectonic inversion of the two but also via the very logic they convey. The technically advanced glass structure, symbolizing the Zionist modernization of the country, provides the economic and historic basis for the realization of a Jewish nation-state, which in turn is embodied in the seemingly archaic stone of the assembly hall building. The modern Israeli linkage to the ground is facilitated by technological advancement that provides the basis for the monumental, allegedly timeless presence of the nation.[54]

While the contradictions of the Israeli context arguably necessitated such a paradoxical design, Sierra Leone allowed Karmi to bypass them and project his image of a desired nativity onto the newly decolonized state by envisioning a unified building that, according to him, "grows from the ground."[55] In a curiously classical gesture, the architects topped the parliament building with a faintly golden shallow dome recalling that of the capitol building in neighboring Liberia, which had been completed in 1956, or perhaps gesturing to Freetown's large Muslim population by echoing the Dome of the Rock mosque in Jerusalem. When observed from the historical nucleus of the city, however, the dome is hardly discernible, while the building's terraces gain prominence as the visual lead-up to the

FIGURE 1.5 Ram Karmi, Sierra Leone parliament model, Freetown, 1960. Courtesy of the Azrieli Architectural Archive; Dov and Ram Karmi collection, 8267357058013.

building. In contrast with the Israeli Knesset, the integration of the terraces with the main building creates an effect of organic continuity between the two parts—an effect achieved by the repeating horizontal lines of the cantilevers that hang over the window strips. Their perspectival rendering unequivocally recalls Frank Lloyd Wright's Fallingwater (see fig. 1.2).[56] According to Karmi's series of drawings and model, a pedestrian route leading up the slope would have extended these horizontal lines down the hill in accordance with the site's topography (fig. 1.5). Projecting surfaces coated with white plaster were interleaved between the laterite stones whose earthy reddish tones dominate the building's facade to create a sense of visual dynamism and accentuate the projected massing.

While Klarwein's use of stone in Jerusalem served to denote a linear continuum between the state and an ancient Hebrew civilization, in Freetown Karmi carved out an image of nativity from the ground, bypassing any reference to local history, recent or ancient.[57] Following their professional experience in Israel, where modernist Jewish architects had difficulty borrowing directly from Palestinian building crafts, Karmi and Zvi Meltzer, the architect on-site, did not consider the wooden-slat multistory houses in Freetown, or the mud and thatch structures of the country's rural areas, as sources for their design. Karmi and Meltzer instead "invented" a tradition by converting the local laterite stone into cladding.[58] Although it had been used as building material for the base of structures,

FAST-TRACKING THE NATION-STATE 41

and, when combined with lime mortar, for office buildings or houses of three to four stories, the architects elevated laterite stone to become the parliament facade's most dominant feature. Moreover, unlike contemporaneous UNESCO conservators' missions, which appreciated that laterite stone comes out of the quarry in ready-to-use block form and noted its role in monuments such as the Angkor Wat temple in Cambodia,[59] the Israeli architects were not interested in the skills and forms associated with it. While they also used laterite blocks in the assembly chamber, laterite's use as crushed stone embedded in concrete plates on the cantilevered exteriors symbolized more than anything Karmi's autochthonous vision of a building "growing from the ground" (see plates 1–3). As we shall see later in this chapter, this de-skilling—like the introduction of concrete in Palestine, which allowed unskilled Jewish laborers to take over the building industry and supplant skilled and cheaper Arab builders—was used to unite a cohort of Sierra Leone laborers across ethnicities and classes in a spectacle of national becoming.

The autochthonous effect became more pronounced over time as the iron-rich stone on the building's exterior gradually deepened its rusty shade due to its perpetual exposure to the elements. By crushing the stone and fixing it into concrete plates, the architects both preempted the stone's tendency to corrode and disintegrate and hastened its color transformation by increasing its surface area.[60] Like the contemporaneous parliament buildings designed by Louis Kahn in Dhaka and Le Corbusier in Chandigarh, the weathering of the stone instilled an aura of archaism and authenticity while also asserting the building's modernity.[61] Through this method, the architects ensured that the parliament would convey the paradoxical temporality of the postcolonial nation-state, in which autochthony converges not only with the newness of the present but also with the future in which the building's surface would increasingly merge with the land's rusty shade. That the excavated stone, an ostensibly unequivocal symbol of autochthony, was nonetheless subjected to a process of acclimatization attests to the architects' unwitting acknowledgment that nativity is not a given autochthonic fact but is subject to becoming. While the architects' aesthetic of nativism sought to bypass ethnic rivalries and historical divisions in Sierra Leone, it also drew directly on Zionist anxieties, in which connection with the ground and the environment at large was imagined as part of a process of cultural unification under the banner of a shared territory and natural belonging. The adaptation of the design for the Israeli parliament in the Sierra Leonean context can thus be understood as a projection of Karmi's desire for a modern nativism, one that encapsulated Zionist yearnings and anxieties, but that could paradoxically be materialized only on, and literally by means of, foreign grounds.

According to the architects, Sierra Leonean government officials welcomed this blend of nativist modernism and classicism, which affirmed the hegemony of the former protectorate members in what had once been an "Enlightenment colony." However, not all welcomed the design equally: one administrative official, who was most probably of Krio descent, asked Ram Karmi when the Carrara marble would arrive to complete the finishing. For this official, the building evidently seemed bare and incomplete. He also warned the architect, in a hypersexualizing gesture typical of his overidentification with the former colonizer, that the offices he was designing would eventually serve as places for the uncultured ministers, who "just came off of the trees," to host prostitutes.[62] While this concern should be understood in the context of the administrator's resentment of the protectorate's rise to power, his first concern regarding the incompleteness of the building was not without grounds. As we shall see in what follows, the logic of incompleteness, and the emphasis on process that it entailed, characterized the modus operandi of the parliament's construction.

Performing Construction

On April 27, 1961, the date of independence, the parliament was still under construction. A fully furnished and air-conditioned assembly hall welcomed the Duke of Kent, then Prince Edward, the member of the British royal family who inaugurated the building (fig. 1.6). Yet the exterior of the assembly hall resembled nothing so much as a concrete water tank (fig. 1.7). To compensate for this deficiency, a model of the complete building was presented to the duke and other dignitaries as they passed underneath the scaffolding (fig. 1.8).

This curious inversion, in which the assembly hall's interiors were fully furnished and operational before the building was completed, was the result of the pressing timetable. The speed of construction was a matter of national importance for both the Sierra Leoneans and the Israelis. The *Davar*, the Israeli Labor Party daily, proudly reported that Solel Boneh won the project because no English firm the Sierra Leonean government had approached was willing to commit to a seven-month deadline.[63] The commission was a matter of national pride because it proved that an Israeli construction company could compete with and outdo those of the

FAST-TRACKING THE NATION-STATE

FIGURE 1.6 The Sierra Leone parliament assembly hall interior, Freetown, April 1961. Courtesy of Zvi Meltzer.

former colonial empire. The spectacular effects of Israeli workmanship were indeed part of the reason for Solel Boneh's commission: "Members have seen the work of an Israeli construction company in Monrovia and felt that the quality of workmanship and the speed of execution could not easily be bettered."[64]

Contrary to what one might suppose, the partial construction of the

FIGURE 1.7 The Sierra Leone parliament under construction, Tower Hill, Freetown, April 1961. Courtesy of the Azrieli Architectural Archive; Ram Karmi collection, 8267357058013.

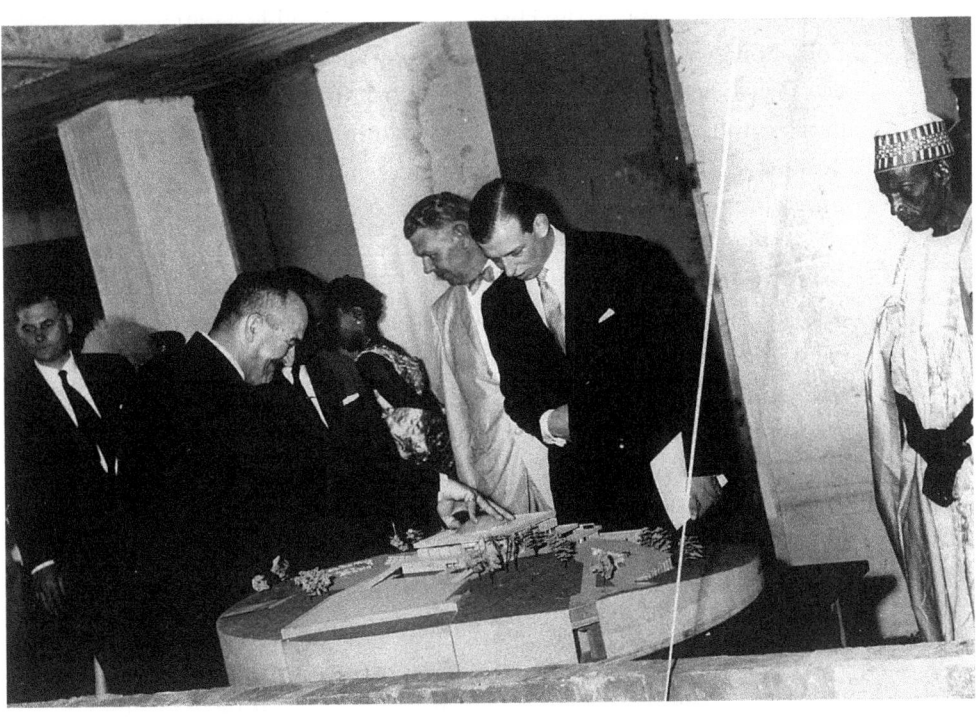

FIGURE 1.8 Dov Karmi (second from the left) presents the model of the parliament to Prince Edward, the Duke of Kent, with Sierra Leone prime minister Sir Milton Margai on the right, Freetown, April 1961. Courtesy of Zvi Meltzer.

parliament was not a breach of contract or a failure to deliver in time. The contract stipulated that the construction take place in three phases: The first phase included "the Chamber, with such other work as the Contractor is able to complete but at least sufficient to give access to the various levels of the Chamber by Independence Day." It was expected that "temporary decorations" would be needed to mask the work still under construction. Stage two included the remaining structural work, and stage three the finishing.[65] As this breakdown of the phases demonstrates, the reversal of the construction order was a calculated strategy to rush the operational capacity of the building. In this sense, the Israelis *did* manage to build the parliament in time for independence; they just employed a logic that favored making the building functional as quickly as possible over finishing the details and making it presentable in order to meet that goal.

This emphasis on speed is a classic example of how Israelis defined their development expertise in relation to the development methods of former colonial powers. As David Hacohen, Solel Boneh's former manager and Israel's first envoy in Burma in the 1950s, explained, if the colonial powers taught their colonies how to be patient, the time was ripe for them to become impatient, and Israel could assist with that.[66] In this respect, Solel Boneh was the perfect institution to mediate Israeli development expertise. Established in 1924 by the Histadrut, the General Federation of Laborers, Solel Boneh played an instrumental role in demarcating the territory of the Jewish settlement by laying infrastructure rapidly, often with disregard to the authority of the British administration, and facilitating the occupational shift of the New Jew from commerce to productive labor.[67] By providing the immigrant Jews with the technical skills that enabled them to supplant the lower-salaried Palestinian workers, Solel Boneh created a Jewish workforce and industry in the field of construction and played a crucial role in implementing the ideology of the Zionist labor movement, crystallized in expressions such as "the conquest of labor," "Hebrew labor," and "to build and be built," which encapsulated the ideology of national transformation. The Israeli example thus conveyed to postcolonial countries that it was possible to close the gap between developing and developed nations by circumventing long historical processes rather than dutifully repeating Western historical phases. If the former colonizers used this gap, and the task of closing it, as a tentative promise and a technique of governance, the Israelis offered a completely different approach that compressed the established timetables of development.

Such, for example, was the case with the establishment of Black Star, a

Ghanaian shipping company, in partnership with the Israeli Zim, a large shipping company co-owned by the Histadrut, the Jewish Agency, and the Israeli state. According to an Israeli official, while the British tried to dissuade the Ghanaian leadership from their plans to ship cocoa in their own vessels, claiming that "the establishment of a merchant fleet would consume hundreds of millions of Sterling pounds and many years for the training of seafaring personnel," the Israeli Foreign Ministry took up the challenge, just as it did when it offered the services of Solel Boneh for the rapid construction of the Sierra Leone parliament. Within six months the first ship had been bought, and Black Star became the first African shipping company of the new postcolonial state. To sustain this enterprise—and against their British advisers' warning that they would need "about forty years" to train a Ghanaian ship's captain—a nautical college following an Israeli model was established to prepare young Ghanaians for the task.[68]

Training local personnel while companies were being set up was important to the speed of execution the Israelis had promised. In February 1961, six months after the establishment of the National Construction Company, an Israeli trade delegation visited Sierra Leone and raised the possibility of venturing into other industries. Among these were a national shipping line like the Ghanaian Black Star, airlines, and a number of light industries, such as printing, medical supplies, and the manufacture of clothing, umbrellas, and footwear.[69] Labor-intensive, consumer-oriented, and requiring low capital investment, light industries were seen as the most efficient way to create an infrastructure for local manufacturing within the limits of Israeli aid, which, because of lack of funds, focused on capacity building rather than on capital infusion.[70] Rejecting the classical colonial economy based on the extraction of raw materials, the proposed industries were intended to reduce the need to import consumer products from developed countries.[71] At the same time, a dependency on Israeli products was entailed in the founding and maintenance of these industries.

To save time while the factories were being installed, the trade delegation offered to train Sierra Leoneans as foremen in similar manufactory plants in Israel that used machinery and production techniques equivalent to the ones that would be constructed in Sierra Leone.[72] This model of cooperation was tailored to present an alternative to the colonial "not yet" paradigm that continued to undergird the relationship of the former colonies with the British metropole and measured the colonies according to a universal linear narrative of historical progress.[73] Its objective was to hasten the knowledge transfer process while ensuring that training abroad would be effective once the trainees returned to their own country. The concurrent training of workers and construction of plants addressed the African states' desire to streamline the Africanization of their institutions and to loosen their ties to the colonial infrastructure on which the African economy continued to depend for lack of better alternatives.

Solel Boneh's unique model of cooperation was also key to its advantage over other more experienced and better-financed British competitors in the area. Solel Boneh had developed this model in Ghana, where the Ghana National Construction Corporation was established in 1958, and in Nigeria, where both the east and west governments followed suit a year later. In these companies, Solel Boneh held between 40 and 49 percent of the shares, and the local governments held the majority shares. To alleviate fears of neocolonialism, the contract was limited to a set number of years, typically five to seven, with an option to sell Solel Boneh's shares and remove its personnel. When Hanan Yavor, Israel's ambassador in Monrovia, Liberia, first initiated this joint venture to the Sierra Leone government, the latter was considering a competing offer by the local branch of Woodrow-Taylor, one of Britain's largest construction companies. J. C. Mitchell, the general manager of Woodrow-Taylor, was willing to secure loans to the Sierra Leone government jointly with the United Africa Company, a British trade company. But the negotiations did not revolve solely around financial concerns. When asked by Mr. D. F. Pearl, Sierra Leone's development secretary, about their policy of training African personnel, Mitchell assured him that the company highly prioritized the Africanization of senior managerial positions and welcomed civil engineering graduates, as was common among British companies who wished to adapt to the new realities of decolonization. Yavor's proposition, however, specified the training of "technicians and administrative staff" as well. Aiming at the training of all levels of personnel, rather than strictly managerial positions for educated Africans, the Israeli proposal dispensed with education as a hiring prerequisite. Importantly, however, Sierra Leone officials removed the clause of welfare of the worker—a fundamental aspect of Histadrut's institutions—from the Solel Boneh draft proposal.[74]

Unlike the Black Star shipping line in Ghana that required a nautical college, or the factories that required the training of foremen in Israel, the urgent task of building the parliament presented the opportunity to train a mass of laborers on-site. Continuing Solel Boneh's decades of experience in training Jewish immigrants in Palestine, in 1950s Israel the construction industry was seen "as a natural vocation school for new immigrants," as one planner of the Israeli Housing Ministry explained. "The majority of new immigrants come from the middle classes and are not accustomed to physical labor.... Under such circumstances the construction industry acts as an important and desirable transitional change."[75] While addressing the housing shortage, the construction industry at the time of state building functioned simultaneously as relief work, a vocational school, and a tool for social modernization. The discourse about workers' "transitional change" had racist undertones, as immigrants to Israel were identified according to their country of origin's level of westernization and their assumed corresponding potential to acquire technical skills. Immigrants arriving from North Africa and the Middle East, perceived as "primitive" or backward, were the main, yet not exclusive, subjects of a racialized division of labor. Earlier in the century, for example, Solel Boneh took pride in its ability to train even Yemenite Jews in technical occupations. It was implicitly assumed that Solel Boneh could deploy its "magic" on African subjects in order to populate all levels of technical competency on the building site. In Sierra Leone, this "transitional phase" was aimed mainly at the influx of rural immigrants to the capital; the construction industry became the foremost industrial employer in the country, second only to public administration.[76] With no need for the light industries' spatial and temporal separation of training and employment, the parliament's construction became the paradigmatic site of Sierra Leone's alternative to the colonial "not yet."

By refusing the British claim that the building could not be built on time, the Sierra Leoneans practiced the "impatience" that the Israelis preached. The insistence of future foreign minister John Karefa-Smart on building a new parliament to commemorate independence speaks to a determination to shake the population out of the ideological lethargy that characterized the country's peaceful transition to independence. With no strong anticolonial movement, the country lacked a common national imaginary. It was missing a "productive" crisis, one that would unite its people and bond them with the state, as well as ease the collection of taxes and the mobilization of the population.[77] While the parliament offered a national collective symbol, the impossible deadline for its construction required the quick mobilization of labor. This "productive crisis" was mediated by the front pages of the *Daily Mail*, which, as we have already seen in relation to the independence celebrations, facilitated the public's transformation from colonial subjects to sovereign citizens.

During the transition to independence, one *Daily Mail* headline announced, "The New House Will Be Ready in Time!" Appearing on September 28, 1960, seven months before independence, the article preempted readers' skepticism over the new government's promise:

> You—like me—may have said "oh, yeah?" when you heard that. But yesterday I went to see what progress has been made so far, and I'm telling you this: THE NEW HOUSE WILL BE READY IN TIME—or I'll eat my hat (my best Sunday one). . . . The progress that has been made in just a few weeks is STAGGERING. The whole site is one scene of hustle and activity. Streams of labourers are moving earth, carpenters and other skilled men are busily working in unison. And it goes on for TWELVE HOURS A DAY.[78]

This report helped instill confidence in the new government's ability to measure up to colonial demonstrations of technological prowess. The reporter's promise that the building would be constructed in time for independence attests to a feat reminiscent of the spectacles of infrastructure in the latter years of colonial rule that produced what anthropologist Brian Larkin has named the "colonial sublime." According to Larkin, in the colonial context the grand opening ceremonies that accompanied infrastructural objects such as power plants, bridges, dams, and railroads were used to assert the superiority of European civilization, as a means to legitimate its continuous rule.[79] In extreme cases, technology was used to incite awe and thereby ratify the colonial difference between "those who understand and control machines and those who do not."[80] But it also presented a soft version of the colonial "not yet," implying that, through education and training, this technology could be made attainable and its sublimity domesticated.[81] In Larkin's account, the rift of difference opened by this form of spectacular representation was dynamic and dialectic; it also carried with it the possibility of fusion and the promise of equality. In this way, the "cultivation of sameness," achieved through the education and training of colonial subjects, was made to seem attainable and yet was constantly deferred, suspended between the spectacular present and its domesticated future.

But the *Daily Mail*'s report departs from its colonial precedents in two fundamental ways. First, the depiction of construction as a process, rather than the unveiling of a completed object, attenuated the sublime effect of a building appearing ex nihilo. The reporter's emphasis on the construction process rendered the promise of technology more tangible and attainable. Secondly, the reporter focused on the ensemble of workers rather than on the machinery used. He deliberately chose to underscore the coordination of human effort rather than the imported technology needed for such grand project. The harmonious orchestration of groups of skilled and unskilled laborers of various ethnicities consequently became a salient feature of the completed object. The fact that the design involved crushing laterite stone and embedding it in concrete frames resulted in the appearance of a makeshift prefabrication plant on-site, where a mass of unskilled workers participated in construction. Through the newspaper's coverage, the project was represented as a national event in which the workers were the main protagonists and the building—to borrow from David Nye, who wrote about similar coverage of the construction of the Empire State Building—was a "monumental proof of hopefulness."[82] The hopefulness attached to the Sierra Leone parliament, a building that represented more than any other the nation's imminent independence, was achieved by two revisions to the colonial sublime: a focus on the present rather than on the perpetually deferred future, and a focus on the workers that was reinforced by an emphasis on labor-intensive methods rather than on the machinery used.

The *Daily Mail* report staged the construction of the parliament by the Sierra Leone National Construction Company (SLNCC), the joint company Solel Boneh established with the local government, as a national event and its workers as national heroes. The coverage of the workers' ability to work twelve-hour shifts was meant to attest not to unjust labor conditions but to their dedication and stamina. This appreciation was mediated through the authoritative expertise of the Israeli supervisors: "A word of praise to the Israeli supervisors. They are really bringing out the best in *our workers*. And this is what one Israeli to whom I talked to yesterday said: 'we find the Sierra Leoneans are very co-operative and very willing to learn. They are working well, as you see for yourself. Lazy? Not a bit of it! I for one am very pleasantly surprised by the way *your people* get on with the job.'"[83]

In the post-independence context, this public appreciation of the local worker served two purposes: to refute the colonial stereotypes of the "idle natives" and to heighten the morale and productivity of the workers. Productivity per se, however, was not the sole objective at stake here. The reporter and the Israeli supervisor's joint didactic effort, as performed on the newspaper's pages, had an additional ideological effect: the reporter's "our workers" was reformulated by the Israeli supervisor and transformed into "your people." This succinct dialogue ideologically addressed the workers, and by extension the readers, as national subjects and as one people.[84]

The Israeli supervisor's authority was thus extracted and metonymically expanded from the realm of construction to the realm of nation building; his approval of the workers' performance was elevated into an acclamation of the Sierra Leonean newspaper readers as a nation. (As both a byproduct and precondition, the Israeli manager's own nationality and his foreignness were also reaffirmed.) Skilled and unskilled workers of differing ethnic backgrounds, from the colony and the protectorate, became a national cohesive body through this process of signification. This process of national becoming, which needed to be repeatedly ratified in order to maintain its vitality, divested the workers of their previous, colonially defined loyalties and molded them into a homogenous, productive national whole.[85]

The staging of the figure of the manual worker as a national hero needs to be understood as an attempt to redress the acute problem of workforce mobilization that postcolonial states faced at the end of colonial rule. By encouraging students to pursue careers in the civil service, colonial missionary and administrative education created a rift between the liberal arts and vocational training, and as a result manual labor was perceived as undignified.[86] In Sierra Leone, this divide was inscribed geographically and ethnically as the westernized, educated Krio, mostly of freed slave descent, was concentrated in the capital and well integrated in the colonial administration, while the rural population of the protectorate, among them recent migrants to Freetown, became a readily available workforce. However, the young people who migrated to the city had a set of expectations that did not correspond to the new state's urgent needs. Their Freetown was a site of cash wages, cinemas, clubs, and access to women, away from the control of their community elders. The chiefs, in turn, criticized the young immigrant generation as lazy and willing to do only the easiest jobs.[87]

Colonial development idealized the well-educated, white-collar administrator sitting in a modern office, not the construction worker laboring onsite.[88] In the narrative of late colonial modernity, acquiring an education and moving to the city were efforts to be rewarded with a comfortable life, not manual labor. With the shift to independence, the question was how to engage the masses in work and transform their relationship to modernity, so that they would no longer be passive consumers of its commodities and lifestyle but instead active agents in its formation. In *The Wretched of the Earth*, Frantz Fanon addresses this problem with his characteristic poetic poignancy:

> If the building of a bridge does not enrich the consciousness of those working on it, then don't build the bridge, and let the citizens continue to swim across the river or use a ferry. The bridge must not be pitchforked or foisted upon the social landscape by a deus ex machina, but, on the contrary, must be the product of the citizens' brains and muscles. And there is no doubt architects and engineers, foreigners for the most part, will probably be needed, but the local party leaders must see to it that the techniques seep into the desert of the citizen's brain so that the bridge in its entirety and every detail can be integrated, redesigned, and reappropriated. The citizen must appropriate the bridge. Then, and only then, is everything possible.[89]

Rather than denouncing foreign techniques as continuing neocolonial subjugation, Fanon levels his critique at the local leadership. This expresses the sentiment of the day among anticolonial thinkers and postcolonial leaders such as Jawaharlal Nehru in India and Julius Nyerere in Tanzania, who did not reject modernization but sought to appropriate it to their countries' ends. While technological competency continued to be desired, in the postcolonial era its manifestation was displaced from the spectacular effect of objects to their human mastery. "The figure of the engineer," Dipesh Chakrabarty observed, was "one of the most eroticized figures of the postcolonial developmentalist imagination."[90] While the desire for technological advancement that had been displaced from objects to their human makers may have been directed toward a privileged few engineers, it nonetheless had a popular appeal since the effects of this technological capacity were now imagined at the level of entire populations. In his report on the Bandung Conference, the African-American author Richard Wright commented, "Indonesia has taken power away from the Dutch, but she does not know how to use it. . . . Where is the *engineer* who can build a project out of eighty million human lives, a project that can nourish them, sustain them, and yet have their voluntary loyalty?"[91] The figure of the engineer was intimately tied to the question of governance. The task at hand was the social engineering of populations who, according to Chakrabarty, "were already full citizens—in that they had the associated rights—but also . . . were not quite full citizens in that they needed to be educated in the habits and manners of citizens."[92]

Fanon argued that, in order to fulfill the needs of the postcolonial state, foreign techniques should not be simply learned, but fully embodied by the masses' "muscles and brains." The problem was not merely that of mastering knowledge or possessing skills, or even determining whether these should be the privilege of a few or the right of the masses. At stake was the voluntary, even passionate, participation of peasants and workers in state-building projects, and their full transformation—body and mind—in the process. To be ready to play their role, the masses needed to understand their stake in this appropriation: "To politicize the masses is not and cannot be to make a political speech. It means driving home to the masses that everything depends on them, that if we stagnate the fault is theirs, and that if we progress, they too are responsible, that there is no demiurge, no illustrious man taking responsibility for everything, but that the demiurge is the people and the magic lies in their hands and their hands alone."[93] Chakrabarty associates the image of the engineer with the "pedagogical style" of Third World leaders who saw themselves as "teachers to their nations."[94] Fanon introduces nuance to this paternalistic approach by emphasizing postcolonial leaders' responsibility for conveying that development depended solely on the efforts of the people as a collective, not on foreign aid or an educated elite.

Following Fanon, one could extend the category of the "pedagogical style" to include "showing by doing." George Roberts, an American social scientist born in Sierra Leone, attributes this pedagogical function to foreign aid, which, depending on its technique, might set an example that could foster "changes in attitudes, aspirations, and commitments" inherited from the colonial period. For him, the problem of manual labor's degraded status could be resolved by presenting an alternative image of foreigners' attitudes that would serve as a didactic instrument to rival the ideological and material heritage of colonial administration:

> For Sierra Leoneans still laboring under the strict separation of the educated from activities requiring manual labor (a heritage of the colonial period which has retained the respect of even the indigenous leaders and role models), the presence of manually-active, although educated, aliens is a beneficial lesson. Unlike the aloof and white-shirted image of the British, Sierra Leoneans now see *in action* more aliens who are not hesitant to "roll up their sleeves" and perform tasks traditionally perceived as demeaning for an educated person—particularly when that person happens to be non-negroid [sic] also.[95]

In postcolonial Sierra Leone, the image of a white man working side by side with a black man could not be overestimated in its power. Roberts cites in particular the example of two foreigners: a Chinese horticulturalist who tends crops alongside manual laborers, and the Israeli ambassador who walks rather than riding in a limousine.

This unmediated approach was exactly the self-image the Israeli foreign ministry wished to project in setting the state and its people up as a living example of an egalitarian, productive, and dynamic society united in pursuit of national development. Solel Boneh personnel prided themselves on their unpretentiousness and thereby differentiated themselves from colonial work-relations: "We worked with the local people and wore the same work clothes they did . . . we let them come into our hut, *which no Englishman would do.*"[96] In newspaper photographs depicting the construction of the parliament, the Israeli management was portrayed wearing simple shirts with short or rolled-up sleeves.[97] Sierra Leonean students in Israel, in turn, took pictures wearing the "kova tembel," a short-brimmed version of the British bucket hat, which became an Israeli national symbol associated with the *halutzim* (the Jewish pioneers in Palestine).[98] This egalitarian image came in lieu of the late colonial version of aspired similitude in which both black and white workers wore the most up-to-date, crisp Western suits and ties.[99] The ideology of Labor Zionism, mediated by Solel Boneh's personnel, offered a way out of the inherited colonial incongruity between the modern subject and manual work; it cultivated a new image of ideal national subjects who literally took the task of development into their own hands.[100]

Alongside the problem of how to mobilize workers, there was the question of how to unite them, direct their efforts in the interest of the state, and demand sacrifice toward the abstract goal of building the nation. While wage work provided the site for the divesting from colonial and precolonial alliances, it also introduced new alignments that threatened the construction of a homogenous national whole. Anthropologist Michael Banton observed in 1957 that class solidarities supplanted ethnic loyalties in the workplace: "Tribal people may in some situations feel themselves united in opposition to Creoles, but at work the opposition is between employers and employed, so that tribal immigrants readily accept the leadership of Creole trade unionists."[101] The rise of a working class and trade unions was a broad phenomenon in late colonial development that cut across the British and French colonies. The political opportunity for the people of the protectorate and the Krio population to unite around shared goals was indeed realized in the 1955 general strike, but this union did not last long.¹⁰² By the time of independence, trade unions had become branches of political parties, and workers' demands were subsumed under, if not repressed by, broader national goals.¹⁰³

The Israeli Histadrut, Israel's national federation of trade unions and the owner of Solel Boneh, served for many of these trade unionists as a role model. Many of them met with Histadrut members in international congresses even prior to their countries' independence in order to learn how socialism and nationalism could be integrated under the banner of "constructive socialism." This ideology was propagated by the Histadrut in periodical seminars it tailored to trade unionists from "developing countries." In his address at the opening of the first Afro-Asian Cooperation Seminar held in Tel Aviv on November 20, 1958, Reuven Barkatt, head of the political department of the Histadrut, described pioneering and volunteerism as the compelling force of Zionism: "Embodied in this nation is a creative and pioneering force, vibrant and dynamic, which turns miracles into everyday practice and raises every transformative mission and constructive effort to the level of example and symbol."¹⁰⁴ In an unwitting echo of Fanon, the Israeli Labor Party's technological sublime is performed by people, so that miracles are achieved through everyday practice, and everyday practices are elevated, in turn, to examples or symbols. This success, Barkatt argued, could be repeated in Asia and Africa if nations adhered to Israel's societal values and cooperative forms.¹⁰⁵ Three months later, at the closing of the seminar, the general secretary of the Histadrut, Pinhas Lavon, explained to the Afro-Asian trainees that the interests of the workers and those of the state are in fact mutual: "We are trying to integrate in our work three elements: concern for the well-being of the worker, concern for the development of the country, and unity between the worker and the state. It is characteristic of our work to concern ourselves with the development of the resources of the country because without that development there cannot be well-being for the workers . . . *our basic conception is that the interest of the working class and the interest of the nation are not contradictory.*"¹⁰⁶

Solel Boneh, a cooperative subsidiary of the Histadrut, represented a model of management that ostensibly mediated between the new African governments' needs and the rising class of workers. Its managerial ideology, as developed in Palestine during the prestate era, drew an inextricable link between national ideology and productivity. Unlike the American managerial ideology that was based on rationality and efficiency, the industrial development of the Jewish settlement in Palestine from 1920 to 1948 was based on an affective concept of productivity.¹⁰⁷ In Palestine, the

Jewish workers' identification with their employers' hardships derived from the shared pioneering role they assumed in the grand narrative of Zionism. Like the North American pioneer, the mythical figure of the prestate *halutz* displayed toughness in the face of new living conditions, a harsh climate, and the necessity of manual labor. However, unlike his American counterpart, the Zionist pioneer was not an individualistic entrepreneur. He was portrayed as an ascetic figure taking part in a national collective goal.[108] In this collective endeavor, sacrifice was demanded from all levels of the managerial chain. In a market dominated by the Labor Zionist hegemony, even entrepreneurs in the private sector had to employ nationalist rhetoric in order to ensure a sufficient supply of motivated workers. The workers, in turn, had to comply with lower wages when they were "told that the firm—whose importance to national needs is undeniable—is under enormous hardship and therefore they should set aside their 'private' demands."[109] Such compliance was expected all the more at Histadrut's own institutions, Solel Boneh included.[110]

In the construction site in Sierra Leone, this Labor Zionist culture of productivity and purpose appeared at different levels of personnel. Even architect Zvi Meltzer, who was not officially part of the Solel Boneh management but worked closely with them, experimented with managerial-educational techniques in his conversations with the laborers on-site. He used to approach workers and explain, for example, how each hole they drilled connected with another and what their functions were. Making technical drawings not only concrete but also purposeful, Meltzer imbued the workers with a practical understanding of the process, as well as their particular role in it. To energize them during the long shifts, he would exclaim, "This is for you: you're working to build your own parliament," reminding them of the final goal and not only rendering it attainable but also underscoring their personal investment.[111] In this sense, Solel Boneh's affective concept of productivity helped to extend control over workers through interpersonal forms of authority, even when groups within the labor force preserved religious identities that ostensibly challenged the abstraction and homogenization of labor.[112] For example, Meltzer took pride in the success of his improvised managerial skills when a group of Muslim workers assured him they would finish with their job before the start of Ramadan.[113] Taking personal responsibility over their production capabilities, the workers managed their competing alliances when they could no longer meet the basic capitalist presupposition that they would be able to "work tomorrow with the same normal amount of strength, health, and freshness as today."[114] However, without the social benefits inscribed as workers' rights, there was no guarantee that the employer would treat them with the same respect and sense of responsibility in return. As we shall see next, the emphasis on the performance of productivity had negative effects beyond the one-sided expectation that workers relinquish their own interests, whether based on class or religion, to the greater purpose of building the nation.

### Start Building without a Plan

The blurring of lines between the resident architect and the building managers reflected the ambiguous status of architects in this collaborative vision of national development. This muddled division of labor between design and construction meant that construction took place without plans. Mr. R. L. Armstrong, the Sierra Leone government's director of public works, was alarmed about the lack of formal distinction between the functions of the architects and the contractor, which British regulations had formerly instituted. When he asked for the delayed drawings for the first stage to be sent from Israel, Solel Boneh, to his surprise, responded to SLNCC and shifted responsibility to them: since "part of the Structural and Architectural design is now carried out on the site and co-ordination of service design and supply is in your hands you are in a better position to give the Director of Public Works the latest up to date information." According to Armstrong, the lack of separation between design and construction resulted in confusion about who needed to approve the design, and lack of supervision, since the architects were supposed to keep the contractor in check. This was not a one-time occurrence. While he waited in vain for drawings of the design or specifications of the roads and parking areas, Armstrong commented, "I cannot help but record the irregularity which shrouds the whole work," emphasizing that he would like "to record my concern about the unorthodox method in which the whole affair has been, and is being conducted."[115]

This critique was not new: the Histadrut Executive Committee expressed similar concerns about the lack of checks and balances among Solel Boneh's functional arms, which led to the company's subdivision in 1958.[116] The *Daily Mail*, in contrast, was far less critical about the lack of a clear division of labor, reporting enthusiastically that "work is going on so fast that the planners are having a job to get their drawings out ahead of the work that's being done!"[117] With this hyperbole, the reporter crystallized an intrinsic Labor Zionist practice that originated in the settler colonial, prestate years: the privileging of action over planning that was used as part of a political strategy to establish a territorial foothold through the setting up of "facts on the ground." As I have shown, the national managerial ideology demanded sacrifice from all workers, regardless of their position. For the architects, this meant, on the one hand, their direct involvement in managing the workers and making impromptu decisions on the construction site.[118] On the other hand, it also meant the subordination of their professional knowledge to their clients' agendas, which were often political, militaristic, and territorial. A frequent result was the erection of incomplete buildings—as would turn out to be the case with Sierra Leone's parliament building.[119]

One of the prominent promoters of these work methods was the engineer Shlomo Gur. By the time of Israel's establishment, he had become a sort of a "national project manager"—feared by architects, admired by contractors—who was involved in the state's first grand projects. As a member of the implementation committee for the Knesset building in Jerusalem until the mid-1960s, Gur ordered the beginning of construction while its architect, Joseph Klarwein, was still in Europe on a study trip to rework his winning but contested design.[120] Upon his return, Klarwein discovered that construction had begun with disregard to his plans. Gur explained these contentious actions—which became known in the field of construction as "fast-tracking"—by claiming, "The principle is to start building without plans. All you need is someone who has decision-making power to take upon himself the responsibility and get the wheels turning."[121]

Solel Boneh had been well acquainted with Gur's methods since their conception in the late 1930s, and mastered his techniques. Gur first developed this methodology during the Arab uprising of 1936–39, when he conceived the Tower and Stockade (Homa Umigdal) guerrilla settlements operation in consultation with Yohanan Ratner, a prominent architect and educator, and a chief member of the National Command of the Haganah (literally, "Defense"), an illegal Jewish paramilitary organization. The operation's objective was to erect a network of fortified settlements to rapidly seize control of land that had previously been purchased by the Jewish National Fund but that could not be settled due to the local Arab population's objections and British restrictions on Jewish territorial expansion. The Tower and Stockade operation forcefully contested these restrictions by setting up prefabricated settler outposts that were rapidly assembled on-site.[122] Solel Boneh provided the logistics for this operation by constructing the road network connecting these new settlements; preparing their wooden structures, walls, and towers; transporting the prefabricated elements and construction equipment; and having its workers actively participate on-site, whether in building or as guards.[123] Displayed as a "'work in progress" and a permanent construction site, Tower and Stockade was not measured by its aesthetic qualities but rather by the lack thereof; the simplicity of its objects corresponded to the extemporaneous manner of their execution and the cheap raw materials used.[124] Yet despite their meager appearance, Tower and Stockade settlements did present a spectacle comparable to that of the colonial sublime. Against the perpetual deferral of the "not yet," here was the element of surprise: the appearance of settlements ex nihilo within a day or sometimes even overnight.[125]

As the construction of the Knesset demonstrates, prestigious public buildings did not escape this militaristic operational logic, where emergency conditions were privileged over gradual and sustained undertakings. Binyanei Ha'Uma (the Nation Buildings), founded to host the Zionist Congress and other national and international conferences for world Jewry and thereby to reinforce Jerusalem's status as the capital, is another case in point.[126] While construction began in 1950, the convention center was not completed until the end of the decade due to the state's austerity measures. Yet its unfinished condition, which awarded it the nickname "H̲irbat el-Uma" (Arabic for "Ruin of the Nation"),[127] did not hinder its use, as for example when it hosted the "Kibush HaShmama" (Conquest of Wasteland) international exhibition at the end of 1953.[128] The building's frame was covered with a temporary facade for the occasion, while an electricity tower was exhibited in the partly landscaped plaza—a setting that conveyed "development in progress" perfectly appropriate for the exhibition inside (figs. 1.9 and 1.10).

The Sierra Leone parliament followed this "bare necessity" logic: the assembly hall was fully functioning though the building itself was still underway at the time of inauguration. The Sierra Leonean workers, who were quite embarrassed by the structure's rough appearance, covered up the walls with flags to mitigate their bareness.[129] These flags did not escape this crude operative logic either, as they were used to absorb the water of an unfortunate flood a week before Independence Day. The road leading to the parliament, also constructed by SLNCC, collapsed completely during the flooding, but was repaired swiftly for the celebrations.[130]

What could be the raison d'être for such inglorious spectacles of deficiency, exposed bareness, and incompleteness? While Solel Boneh's deficiencies served to extend the company's own work while causing unnecessary crises and draining governments financially, I propose to read its half-finished projects as successes conditioned by momentary failures. They were heroic because they demanded hard, visible work. As an American ambassador commented sardonically to Israeli agriculture experts in Togo in relation to another flood, they must have arranged the flooding especially for the occasion to demonstrate their efficiency.[131] The building's ruptures and exposed scaffolding emphasized human agency rather than reifying the machinery used; they displaced fetishistic desire from the technological object to the body of the worker. The Israeli supervisors' achievements were heightened because they managed to be productive "despite" unfavorable conditions that, in hindsight, could have been avoided.[132] The construction of the parliament and the road leading to it served as a platform for Solel Boneh personnel to exhibit their strength, not in careful, informed planning but in the mobilization and training of manpower and improvisation under emergency conditions. Cartoons about their clashes with their British supervisors in Abadan, Iran, demonstrate Solel Boneh's dismissal of drawings and specifications; the company took pride in its quick and extemporaneous mode of operation and considered it a positive characteristic that distinguished its way of working from the formal but, according to Solel Boneh, pointless approach of the British (figs. 1.11 and 1.12). Much cheaper than the colonial spectacles that needed to be constantly enhanced in order to legitimize the continual British presence, the magic cycle of urgency, provisional failures, and the crises they generated perpetuated a dependency on Israeli aid.[133] At the same time, this cycle enabled local governments to extract international development funds for repair, as one Israeli foreign ministry delegate who criticized Solel Boneh's unfinished road in Ethiopia assumed. According to him, the Ethiopian government was unwilling to repair a road that had opened prematurely because it was using it as a pretext to solicit more funds.[134]

Solel Boneh's method of operation utilized crisis to extend its professional capital, if not its economic gain. Golda Meir's call not to take financial advantage of African governments seems redundant, given that SLNCC—not unlike other Solel Boneh joint companies in Africa before it took a more business-oriented, pragmatic approach in the mid-1960s—proved an economic disaster. By November 1961, the initial estimate for the parliament had more than doubled, to almost a million British pounds. The Sierra Leone Ministry of Finance closely monitored SLNCC's imprudent spending. When SLNCC requested an advance for construction machinery

FIGURE 1.9 *The Conquest of Wasteland* exhibition entrance, Binyanei Ha'Uma, Jerusalem, 1953. Courtesy of the Central Zionist Archives, PHPS\1331052.

that exceeded the company's authorized capital, the minister of finance commented that "this procedure is neither sound commercially nor honest practice. In effect the Government is paying for one hundred per cent of the cost of equipping the Company but it retains only sixty percent ownership. . . . We are in effect making a present of forty per cent of the equipment acquired in this way to the Israelis."[135] The fact that construction began without a bill of quantities did not help either, as the company could have avoided purchasing equipment and materials at higher rates. In fact, its mission to train unskilled workers may have been financially detrimental as well, as Windell and Trollope, the local quantity surveyors assigned by the Public Works Department, claimed in retrospect.[136] While agreeing with some of these criticisms, Mr. D. F. Pearl, the development secretary at the Ministry of Internal Affairs and Development, reminded the Ministry of Finance "that it was the government's decision which created the emergency, and that government's credit is involved in getting the work done in time."[137]

Justifying expenses with national urgency was Solel Boneh's modus operandi in the prestate period as well, when it served Zionist institutions by building under danger and duress.[138] Solel Boneh was so used to this method of government backing that it expected the Sierra Leone government to continue the flow of funds the joint company needed to keep afloat and complete the parliament building. Moreover, as in its operation in Israel, where the various Solel Boneh branches relied on unchecked mutual assistance, it took for granted that help would come from the "Public

FIGURE 1.10 *The Conquest of Wasteland* exhibition entrance, Binyanei Ha'Uma, Jerusalem, 1953. Courtesy of the Central Zionist Archives, PHPS\1331083.

FIGURE 1.11 "He tells *me* this." Solel Boneh, Abadan, 1943–45. Courtesy of the Labour Movement Archives, Lavon Institute for Labour Research, Tel Aviv, IV 320-6.

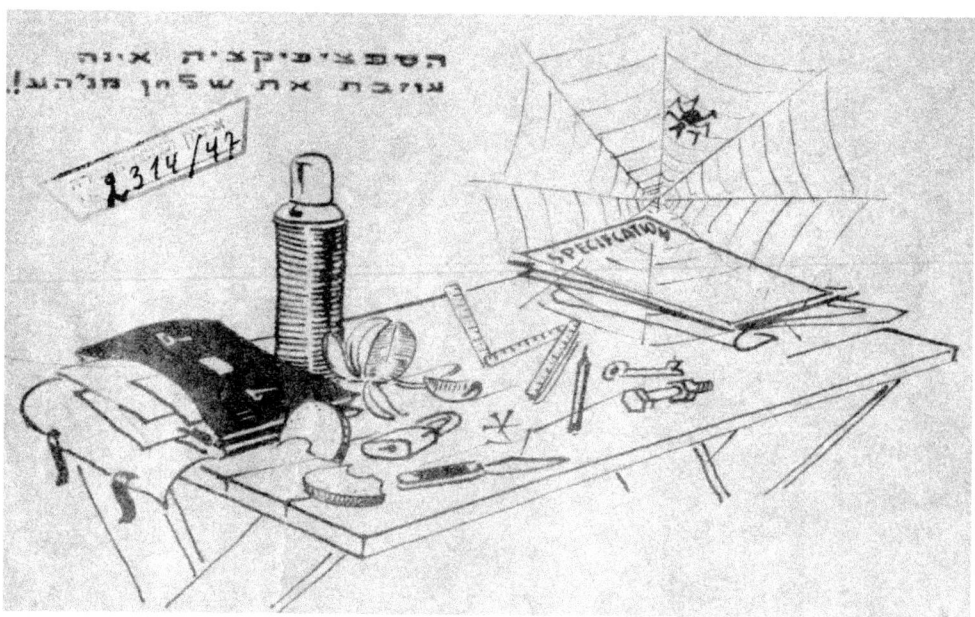

FIGURE 1.12 "The specification never leaves the manager's desk!" Solel Boneh, Abadan, 1943–45. Courtesy of the Labour Movement Archives, Lavon Institute for Labour Research, Tel Aviv, IV 320-6.

Works Department Quarry and the Public Works Department Unallocated Stores which supplied badly needed Timber to the National Construction Company at a time of urgent need."[139] Without these supplies, Armstrong argued, "it is quite certain that the work on the Main Chamber would at the moment be even more retarded."[140] Taking advantage of its partnership with the government, SLNCC managers used what the Ministry of Works called "back door methods," "snarling up relations between Ministers and expatriate officials," and sending out circular letters to ministers without going through "the proper channels." They also criticized SLNCC's reluctance to seek jobs outside the ones commissioned by the government. As in Israel, where the government tried to contain Solel Boneh by opening its bids to the private market, Solel Boneh used informal and uninhibited modes of operation. By 1966, funds from Sierra Leone were not enough to cover the company's losses. The Israeli embassy had to step in to cover the losses and fix embarrassing accounting discrepancies.[141] Since Israel's national image as a creative force and miracle maker depended on the performance of crisis management rather than on careful planning, it needed to pay the price for this cover-up.

While full of financial and construction deficiencies, the "operative emergency" of the parliament's construction did political work by highlighting the workers as well as the Israeli supervisors who took credit for their mobilization. The local workforce, in turn—now homogenized, deskilled, and re-skilled to constitute "a people"—became the ideological *and* physical foundation that could support national development in spite of meager technological means. "Technical transfer" in this case meant imbuing the workforce with "national spirit" as a managerial technique to subdue class struggles and to increase productivity, while forging a cohesive body of workers as a national resource. Thus while journalist and historian Basil Davidson's sweeping statement that African societies did not want flags but food and shelter may be correct, the Israeli managers exported the notion that the road to food and shelter is paved with national ideology.[142]

Evidence of the work in progress—the incomplete parliament building and the rough finishing of its stone-plated facade—became a metonym for the human labor invested in it. Having learned from the Israelis, Henry Josiah Lightfoot Boston, the Speaker of the House of Representatives, turned the construction company's deficiency into a national moral in his Independence Day speech. Speaking from inside the fully furnished infrastructural island of the assembly hall, where generator-powered electric lights were on, yet directing his speech to the majority of the population, who could only enjoy the building's incomplete exteriors from outside, he explained, "It is symbolical that at Independence only the chamber of our Parliament Building is as yet in a state of readiness and that [a] vast amount of work has still to be done before the entire structure will be complete. This reminds us that as a new nation the attainment of Independence is only *a start on the road, probably hard and long*, by which we can ever hope to fill a worthy place among the great nations of the world."[143] The tension between the completeness of the interiors and the incompleteness of its exteriors is resolved in Lightfoot Boston's invitation for the public to head down the arduous path of national becoming. The fact of independence was not enough, he implied, but demanded the hard work of the government and the people, working in concert.

Coda

After the celebrations were over, the government ordered the slowing down of construction, and the *Daily Mail* stopped covering it.[144] The SLNCC, finding that the building was no longer a pressing concern after independence, finished part of the plan, while leaving less visible areas such as the basement unattended, or, as in the case of the MP offices' wing, unrealized. Following Dov Karmi's sudden death in 1962, there was a change of personnel in the architects on-site, and Ram Karmi, who went on to become one of the most influential architects in Israel, seems in retrospect to have abdicated his responsibility for the final outcome.[145] In fact, it appears that the logic of process and incompleteness had absolved all involved—the government, the construction company, and the architects—of responsibility for the building, which was relinquished instead to the amorphous body of the Sierra Leone people.

Although Sierra Leone did not sever relations with Israel until October 1973, under pressure from the Arab League, the year 1967, when Israel occupied the Palestinian territories, also marked the beginning of a long, turbulent period in the history of Sierra Leone, including military coups, a dictatorship, and a bloody civil war. In 1996, during a cease-fire, Sierra Leone held its first multiparty elections since 1978. One of the tasks the elected president determined to pursue as part of the rehabilitation of democracy in the country was the parliament's completion.[146] As if time had not elapsed, the government approached a descendant of Sonitra, the joint company Solel Boneh established in Cote d'Ivoire, with the expectation that it would finish the work that SLNCC had begun more than thirty years ago. A year later another military coup put yet another end to this plan. In 2004, a Chinese construction company volunteered for the job. It built a new MPs' office building on the cleared and leveled site that was left for the expansion of the original plan and refurbished some parts of the original chamber. It could not, however, locate the source of some major leaks.[147] While the refurbished parliament functions, if not optimally, to this day, it also continues to serve as a symbol of perseverance and hope. Although motivated by national ideology rather than neoliberal economy, Solel Boneh's privileging of emergency situations over a gradual technical transfer resulted in yet another example of the long history of infrastructural violence brought about by fickle geopolitical solidarities across the continent.[148]

# two

# rootedness and open-ended planning

The Sierra Leone National Urbanization Plan

IN DECEMBER 1965, the Institute for Planning and Development (IPD) in Israel, headed by Aryeh Doudai, published a large booklet titled *Sierra Leone National Urbanisation Plan.* Initially conceived as a survey, the plan reconfigured Sierra Leone's territory by introducing a hierarchical network of urban centers across the country. As we saw in the previous chapter, the Sierra Leone parliament design projected an Israeli settler colonial yearning for nativism. This image of nativism and the staging of the parliament's construction as a national event were meant to bridge the social and cultural differences between the residents of Freetown and those of the former protectorate, however much they fell short of that goal. This chapter turns from the capital, the locus of Sierra Leone's modernization, to the rural hinterland, and from the design and construction of a representative architectural object to territorial planning. At stake in the Sierra Leone national urbanization plan was the respatialization of the colonial bifurcated state—that is, unifying the Freetown peninsula with the interior of the country as well as balancing development across all of its regions. A temporal schism between a desire for nativism and the acceleration of development, like that expressed in the design and construction of the Sierra Leone parliament, also informed the urbanization plan. Doudai used Israel's recent experience in redirecting an immigrant population to the country's contested areas as the basis for the plan, but reformulated it in response to the Sierra Leone government's dependence on the cooperation of paramount chiefs to govern the inland areas of the country. In this case, accelerating processes of urbanization were paradoxically contingent on strengthening the chiefdoms and their rural domains.

By the 1960s, Israel had become a prominent site of pilgrimage in the global development theater. Identifying national physical planning as one of Israel's flagship areas of expertise that could be exported to other developing countries, the Division of International Cooperation (Mashav) at the Ministry of Foreign Affairs established the IPD in July 1962 as a joint department of the Ministry of Interior, Ministry of Work, and Ministry of Housing; it was to serve as a center for the coordination and dissemination of Israeli planning expertise abroad. The Jewish Agency Settlement Department, an extragovernmental body in charge of setting up agricultural settlements, joined the partnership soon after. The IPD's twofold mission included, on the one hand, guiding and implementing planning in developing countries and, on the other, producing knowledge by gathering and evaluating data from experts' experiences upon their return.[1] The IPD's objective was to ensure that Israeli experts gained a foothold—initially as government contractors, and after 1967 as private entrepreneurs—in this growing development market.[2] As a public institution it avoided competition with Solel Boneh's planning subcompany AMY (an acronym for "Architects, Engineers, Consultants" in Hebrew), whose planning tasks sometimes overlapped with those of the IPD; both agreed to steer appropriate projects toward the other if they came in their direction.[3] In addition to providing professional guidance and follow-up, the IPD monitored the behavior of its experts abroad; as Doudai explained, in their capacity as representatives of the state of Israel, the responsibility of IPD affiliates extended well beyond the delivery of professional services.[4]

As the case of the Sierra Leone national urbanization plan demonstrates, the IPD's mode of operation was not limited to the passive receipt of existing projects, but also involved the creation of opportunities for their conception in the first place: the IPD identified funding opportunities for development projects and conveyed them to interested governments.[5]

Although it was not one of the institute's stated roles, the IPD mediated between developing countries' governments and international or multinational bodies, such as the UN, the United States Agency for International Development (USAID), the Organisation for Economic Co-operation and Development, and the European Economic Community.[6] Establishing working relationships with key figures in these organizations was essential to the IPD's success. The IPD's relationship with UN planning committees had first been established when Doudai participated in a meeting on housing and urban development held at the UN headquarters in New York in 1962, in his capacity as the director of the Planning and Engineering Department at the Israeli Ministry of Housing.[7] In 1963, the Sierra Leone housing and planning minister, G. Dickson-Thomas, accompanied by a representative of USAID, visited Israel to discuss the IPD's commission. The project that Doudai and his frequent collaborator, Ursula Oelsner,[8] proposed was based both on their planning experience in Israel and on Doudai's work as a planning advisor in Sierra Leone in 1960 and 1961, during which he had developed a good professional relationship with Reuben Johnson Oluwole Wright, secretary and town planning officer at the Ministry of Housing and Country Planning. An off-the-record proposition that the UN Special Fund might have funds available for such a project by the end of the year gave the proposal extra impetus and instilled urgency in Dickson-Thomas, the Sierra Leonean client.[9] The timing was opportune for the Sierra Leonean government, as it was preparing to draft a *Five-Year Plan of Economic and Social Development* that would be published in 1965 and would elaborate on its *Ten-Year Plan of Economic and Social Development* from 1962.[10] In March 1964, Sierra Leone's government decided to allocate four thousand British pounds for Doudai to draft a survey; they specifically asked him to take on the job because of his previous consulting experience in Sierra Leone.[11]

This chapter shows how Doudai fashioned the Sierra Leone national urbanization plan following Israeli population distribution schemes that, in turn, drew on British New Towns and on German and Italian internal colonization models in order to reach strategic, political, and economic objectives. Unlike these precedents, however, the Sierra Leone plan did not entail the creation of new settlements in a fixed, projected master plan but instead emphasized open-ended and dynamic reciprocal relations between town and country, using the plan as a catalyst for policy making. In order to understand how planning concepts traveled and were reshaped in their translation from Israel to Sierra Leone, this chapter begins by examining population distribution plans in Israel in the early state period, specifically the country's first master plan (1951) and the Lakhish region project (1954–59). I locate the appeal of these plans to African governments in their promotion of Israel's predominantly rural interior as an engine of development and a viable alternative to urban concentration in the capital. Next, the chapter turns to the challenges planners faced in Israel due to pressure for rapid implementation, and how Doudai negotiated these pressures and extended lessons from this experience to other developing countries. Central to the discussion is anthropologist James Scott's distinction between high modernism, the realm of scientific state planning, on the one hand, and "metis," the alternative category he proposes for informal knowledge that derives from working under strenuous, high-stakes conditions, on the other.[12] The Israeli experience challenges this formulation: though Israeli planners' settler colonial mode of operation better fits the metis approach, planning was put in the service of the state. In lieu of Scott's categories, which risk pitting top-down and grassroots forms of knowledge against each other, I turn to anthropologist Claude Lévi-Strauss's concept of the bricoleur, which better characterizes the operative logic of the Israeli planners and how they perceived themselves in relation to the more established Western international development experts and their formal procedures.[13] Like the accelerated construction of the parliament, which caused disciplinary tension between designers and builders, in this case the desire to accelerate regional development caused disciplinary anxiety in the urban planning profession, specifically in relation to its sequential procedures of surveying, planning, and implementation.

Finally, I analyze the rhetorical structure of the *Sierra Leone National Urbanisation Plan*, arguing that, while master plans typically prescribe particular courses of action, this plan's main significance lay instead in its use as an open-ended device for governing and decision making. The plan served as a tool for negotiation between various stakeholders, particularly the country's chiefs. The chapter concludes by identifying the establishment of four "regions" as the plan's main objective. As a flexible spatial-temporal unit, the region emerged in the plan as a tool of governmentality that allowed for the continuation of customary rule and small-scale agriculture alongside medium-sized urban developments.[14] The concept of the region thus implied that economic interests would bypass cultural and ethnic divides.

### Becoming "Rooted"

In the 1950s and 1960s, UN experts in general considered the rapid urbanization of the Third World a ticking bomb about to explode. In his introduction to the plan for Sierra Leone, Doudai conformed to this discourse and posited the African city—the prime locus of African societies' rapid modernization process—as an emergent problem. While only 7 percent of Africa's population had lived in urban areas in 1940, urbanization proceeded more rapidly in Africa than any other continent over the next two decades, so that by 1960 almost 20 percent of Africans were city dwellers.[15] Under British colonial rule, the role of cities was primarily administrative: they were nodes that connected the colonies to the metropole through the collection of taxes and the transfer of raw materials and cash crops. With little or no colonial investment in local industry and urban infrastructure, the colonial city could not accommodate this influx of rural migrants. The British Colonial Office only gradually and reluctantly came to terms with the need for urban planning in its African territories in the interwar and postwar periods. When British administrators finally did confront this issue, they aimed to prevent colonial unrest rather than to encourage urban growth. This preventative approach continued to some degree in the UN discourse of the 1950s and early 1960s, not least because of the continuity in personnel from colonial institutions to postwar international development ones.[16] In addition to such lingering colonial precepts, UN discourse was informed by the image of crisis associated with the American city, which was perceived as a hotbed of poverty and racial conflict, as well as by lessons drawn from the world wars that explained the rise of fascism in Europe as the result of a failure to balance technological progress with cultural preservation.[17] For international development agencies such as the UN, Third World cities presented a historical opportunity to preempt such unfavorable outcomes by intervening and directing the process of urbanization and by mitigating the downsides of change through cultural preservation. The Soviet Bloc's growing influence in Africa made this task especially urgent. The key word was "stability," and the question was how to facilitate modernization while avoiding the dangers entailed in the abrupt collapse of traditional social and economic systems.

In Doudai's reformulation of the problem, however, the city had an important role to play in African countries' development. In his diagnosis, the problem was not located in the African city per se but rather in the relationships between cities and their surroundings: "Although the role of cities as catalysts and levers for national development is of vital importance in the developing countries, their function as such is being impeded. The cities are separate, insular entities sharply differentiated from the country of which they are an element. The physical, social, economic and political linkage between town and country, that is essential tor [sic] balanced and optimum development, is lacking."[18] By redefining the postcolonial problem of urbanization, Doudai enlarges the framework through which the city should be addressed. Unlike the administrative islands of colonial urbanization, postcolonial cities should serve as catalysts for the development of the countryside. The colonial city's insularity was further aggravated, according to Doudai, by the "tendency of the cities to be oriented outwards towards factors beyond the borders of the country, rather than to the hinterland of their country."[19]

In Sierra Leone, as in many other former colonies, Doudai's diagnosis touched upon one of the most dramatic territorial inheritances of colonialism: that is, the divorce between capital cities—which, as in the case of Freetown, were often located on the coast—and vast inland territories. While colonial control over Africa's interior was technically declared at the Berlin Conference of 1884–85, several decades passed before the colonial powers managed to exercise formal authority over the territories.[20] In Sierra Leone, as in other territories under British rule, this division was codified formally by differences in assigned status: in 1924, the western peninsula, including the port city Freetown, was made a colony, while the hinterland was made a protectorate. This administrative distinction further deepened the occupational, social, and economic divide that already separated the Krio British subjects of the colony, concentrated in the Freetown peninsula, from the "protected aliens" of the protectorate.[21] This division also entailed two simultaneous land tenure systems that still predominate today: statutory tenure in the former Freetown peninsula colony and customary law in the rest of the country.[22] Under indirect rule, the protectorate was divided into 146 chiefdoms; in 1946, as part of the Colonial Welfare and Development Act, these chiefdoms were consolidated into twelve districts to administer funds efficiently and carry out large-scale projects, with some towns coming to serve as district headquarters.[23] The orientation of towns outward, as collection nodes for taxes and raw materials that were shipped to the metropole through Freetown's port, largely continued even in late colonial development policy. As late as 1944 and 1948, reports show that, besides Freetown, only one town in the protectorate, Bo, was chosen for urban renewal, and there is no evidence that any plans were actually made for it. Clearly, little effort was put into the planning of these administrative towns.[24]

Doudai's critique of colonial urbanization in Sierra Leone derived from Israel's disavowal of its own settler colonialism, as it was reflected in Israeli planning discourse. Prominent town planners in Israel deplored the unbalanced concentration of Jewish settlers in the coastal cities and turned to the regional distribution of population—an approach that dates back as early as 1919 in Jewish planning circles in Palestine.[25] They attributed the problem to settler colonial patterns such as those found in Argentina and Australia, where dense coastal cities contrast with the vastly dispersed population in the hinterlands. Under the British mandate, 82 percent of the Jewish population concentrated in urban settlements on the coast, while 18 percent lived in rural settlements. Seeking to differentiate Israel from these other settler colonial societies, architect and town planner Arieh Sharon, who headed the Government's Planning Department (Agaf Hatikhnun Hamemshalti) at the Prime Minister's Office from 1948 to 1953, based Israel's first national master plan on the assumption that small countries in Central and Western Europe were more appropriate examples to follow.[26] Unlike the unbalanced distribution of population in the "rich colonial countries," where the majority of people lived in large coastal cities "without taking root" and at the expense of the hinterland, he deemed the population distribution of small European countries, where people covered the entire territory, a more appropriate model for Israel.[27]

By referring to the European model as one that should dictate Israeli settlement patterns, Sharon unwittingly disclosed Zionist labor and settlement strategies that legitimized the permanent removal of Palestinians. His criticism of other settler societies for failing to "take root" was in fact a condemnation of these other settler colonial projects for their failure to attach themselves physically and emotionally to land, and thereby to naturalize themselves as its natives. In this critique, he drew from the hegemonic Labor-Zionist ideology of agricultural settlement to which he had subscribed as a young man, when he was a founding member of kibbutz Gan Shmuel. In the "pioneering" period of the second and third waves of Zionist immigration (1904 to 1914 and 1919 to 1923, respectively), "taking root" meant establishing an unmediated relationship with the land through communal Jewish agricultural settlements.[28] Though the Jewish National Fund was established in 1901 to purchase land, formal ownership was deemed insufficient: only actual settlement and the physical presence of Jews who were engaged in productive labor could give moral and political weight to the claim of rights to land.[29] In the 1930s, this "facts on the ground" approach was further extended by the so-called Tower and Stockade operation, in which ad hoc settlements motivated by security and strategy were thrown up quickly.[30] The logic underlying this form of settlement involved dispersing a minimum of population to cover a maximum area of land.[31] The proliferation of kibbutz and moshav (cooperative village) agricultural settlements that began in the 1930s continued through the 1940s and into the first years of Israel's establishment.

With statehood, the aim of becoming "rooted," unlike the settler colonial societies that Sharon had deplored, came to justify the Israeli government's agenda to rapidly settle the territories that were not included in the Israeli state according to the 1947 UN Partition Plan for Palestine. At this time, national planning was coordinated with the military establishment's planning division. Following the massive displacement of the Palestinian population in the 1948 Arab-Israeli War, rapid planning and the settlement of "empty" territories were used as preemptive strategies to counter Palestinian refugees' claims to the right of return. In 1953, for example, Lieutenant Colonel Yuval Ne'eman, the head of the Planning Division of the Israel Defense Forces, explained that immediately after the 1948 war, "it was clear to us that the war was not over, and as long as the country was not fully settled and [agriculturally] cultivated, we would not have control over its entire territory. It was clear to us that every territory we neglected would be invaded by an Arab, whether a resident of the country or from across the border, who would stick a peg in the ground and re-root himself."[32]

Sharon and his peers saw the immigrants who flooded the country after the establishment of the state as an instrument for occupying contested areas and achieving a balanced distribution of population over territory. Following the British postwar New Town program, Sharon's plan emphasized new mid-sized and small towns as intermediary forms that would even out the urban-rural polarization of Jewish prestate settlement patterns. In Israel, Sharon claimed, it would be easier than in England to create new towns since this would not involve relocating Jewish citizens but simply funneling the expected influx of immigrants to these towns, thus turning the voluntary practice of prestate "pioneering" into a state-directed project.[33] In the 1952 physical plan, the agricultural sector continued to consist of 20 percent of the population; of the remaining urban population, 45 percent was expected to reside in the three existing major cities, and 55 percent in mid-sized and small new towns spread across the country.[34]

In addition to British New Towns, experiments in internal colonization in Germany and Italy in the 1930s also influenced the Israeli planners. The hierarchy of settlements in Sharon's plan is reminiscent of the German geographer Walter Christaller's central place theory, which became influential in the West in the 1950s and 1960s, and in the Third World by the 1970s.[35] Initially conceiving his thesis for southern Germany in 1932, Christaller had modified it to correspond with the National Socialist agenda to create a "folk community" (*Volksgemeinschaft*) by the mid-1930s. From 1939 on, he applied his theory to the colonization and Germanization of the occupied East through his role in the Planning and Soil Office headed by Heinrich Himmler.[36] While Christaller's planning method was based on rational geometric patterns, with small villages organized around larger villages (*Hauptdörfer*) that in turn connected to urban centers, it was inspired by medieval settlement patterns that were romanticized as a healthy symbiosis between urban and rural life.[37] This nostalgic yearning to restore the putative harmony of preindustrial life stemmed from the mid-nineteenth century Völkish movement, whose thinkers exalted the notion of "rootedness" (*Verwurzelung*)—that is, the connection of the folk to their native soil and landscape.[38] Christaller's planning method was perceived as particularly appropriate for the German occupied territories, where, as part of the German Lebensraum, it could regenerate this rootedness by superimposing a landscape of settlements over the ethnically cleansed space.[39] Like Christaller's methodology, Sharon's plan simulated an accelerated historical process that erased traces of Palestinian communities while nationalizing the territory via an ideology of organic rootedness, albeit created ex nihilo.

The historical homology with Christaller's methodology is even more apparent in the planning of the Lakhish Region settlement project from 1954 to 1959. Located west of south Mount Hebron and northeast of the Gaza Strip, the Lakhish Region became Israeli planners' flagship project for marketing to Third World leaders.[40] While the emphasis had been on urban dispersal in small and medium towns in Sharon's plan, the scale of the Lakhish scheme was regional, and the emphasis was on rural and semi-urban settlement clusters. As the diagram in figure 2.1 shows, six villages were clustered around one central village; six such clusters of villages, in turn, encircled a provincial town. Like Christaller's central place theory diagram, the plan was based on the principle of making the distance between the small villages and their central village cores as short as possible.

The Lakhish project was developed by Raanan Weitz, who had studied

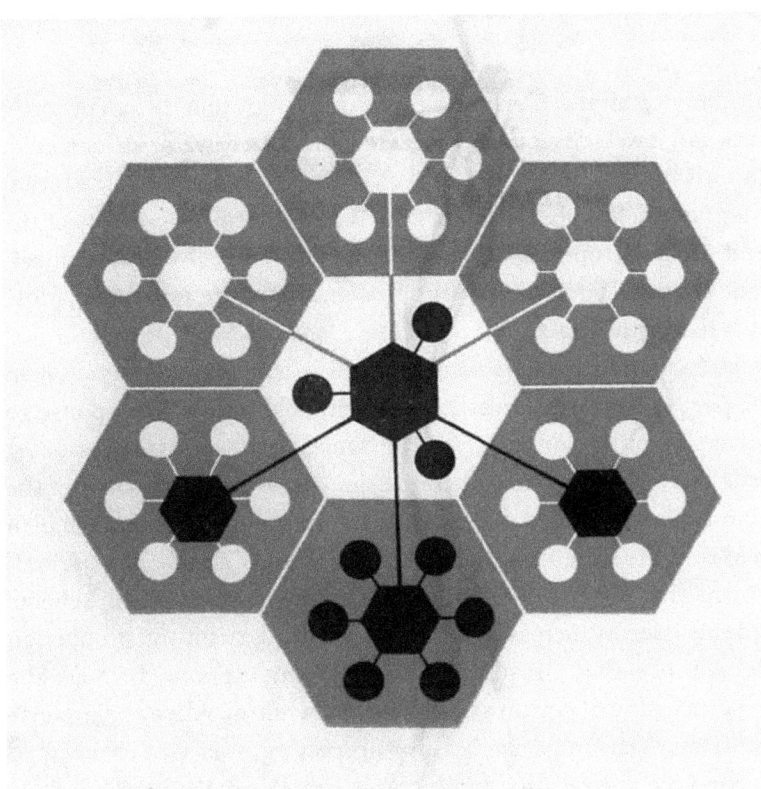

FIGURE 2.1 A schematic model of town and rural settlements in the Lakhish Region. Jacob Dash and Elisha Efrat, *The Israel Physical Master Plan* (Jerusalem: The Israel Government Ministry of the Interior, Planning Department, 1964), 53.

at the agriculture department of the University of Florence in the heyday of fascist Italy's expansive regional planning for both internal colonization in Italy and the colonization of its North African territories.[41] In 1953, Weitz was the general director of the Settlement Department at the Jewish Agency, which, like the Jewish National Fund, was an ex-territorial body funded by world Jewry and, during the prestate period, had coordinated Jewish colonization in Palestine. With the establishment of the state, the Jewish Agency received governing power to manage immigration and set up agricultural settlements. The assignment of these functions to a Zionist body that operated exclusively for the Jewish population was a convenient apparatus the state used to bypass the universalism expected of a democratic regime.[42] Through this legal continuation of colonial institutions in the operative matrix of the state, the Lakhish region project—like the Nazi plans for the Germanization of the East—became an instrument for the Jewification of a previously densely populated Arab territory. Fears that the political situation was reversible, as well as Israel's deteriorating international position in 1953–54, were the prime impetus for conceiving such large-scale settlement schemes, for which masses of Moroccan Jews

ROOTEDNESS AND OPEN-ENDED PLANNING

were especially recruited even prior to their immigration.[43] Concurrently with Moroccan Jews' subsequent resettlement in formerly Palestinian land, Weitz and his father, Yosef Weitz, director of the Land and Afforestation Department of the Jewish National Fund and one of the originators of the Tower and Stockade operation, devised plans to "reroot" Palestinian refugees in new agricultural villages in Libya, and after the 1967 occupation, in El Arish in North Sinai.[44]

These strategic motivations were coupled with economic urgency. In the latter part of 1953, the United States withheld grants in response to Israel's diversion of the Jordan River; the Americans were also pressuring the Israelis to consider territorial concessions and to absorb some of the Palestinian refugees. Thus the Israeli leadership sought an economic plan that would free the state from its dependence on US grants. The agricultural reforms that Weitz promoted as part of the Lakhish region scheme addressed this issue by increasing Israel's domestic agricultural production and its local processing. Creating a self-sustaining economy through the industrial processing of cotton and beet sugar, while avoiding the expense of transporting these crops overseas for processing, was seen as a way to achieve economic self-reliance and increase Israel's export market.[45]

While Israeli settlement programs and ideologies elevated agriculture to the status of a national project largely as a byproduct of their nationalist agendas, its promotion signified economic survival in postcolonial countries. Agriculture had a crucial role to play in the economic development of Third World countries, where the ratio of food production to population growth was a subject of growing concern in international institutions. However, early national development plans had marginalized agriculture in favor of industrialization. Postwar modernization theories perceived rural labor as a large reservoir of "surplus labor" that could be utilized as cheap industrial labor in urban centers.[46] However, rapid urbanization prompted African leaders to reconsider this strategy. African leaders thus welcomed the Labor Zionist ethos of frontier agricultural settlements as a way to mobilize their youth to remain in the countryside. As planners exported Lakhish-inspired projects, the Israeli Defense Forces promoted Nahal (Noar Halutzi Lohem; Fighting Pioneering Youth), a frontier settlement group that helped establish kibbutzim in Israel, as a model for frontier agricultural settlements in African states. Although the Nahal program did not attract the expected youth in Israel, and although the "fighting" component was irrelevant in most African states, where border disputes hardly existed, the model nevertheless traveled to African states as a means of directing unemployed youth and veteran soldiers to agricultural settlements.[47]

Despite the name of Doudai's national urbanization plan for Sierra Leone, one of its main objectives was to bolster the agricultural sector. Doudai's focus on the countryside took the Israeli ideology of organic rootedness and translated it, in the postcolonial African context, into the key to economic self-reliance. In Sierra Leone, the aim was not to relocate populations en masse from urban centers to rural areas, or to ethnically reterritorialize the country, but rather to discourage people from immigrating from the interior to Freetown. In order to address UN concerns and make the most of funding opportunities offered by international organizations, Doudai strategically foregrounded urbanization as the main objective of the plan. As he explained, plans that aimed at urban concentration and transport networks found a more sympathetic ear in international institutions than plans that covered the entire national territory.[48] Following the Lakhish model, however, Doudai's plan in fact identified existing urban nuclei that were to be developed into regional centers in order to keep the young generation "rooted" and the agricultural sector intact. As Doudai explained, these urban centers, unlike faraway Freetown, would provide an opportunity for young men to migrate from country to town seasonally and thus work both on their families' farms and at new jobs in the cities.[49]

## A Laboratory in Action

Sub-Saharan African governmental delegations were frequent visitors to the "Israeli experiment" at the end of the 1950s and the beginning of the 1960s. The new state was presented as a site of experimentation, a "field trial" where planning and development, rather than a fait accompli or a technical projection on a drafting board, could be seen in action. The busy schedule of the tours, in which the Lakhish region was a prime destination, ensured that the spectacle was tightly framed in order to omit the poor living conditions of the *ma'abarot*, the transit camps where the state housed Middle Eastern and North African immigrants, and the deliberate dilapidation of Palestinian quarters in mixed towns. African dignitaries were not the only ones to visit the sites of Israel's experiment in the mass settlement of immigrants; international experts, including prominent UN consultants such as Otto Koenigsberger, came to learn from this laboratory as well. The latter had visited Israel at least twice by the spring of 1962 and had reported on "the value of Israeli experiences for other countries" in a UN study. He was so enthused by what he saw that he suggested addressing his report not only to academic and UN readership but also to administrators and politicians.[50]

Through this spectacle of development in the making, Israel presented itself as a success story that resonated with African leaders and set an example to emulate. An issue that Israel and developing African countries had in common, besides agricultural mobilization and the settling of the hinterland, was the discrepant temporality of planning and implementation. To put it in other words, these new nations were torn between satisfying the state's urgent needs, on the one hand, and undertaking a gradual process of change carefully oriented toward future objectives, on the other. In fact, alongside "the country" and "the people," Sharon's 1952 physical plan cited "time" as its constitutive element.[51] A cause of disciplinary anxiety among Israeli planners in the 1950s, this urgency determined their methods of operation to a considerable extent. In this battle between the professionalism of the planners and the urgent needs of the state, the state had the upper hand, and the planners were obliged to adapt their methods effectively in order to provide cheap mass housing and settle the contested territories quickly.[52]

One of the challenges the planners faced was the time needed for surveying land, which tended to prolong the planning process significantly. As a result, surveys were simply sidestepped in favor of moving ahead without the proper information needed for the task of planning. As Raanan Weitz himself proclaimed, the planning and implementation process for the Lakhish region advanced on a trial-and-error basis, not only at the level of the settlements' inhabitation but even at the level of underlying information:

> One difficulty was getting topographical maps quickly. . . . I called my team and told them that we had a basic map which the British had done, on the scale of 1 to 20,000, with one meter levels. I told them to enlarge it and work on it. The answer was that this was not accurate.
>
> The team said that in order to plan houses, roads, and villages, you need to do topography. I said, "Yes, you do need to do topography. If we mobilize all the certified surveyors in Israel, how many topographies could we produce in a year? The one we need is with levels of ½ meter, 10 centimeters, with details 1 to 1,000."
>
> They said, "Well, maybe between 10 and 15."

I said, "Since this year we are establishing 120 villages, we would have to wait for the topographies. Some of us would have to wait ten years. In the meantime, what will people do? Who will build their houses?"

So, I said, "The mistakes you'll make by waiting to do it without mistakes will be a hundred times bigger than the mistakes you will make by using the maps we have."[53]

The inappropriateness of a rigid plan for the Lakhish project, due to its urgency and the lack of information, led instead to an approach based on "a series of specific actions" and "a planned chain of concrete projects such as bridges, roads, factories, schools; and so on."[54] The phased implementation of the plan combined and at times overlapped with the planning itself. In Lakhish, this method developed ad hoc, in response to the circumstances. From its inception, the Lakhish project was executed in a haphazard, improvisatory manner because of the unexpected arrival of immigrants before the plans were even halfway complete.[55] The villages were populated during planning and construction and before basic infrastructure, such as transportation, electricity, phone cables, and medical and educational facilities, was laid. The electrical and phone lines, to note a couple of examples, were not put in place until July 1955, six months after the arrival of the first settlers; by that time, nine villages had already been established.[56]

Such asynchronous planning methods could also retroactively justify unplanned changes and failures to meet stated goals. As Weitz explained from the safe distance of half a century later, "I once said that, if you expect that after 25 years Lachish will look exactly as we described it in the beginning, then we failed. Implementation is never exactly like plans. It's not a bridge which you are building which must be exact. Because a bridge is a dead thing. A region is a living thing, and living things develop forces from within, which bring some healthy modification to the plan. The planning should be readjusted to reality, and implementation needs planning to direct it."[57]

According to Weitz, the planner's role was to gather information in the back-and-forth movement between planning and implementation, basing changes not only on the plan but also on "forces from within" the region. In this reciprocal process of planning and implementation, the people and the territory should mutually affect each other, as if they were two parts of the same living organism. Through this reasoning, which recalls the reciprocity implied in the Zionist idiom "to build and be built," perhaps Weitz wished to alleviate the artificiality implied in the Jewification of the land.

In the process of Jewish settlers' taking root, according to this logic, the land would transform and lose the imprint of its previous Palestinian owners, while the Jewish settlers would shed their North African characteristics. Weitz's planning scheme for the Lakhish region involved gradually enacting two complementary and correlative transitions: from traditional mixed farming to specialized industrial farming, and from traditional societies to modern ones. According to this scheme, the immigrants, guided by instructors who were veterans of kibbutzim and moshavim, were supposed to go through a transitional period of socialization into the state through farming; only after that would they acquire ownership of the land and become self-governing. To accomplish these goals, the Lakhish region's planners lived in the regional urban centers Ashkelon and Kiryat Gat and supervised the process on-site.[58]

Doudai shared much of Weitz's pragmatism. As Doudai explained in a talk he gave at the Tel Aviv Engineering Club in December 1963, this pragmatic approach should also dictate the planning methodology of other developing countries, where the challenge was to plan despite the unavailability of data. To make his point, Doudai brought up the example of a European planner whose survey in one developing country lasted for three years. By the time he had finished, he realized that the conditions had completely changed.[59] Other cases demonstrate that this was not a one-time incident. By 1963, for example, the 1955 master plan for Singapore was no longer viable.[60] Similarly, French planner Michel Écochard's plan for Dakar, which was commissioned in 1963, had become outdated by the time he completed it and the survey for it.[61] Other examples include the master plan for Abidjan, which was produced in 1961 by the French engineering firm SETAP under the authority of the French program Fonds d'aide et de coopération, and the master plan for Kinshasa, which became obsolete the moment the Mission française d'urbanisme published it in 1967, three years after its commissioning.[62]

These countries, Doudai maintained, could not afford to wait for the planners to catch up: "To establish a national plan takes years. During all that time the country continues to develop and change. I do not believe that such plans must be absolutely exact for what will emerge in fifty, sixty or seventy years. *In my life I have already seen so many enormous and sudden changes that I realize that any plan one makes today will be outmoded in five or ten years.*"[63]

Doudai held that Israeli planners were more competent at planning in developing countries than their colleagues from the developed world because, like him, they were accustomed to drastic changes and thus "found a way to integrate scientific planning with sound human intuition."[64] In the IPD, Doudai explained, their goal was first and foremost to achieve a national comprehensive plan that was based not on scientific exactness but on the knowledge already available in the Third World country.[65] In the Sierra Leone national urbanization plan, "intuitive decisions" became an inevitable tool that compensated for the lack of sufficient data.[66]

Moreover, the construction of professional expertise characteristically drew on informal sources of legitimacy during the prestate period, and effects of this lingered on in the first decades after the establishment of Israel. For example, when introducing Doudai at the Tel Aviv Engineering Club, the club's chairman made a point of the fact that Doudai's background did not consist solely of education at the Technion (Israel Institute of Technology) and in schools in Brussels and London, but was complemented by his experience in the Haganah, a Jewish paramilitary organization: "He was among the few Haganah members that, during the [Palestinian] Riots of 1929, were sent to break the path to Jerusalem. It seems to me," the club's chairman, S. Sirkin, noted, "that learning HOW to break [actual] paths has enabled him to learn how to break [metaphoric] paths in national and regional planning."[67] That the club's chairman emphasized Doudai's role in the Haganah as a significant professional credential is symptomatic of the formation of Jewish elite in Palestine. In the prestate period, diffuse qualities such as initiative, flexibility, and the ability to improvise—alongside clear ideological identification with the labor movement—were seen as essential qualifications for elite positions.[68] Doudai's role in the Haganah demonstrated both his ideological commitment and a set of pragmatic skills that were considered much more useful than formal training. Doudai demonstrated the ingenuity that, in Israeli foreign aid literature, would attain for him the status of a national genius through a story about how he managed to obtain aerial photos from an officer of a foreign country, thus evincing his ability to work outside formal channels and make information available for unintended uses.[69]

The emphasis on expertise that stems from a particular experience or extreme circumstances, such as stealthy paramilitary operations in the prestate period and emergency planning in Israel following the 1948 war, is reminiscent of "metis," the category of knowledge that James Scott, in his influential study *Seeing Like a State*, posited as the "missing link" in high modernism. According to Scott, "Formal order . . . is always and to some considerable degree parasitic on informal processes, which the formal scheme does not recognize, without which it could not exist, and which it alone cannot create or maintain . . . actual work processes depend more heavily on *informal understandings and improvisations* than upon formal work rules."[70] Scott distinguishes between high modernism's abstract "imperial scientific knowledge," which he associates with the state, and the localized, situated knowledge of "metis," which designates practical skills, common sense, and experience, including the ability to adapt to new situations and respond quickly and decisively.[71] While Scott explicitly refrains from using the term "traditional knowledge" because of the negative connotations of "backward" and "static" often attached to it, the distinction he maintains between scientific, generalizable theory on the one hand and local, ungeneralizable practice on the other arguably reproduces the very binary opposition he contests.[72]

The case of exporting Israeli planning experience, based on "hands-on" approaches, presents a challenge to Scott's formulation. While pragmatic planning methods in Israel developed in response to rapidly changing conditions during the prestate period, they continued to be deployed by the state and its technical agencies after Israel's establishment.[73] As prestate Zionist organizations and personnel were incorporated into the state, their metis modes of operation became institutionalized and were put in the service of state domination and control.

Israeli experts in Africa were skilled in the metis practice of appropriating and redirecting whatever means were available to new uses. For example, "When Rumanian tractors turned out to be useless in Zambia, their motors were used to operate water pumps. When the head of the Khajura settlement project [in Nepal] found at headquarters a truck with drilling equipment donated by AID, he drove the drilling equipment to his project and succeeded in finding water and drilling a well."[74] Social scientists Moshe Schwartz and A. Paul Hare characterize these experts as "tinkerers" or "bricoleurs." The latter term derives from Claude Lévi-Strauss's distinction between scientific and mythical thinking, which precedes Scott's attempt to describe practical knowledge and provides a more nuanced articulation of the local "tool box." Unlike the engineer or scientist, the bricoleur can perform a large and "heterogeneous repertoire" of tasks that cut across professional boundaries. However, the bricoleur's freedom is nonetheless limited, since he operates within the spectrum of the given, making do with "whatever is at hand," rather than attempting to invent concepts and break out of his civilization's conditions.[75]

As a lively discussion among Mapai (Labor Party) members in the early

1960s demonstrates, the ideal of the Israeli expert as bricoleur became something of an antidoctrinaire doctrine that informed the export of development and planning know-how to the Third World. While some Mapai members thought it was impractical, uneconomical, and inefficient to operate without a theory, others thought this lack of general theory, and the experts' ability to respond on a case-by-case basis, was exactly the strength of Israeli aid compared to that of other nations.[76] This approach enabled the foreign ministry to respond quickly to African countries' requests to dispatch experts, or to develop specialized training programs in Israel, which often necessitated immediate action. The example that became a leading motif in this particular discussion was the unexpected arrival of "an airplane full of Africans descending from the black skies," whose last-minute notice had required the rushed organization of a welcoming committee and a training program. Complementing this aeronautic metaphor was another Israeli expert's critique of Israeli projects in Africa, which he compared with missiles launched into space from Cape Canaveral.[77] By this he meant that Israeli aid programs were basically reckless, since without cohesive methods, proper supervision, and close follow-up, their results were most likely unsustainable. Unlike the American development economist Walt Whitman Rostow's confident metaphor of Third World countries' "take off," the Israeli metaphors tellingly focused on the anxiety of hitting the ground.

### The Plan as Feedback Mechanism

By the mid-1960s, ten years after commencing the Lakhish region project, Israeli planners grew wary of resettlement projects, as the negative effects of their social management and economic dependency on the government agencies became publicly visible, with the settlers' growing resistance and attempts to relocate.[78] Following the lessons of the "Israeli experiment," Doudai's plan for Sierra Leone did not propose the establishment of new towns or villages—the epitome of high modernist planning—and in fact even raised concerns about "the resettlement nature of some of the schemes" that the Sierra Leone government had introduced. Similarly, Doudai suggested avoiding "major changes in the scale and organization of agricultural production," contrary to the massive industrialization of agriculture that was soon to take place in Asia under the banner of the Green Revolution.[79] Doudai confined his plan to identifying existing urban centers to be developed and improved; it was thus similar to the initial stage of Sharon's plan, in which the first "new towns" were, for the most part, existing towns with a mix of Arab and Jewish residents that, after the 1948 war, the plan aimed to populate with a Jewish majority.

If Doudai proposed neither new towns nor the modernization of agricultural production, what course of action did his plan delineate for Sierra Leone? For Doudai, the answer lay in the entirely novel ontological and epistemic status he attributed to the plan. If the plan was not oriented toward a preconceived future, and if it was destined to become irrelevant in just a few years, the status of the plan as a blueprint in the high modernist sense became obsolete. Instead, Doudai proposed that the plan should act as a catalyst that stimulates feedback mechanisms. In doing so, he updated the process-oriented planning approach developed by the Tennessee Valley Authority—an inspiration for many postwar governments—with the language of systems that prevailed in development discourse in the 1960s.[80] According to this logic, feedback would be translated into information, which in turn would be reinvested back into the plan in a continuous dynamic process:

> The planning process should be multi-dimensional. . . . In terms of time it should be designed not for a predetermined sequence of activities, but on the basis of an ever-deepening process in which the first broad intuitive decisions feed back as information and experience on which to set off another series of processes, in a continuous, on-going, succession. . . . First decisions have to be made on an intuitive basis from an overall comprehensive examination of material available, and studies that are undertaken while the decisions are taking effect should be utilized primarily to deepen the understanding for planning decisions at a later stage. . . . To some degree survey, research, planning, programming, decision making and implementation overlap in all situations, *and in Africa one single and continuous process is particularly suitable. Incorporating research, planning, and implementation interwoven in time and place.*[81]

In this reformulation of the plan's function and operation, it was not only that the survey did not precede the plan, or that planning did not precede implementation, but rather that all of these components were to be linked in a process of simultaneously gathering information and making adaptive decisions. Both information and decisions were to be pursued through local, continuous interventions that would be coordinated step by step, with no fixed, grand master plan. In radically repurposing the master plan, Doudai reacted to trends in governmental administration that rejected "the comprehensive rational approach" of academic experts in favor of short-term decision making.[82] The Sierra Leone Development Plan of 1962 reflected this trend, noting that the plan "should not be interpreted as an inflexible framework, but rather as a plan subject to constant review and modification." It also postulated that "lack of information, as such, is not necessarily a barrier to planning, for the collection of *adequate* data in the form required is itself an objective of planning."[83] Because of this approach, the temptation to proceed from survey to broad intuitive decisions was so strong that Doudai ended up producing a plan while he was only commissioned to conduct a survey.[84]

Doudai's reformulation of planning was a direct response to the logic adopted in the Sierra Leone Development Plan as well as, more broadly, to the epistemic problem that the Third World city presented to Western planners. Because of the rapidly changing conditions in Third World cities, planners came to the conclusion that it was difficult for information gathering to precede and thereby lay sound scientific grounds for planning. But rapid change was only part of the problem, as the main challenge was understanding foreign phenomena and processes and translating them into "adequate"—that is, usable—data. Since the survey served as the substrate through which experts rationalized the planning and implementation of development projects, its use was fundamentally predetermined by Western scientific reasoning. Another look at Lévi-Strauss's distinction discloses that the engineer, though conceptually inventive, is as restricted as the bricoleur in his execution of projects, because he limits himself to the materials and tools "conceived and procured for the purpose of the project."[85] Once the engineer "invents" his concepts and tools, they bind him. Similarly, the ability to plan development projects was conditioned, first and foremost, by the availability of data that could be subjected to the Western experts' methods of analysis. In the early 1950s, the UN had singled out information gathering as an urgent problem, since "defective knowledge and consequent inability to make rational plans was a major constraint."[86] As a result, the task of the development expert expanded from the mere processing of data to the gathering of information in the first place: the production of the "Third World" as a category of knowledge called for the collection of ever more information about it. By the 1960s, as the Sierra Leone urbanization plan demonstrates, planners gradually acknowledged that the gathering of information without planning intervention was futile, since the two were interdependent. The Third World city was constructed as an epistemological problem that Western planning could tackle only by applying its own categories and paradigms of action, which would, in turn, create a framework for gathering information that fit within these categories.

Anthropologists provided planners with important guidance on how to translate processes they observed on the ground into data. In fact, Doudai's use of the term "feedback," borrowed from the language of cybernetics and transposed to planning, may have been mediated by renowned American anthropologist Margaret Mead, who visited the Lakhish region in the summer of 1956 and praised its planners indirectly, teasing them with what at first seemed criticism.[87] Facing such a project, another country, she mused, would have approached the UN, which would have appointed sociologists, anthropologists, historians, and other experts to study the subject, who would then have formed committees under the auspices of UNICEF or UNESCO. These committees would have sat for three years and issued a detailed report in the fourth, explaining ultimately why it would be impossible to build settlements in the area. Amused, she stated, "You skipped all these phases and just went on to build the settlements."[88] She may have found that the Israeli approach resonated with current trends in anthropology as they were applied to development work. Two years prior to this visit, Mead had edited a "manual for technical experts," published jointly by UNESCO and the World Federation for Mental Health, in which she presented the feedback mechanism as a new model of social intervention. In this new model of "participatory" social sciences that emphasized "learning from the ground," the expert created new patterns out of old ones and thus managed development by collaborating with the local population. The expert effectively became a mediating figure who could not only process information into data but also communicate the idea of development across cultural contexts by reducing scientific techniques to their essentials and translating them into a new, accommodating pattern that would become meaningful in the new context.[89]

Following the logic that it did not make sense to complete a detailed survey before planning, Doudai spent less than two weeks on his basic data-gathering mission in Freetown in May 1964, and most probably did not visit, at least not on this occasion, the country's interior, which was his plan's main focus.[90] In his Tel Aviv office, he scaled the state's territory down to a series of unified templates, each the size of a page, that could all fit into a sizeable booklet. Packed in this form, the survey that had turned into a plan traveled back to Sierra Leone and was handed over to the Sierra Leone government; it was also distributed among the international community of experts, particularly representatives of institutions that coordinated and financed such projects.[91] By isolating variables such as soil, agriculture, population movement, and services—based mostly on information from the British colonial administration—on a repeated, homogenous plane, Doudai created a legible template that simplified the presentation of existing information. The booklet also incorporated tracing paper that allowed for the juxtaposition and superimposition of various maps. Reminiscent of the regional surveys that had been developed in Britain in the 1930s, the tracing paper layered over the maps provided a playful platform for processing information and a narrative-like progression from findings to conclusion accessible even to laymen such as the Sierra Leone government officials and possibly the local chiefs.[92]

Lévi-Strauss's characterization of the bricoleur's plan as no more than a sketch is an apt description of the visualization techniques Doudai employed in his plan for Sierra Leone. As a flexible template to be used for ongoing decision making, the more schematic and general the plan was, the better. The book's visual analysis concluded with a series of flow maps titled "Population Movements," "Regional Pattern: Social," and "Urban Framework" (figs. 2.2 and 2.3, and plate 4). While the first two depict existing conditions and patterns, "Urban Framework" instead depicts a desired condition that could be achieved by creating and reinforcing peripheral urban centers whose development potential can be deduced from previous maps. In an almost seamless transition from representing existing patterns to prescribing new ones, "Urban Framework" became a hybrid that both charted the territory as it was and diagrammed the desired relationship among urban centers.

Often conceived as a tool of policy makers rather than physical planners, the plan's significance in the Third World developmentalist context lay not at the level of specific prescriptions but at the rhetorical level. The plan's very existence was often presented as an actual achievement.[93] Because it provided a basis for policy making, its actionable status made it comparable to a speech act. Moreover, the more open-ended the plan was, the more it absolved the policy maker and planner of responsibility for its full and complete implementation, since its success could not be measured in any concrete terms. This flexibility was especially useful in the hands of the so-called weak governments of Africa, where the lack of administrative infrastructure far from the capital presented a challenge of governance. The inheritance of the colonial divide between direct and indirect rule posed a particularly acute obstacle in relation to the implementation of any physical plan since it set in stone the customary land tenure system in the protectorate, which precluded any government intervention without local chiefs' concession of land.⁹⁴ It is exactly for this reason that the plan was more important as a speech act than as a binding document, since it had the potential to set in motion a chain reaction flexible enough to address and include the input of various "populations of interest," from

FIGURE 2.2 "Population Movements." Aryeh Doudai and Ursula Oelsner, *Sierra Leone National Urbanisation Plan* (Tel Aviv: Institute for Planning and Development, 1965).

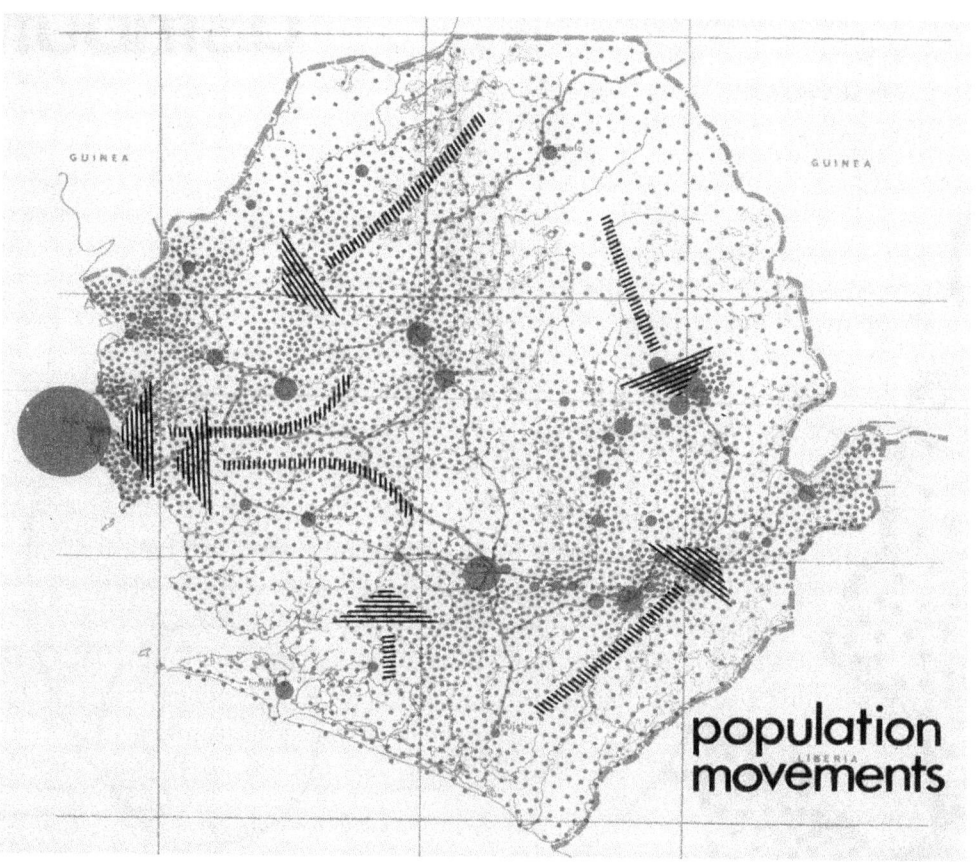

international and national institutions to customary leaders across the country.⁹⁵

A Nation of Regions

As an intermediary category, "a link in a chain between national programming and local activity,"⁹⁶ regions, rather than urban centers, were the ultimate development object of the Sierra Leone national urbanization plan. Four unnamed regions emerged from the concluding flow maps as organic units that were superimposed over the colonial demarcations of the provinces, districts, and chiefdoms.⁹⁷ Presented as the calculated result of both

FIGURE 2.3 "Regional Pattern: Social." Aryeh Doudai and Ursula Oelsner, *Sierra Leone National Urbanisation Plan* (Tel Aviv: Institute for Planning and Development, 1965).

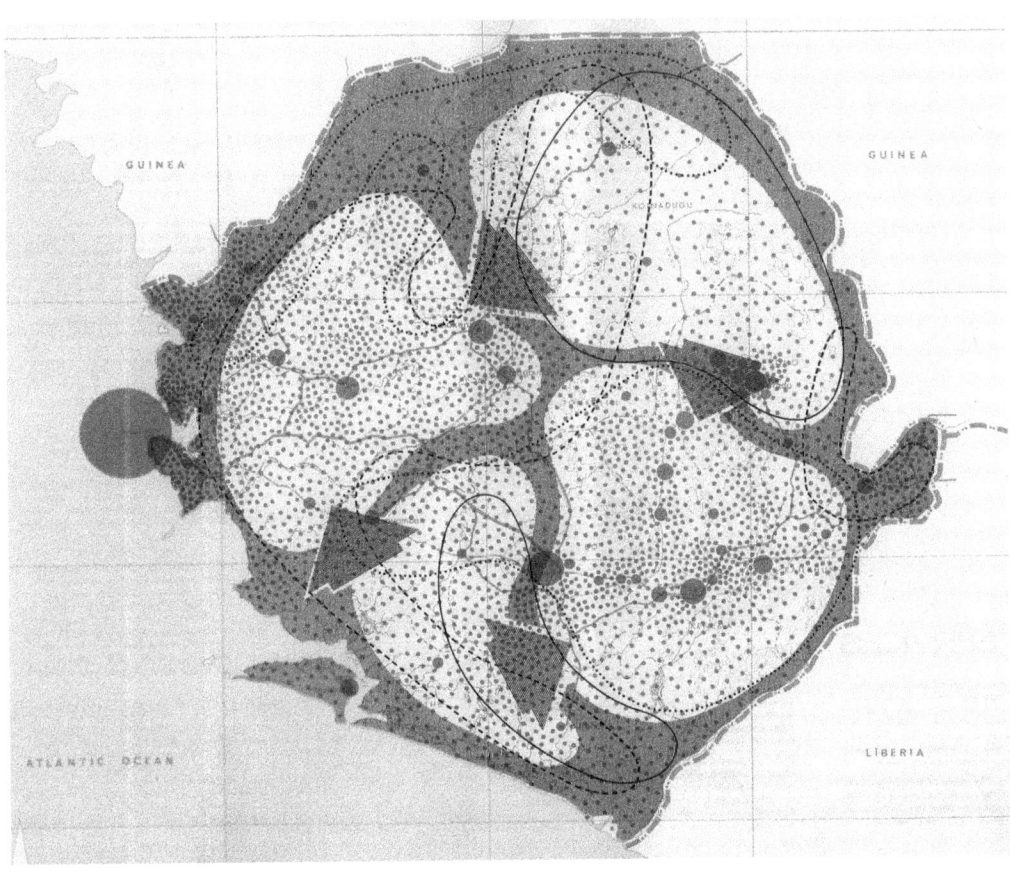

physical variables and cultural data such as ethnicity and language, these regions were constructed as natural economic units of specialized activity that had yet to be consolidated. The urban network, in turn, was conceived in the service of regional development, acting to extend and diffuse it: "The towns constituting the urban framework represent only the upper levels of a total national structure that will have to be developed. As collectors, transmitters, mixers and magnifiers of the diverse material that constitutes a society and generates development, they are selected as the foci most likely to optimize forces between Freetown and the rural hinterland. . . . The role of these towns *is to gather their regional forces and to transmit them* to Freetown and similar towns in other regions."[98]

Understanding towns as "collectors, transmitters, mixers and magnifiers" reflects a shift in planning from the projection of zones of designated human activity on an imagined blank slate to the study of existing territories as complex fields of relations, force lines, and attraction poles.[99] If, in Lakhish, the planning of the urban center had followed the planning of the region, here, in a circular logic, neither did the planning of the regions precede that of the towns, nor vice versa; instead, both were mutually constitutive.[100] This mutually constitutive logic dictated other aspects of the plan as well—specifically, the gradual transformation of society and the economic potential of the territory. Like Weitz, Doudai did not consider the Lakhish region a fixed geographic entity, but a living organism whose economic growth depended on its society's gradual modernization.[101] If, in Lakhish, the settlers were grouped according to their place of origin to maintain family ties and a sense of community, in Sierra Leone traditional ties were to be hardly disturbed at all, since people were not to be uprooted or coerced into modernizing their agricultural practices. Seemingly guided by the invisible hand of liberal economy rather than the state, the regions were expected to transform over time, and their economic differentiation to increase "as urbanisation and industrialization proceed and as natural, human and economic potential known to exist in Sierra Leone are exploited."[102]

Ultimately, the plan was oriented toward maximizing resources while preserving existing customs, including traditional modes of agricultural production in the rural sector, as much as possible. While the urban framework aimed at "stimulating progress in the smallest rural villages," Doudai warned against changes in the scale of agricultural production.[103] The abstract stains that represented the regions stood in for the villages that were practically absent from the plan: "Planning must include factors which will maximize the influence of the town on its surrounding region in order *to encourage the population to remain in rural villages.* Some of these factors are extension into the hinterland of social services, organization of central markets for buying and selling of agricultural products, and establishment of an adequate transportation system between the town and the rural areas. The regional services become an integral part of the regional plan."[104] Located in feasible proximity to the villages, urban centers would strengthen the villages' agricultural production by providing the necessary facilities for their survival in a modernizing economy, albeit without introducing radical social changes. In this process, Doudai promised, "chiefdom units [will] be disturbed as little as possible."[105] Thus, instead of introducing a gradual process of modernization guided by the planner and the anthropologist, as theorized by Margaret Mead and practiced in the Lakhish project, here the objective was to keep traditional society intact.

The discrepancy between Doudai's approach in the Lakhish plan and the Sierra Leone one can be explained by Sierra Leone's particular government structure and land tenure politics. The tension the planner wished to resolve was not simply between modernity and tradition in daily life, as in Lakhish, but also in governance, where the modern state confronted traditional chiefs who acted as "brokers of political power," in J. F. Ade Ajayi's apt phrasing.[106] On top of the twelve paramount chiefs, one for each district, who have seats in the Sierra Leone parliament in addition to its elected members, the government depends on local chiefs for both electoral support and active implementation of governmental policy and projects. Alongside the plan's affirmation of the chiefdoms' status, its emphasis on interregional reciprocity and economic balance was further meant to assist the government in relieving concerns about ethnic favoritism because the prime minister was Mende—that is, from one of the two most powerful ethnic groups in the country.[107]

The structure of Sierra Leone's government and its lack of a strong administrative infrastructure in inland areas weakened its ability to implement development plans. Doudai was well aware of these struggles and deficiencies: "Efforts to organize a hierarchically structured decentralized government are proceeding, but imbalances and conflicts are still severe. Areas of responsibility are ambiguous, leaving some sectors with overlapping authorities and others untouched. Sufficient technical and administrative staff are unavailable. The role of government in development is not clear. A comprehensive operating procedure for government administration is lacking, and a national framework assigning functions and responsibilities to each level and department of government in an integrated hierarchical system, has not been drawn up."[108] As remedy to these challenges, Doudai proposed the region as a device of governmentality, to use Michel Foucault's term for describing how the power of the state operates by encouraging certain trends rather than exercising strict control.[109] In Weitz's formulation, which became known as the "Rehovot Approach" after the Center for the Study of Rural and Urban Settlements that he established in 1963, the region acts as an intermediary category that mediates between the vertical and horizontal levels of state management. By "vertical," Weitz meant governmental decisions that trickle down from the national level to regional and local levels. By "horizontal," he meant the linking of all three sectors by chains of concrete projects.[110] It was assumed that while chiefdoms would be "undisturbed" locally, they would wish to cooperate with the state and other chiefdoms at a regional level in order to benefit from shared regional economic interests. As a larger frame of reference that was defined predominantly in economic terms, the regional framework would encourage the maintenance of cultural or ethnic differentiations only to the extent that these served shared economic interests.

Postscript

A flexible territorial-temporal unit, the "region" emerged in the Sierra Leone plan as a naturally given intermediary scale between the national and the urban (plate 4). In contrast with the artificial character of many national, provincial, or district boundaries drawn under colonial rule, the plan's regions were defined mainly through natural resources and population distribution. Instead of controlling urbanization, as in late colonial and early postcolonial development master plans, the plan encouraged hinterland urbanization while using it as source for regional development. Constructing the regions as natural economic units not only created larger and more coherent areas of governance than the late-colonial districts but also enabled local chiefs to cooperate well beyond their chiefdoms' borders. As a territorial unit, the region included villages whose agricultural production ensured that the traditional power structure would continue. As they did under colonial indirect rule, the chiefs would serve as the central government's local arms. Without the threat of losing their traditional hold, the chiefs' participation and cooperation would extend to the regional level and consequently also to the state.

Unable to truly resolve the conundrum of how to modernize the economy without modernizing society, the plan is filled with self-contradictions and bypasses challenges such as conflicting customs and ethnic tensions. Based on the hope that economic logic will serve as a regulatory mechanism, it assumes that shared economic interests will help varying constituencies overcome their differences and arrive at consensus. The plan thus offers a model of Foucault's governmentality rather than Scott's top-down high modernism. In lieu of delineating detailed, fixed scenarios that assume the state's complete control, the Sierra Leone urbanization plan gives the state the role of identifying and encouraging desirable trends while minimizing interference. The state should appear to be merely facilitating a natural flow of inevitable processes that are led by local agents. By performing governmentality and emphasizing the agency of local stakeholders, the plan helps us understand the politics of planning and implementation in Sierra Leone and other postcolonial developing countries beyond the top-down-versus-grassroots dichotomy.

Furthermore, unlike other contemporary projects, such as Constatinos Doxiadis's national villagization plan for Zambia (1967–69), this plan did not treat the countryside as a homogenous entity.[111] While the regions appear as empty spaces in their highly abstracted graphic representation, the emptiness does not mark disregard for the existing forces operating in them, but rather suggests that even the regions should not be fixed by the government, the planners, or, ultimately, the local chiefs. In this sense, the plan's open-endedness diverges from the colonial fixation of power in the hands of local chiefs, implying instead that even they will relinquish some of their power in favor of economic advantages that, in turn, will lead to the gradual modernization of Sierra Leonean society.

The plan's open-endedness rendered its processes of implementation ambiguous and difficult to detect. Following his submission of the plan in June 1966, together with instructions to the Sierra Leone government on how to apply for a grant from the UN Special Fund, Doudai remarked in frustration that he doubted the government would do anything about it.[112] Doudai's pessimism may have been affected by his resignation from the IPD the same month. In response to the Israeli state comptroller's report the previous year, it had been recommended that the IPD should be terminated due to "its mediocre function" and its failure to raise funds from third parties.[113] Perhaps it was the plan's open-ended character and lack of concrete projects that proved to be uneconomic from the perspective of the Israeli government: the plan did not, after all, prescribe specific courses of action that could be performed by other Israeli planners and contractors.

The fact that the booklet's cost of production far exceeded what the Israeli government had initially agreed to spend probably did not help either. As with Solel Boneh's transformation from an arm of state aid to a purely commercial undertaking in 1964, the IPD changed course to provide Israeli planning services for paying clients, including some in Europe and the United States, just as Israel's relationship with African governments was beginning to deteriorate in the wake of the 1967 war.[114] After the IPD was reorganized in 1967 and then again in 1970, its function was dramatically reduced to a center for information exchange and coordination of Israeli private professionals' work abroad.

The year 1967 was also a dramatic one in Sierra Leone. Siaka Stevens's opposition party, the All People's Congress, won the election by only a minor margin, which led to a military coup. Although Stevens would regain the title of prime minister the following year, it was not until April 1971, when he declared Sierra Leone a republic and himself its president, that the government, now with a one-party system, was stable enough to resume planning operations. As if time had not elapsed and the regime had not changed—and as in the case of the Sierra Leone parliament building, where, after decades of civil war, the new government approached the Ivory Coast's Sonitra, Solel Boneh's former partnership in Africa, to complete the building—the new administration approached the IPD in August 1971, now with the far less ambitious objective of focusing on a "metropolitan structure plan for Greater Freetown."[115] Turning back to the capital, this plan centered on the coastal urban concentration that Doudai's plan had sought to balance by emphasizing rural areas. Yet the logic that guided the IPD's plan continued to influence planning professionals in Sierra Leone, even if they had very little opportunity to exercise their skills during the ensuing civil war that plagued the country.[116]

# planning a postcolonial university campus

## The University of Ife, Nigeria

THE FOLLOWING IMPRESSIONS, told in retrospect, are those of a Nigerian student arriving in 1979 for the first time on the campus of the University of Ife, which was later renamed Obafemi Awolowo University (plate 5):

> What greeted my young mind virtually had me pass out. My eyes were scintillated by the sight of an impressive stretch of well laid lawn garnished with floricultural species carefully arranged . . .
>
> After about a ten minute drive on that beautiful road—the famed Road One, . . . were gigantic architectural masterpieces all linked by lush green lawns, décors, walk ways, elevations and subways. I was later to realize that the intimidating architectural array warehoused the famous Oduduwa Hall, the Hezekiah Oluwasanmi library, the Senate Building cum Administrative building and the Humanities faculty.[1]

Had the student continued the drive northeast, he would have seen the elegant agriculture faculty and, further north, its experimental farms.

Scattered between the farms and the agriculture faculty were detached or semidetached one- and two-story faculty houses. To the west of the academic core, which the student described as full of "gigantic architectural masterpieces," were the students' dormitories. More modest and orderly, their main attractions were the spacious and strikingly modern study halls. "Was I in Nigeria?" the student recounted his amazement. "No I must be elsewhere." "Did Nigerians think this place up? . . . Was I indeed in the same country where confusion is a festering norm?" "It must be different Nigerians that planned this Ife," he concluded. These "different Nigerians" were in fact a team of Israeli architects headed by Arieh Sharon, a Bauhaus graduate and one of Israel's most prominent architects and planners at that time. The team worked closely with the Nigerian university committee from the university's inception in 1960 through the early 1980s.[2]

The University of Ife was the most ambitious governmental project of Nigeria's western region and a crowning symbol of independence. The university's goal, according to its historians, Olufemi Omosini and 'Biodun Adediran, was "to produce graduates who will be able to adjust themselves to life in the communities they may be called upon to serve and not reproduce an elite which is divorced from the rest of the community."[3] The site chosen for the campus location—next to the town of Ife, also known as Ile-Ife and the cradle of the Yoruba, the predominant ethnic group of the region—was deemed appropriate to fulfill this goal because of its semirural characteristics and the vast agricultural land Ife's *ooni*, the Yoruba king, made available for the institution. While the University College Ibadan (UCI), which had been established by the British colonial administration at the outskirts of a great metropolitan area in 1948, followed the Oxbridge model and aimed to cultivate a Nigerian elite, the University of Ife—much like the other two regional universities that were established immediately upon independence—was instead modeled on the American land grant university. In its democratic goals and rural setting, as well as its emphasis on applied research in agriculture and technical fields, the Nigerian university committee found a precedent better fit to address the immediate development needs of the region.

As historian and university administrator Cornelius de Kiewiet, who became involved in higher education in postindependence Africa, wrote in 1971, the university in Africa was the primary tool in decolonization and development, second in importance only to the government itself.[4] The government of West Nigeria recognized this when it announced the establishment of its own regional university at the same time that Nigeria gained independence in October 1960. In doing so, the West Nigerian government disregarded the recommendations of the Ashby Committee, a federal university planning committee, which limited the building of regional universities to the northern and eastern regions alone.[5] This regional competition over the allocation of higher education resources was intertwined with ethnical rivalry, as each region was associated with one of Nigeria's dominant ethnic groups. Originating from this act of defiance against the Ashby Committee, the University of Ife was the West Nigerian government's most ambitious project. With an estimated capital expenditure of twenty million pounds in the first ten years, the university was to be the western region's showpiece and continued to be a top priority in the following decades, withstanding radical shifts in both local and federal government.[6]

Persistence in planning and constructing the university campus over the next twenty years attests to the determination of West Nigerian politicians and educators and their commitment to building the university despite fickle geopolitical alignments, political crises, and corruption. The decision to establish the university was made under the leadership of chief Obafemi Awolowo of the ruling party, Action Group, but in 1962 a political crisis in the region brought his incarceration and the dissolution of the party.[7] At that time, the university provincial council requested that the Israeli architects discontinue designing most of the buildings, with the expectation that the regional Ministry of Work would complete the task. However, claiming that this would jeopardize the integrity of the master plan, the Israeli architects insisted on continuing to oversee the design.[8] Work resumed as soon as the federal military coup of 1966 stabilized the region. Despite the civil war that broke out the following year and continued until the end of the decade, the construction of the university carried on almost without interruption well into the 1970s.[9] In fact, it did not halt even in 1973, when Nigeria severed formal diplomatic relations with Israel, whose Solel Boneh was in charge of most of the undertaking, initially as Nigersol, a joint company with the government of West Nigeria, and after 1966, as a private local branch of Solel Boneh.

As in the case of the Sierra Leone parliament building, the western region's government, while determined to establish a regional university, had no concrete vision for its physical manifestation. With no prescribed model for a postcolonial African university, the program and master plan unfolded in tandem as Sharon started to search for a site and began preliminary planning while the university committee deliberated on the university's character. Although this was the first university to be planned by an all-Nigerian committee, foreign aid nevertheless affected the university's formation.[10] Between 1960 and 1962, Nigeria received loans from the United Kingdom, the United States, the International Bank for Development and Reconstruction, and Israel.[11] Nigeria's shift from the model of Oxbridge to that of the American land grant university reflects this development theater: while the influence of the World Bank and the United States was growing, that of the United Kingdom was waning. Although Israel's aid was miniscule compared to that of both the declining British Empire and the rising United States, in practice Sharon and his team played a decisive role in planning and designing the university. Sharon's architects drew on their experience in Israel and negotiated American influence, particularly the recommendations made by a team from the Department of Landscape Architecture at the University of Wisconsin-Madison, who served as consultants from 1966 to 1969.

This chapter tracks the planning of the university campus from its early inception; I open by showing how regional rivalries and the politics of foreign aid together led to the awarding of the project to Nigersol, Solel Boneh's partnership with the western region government. The chapter then turns to the choice of site, the reasons for the committee's rejection of the Oxbridge collegiate model, and the search for an alternative model. I delve into the history of UCI's planning in order to show how the Oxbridge model was used in Nigeria and explore why the University of Ife committee rejected it. The chapter concludes with Sharon's turn to kibbutz planning as a way of integrating agricultural facilities with the representative university core. Influenced by the recommendations of the University of Wisconsin consultants, Sharon adapted the collective principles of kibbutzim to American-inspired suburban living. Both the kibbutz and suburban models addressed the university's need to elevate the standard of living in the countryside so that it could attract faculty who preferred the urban environs of Ibadan and Lagos, and discourage students from leaving the rural hinterland following graduation.

The problem of reconfiguring the countryside so it would become a desirable alternative to the city builds on the discussion in chapter 2, where I showed how strengthening Sierra Leone's interior was proposed as a strategy to preempt rural-urban migration to the country's capital, Freetown. However, the plan for the University of Ife's campus diverged greatly from the Sierra Leone national urbanization plan in both the audience it addressed and the image of the countryside it produced. While the plan for

Sierra Leone addressed mainly chiefs and assured them that the customary social structure would not be affected by the modernization of the country's economy, the plan for the University of Ife campus addressed university professors and students, who for the most part associated modernity and education with an urban lifestyle. As we saw in the first chapter, African governments also faced the challenge of mobilizing their workforce. While the first chapter focused on the unskilled labor used to build the Sierra Leone parliament, this chapter addresses how the University of Ife's curriculum was designed to produce the much-needed skilled manpower that was especially lacking in the countryside. In order to do so, the university campus needed to radically break with the backward image of the countryside so that it could present a competing vision of modernity. Unlike in the Sierra Leone plan, therefore, the aim was not to balance the traditional countryside with urbanization but rather to radically transform the countryside both by professionalizing agriculture and by changing the lifestyle associated with it. However, as this chapter demonstrates, this attempt failed to extend beyond the boundaries of the campus, which continued to grow as a self-contained economic and cultural unit.

National Politics, Regional Ambitions, and International Aid

The decision to establish a regional university in Nigeria's western region followed a series of higher education reforms that the British colonial government had initiated in the 1950s, culminating in the Ashby Committee's report on the eve of Nigerian independence. Recommending the establishment of two regional universities in the east and north as well as a federal university in Lagos, the Ashby Committee assumed that the existing University College Ibadan, the first university in the country, which had been established in 1948 in the capital of the western region, would address that region's educational needs. However, the western region government argued that UCI's capacity was too limited to fulfill these needs. In 1960, there were close to three thousand students from West Nigeria, supported by government scholarships, in the United Kingdom alone.[12] Furthermore, due to its status as a federal university, UCI enrolled equal numbers of students from each of the three regions, and therefore even if it grew, it could not assure sufficient space for students from the western region.[13] Not only UCI but also other federal educational institutions, such as a branch of the Nigerian College for Arts, Science and Technology in Ibadan and the Yaba College in federal Lagos, were located in the western region, but, in effect, the privilege the region had enjoyed during the late colonial period became a hindrance with the approach of independence. Protesting against these recommendations, Sanya Dojo Onabamiro, the western region's minister of education and its representative on the Ashby Committee, submitted a minority report and withdrew from the committee in protest.[14] From that moment on, the western region's government unilaterally pursued its decision to establish a university in the region that would cater first, if not exclusively, to students who were predominantly of Yoruba origin.[15]

In April 1961, when the federal government formally accepted the establishment of the university, its planning was already underway.[16] By that point, the western government had formed the University Planning Committee in October 1960, published a white paper announcing the search for a suitable site in November, and then sent a delegation on a study-tour of campuses overseas.[17]

By the time the decision to establish a regional university had been made, Nigersol had already been in operation for almost two years and was waiting for a commission of such magnitude. Although Britain blocked the opening of an Israeli consular office in Lagos until March 1960, Israel had already initiated trade relations and technical assistance programs with Nigeria.[18] In 1957, when the eastern and western regions became self-governing (the northern region postponed it until 1959), initial trade relations were formalized.[19] These trade relations were mediated mainly through the Israeli export company Dizengoff West Africa, which was established the same year and opened branches in Ghana, Sierra Leone, and Nigeria.[20] As early as 1957, Chief C. D. Akran, minister of development for Nigeria's western region, visited Israel to negotiate trade and technical assistance.[21] Chief Akin Deko, minister of agriculture and natural resources for West Nigeria, visited the following year.[22] In the wake of these visits, Solel Boneh personnel and Israeli foreign ministry delegates stationed in Accra frequented West Nigeria to discuss the establishment of a joint company modeled on an Israeli-Ghanaian partnership, the Ghana National Construction Corporation.[23] These negotiations resulted in an agreement, signed on January 14, 1959, between the Western Region Production Development Board and Solel Boneh to establish the Nigersol Construction Company. Solel Boneh held 40 percent of its shares.[24] By September 1959, eleven Solel Boneh personnel were stationed in Ibadan, while two more were on their way; Nigersol employed 270 local workers.[25] In December 1960, just two months after Nigeria celebrated its independence, there were sixty-two Solel Boneh personnel stationed in Nigersol branches in Ibadan and Lagos.[26]

Through the Western Region Production Development Board (later renamed Western Nigeria Development Corporation), the government was involved in the Nigerian construction market. Its involvement was based on what the political scientist Crawford Young has called the "pragmatic socialism" of the late 1950s, in which a nationalist "nurture-capitalism," whereby the government encouraged the growth of a local entrepreneurial class, was combined with state-capitalist and welfare tendencies.[27] The *1955–60 Economic Plan of Western Nigeria* outlined the following priorities for the Development Corporation: "(a) the undertaking of those projects for which individual initiative and private capital are not forthcoming, i.e.[,] to be complementary to, and not competitive with, private enterprise; (b) the undertaking of those types of enterprise for which the minimum economic unit and, so, the capital requirements are large; and (c) the attraction, so far as possible, of outside capital to these enterprises subject to adequate safeguards."[28]

In the absence of a strong indigenous private sector, this parastatal sector assumed the role of an entrepreneur, while the government attracted foreign investment with various incentives such as tax relief and protective tariffs.[29] This may help to explain why the western region, alongside federal Lagos, attracted most of the country's foreign investment, despite the fact that its first premier, Obafemi Awolowo, advanced nationalization as part of his opposition to foreign domination of the economy.[30] In this context, a continuous influx of foreign investment was not perceived as a new economic subjugation. On the contrary, relationships with non-British investors were welcomed as a means of loosening British companies' grip on the economy and therefore as steps toward economic independence.

Attracting foreign investment also presented a strategic advantage in domestic rivalries. Against British attempts to thwart the Israeli initiative because it would decrease dependence on British contractors, the western region government was keen to establish the joint company before the impending federal elections of 1960. Awolowo wanted to boost the region's economy in order to bolster his party's competitiveness against a potential coalition of the northern and eastern regions.[31] This regional competition, however, did not deter Solel Boneh from establishing a parallel joint company with the eastern region government, the Eastern Nigeria Construction and Furniture Company, in November 1959.[32] The booming state construction industry, which had opened to private contracting in 1950, offered a particularly lucrative opportunity. From 1950 to 1963, construction costs rose 285 percent while overall prices increased only 36 percent.[33] As the Israel foreign ministry official A. Tzur reported on the eve of 1959, "Just today the newspaper published the figures that English contractor companies' estimated jobs in Nigeria in 1957 is 157 million pounds."[34] At the time of its inception, Nigersol expected its work over the following five years to yield twenty million British pounds.[35] Nigersol's establishment as a government-owned company was therefore an attempt to return to the western region's government, now fully Nigerianized, some of the profits from the region's construction industry, if not control over it.[36]

Indicating Nigeria's entrepreneurship, Nigersol's "Memorandum and Articles of Association," dated September 29, 1959, nowhere declare that the company was state-owned. The company's mission statement was grounded purely on a market-based economy, and the scope of its activity was by no means limited to the western region, or even to Nigeria.[37] Off the record, however, Awolowo's government assured the Israeli delegates ("without blushing," as one of them reported) that Nigersol would be given priority over other contractors in state projects and would sometimes even be able to bypass formal tenders.[38] In the negotiations over the establishment of the Eastern Nigeria Construction and Furniture Company, a similar company in the eastern region, the Israeli representative made it clear that securing a few head-start projects was a precondition for any such undertaking.[39]

The low interest loans that Israel offered to Nigeria's federal government also played a role in Nigersol's establishment in this parastatal sector. While the loans were only occasionally directed toward the implementation of specific projects, as in the case of the loan for the Sierra Leone parliament, it was generally understood that the majority of the loans would be used for the projects that Israeli-African joint companies were undertaking. Furthermore, even if African governments did not condition the establishment of joint companies on Israel's granting of loans, their establishment served as an incentive for such granting, in order to ensure the joint companies' success in securing and carrying out projects. Israel and the future federal government of Nigeria signed their first loan agreement in Lagos in July 1960.[40] In a draft dated a month earlier, the three-million-British-pound loan was to be divided equally between the northern region (whose pro–Arab League government Israel had been persistently courting), the eastern region, and the federal government. Eventually, the signed agreement specified the allocation of one million British pounds to the Eastern Nigeria Construction and Furniture Company to complete construction of two hotels in Enugu and Port Harcourt, and the remaining two million pounds were left to the discretion of the federal government, provided that it would use half for the purchase of Israeli goods and the other half for development projects. It was assumed that Israeli-Nigerian joint companies would carry out at least some of these projects. In later correspondence, the federal minister of finance, chief Festus Samuel Okotie-Eboh, confirmed that he would ensure that 500,000 British pounds would be allocated to the government of West Nigeria and be used "exclusively for paying outstanding Bills to the Nigersol Construction Company and the Nigerian Water Resources Developments Limited," both Israeli-Nigerian joint companies.[41]

The western region's university project, with a capital expenditure estimated at twenty million pounds for the first ten years, was by far the largest project Nigersol could have hoped for.[42] With Nigersol readily available, the University Planning Committee did not issue a public tender.[43] It was clear that Nigersol would be the contractor for the bush clearing, road paving, and eventually construction of the buildings. Before this commission, Nigersol's contracts included civil engineering projects such as the construction of roads, industrial sheds, and warehouses.[44] It was assumed that once major architectural projects arrived, they would boost the company's experience and prestige, increase the number of its workers, and utilize machinery on which the company had spent over a million British pounds.[45] The first such job Nigersol undertook was the Premier Hotel in Ibadan, for which Solel Boneh subcontracted the Haifa architect Shmuel Rosoff, known for designing luxury hotels and villas.[46] Planning and construction were perceived as linked, and there was no institutional separation between the trades: Solel Boneh employed its own architects, who were in charge of planning tasks for the African joint companies. When commissions for more complicated and prestigious projects arrived, Solel Boneh often subcontracted prominent Israeli architects specifically for the job.[47] As a result, there was no clear, formal division between the designers and the construction contractors, as both were employed by Solel Boneh. Moreover, when design and construction were divorced, that could doom the project: on one occasion, the prominent Israeli architect Alfred (Al) Mansfeld was to design the University of Nigeria in the eastern region, but planning for the university was aborted due to disputes with the local contractors.[48] As the diplomat reporting on the fiasco argued, Israel had no interest in designing projects without also handling their construction.[49] The dependence of the former on the latter reflected the need to show concrete results through the execution of such projects, as well as to ensure that Israeli loans returned to Israel through the construction company's purchase of Israeli products.

Following Solel Boneh's habit of subcontracting external architects for complex and prestigious jobs, Nigersol commissioned prominent architect and town planner Arieh Sharon to design the master plan for the University of Ife's campus. Given Sharon's long-established professional connections with the Histadrut and Solel Boneh, and the fact that he had created the winning design proposal for the new campus forum at the Technion (Israel Institute of Technology), this commission is not surprising. However, since the architectural firm Karmi-Meltzer-Karmi, who designed Sierra Leone's parliament, had an equally important commission on the Hebrew University campus in Givat Ram, as did Al Mansfeld, who was commissioned to design the University of Nigeria in the eastern region, it appears that Solel Boneh did not concentrate its projects in the hands of one particular external firm for strategic reasons—so that Solel Boneh itself would remain in control of the receipt of commissions in Africa. Perhaps following the Sierra Leone Public Works Department director's criticism about the lack of checks and balances between design and construction in the operation of the Sierra Leone National Construction Company (see chapter 1), Solel Boneh further divided up the work in Ife. In designing the University of Ife, Sharon collaborated with Solel Boneh architects who were employed by a subcompany under the acronym AMY (architects, engineers, consultants).

Site Selection

Because it was already the seat of University College Ibadan, the western region's capital, Ibadan, was automatically annulled as a site option for the western regional university. With no obvious alternative, the choice of site became a subject of intense competition among Yoruba towns, whose economies—except for that of industrialized Lagos—depended mainly on trade, craft, and agriculture.[50] While the university was seen as a motor for the development of the region in general, it would benefit its immediate environment most promptly, boosting the economy of the town selected by increasing commerce and providing jobs and services. This had been the case with the opening of UCI; together with the teaching hospital's well-paid employees and the concentration of government ministries, UCI substantially increased purchasing power in Ibadan and stimulated rapid growth in commerce and employment opportunities.[51] To preempt a political crisis and relieve the tension between rival towns, the planning committee issued a white paper announcing that the choice of site would "be guided by the advice of experts who will conduct a survey of all possible sites in various parts of the Region."[52]

Serving as such an impartial expert, Sharon had already arrived in Nigeria shortly before the white paper meeting took place to conduct a preliminary survey of eight towns, based on a list from the minister of education, Dr. Onabamiro.[53] The list included Abeokuta, Ado-Ekiti, Akure, Benin City, Ile-Ife, Ijebu-Ode, Ondo, and Owo, to which Sharon added the town of Oyo. Sharon submitted his report on the first day of the white paper meeting, and its criteria were based on his conclusions. Sharon listed five factors that he deemed decisive in the selection of a campus site. First, the town and district selected should be centrally located within the western region and in relation to other regions, and should be easily accessible by road, railway, and a future airport. Second, the site should be adjacent to a medium-sized town of 100,000 people (to be expanded in the future to 150,000 people) that should be "well-developing and if possible, quite attractive." Third, the size of the site should be about five-by-five or four-by-six miles, and it should be located two to three miles from the boundary of the town. Fourth, in addition to infrastructural amenities such as water supply, electricity, and telecommunications, which had already been constructed or were near completion in most of the towns in the survey, Sharon added soil conditions "and other fertility factors" as equally decisive in the choice of a site for a university where one of the main fields of research and study would be agriculture.[54] The fifth and final factor pertained to the "microphysical conditions," by which Sharon referred to the kind of landscape he envisioned as the ideal setting for a university campus. Attached to his report was a comparative table containing data on location, communications (quality of roads, railway station, and airport), geographic factors (altitude and climate), existing services and amenities (water supply and electricity, hospitals, schools, shops), population figures and occupation, and general characteristics relating to the local and physical environment.

The white paper incorporated most of Sharon's recommendations, but, tellingly, inverted their order when presenting them to the larger public. Sharon's fifth and most subjective point regarding "the physical setting appropriate to a University environment" moved up to the top of the list of prerequisites, while soil conditions suitable for agricultural experimentation moved to the prominent second position. The white paper positioned the centrality of the town in relation to the region as the third condition, leaving out Sharon's concern about the centrality of the chosen town in relation to the entire country. These modifications bring to the fore what the western regional government wanted to emphasize: that the university would serve the western region first and foremost, rather than the entire country, and that it would be dedicated to agricultural experimentation as one of its flagship research fields. By moving the least objectively measurable parameter—"the physical settings appropriate to a University environment"—to the forefront, the white paper left the final say on the site to the architect, rendering the decision-making process opaque enough that his professional authority would override any possible grievances.[55]

After returning for another visit and surveying seven more towns—Badagry, Ilaro, Ilesha, Ogbomosho, Oshogbo, Shagamu, and Sapele—Sharon chose the town of Ife (Yoruba: Ifè, also Ilé-Ifè).[56] More centrally located within the region than the region's capital, Ibadan, Ife was nonetheless connected to Ibadan's "first-class" fifty-one-mile road and could benefit from its proximity. Ife's geographical centrality was further reaffirmed after the midwestern region formed its own government in 1963; its separation from the western region reduced the latter's size by approximately one-third to the east. Ife satisfied other conditions as well, as it was a medium-sized town of 110,000 thousand people and a prominent producer of cocoa, the staple product of the region, as well as palm kernels and timber.[57] In terms of infrastructure and services, it had electricity and a local water supply, along with a new water scheme that was underway. In addition, it had "many schools, a modern hospital, banks and lively shopping streets."[58] Sharon found its geographic and climatic settings favorable due to its location in the high-forest belt of the region, eight hundred feet above sea level, with a temperature varying between 60 and 80 degrees Fahrenheit and a mean relative humidity of 70 percent. Portraying the site as "an attractive slightly undulated wooded countryside, rich in agricultural plantations, which form also the economic basis for Ife's economy and future development," Sharon linked the relatively pleasant climate with the aesthetic qualities of the landscape and its economic potential—a subject that I will return to in the next chapter, and which explores the Sharon team's design of the campus core in relation to the area's tropical climate.[59] Referring specifically to the wooded site, bounded by a series of hills and a river on the northwest edge of town, Sharon qualified his choice by mentioning that despite its economic potential, the area was relatively unpopulated, and therefore the project would not involve a massive displacement of farmers.[60]

To these favorable factors, Sharon retroactively added the town's cultural and historical significance: Ife is considered the cradle of Yoruba civilization and the seat of the ooni. Sharon added these comments after the site was chosen, suggesting that they served post hoc to rationalize and buttress what was, at bottom, a political decision.[61] Categorized as "third-class" under the colonial administration, Ife had received fewer services than many "second-class" towns (Lagos was the sole "first-class" town).[62] There were other strong candidates: the towns of Oyo and Ilesha were also singled out by the planning committee.[63] However, since ooni Adesoji Aderemi (Oba Sir Titus Martins Adesoji Tadeniawo Aderemi, king of Ife, 1930–80) was a supporter of the Action Group and the town served as a stronghold of the ruling party, Ife's political capital was unmatched by that of its better-serviced competitors. With such a powerful figure on its side, the university would benefit both from the extensive communal lands the ooni could grant to it as well as Aderemi's assurance that the town would collaborate fully with the university endeavor.[64]

### The Search for a Model

Conceiving of their regional university as an alternative to the federal UCI, the University of Ife's founders took both UCI's curriculum and its architecture as negative reference points. As the first university in Nigeria, UCI served as a testing ground for higher education in the country. Many of the founders of the University of Ife drew their conclusions directly from their intimate experience of UCI's formation.[65] Established in 1948 by the British as part of colonial educational reform, UCI was one of a few new university colleges established in the West Indies, Malaya, Uganda, and the Gold Coast (Ghana).[66] The two universities in West Africa, UCI and the University College of the Gold Coast, joined the existing Fourah Bay College in Freetown, Sierra Leone, which had been founded in 1827 and, until 1948, was the only university in the entire region to serve the growing demand for higher education. Because of this, Yoruba of Nigeria had been sending their children to British universities since the 1870s. Due to a shortage of places available in Britain after World War I, from the 1920s on Yoruba turned to North American universities and colleges as well; beginning in the 1930s, Nigeria's other ethnic groups followed suit.[67]

University College Ibadan succeeded Yaba Higher College, whose staff, students, and equipment it inherited when the college closed in December 1947. Officially opened in 1934, though it had been in operation since 1932, Yaba Higher College was established on the outskirts of Lagos municipality mainly to cater to the manpower needs of the colonial governmental departments by training personnel for intermediary civil service posts.[68] The Nigerian elite criticized it for its vocational emphasis; its very limited enrollment, which was directly tied to anticipated vacancies; and its failure to fulfill any educational qualifications recognizable outside Nigeria. Arguing against what they interpreted as false standards, they accused the colonial administration of deliberately deterring Nigerian youth from pursuing education abroad.[69] To correct this, the British administration set up UCI as an institute of higher learning and included courses in the arts and sciences as well as professional schools, such as medicine, dentistry, agriculture, forestry, veterinary science, teacher training, and engineering, to respond to Nigeria's specific needs.[70] To ensure high standards, UCI granted degrees under the authority of the University of London until it gained academic independence in 1962; it subsequently changed its name to the University of Ibadan.[71]

Rising standards conflicted with demands to increase enrollment and the anticipated growth of the university. Ibadan was chosen for its advantages over Lagos' lagoon geography and its ability to accommodate and sustain the university's expected expansion. Ibadan's population was estimated at four hundred thousand at that time; it was the fourth-largest city in Africa and the largest in tropical Africa, larger even than neighboring Lagos. The local chiefs contributed more than 2,550 acres of land five miles away from the city for the university's site.[72] Despite these favorable conditions, however, consultants for the International Bank for Reconstruction and Development, who had frequented the country since the early 1950s, criticized UCI's slow growth rate: six years after it opened, it had an enrollment of only four hundred students. While this number represented nothing short of a failure for the American advisors, who had envisioned a university capacity of twenty thousand students, for the university's English founders this number optimally reflected the growth rate they had cautiously envisioned—they expected just "more than 600 students" by the end of the 1948–57 period.[73]

By the time of independence, as Omosini and Adediran argue, it had become clear that UCI was inadequate to meet the needs of "a country moving towards political sovereignty and with an articulate political elite desirous of decolonizing the public service economy."[74] In addition to curricular standards that inhibited UCI's growth, the planning of its campus along the lines of an Oxbridge residential collegiate model presented a major obstacle to expansion. The British Asquith Committee presented its argument for the necessity of a residential university model in the African context in 1945 because of "the unsuitability of off-campus accommodations and the necessity to supervise the health of the students closely." This emphasis on a healthy living environment must have had a particular resonance for Kenneth Mellanby, who, prior to becoming UCI's first principal, was trained as a medical entomologist at the London School of Hygiene and Tropical Medicine. The Asquith Committee's other points included "the widely different backgrounds of the undergraduates and the need to promote unity"—that is, the university would be an elite melting pot where the governing class would be groomed to overcome ethnic divisions—and "the opportunity offered for broadening their outlook through the sharing of experiences and through extra-curricular activities." Thus, the residential college model would allow the university to shape students' entire social lives and habits.[75] All points expressed the Asquith Committee's conviction that students had to be shielded from realities outside of the university campus.[76]

Following Mellanby's instructions, UCI was modeled on Oxbridge residential colleges. The initial site plan, designed in 1949 by British modernist architects E. Maxwell Fry and Jane Drew, comprised two halls of residence that accommodated 150 students each. The halls had their own courtyard and a dining hall, and each student enjoyed a private study-bedroom and a veranda.[77] UCI maintained exclusive standards suitable for the cultivation of a British-educated Nigerian elite—the designated "heirs of empire."[78] As a secluded space of privilege, UCI continued Oxbridge's ivory-tower elitism, which had emerged historically from "town-gown" antagonism and the necessity of segregating students for their own protection, especially after the Reformation.[79]

In November 1952, UCI's new halls of residence, laboratory, classroom blocks, and staff houses formally opened and presented a spectacular image of architectural modernism unrivaled in the area.[80] However, criticisms about the cost and restrictive capacity of the facilities were soon to follow. In 1954, Dr. Nnamdi (Zik) Azikiwe, the renowned Nigerian nationalist who would become Nigeria's first president, argued in the House of Representatives that "what this country sorely needs today is a first-class institution of learning and not a first-class exhibition of streamlined buildings." He went on to propose the use of prefabricated houses for junior and senior staff and the admission of nonresidential students.[81] Around the same time, International Bank for Development advisors criticized UCI's accommodations as "luxurious" and suggested pairing students in rooms to double capacity, pointing to Indian universities recently built with American guidance as alternatives to the Oxbridge model.[82] Even the Inter-University Council of England, which had been established in March 1946 to supervise the colonial universities' "special relationship" with universities in England on the Asquith Committee's recommendation, criticized the excessive emphasis on halls. The collegiate model was gradually abandoned, and, in the early 1970s, the University of Ibadan ceased being exclusively residential.[83]

With the negative example of UCI in mind, Sharon addressed the "town-gown" relationship in Ife, arguing that the town's medium size—with a population of just over one hundred thousand compared to Ibadan's four hundred thousand—would ensure a mutually beneficial relationship between the town and the university and prevent "the danger of social sterility and intellectual superiority."[84] With a projected figure of three thousand students in the first decade compared to "more than 600" in Ibadan,[85] the ratio of students and faculty to town residents would ensure interrelationships between the two groups and preclude any elitism. As the projected student population and the desirable size of the campus grew following the university committee's study trip to universities in the United States and Latin America, the distance between the campus and the town was reduced from two to three miles to one to two miles, further emphasizing the campus' potential connectivity with the town, as against the five-mile distance between UCI and Ibadan. Sharon recommended that the university's campus plan be incorporated into Ife's town plan, if such a plan existed, so that their growth could be coordinated.[86] Finally, Sharon's plan implied that the university's facilities, services, and infrastructure would raise the standard of living in the town.

Starting out with 244 students and about eighty teaching staff in October 1962, by the end of 1978 the University of Ife comprised 9,097 students and 1,346 academic and senior staff.[87] Given this growth rate, the enrollment goal of twenty thousand students set by the International Bank for Development advisors, which may have been based on their experience in India, was not an overestimate. From 1951, when the United States started the Technical Cooperation Mission, to 1972, the International Bank and other organizations were involved in establishing agricultural universities in India modeled on American land grant universities.[88] Seen perhaps as a convenient mechanism for appropriating land under customary tenure, the land grant university also brought, along with its democratic ideals, some of the American settler colonial history that undergirded it.[89] In 1961, when the US Agency for International Development (USAID) took over, it extended this university development program to Nigeria.[90]

The land grant university model was not a unidirectional imposition. In fact, Nnamdi (Zik) Azikiwe, who served as the premier of the eastern region before he was named general governor in 1960 and, subsequently, president of the country in 1963, first imported it to Nigeria. While Ife was the first Nigerian university to be established on the recommendation of an all-Nigerian committee, the University of Nigeria in Nsukka, East Nigeria, was the first to introduce a model that radically diverged from that of UCI in order to accommodate the postindependence era.[91] Unlike Obafemi Awolowo, the first premier of the western region, who was educated in Nigeria and England and therefore had not experienced the American university system firsthand, Nnamdi Azikiwe had received his degrees from Howard University in Washington, DC; Lincoln University in Pennsylvania; and the University of Pennsylvania. As early as the late 1930s and 1940s, Azikiwe organized sponsorship programs from American institutions for the education of Nigerian students.[92] Following the eastern region's initiative to establish a regional university, advisors from Exeter University in England and Michigan State University in the United States arrived in East Nigeria as early as 1957; their recommendations set a precedent that the West Nigerians would follow.[93] These advisors suggested the establishment of a provisional council and a visit to universities in England and the United States.[94]

Members of the University of Ife Planning Committee, who had already visited Oxford, Yale, Harvard, and MIT, added to their study tour universities in Mexico City, Rio de Janeiro, and Caracas—the last of which was eventually dropped.[95] It is possible that the decision to visit universities in Latin America was made on the recommendation of the Harvard architecture dean José Luis Sert, whom the Nigerian delegation had met on its preliminary tour and who had considerable planning experience in Latin America.[96] This initiative certainly did not come from Sharon, whose first impulse was to examine contemporary university planning in the Netherlands, Denmark, and Germany.[97] Although Sharon cited the Israeli universities—the Hebrew University of Jerusalem and the Technion in Haifa, both of which he had a hand in designing—as having made a most positive impression on the delegates, these were not part of the official itinerary and were not visited by the entire delegation.[98] Two members of the Nigerian delegation arrived in Israel at the end of the tour primarily to discuss the construction and financing arrangements, and Sharon used this opportunity to show them the newly built campuses.[99] Writing for the entire delegation, Sharon stated that in Latin America, "the greatest lesson was given to us by the Aztecs and the Mayas' old towns," although it was the modern university in Mexico City that in fact impressed the West Nigerian delegation.[100] The disparate opinions did not center around form as much as scale. Although the planning of the National Autonomous University of Mexico was inspired by Aztec towns, its scale was more reminiscent of the monumental modernity of Brasília.[101] Sharon instead proposed the compact scale of Israeli campuses, neglecting the extreme disparity between the population of Nigeria, which was much closer to that of a large Latin American country, than to that of a country as small as Israel.

In terms of program, the university planners clearly preferred the American university model over the European one. Comparing the two, the unofficial committee of intellectuals set up by premier chief Samuel Ladoke Akintola agreed that the latter produces a "scholar" with "specialized knowledge" and thus caters to only a small section of the population, while the American model aims at "breadth and balance in scholarship . . . makes genera [sic] education an integral part of University curriculum[,] . . . provides for a much higher percentage of the population[,] . . . [and] have managed to combine quality with quantity."[102] Envisioning a radical reorientation of UCI's curriculum to make education relevant to the needs of the region and to rapidly Nigerianize the public service, the university planners had a nonelitist institution in mind, for which the North American land grant university and its Latin American counterpart, the reformed university, could serve as models.[103] Both of these democratized models emphasized public access to education, applied research, and community enhancement as formulated in the tripartite mission of teaching, research, and off-campus extension.[104] The goal of the new university, according to its historians, was "to produce graduates who will be able to adjust themselves to life in the communities they may be called upon to serve and not reproduce an elite which is divorced from the rest of the community."[105] In order to facilitate this transformation rapidly, the Akintola committee recommended to supplement university education with evening classes, correspondence courses, and training programs.[106] Furthermore, in contrast to British emphasis on training civil servants, the committee aspired for an enrollment ratio of 65 percent in the sciences and 35 percent in the humanities.[107] At its first meeting, the western region university planning committee decided that the faculties of agriculture, arts, science, engineering, and social science would be set up in the first five years, followed by the faculties of medicine, veterinary science, dental surgery, and law. In addition, the faculty of engineering would later be expanded to include architecture, town planning, quantity surveying, and estate management.[108]

Recognizing the opportunity for extensive involvement in the concurrent development of all three regional universities, USAID launched what was then its largest US assistance program in Africa. This assistance involved pairing a major American land grant university with each regional university: Kansas State University partnered with Ahmadu Bello University in the north; Michigan State University with the University of Nigeria at Nsukka in the east; and the University of Wisconsin with the University of Ife in the west.[109] While the American universities differed in the scope of their involvement, the main impetus behind the partnerships was to establish agricultural research institutions in Nigeria. The American land grant university model was especially attractive to Nigerian regional governments since it addressed the needs and concerns of the local community, often by establishing off-campus extension programs.

Since American aid focused on agriculture, it depended on access to land. Through the professionalization of farming, university-level applied research, and extension services for the surrounding population, the university system presented the most viable channel for American intervention in what was the largest production and export sector in Nigeria before the 1970s oil boom. While the western and eastern regional governments did manage to acquire land for rural resettlement projects, the customary land tenure system made it difficult to acquire the large tracts of land necessary for agricultural experimentation.[110] Land was traditionally the property of the community and was subdivided among families and individuals for cultivation. It could not be bought or sold, and thus large projects required a special grant of land from a local chief.[111] Oladele Adebayo Ajose, the first vice-chancellor of the University of Ife, managed to acquire a 13,500-acre site from the ooni of Ife, Adesoji Aderemi, who also served as the governor of the western region from 1960 to 1962. Of that area, three thousand acres were allocated for experimental use by the agriculture faculty, compared to just five hundred acres at University College Ibadan.[112] The University of Ife's agricultural facilities included a farm center, a swine research unit, a poultry research unit, a greenhouse, a nursery, cropping systems, and research units for cattle, sheep, dairy goats, and turkeys.[113]

## Rebranding the Rural

While Nigerian agriculturalists shared American assumptions about the benefits of modernizing agriculture, it was more difficult to recruit the younger generation to this task in a society in which modernization, high standards of living, and social status were associated exclusively with the city.[114] In his 1971 address to the university, vice-chancellor Hezekiah Oluwasanmi, himself a professor of agricultural economics, deplored the flight of university graduates, who "loathed the rural areas," to the city. The problem, he explained, was that the urban migration of educated young people left rural areas in the hands of non-Nigerians who did not understand Nigerian rural culture. This was, Oluwasanmi stressed, "our chance of effecting a rapid but orderly social change."[115] Similarly, Akintola Agboola of the Faculty of Agriculture at the University of Ife complained in 1967 that school "graduates from any level regard farmers as those at the bottom of the economic ladder."[116] Due to British colonial prejudices built into the educational system, the sons of farmers did not return to their families' farms after acquiring an education because they associated farming with backwardness and illiteracy.[117] To reform agriculture successfully, Agboola argued, adult education for practicing farmers was not enough. Educated young men, who "will be easier to reach than the old illiterate farmers," were needed, and therefore incentives had to be created to induce them to return.[118]

Both the status of the farmer and rural living conditions needed to be elevated to present a desirable alternative to the lure of the city. On top of providing land for experimentation, the regional university campus served as the ideal setting in which to demonstrate modern rural living. Just as the university's agricultural land functioned as a demonstration farm for nearby farmers, so the residential quarters of its staff, dispersed in the bucolic landscape between the agriculture faculty and the university farm, demonstrated high-quality living in a rural area.[119] As in other places, architecture here made visible the benefits of modernized agriculture.[120] For those who did not frequent the campus, a photograph of a house of the largest type among the university's 130 units for senior staff appeared in the *Nigerian Daily Sketch*, a western region newspaper published in Ibadan.[121] It looked no less comfortable than the houses of the Bodija Estate, the first planned housing estate in Ibadan, built in the early 1960s and modeled after colonial residential districts specifically reserved for Europeans. The Bodija Estate served as a model for the senior staff housing of the nearby University College Ibadan and presented a desirable standard for faculty housing.[122] Like the hierarchy of housing types, corresponding to a modern class system, that the Bodija Estate offered in order to attract both high- and middle-income residents, housing on the University of Ife campus was diversified to serve senior and junior faculty as well as staff (see plates 6–8).[123] By filling the campus site with varied housing, the university aimed to preempt the "villagization" of the campus—that is, the informal settlement of workers and displaced villagers on campus grounds.[124]

On top of providing housing for faculty, staff, and students, the university needed to supplement the city's services in order to maintain high standards of living and working. Sharon's evaluation of the existing infrastructure in his surveys proved too optimistic, as he could not foresee the internal political crisis that would halt regional development and campus construction from 1962 to 1966, when the new military government stabilized the region. When Hezekiah Oluwasanmi, the second vice-chancellor, arrived to inspect the site before the university's relocation from its temporary facilities in Ibadan, he found no telecommunications infrastructure in the area.[125] In addition, the university needed to construct a dam to supplement water supply, install emergency diesel generators for uninterrupted electricity service, and build a sewage treatment and disposal plant.[126] It also catered to the needs of the faculty and staff by establishing schools for their children. Thus the University of Ife campus in some ways replicated the "reservation," as residential quarters designed for Europeans came to be called during the colonial period. The small houses for "houseboys," or servants, that were built adjacent to faculty housing further reinforced this impression. By the beginning of the 1980s, the Israeli team of architects in charge of the updated master plan had already abandoned the language of symbiotic development with the town of Ife, arguing that, "located in a rural area, the University must develop self-sufficiency in terms of services, housing, recreation, schools and shopping and in terms of infrastructural capabilities such as electricity, water, sewage, disposal and treatment, communications and transportation."[127]

The University of Ife faced an image problem not only because of the status of farming as a profession and the need to improve standards of living in rural areas but also because social mobility, cultural capital, and sophistication were associated strictly with the city. In addition to drawing the sons of farmers back to their family farms, the university had to attract Nigerian and international professors—rare commodities subject to competition from other new universities—to its rural setting.[128] In the western region, the University of Ife competed in particular with the federal universities of Ibadan and Lagos, the latter established in 1962. Although Ife was only fifty-one miles away from Ibadan, it was considered so remote that even Ife's own faculty, who initially taught in temporary structures in Ibadan, were reluctant to move to Ife when the campus began its operation.[129] Among his reasons for choosing Ife, Sharon had mentioned the cultural and historical value of the museum of Ife, established in 1954 to house Ife's antiquities. Although Ife was a center for traditional craftwork, it did not have the vibrant art culture that characterized Ibadan and was developing in its nearer neighbor, the town of Oshogbo.[130] While Sharon acknowledged that Ibadan was the regional university's closest metropolitan center, he envisioned Ife as a cultural center in its own right, which would be revived by the activities of the university. The university's founders shared this vision. In fact, one of the tasks of the University Town and Gown Committee was to manage Ife's Ori Olokun Cultural Center, which provided space in town for the university's theatre company. However, by the end of the 1970s, most of the cultural activity organized by the university had relocated to campus, as it offered better facilities in the newly built Institute of African Studies, designed by E. Maxwell Fry, Jane Drew, and J. Robin Atkinson, and Oduduwa Hall, designed by Harold Rubin for Sharon.[131] As a result, while students and faculty "went to town" in Ibadan, most likely against the university administration's wishes, at Ife, the town came to campus.[132]

Campus Plan: Marrying the Rural with the Urban,
Kibbutz with Suburbia

Early designs for the campus reflect the equal weight given to culture and agriculture as two distinct components of the university; these designs rely on a basic separation between the academic core and the Faculty of Agriculture, which formed a semienclosure of its own (see plate 9).[133] Sharon, who had no experience in designing a university campus that included a large agriculture faculty and its experimental facilities, approached Hebrew University's Faculty of Agriculture to consult on planning. Although also developed on the basis of the American land grant university model, Hebrew University's agriculture faculty did not provide an example of an integrated campus. Originally established as an independent research institute and later incorporated into the university, it is located on a separate campus in Rehovot, away from the main campus in Jerusalem.[134] Similarly, the siting of schools of agriculture at American land grant universities was more often the result of historical contingency than deliberate planning. With no comprehensive model for the rational integration of agriculture in campus planning, Sharon struggled with siting the Faculty of Agriculture and its farms in relation to the rest of the faculties, especially the representative academic core. As a series of plans between June 1961 and June 1962 demonstrates, Sharon treated the academic core—which included the faculties of the humanities, the social sciences, and education, as well as the administration building, the central library, and the assembly hall—as one unit, around which other faculties were to be placed to its north, east, and west. The agriculture faculty, however, was part of neither the core nor the periphery. Located northeast of the central core and separated from it by stretches of land, Sharon designed it as a discrete unit that consisted of three orthogonal parallel buildings connected by a shaded pathway and a bridge (see plate 10). As a few of the first buildings to be built on campus grounds, this architectural ensemble is stylistically distinct; later buildings would mostly do away with its rectangular blocks and articulated sun shades, as I discuss in the next chapter. Designed before Sharon's partnership with Benjamin Idelson was severed in 1964, these agricultural facilities are more reminiscent of contemporaneous work in Israel than any of the buildings Sharon would later design for the campus.

In separating the agricultural faculty geographically and programmatically from the university core, Sharon drew on the basics of kibbutz planning with which he was very familiar, first from founding a kibbutz, and later from serving as a planner for the Kibbutz Artzi movement. Kibbutzim, or Jewish collective settlements, began as agricultural settler communities with residences and farms at either end of a rectangular courtyard that served as a common yard.[135] With the growth of kibbutzim in the 1940s, their basic scheme came to involve a division between a social zone and an agricultural zone, which were separated by a green belt. Social zones housed residential and educational facilities and featured a cultural core, while agricultural zones later came to include industry as well.[136] Imagining the kibbutz as a city-village hybrid, kibbutz planners rejected both the alienation and pollution of the city and the abjection of rural life as many kibbutz founders had experienced it in Eastern Europe. Conceiving it as a kind of "new village," kibbutz planners also rejected the idyllic images of rural life linked with early kibbutzim, on the one hand, and the industrialized image of the Soviet *kolkhoz* (collective farm), on the other.[137] Since ideological commitment was pertinent to the survival of a kibbutz's collectivist principles, education and the cultivation of intellectual and cultural life were considered of prime importance. Therefore, the core of a kibbutz often features cultural institutions, such as libraries and performance halls, surrounding a central lawn.[138] Addressing this kernel of kibbutz public life and the challenge of integrating public buildings into a kibbutz's bucolic landscaping, Sharon writes,

> The main planning problem in kibbutzim, as in old and new towns, was—and still is—how to create an architecturally attractive, social and cultural centre. How can the building elements of the dining-hall, the club-houses, the lawn and gardens, be combined into one architectural entity? How can a balanced space relationship between the strong cubes of buildings, the tall trees, and the open spaces and lawns be created? . . . I believe, however, in the clear and simple solution of a central lawn-piazza, surrounded by trees and pergolas, leading to the various public buildings, consisting of dining hall, administration, club and reading rooms. From this central area, all the other building zones would radiate centripetally: the residential and children's quarters, the farm buildings and the small, organic children's society.[139]

Substitute students for "children," a library for "reading rooms," and Oduduwa Hall for the "club," and you have a description of Sharon's vision for the Ife campus. Based on pedestrian-vehicular separation and designed for a growing community that would preserve its original close-knit character, Sharon saw in the kibbutz an appropriate model for a university campus that promoted modern rural living and the marriage of culture and education with agriculture.

The kibbutz model, however, did not entail importing the collective ideals that guided kibbutz founders. Although there was some pride in using a Histadrut contractor, as reflected in a 1973 publication on the university, and perhaps in Sharon's kibbutz background, which is mentioned in the retrospective account of professor of architecture Bayo Amole,[140] there is no indication of any collectivist ambitions for the campus in either Sharon's or the university's publications and correspondence. The applicability of the kibbutz model to the university campus derived from the fact that these two city-village hybrids shared common origins in Enlightenment and anarchist planning traditions that emanated from it.[141] Developed in North America, the university campus was ideally situated in the countryside; this was supposed to allow for expansion and to separate students from the putatively unhealthy and corrupting effects of the city by instead

FIGURE 3.1 Arieh Sharon, University of Ife, academic core, perspective (undated). Courtesy of the Azrieli Architectural Archive; Arieh Sharon collection, AES-1-217.

immersing their young bodies and minds in a salubrious natural setting.[142] Sharon was well aware of the interchangeability of kibbutz and campus planning models. For example, when he planned the boarding school in kibbutz Beit Alpha, he based it on the American campus tradition, with a three-sided quadrangle from which the school expanded horizontally around symmetrical courtyards. Sharon's plan for Ife was much looser in character and retained the three-sided open courtyard logic only in the central piazza of the academic core (see plate 11 and fig 3.1). Even then, its loose grid seemed rigid to the University of Wisconsin landscape architecture team that arrived in Ife in 1966 as USAID consultants. They were more accustomed to American universities' generously spread, Beaux Arts or Gothic bucolic campuses than to the modernist planning principles to which Sharon had adhered since his education at the Bauhaus in interwar Germany, under the famed modernist architects Walter Gropius and Hannes Meyer.[143] The Wisconsin team also criticized the vast open space and the monumental character of the buildings in the plaza, proposing instead the Beaux Arts model of the four-sided quadrangle with a domed structure as its focal point.[144]

The group of detached faculty houses, designed in collaboration with the Wisconsin consultants, adhered most closely to the picturesque image they had in mind. Located far from the university core, between the Faculty of Agriculture and its farms, the loose grouping of houses without fences was reminiscent of kibbutz shared property principles, or, alternatively, of American suburbia. Lush vegetation and some screened patios sheltered the houses from each other slightly, since, as Sharon had learned, even in a kibbutz people need a sense of privacy.[145] Yet the cars parked in front of the houses, and the distance between them, situated them in an individualist, consumerist society rather than in a collective kibbutz, while the adjacent small houses for the "houseboys" disclosed the persistence of a colonial, racialized class structure even in this progressive modern enclave.[146]

Postscript

In both appearance and function, the campus presented a complete alternative to life in the town of Ife as well as in other Yoruba towns and villages. In a report on its involvement in the three regional campuses, USAID emphasized the University of Ife's striking buildings and how they stood out from their surroundings: "The architecture is world-class and spectacular and contrasts starkly with the nearby, typically Yoruba city of Ile-Ife, with its densely clustered earthen buildings topped by rain-rusted tin roofs."[147] The campus contrasted not only with the town of Ife but with practically anything else familiar to the average Nigerian student as well. The description that opened this chapter, by a graduate who is now an agriculturalist and media consultant in Lagos, demonstrates the dramatic impression that the university made on new students.

A self-sufficient island that simulates suburban living (the university offers its houses for subsidized rent, not for sale), the campus brings to mind contemporary foreign resource-extractive enclaves in Africa. Like these transnational suburban gated communities, the campus serves as a governmental civil servants' enclave. However, whereas these foreign extractive company towns only pay lip service to the surrounding community through defunct infrastructure and white elephants, the university's commitment to the larger community was part of its raison d'être.[148] Nevertheless, its ambition to cooperate with the town and serve the regional community eventually turned into the opposite: the university supplanted the town, which, as the campus's planners implied, has failed to develop in tandem with it.[149]

In addition to shifting cultural activities from the town to campus, the 1970s saw the establishment of a commercial farm on campus grounds as an arm of the Faculty of Agriculture in partnership with the private sector. By 1980, however, this commercial farm was run solely by private parties who sold its produce to customers from the university and beyond from a booth west of the student residential areas. In 1979, fifty tons of maize, vegetables, plantains, and eggs were sold. This, in turn, threatened to strip the Yoruba town of its traditional market role and its main source of income. With its favorable road connections to nearby towns, the university's commercial farm could bypass Ife altogether.[150] The self-sufficiency of the campus had developed into an inverted relationship in which, rather than extending its knowledge to the surrounding community, the university instead left the town to catch up with it. The acquisition of a further 15,459 acres of land by the end of the 1970s continued this trend. The planners reported,

> This acquisition is very important to the University and the region . . . For attracting high-quality students, academics and professionals, the University has to create outlets for the application of acquired skills and the means of livelihood for supporting these people in the area. The new lands offer an opportunity for doing this with development in agriculture, science and industry, forestry and paper mills, and archeology. In addition to serving the University, these new developments will supply local manpower and may well serve as a model for other developments in the region. *The university, as a repository of great planning, management, training and research capabilities, will become the centre of regional planned development.*[151]

Facing a lack of sufficient jobs for its graduates, the university's role was now extended to the creation of such jobs. Vice-Chancellor Oluwasanmi did not hold the students, who preferred to migrate to the city, solely responsible for abandoning the countryside. The problem was the lack of employment opportunities when they left the university: "Out of the 85 Agriculture graduates that this University turned out between 1966 and 1970, 25 could find nothing else but schoolroom jobs in this country." Oluwasanmi directed his appeal to the military government, which "must re-examine their priorities for agricultural development in a bold and imaginative manner . . . it is only through such cooperation that the State and the Nation can receive the maximum benefit from their investment in this University."[152]

The fact that the University of Ife was built on the principles of kibbutz planning allowed it to expand while maintaining a coherent structure and relative autonomy. Ironically, this influence contributed to a historical homology wherein both the kibbutz and the university found themselves in fraught positions vis-à-vis the state for whose development they were meant to serve as primary engines. With the establishment of Israel, the kibbutz struggled to maintain its prestate status as a pioneering institution. Rather than integrating socially into the state's regional development efforts, which created new towns as regional centers, kibbutzim instead employed the new immigrants who settled there as wage laborers, thus undercutting their socialist foundational principles. As in British universities' town-gown conflict, kibbutzim closed themselves off from and alienated the new towns.[153] Like the University of Ife, kibbutzim have also continued to maintain a high standard of living compared to neighboring towns and villages, which, by the 1980s, led to severe criticism. One critique specifically targeted a certain kibbutz's lifestyle by comparing it to that of a luxurious American residence.[154] As we saw in this chapter, despite their radical differences, this comparison was not completely far-fetched, as the two models of the kibbutz and the American suburb harmonized in the design of the University of Ife's campus. By this time, and concurrently with parallel developments in the Nigerian university, the disparity between kibbutzim and the rest of Israeli society, coupled with the neoliberalization of the Israeli economy, resulted in their privatization and suburbanization, which only enhanced their image of exclusivity.

Following the 1975 coup that turned the University of Ife into a federal institution—a year also marked by the end of Oluwasanmi's tenure as its vice-chancellor—the university continued to expand territorially, not only to bypass the town but also to overcome the deficiencies of the state. While up until 1966 the Nigerian economy had enjoyed a relatively close alignment between internal revenues and expenditures in each region, with the arrival of the military government in 1966 and the growth in oil revenue, especially after the 1973 oil crisis, this balance was disturbed. The country's division into additional states (from four regions in 1964 to twelve states in 1967 and nineteen in 1976) exacerbated competition over federal resources and resulted in overstaffing in the public sector and the disproportional establishment of state universities.[155] In this climate wherein oil revenue took precedence over production, and administrative jobs took precedence over professional ones, the University of Ife attempted to continue its mission as a privileged site from which to encourage and manage development almost autonomously. The university aimed to become the region's prime producer, marketer, and distributer of agricultural goods, as well as the main human resources developer and employer. In other words, the university used the privileged position that was granted to it by the state, to develop *despite* the state.

# designing the university of ife

Climate, Regeneration, and Ornament

IN HIS 1970 university convocation address titled "The Technological Gap," Hezekiah Oluwasanmi, an agricultural economist and the second vice-chancellor of the University of Ife, stated, "the human material rather than the constitutions, is in reality the greatest determining factor."[1] These words encapsulate the ideal of the university as a dynamic entity that exceeds its institutional form, and where national development is contingent on the students becoming productive subjects. At the core of this ideal is the mutual transformation of human subjects and their natural surroundings, which, as this chapter demonstrates, was intimately tied to how its Israeli and American designers approached the campus's relationship with its environment. As the previous chapter showed, the site was selected for its physical properties, both aesthetic and agricultural. While the collegiate model of the University College Ibadan campus, designed by British architects E. Maxwell Fry and Jane Drew, disavowed the surrounding environment, at the University of Ife the tropical landscape served as a visual backdrop and an economic point of reference. The two campus designs dramatize a shift from British colonial precepts about the tropical environment and its purportedly detrimental effects on its subjects to an approach that postulated a mutually beneficial relationship between the tropical environment and its inhabitants. Although not specifically referring to climate, Oluwasanmi's words register the turn from British colonial environmental determinism, as it was reinscribed in the late colonial period by Fry and Drew's tropical architecture approach, to contrasting Labor Zionist and American convictions that the economic potential of the tropical environment hinges on the cultivation of postcolonial subjects.

Focusing on the buildings that Arieh Sharon's team, in consultation with landscape architects from the University of Wisconsin, designed for the University of Ife's representative campus core from the beginning of the 1960s through the mid-1970s, this chapter examines how national subjects' productive capacity was imagined as "human capital" vis-à-vis their relationship with the tropical environment. The term "human capital," popularized by American economists in the 1960s, emphasized higher education as central to economic growth in both the First and Third Worlds.[2] Although this concept shared the colonialist premise that Western science and technology are essential to mastering and manipulating natural resources in decolonizing countries, it shifted from the paternalistic assumption that indigenous subjects are inherently incapable of technological mastery to a new emphasis on postcolonial subjects as the prime agents of their own countries' economic transformations.[3] Access to higher education was thus the key. Oluwasanmi, a Harvard graduate, was quite familiar with this discourse, but his use of the term "human material" may also indicate the influence of its Labor Zionist conceptual counterpart. In Israel's prestate and early state period, "human material" was imbued with social-ideological dimensions that did not resonate with the American term's purely managerial focus. In the Zionist case, the construction of the human as resource depended upon the role immigrants played in the nation-building project. In contrast with "human capital," the term "human material" implied the human body's malleability and expressed the corporeal as well as vocational and social transformation of the New Jew.

In Labor Zionist ideology, this multifaceted remaking of the human was imbricated with the economic transformation of national territory; it was based less on knowledge or skill than on socialization and ideological leaning, particularly the social capital accumulated through participation in Zionist youth movements in Eastern Europe or in kibbutzim, the Haganah, or the Histadrut. During the early days of Israeli aid to African countries, this social capital was the primary criterion by which Israeli experts were selected to represent the state, taking precedence even over technical skills and professional knowledge.[4] Similar concerns were evident as early as the 1940s in Solel Boneh's selection criteria for workers sent to Abadan, Persia, the seat of the Anglo-Persian Oil Company, who were to be "top-quality human material."[5] If these workers were not already "top quality," Histadrut leaders suggested that the intense collective experience of living and working in Abadan could help them become so. Simply put, Abadan could compensate for the intense pioneering experience that petit bourgeois workers may have chosen to avoid in Palestine. Such discussions implied that the shaping of the Hebrew Pioneer could also occur beyond the borders of the national territory. Just as Jewish immigrants were malleable in terms of skill acquisition, so—under the right conditions—could they be socialized into Labor Zionist ideology.

Even if this "top-quality human material" could provisionally be molded outside the national territory, one of the prime conditions for settlers' ultimate transformation into New Jews was their relationship with the national territory's environment. This environmental aspect of the settler colonial experience in Israel is essential to understanding why Sharon replaced tropical architecture's ubiquitous sunshades with what he called a "self-protecting building." Originating in discourses on tropical medicine and hygiene, tropical architecture was intended to protect colonizers from the environment's physically and morally "degenerating" effects; it emphasized the prevention of disease and moderate insulation. By contrast, Labor Zionism emphasized symbiotic, mutually transformative relations between humans and the environment, as epitomized in the idiom "to build and to be built" (*livnot u'lehibanot*). If, for the British, colonies entailed the danger of degeneration, for Jewish settlers such as Sharon, who cofounded a kibbutz in 1921, a "return" to the land of the patriarchs promised national regeneration.[6] This discourse emerged in reaction to the late nineteenth-century European perception of Jews as an effeminate and degenerating race. Max Nordau, a journalist and physician, was responsible for what historian Boaz Neumann has called Zionism's "bodily turn."[7] Before becoming a Zionist leader, Nordau authored a seminal volume on fin de siècle art and society, *Degeneration* (*Entartung*, 1892). Nordau's analysis of material culture influenced the likes of protomodernist Viennese architect Adolf Loos, who in turn saw architecture at the turn of the twentieth century through its lens. Casting ornamentation as a sign of degeneration, Loos advocated the blank white wall, which would become the signature of modernist architecture. In order to understand how modern architecture, Zionism, and the discourse of degeneration intersected before they were transplanted to and transfigured in the Nigerian context, this chapter traces the role that the modernist white wall, and its adaptation to Palestine's climate, played in creating an architecture conducive to the Jews' regeneration in the land of the patriarchs. This chapter travels from Nigeria back to the origins of the modernist white wall in Vienna and its adaptation in Tel Aviv in the 1930s through the 1950s before returning to the University of Ife, where Sharon and his team readapted their European-influenced Israeli experience to the local climate and culture. Ife offered Sharon not only a path to architectural regeneration free from Zionist settler colonial anxieties about acclimatization but also a nonornamental way of "solving" the modernist predicament of how to integrate local identity with a building's form.

Environment, Architecture, and "Human Capital"

When Arieh Sharon arrived to design the University of Ife, the tropical architecture discourse promoted by Fry and Drew was so prevalent, even among laymen, that Sharon was expected to address tropical climate as a problem that demanded serious design solutions. Oladele Ajose, a specialist in preventive medicine who had been educated in Great Britain and was one of the first African professors at UCI and the University of Ife's first vice-chancellor, requested that Sharon visit the Building Research Station in Garston, England, to consult with its experts about designing for a tropical climate. Sharon wrote in response that his visit had confirmed his design calculations, perhaps in defiance of the presumed British authority in this field.[8] While discourses of tropical architecture were employed by British architects and builders as a gatekeeping mechanism to ensure continuing dependence on the colonizers' knowledge, they were nonetheless open to reinterpretation and reformulation in the postcolonial period.[9] Since the University College Ibadan campus was both the quintessential embodiment of Fry and Drew's approach and the primary negative reference point for the University of Ife's founders, Sharon's task was to devise an architectural language that would be modernist and climatically responsive, as Fry and Drew's tropical architecture was, yet also visually distinct from it. Since Fry and Drew's approach implied that "form follows climate," their reformulation of modernist principles embedded design in a quasi-scientific methodology that treated climate as its empirical base.[10] Sharon's challenge, therefore, was to use the same climatic base to create an entirely different architectural form. Differing architectural "solutions" to the same empirical parameters demonstrate how ideology shapes the translation of empirical climatic data into architectural form—specifically ideologies about the desired relationship between man and environment, or, in this case, between the Nigerian students and their campus. If architecture was supposed to solve the problem of climate, this analysis asks how, for each of the proposed solutions, architects discursively constructed climate as a problem in the first place.

Fry and Drew's approach to tropical climate is encapsulated in their publication *Tropical Architecture in the Humid Zone* (1956): "Caught within the magic circle of growth, lulled by its constancy, controlled by disease and warfare, the people of the tropics have slumbered on for centuries, little touched by what took place in the world outside them, maintaining themselves in a varying balance against the forces of nature at once so propitious yet so insidious."[11] This description resonates with the language of British colonialism in Central Africa at the turn of the twentieth century, which social scientist Jonathan Crush characterizes as "traumatic not romantic—the area was practically in 'chaos,' virtually uninhabited and uninhabitable, racked by internal violence and insecurity."[12] More than half a century later, Fry and Drew used this language of perpetual crisis to represent the tropical climate as the cause of stasis of development in West Africa and the primary impediment to its embarkation on the linear course of world history. In such discourses on tropical Africa, development offered a way out of the "magic circle." According to Crush, development meant "the *rebuilding* of the landscape and the *reclothing* of its benighted inhabitants."[13] Tropical architecture proposed to do exactly that. Colonial subjects had to be "reclothed" in tandem with the "rebuilding" of their surroundings, so that mutual human and environmental transformations would enable Africa's reintegration into world history. As an ordering mechanism, the discourse of tropical architecture offered a way to manage natural and human resources and redirect economic growth beyond the destructive cyclicity of tropical climate.

Although Fry and Drew were latecomers to the colonial project, their approach to the tropics and to the redemptive qualities of architecture drew its logic directly from colonialist discourses. The couple's tropical architecture had its origins in colonial architecture, which developed alongside discourses of tropical disease, hygiene, and colonial medicine, which consisted mainly of preventive measures to help colonial administrators and soldiers survive in what they perceived as hostile environments.[14] As the "other of Europe," "tropicality" was a powerful construct in the European imaginary, comparable to the one Edward Said theorized—Orientalism. Unlike the latter discourse, which emerged from the humanities, tropicality was based on the natural sciences.[15] Lethargy, disease, and corruption were among the attributes the term "tropical" evoked; this discourse led to the wholesale association of the tropics with antidevelopment forces. At the heart of colonizers' insistence on their own physical and psychological separation from the tropical environment lay the fear of racial degeneration. Acclimatizing too well ("going native") would not only lead to moral and physical degeneration but would also belie the alleged racial superiority that justified colonization.[16]

In the 1950s, tropical architecture was systemized into a body of knowledge through the publication of manuals, a conference held at University College London in 1953, and the establishment of the Department of Tropical Architecture at the Architectural Association in London in 1955. Scholars have explained tropical architecture's consolidation during the period of decolonization as a means of securing the British building industry's hegemony in its former colonies.[17] Significantly, tropical architecture's institutionalization at the time of decolonization highlights its discursive insecurities rather than its persuasive power.[18] If tropical architecture was to remain relevant, it had to be cleansed of its racial postulates and reformulated so that it could serve not only its traditional clients—the European colonizers—but also postcolonial citizens. Unable to revise the discourse's causal foundation—that tropicality was the reason for the backwardness of "tropical people"—Fry and Drew found themselves in a predicament. In a sketch that appeared in *Tropical Architecture in the Humid Zone*, black figures personify each of the categories of clothing, health, and acclimatization.[19] While the first two figures are portrayed standing, the second even dancing freely, the last one sits bent over in misery, with his hand supporting his leaning head, overwhelmed by the beating rays of the sun and what might be drops of rain (fig. 4.1). Instead of reframing the problem of acclimatization, which obviously could not apply to natives of the tropics, Fry and Drew displaced the problem from foreigners to West African elites. While lamenting the fact that modern tropical subjects prefer to dress in Western suits unfit for the climate, they ultimately represent alienation from the native environment as an inevitable process; their task was to create microenvironments that would facilitate this transformation.[20] These microenvironments, in turn, would help create a productive society. Tropical architecture was to remedy the "reclothed" subjects by rebuilding their environment (fig. 4.2).

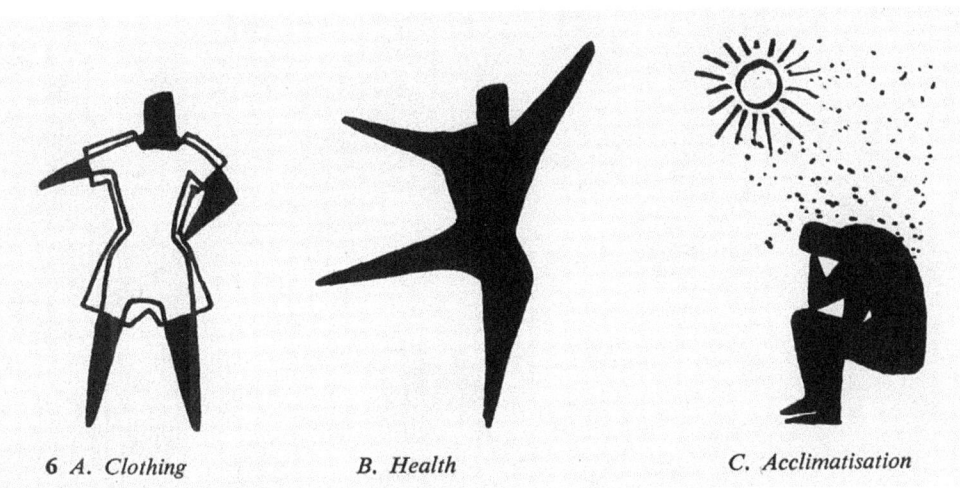

FIGURE 4.1 Maxwell Fry and Jane Drew, "A. Clothing, B. Health, C. Acclimatization." Maxwell Fry and Jane Drew, *Tropical Architecture in the Humid Zone* (New York: Reinhold, 1956), 31.

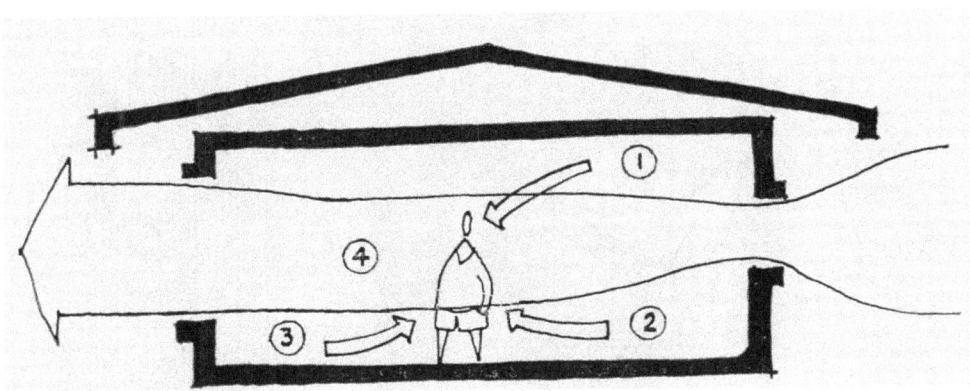

FIGURE 4.2 Maxwell Fry and Jane Drew, "Key: 1 humidity, 2 temperature, 3 radiation, 4 air movement." Maxwell Fry and Jane Drew, *Tropical Architecture in the Dry and Humid Zones* (New York: Reinhold, 1964), 29.

For Zionist thinkers who responded to anti-Semitic European discourses of degeneration, environmental conditioning was also the answer. While such thinkers accepted the idea that the Jews were a degenerate and degenerating race, they deemed Jewish degeneration reversible through geographic transplantation back to the land of the patriarchs.[21] Drawing from German discourses of life reform *(Lebensreform)* and body culture *(Körperkultur)*, Zionist thinkers traced the problem to unhealthy living

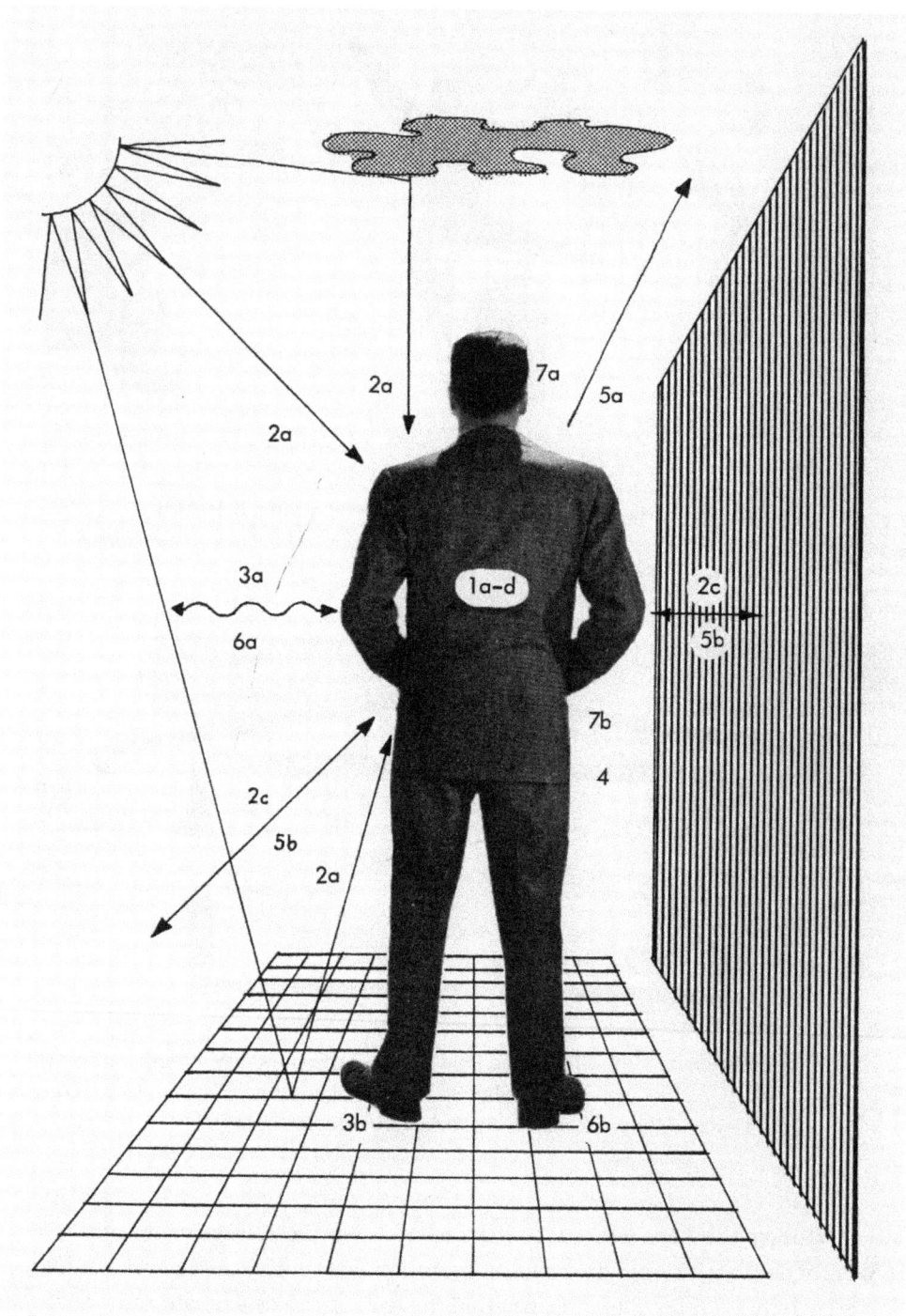

FIGURE 4.3  Victor Olgyay, "Heat exchange between man and surroundings." Victor Olgyay, *Design with Climate: Bioclimatic Approach to Architectural Regionalism* (Princeton, NJ: Princeton University Press, 1963), 16.

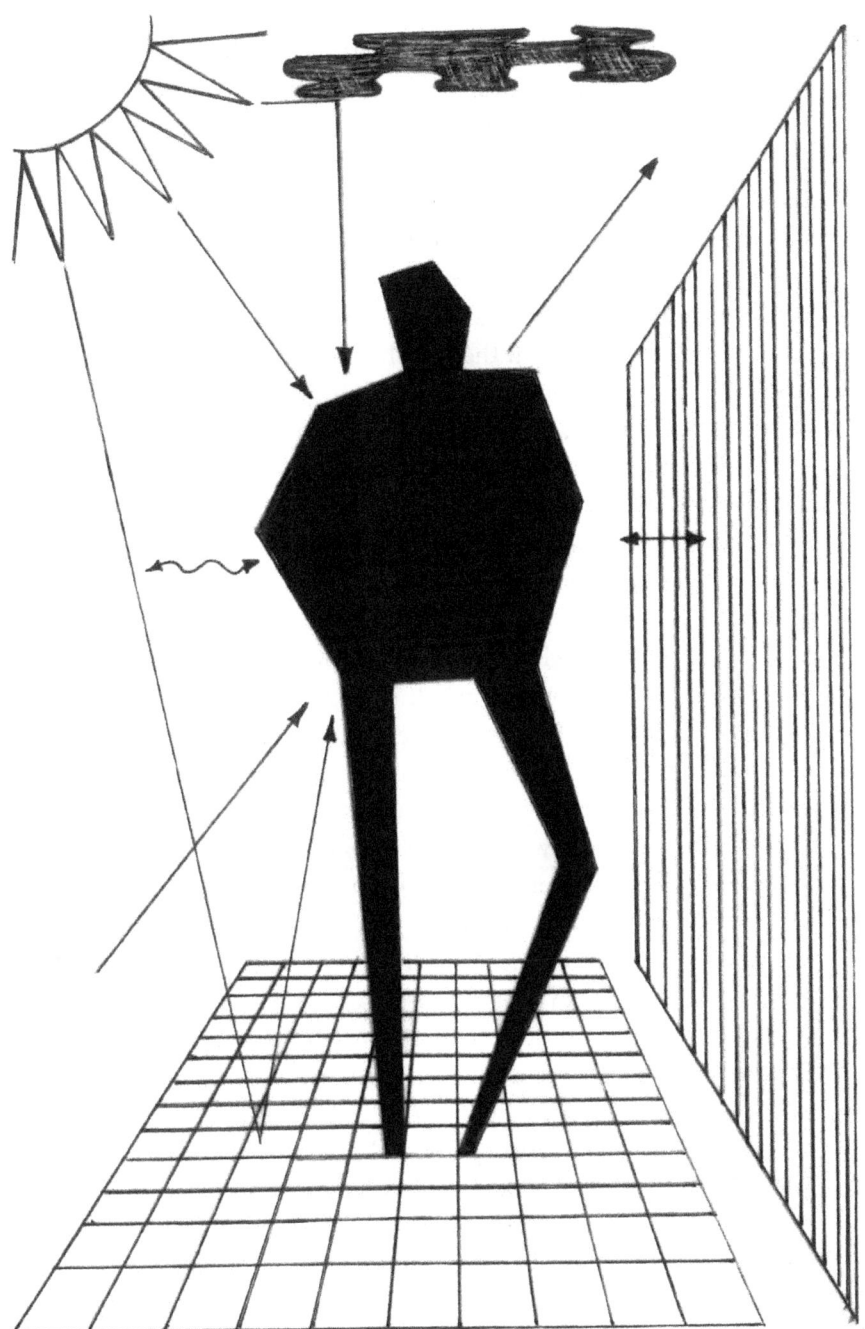

FIGURE 4.4 Bernard J. Niemann and William H. Tishler, "Heat exchange between man and his surroundings." Redrawn from Bernard J. Niemann and William H. Tishler, *University of Ife Physical Development Plan, Ife, Nigeria* (Madison, WI: Department of Landscape Architecture, School of Natural Resources, College of Agricultural and Life Sciences, University of Wisconsin, 1969), 26.

conditions in the Eastern European shtetl and the modern, alienating cities that were home to most Western European Jews. Zionism was construed explicitly as an antidote to moral and biological degeneration: in Palestine, the Jewish body would be rejuvenated as a productive body. The same pathology was extended metaphorically to the land of Palestine, which was perceived, in a typically Orientalist way, as "dead" land, infertile and unproductive physically, economically, and culturally. Degeneration was thus displaced onto the Arab inhabitants and their "degenerate agriculture."[22] In this formulation, only if the Jewish people reconnected with their land would the two be regenerated and "cured." If tropical environments represented the threat of degeneration for British colonists, for the Zionist settler the arid Middle Eastern environment not only presented a challenge of acclimatization and fertilization but also entailed the promise of a national regeneration in which both the people and the land would regain their productive capacities.

Productivity was also a primary concern for the University of Wisconsin landscape architects who arrived in 1966 to consult on the design of the University of Ife campus on behalf of USAID. Providing "resource-based management plans," they emphasized "the procedures for integrating human needs and resources goals into the design-formulation process."[23] The Wisconsin team, which based its study on both Fry and Drew's *Tropical Architecture in the Dry and Humid Zones* (1964) and on the US-based Hungarian émigré Victor Olgyay's *Design with Climate* (1963), did not represent tropicality as a hazard from which people need to be protected, but rather as an array of resources, including sun radiation and soil, that could be maximized through proper coordination and management. Instead of viewing the tropics as an inimical climate in which "all is overdone," as Fry and Drew did,[24] the Wisconsin team rationalized climate to make it calculable and manageable as a resource.

Among the resources developed and managed were the students themselves. The marriage of education and resources was indebted to the mid-century American "human capital" theory, which postulated that human resources, once invested to become human capital, determine development more than natural resources do. This theory assumed that, while natural resources are limited, there is no limit to economic growth via skill acquisition and university education. In the Third World, however, founding universities and setting up programs for knowledge transfer were not enough, since these institutions required healthy surroundings, including "additional food and better shelter," to succeed.[25] The American landscape architecture consultants therefore had to carefully consider the living and working environments of students and faculty. Using a diagram drawn by Victor Olgyay, the team substituted Olgyay's "universal" man—an average-size male portrayed from the back, presumably white, dressed in a business suit—with the abstracted figure of a black man (figs. 4.3 and 4.4). Unlike the arrows in Fry and Drew's cartoons, which depict the unidirectional effect of the environment on the human body, Olgyay's arrows of heat absorption and emission are multidirectional. The Wisconsin team, following Olgyay, situated the African body in relation to the environment, not only as its passive victim but also as an active participant in it.

## Tropical Zionism

Given his experience working under Berlin architect Hannes Meyer, who was famous for including climatic conditions in his multiple calculations, as well as for adapting modern architecture to conditions in Israel, Sharon was no stranger to climatic considerations. However, despite recurrent calls to synthesize Israeli research on the effects of hot climate on building technology, these concerns were not discursively consolidated into a body of knowledge until the late 1970s.[26] Similarly, the British colonial discourse of tropical architecture did not include Palestine. In fact, when a British physician stationed in Nigeria arrived to examine indoor climate in Palestine in 1947, the chilly January weather led him to recommend focusing on warmth in winter rather than heat reduction in summer.[27] By the mid-1970s, however, when Sharon wrote his monograph *Kibbutz + Bauhaus*, he had appropriated the language of tropical architecture, only to give Israel a privileged position in this discourse as a "microclimatic pilot country."[28] Yet both the preventive approach of the British tropical architecture discourse and the resource management approach of the Wisconsin team were very different from what Sharon had in mind when he first arrived in Nigeria. Embarking on his first survey tour, Sharon hoped "to receive a direct and immediate visual impression" of the towns and "to get in immediate contact with nature," which varied from savannah areas in the north to rain forests in the south.[29] By the end of his tour, Sharon had concluded that he preferred lush tropical vegetation and wooded hills threaded with streams over the savannah's flat highlands.

In his initial survey, Sharon so thoroughly idealized what he saw that he even naturalized cash crops as a sort of biblical scene of primal abundance. For Sharon, who originally arrived in Palestine from Eastern Europe to form an agricultural settlement in a difficult environment, tropical abundance stood for an inexhaustible source of natural riches and the fantasy of a Zionist revival of the biblical "land of milk and honey."[30] This vision of reclaimed biblical richness found its expression in the iconic Israeli landscapes of kibbutzim, public parks, and university campuses designed by landscape architects Lipa Yahalom and Dan Tzur.[31] Sharon, who had worked with the two on numerous occasions, invited the first to consult on the landscape design for the University of Ife's campus early in the process.[32]

In an essay published in 1940, Sharon argued that, in kibbutzim and rural areas, public buildings should be situated in a landscape "with maximum humility and harmony, because nature is more significant than human deeds," obfuscating the fact that the "natural" landscape of the Jewish settlement in Palestine was for the most part a product of intense human intervention. "The true talent of the architect," he elaborated, "is expressed in his ability to maximize the building's correspondence with the landscape, with a minimum of exaggeration, in spite of the scale and solid blocks of a big public building."[33] The tropics gave Sharon an opportunity to "work with" the landscape as a constant rather than a manipulable variable and thus to achieve the authentic relationship of "humility and harmony" with the environment that he sought. Sharon's description of himself "intruding into the bush, by footpaths or narrow ways" encapsulates his idea that his architecture, though "intruding," would delicately carve the wooded, hilly landscape from within rather than impose transformation upon it through grand gestures.[34]

Golda Meir, Israel's foreign minister and the primary force behind Israel's diplomatic relations with African countries in the 1960s, expressed a similar sentiment about African natural abundance in a talk she gave at Haile Selassie I University in Addis Ababa. Though Addis Ababa's high altitude and dry climate is a far cry from the rain forest Sharon found in West Nigeria, Meir was nevertheless impressed by the lush but carefully manicured garden of the university campus. She told the students emphatically "how they [in Israel] worked hard to develop the country . . . how they squeezed water out of the desert soil . . . to give life to the barren and uninviting Negev Desert and other dry parts of the country," according to one student's report. Comparing Ethiopia's and Israel's conditions, while ignoring the droughts that the former had repeatedly suffered, she continued, "You have no problem of water here . . . in fact, I see a country that is full with beauty ... unlimited beauty and unlimited possibilities—water, sunshine, soil and *everything grows by itself*, even without planting."[35]

Directing her motivational speech to students who were about to embark on a university service program for rural areas, Meir's words emerged from Jewish settlers' debate with the British Mandate authorities over Palestine's capacity to absorb newcomers economically. Her speech implied that the problem was not Ethiopia's lack of natural resources but the attitudes and capacities of its people. If, for Fry and Drew, the climate of the tropics was the cause of all its socioeconomic ills, then conversely, according to Zionist logic, generations of Arab residents in Palestine were responsible for dilapidating the country's natural resources. Once the land was returned to its rightful owners, Zionists argued, it would regain its biblical economic potential.[36] Thus, in what would later become Israel, experts and technology were tasked with a Promethean reshaping of the environment, as in James Scott's characterization of high modernism, but one that would return it to its imagined original capacities.

Following this logic, the team of Israeli architects did not see Ife's nature as a force from which humans, whether foreigners or locals, needed protection. On the contrary, Sharon attempted to keep his intervention in the landscape to a minimum, for example, by leaving all the tall trees standing.[37] Sharon added covered pathways more for aesthetic reasons, to connect the buildings visually, than for protection from sun and rain. Yet Sharon's insistence on open envelopes for the buildings marked most distinctly how much his approach diverged from that of British tropical architecture. While Fry and Drew limited openings in order to minimize the infiltration of natural menaces—including insects, their "insidious enemies"[38]—Sharon downplayed the possible threats such openings presented and even transfigured potential intruders into joyful creatures such as birds and butterflies: "There was considerable discussion about the dining-hall, the upper space of which is left open below the folded roof, cantilevered for sun and rain protection, without any windows. Some of the professors were afraid of the open spaces, arguing that birds and butterflies might disturb the students, but in the end they agreed to leave the hall open, with the possibility of installing windows in the future, if needed. To this day, the space has remained open and everybody enjoys it, even the few birds and butterflies."[39]

The professors' concerns about the open spaces probably had more to do with the dining hall's hygiene and fear of mosquito-borne malaria than

FIGURE 4.5 Arieh Sharon and Vice-Chancellor Oladele Ajose during Sharon's first visit to the University of Ife site, 1960. Yael Aloni Photo Collection. Courtesy of the Azrieli Architectural Archive; Arieh Sharon collection.

with occasional birds or butterflies. It was not that Sharon was unaware of the threat of malaria; he was familiar with it firsthand from his pioneering days at the kibbutz he helped establish in 1921. By 1931, infectious and parasitic diseases such as malaria had become the third most common cause of death in Palestine.[40] Yet it was precisely this firsthand experience that precluded Sharon from using architecture as a preventive measure against it. Settler-pioneers such as Sharon engaged in the national project of eradicating swamps, often against the advice of the Jewish medical establishment. Before pioneers were co-opted into institutionalized antimalaria campaigns in the late 1920s, they viewed their unmediated encounter with the environment despite the high risk of infection as a heroic rite of passage and self-sacrifice.⁴¹ In 1921, Dr. Isaac M. Rubinow, the first director of the American Zionist Medical Unit in Palestine, commented that the medical establishment's insistent pleading that settlers use mosquito veils and gloves "shows an utter lack of familiarity with the habits and psychology of the *Halutzim* [pioneers]."⁴² Although the high modernist projects of population management and land reclamation eventually eradicated malaria in Israel, in Sharon's recollections such ills were instead overcome with group spirit and singing.⁴³ A photo of Sharon next to Vice-Chancellor Ajose sums up this stance: Sharon is wearing a short-sleeved shirt, unlike his Nigerian counterpart, and leans back confidently, as if to say, "difficult climate, malaria, I've been through it all—it's not so bad" (fig. 4.5).

Architecture of Regeneration

The first group of buildings designed for the campus core was the Humanities Faculty (fig. 4.6). Consisting of three parallel, four-story blocks with ancillary auditoria, the design evolved over the course of one year, 1961 to 1962, from orthogonal, elongated rectangular blocks to inverted pyramids (figs. 4.7–4.9). The series of three inverted pyramids, painted white and dark grey, produced a unique architectural image that diverged

FIGURE 4.6  Arieh Sharon, Humanities Faculty, University of Ife, c. 1966. Courtesy of Amos Spitz.

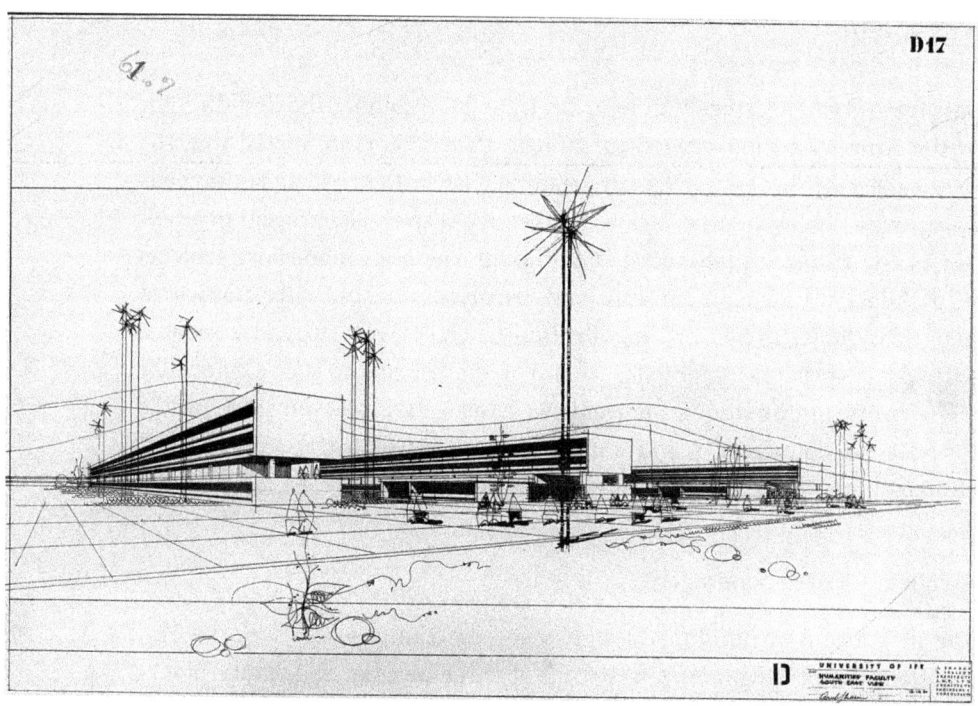

FIGURE 4.7  Arieh Sharon, Humanities Faculty, University of Ife, 1961. Courtesy of the Azrieli Architectural Archive; Arieh Sharon collection, AES-1-233.

FIGURE 4.8  Arieh Sharon, Humanities Faculty, University of Ife, 1962. Courtesy of the Azrieli Architectural Archive; Arieh Sharon collection, AES-1-233.

completely from that of Fry and Drew's neighboring University College Ibadan, which consisted mainly of dense webs of interlocking orthogonal volumes, adorned with patterned sun-shading devices. At Ife, the Humanities buildings prescribed the architectural tone of the entire core, including the buildings that other architects would design over the next decade, and contributed to the University of Ife's reputation as "the most beautiful campus south of the Sahara, north of the River Limpopo."[44] Yet in addition to these formal differences, Sharon distinguished his design from that of UCI and other works by British and local architects through his claim that the inverted pyramid was "self-protective":

> One of the main planning considerations was to relate the building design to the climatic factors. Most of the public buildings in Nigeria are oriented from east to west, their main elevations facing north and south, thus being protected from heat and glare. This also ensures cross-ventilation by prevailing breezes, coming mainly from the south. Many of these buildings erected by English or local architects use as sun protection either concrete canopies and frames around the windows, or louvers and precast ornamental elements around the terraces.

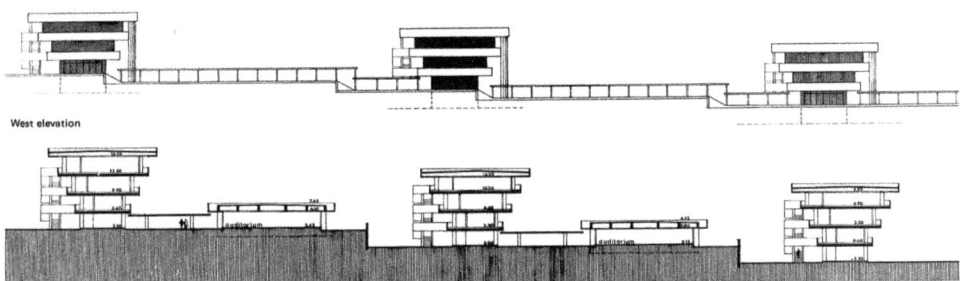

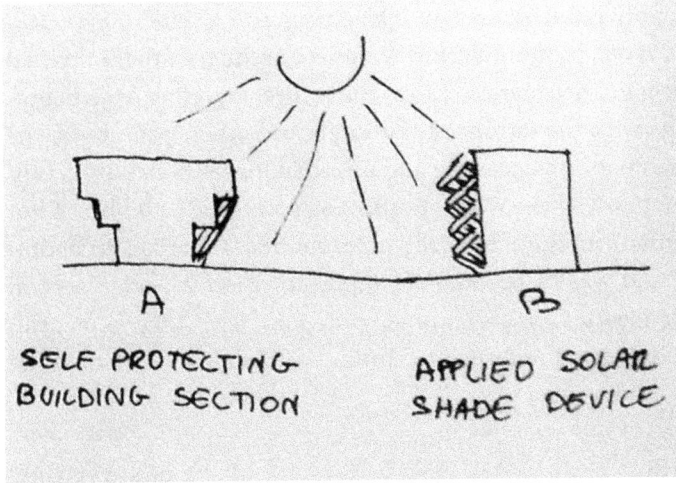

FIGURE 4.9 Arieh Sharon, Humanities Faculty complex, section. Yael Aloni Photo Collection. Courtesy of the Azrieli Architectural Archive; Arieh Sharon collection.

FIGURE 4.10 Arieh Sharon, "Self Protecting Building Section" vs. "Applied Solar Shade Device." Egboramy, Arieh Sharon, and Eldar Sharon, *Ife University Master Plan, 1980–85*, 62. Obafemi Awolowo University Planning Department Archive.

We proposed to make the buildings *self-protecting* against the monsoon rain and the intensive sun and glare by cantilevering the floors one over another. . . . This solution proved useful and efficient, because all the continuous openings protected by simply turning glass louvers are, de facto, open and they can catch the breezes along the whole elevation line. At the same time, they are protected from sun and rain by the cantilevering terraces.[45]

In a drawing, Sharon differentiates between a building with sun protection devices and a building whose sheer mass protects it from the elements. This performance of expertise asserted Sharon's settler colonial experience in the theater of development: he contrasted his "self-protecting building" with tropical architecture's "applied solar shade device," interpreting the latter as an addition that, like applied ornamentation, can be removed without affecting the building's function (fig. 4.10). A few years earlier, Sharon had warned against Israel's wholesale importation of the brise-soleil, a dominant sun-shading device that had originated in Latin America: "The climatic approach is basically correct, but the problem is to differentiate between mere fashion and the organic solution."[46] By "organic," Sharon referred to the fundamentals of interwar modernist architecture: the open plan, its continuous volumes, and their correspondence with the building mass, which was seen as a body whose organs function harmoniously and efficiently as part of a unified whole. It seems that Sharon pursued modernist functional and aesthetic purification even further than the master Le Corbusier, one of the hero-architects of the modernist movement, who embraced the brise-soleil and even claimed it as his own invention.[47] Sharon's critique touched upon the modern movement's underbelly, namely, its construction of ornament as a symptom of degeneration.[48]

The discourse of degeneration connects modernist architecture and Zionism. In his highly influential essay "Ornament and Crime" (*Ornament und Verbrechen,* 1908), protomodernist Viennese architect Adolf Loos had applied the concept of degeneration to architecture. Equating ornamentation on buildings with the tattoos of criminals and other "primitives," he argued that ornaments are excessive and unproductive.[49] Loos's argument is reminiscent not only of the work of criminologist Cesare Lombroso but also of Max Nordau's monumental *Degeneration* (1892). Nordau was Lombroso's disciple and was to become an important Zionist leader, second only to Theodor Herzl, Loos's Viennese contemporary.[50] Like Loos after him, Nordau expanded Lombroso's criminal anthropology to material culture, critiquing fin de siècle Europe's cultural degeneration, which he saw as manifested in such interrelated phenomena as makeup, dress, and interior design.

Although he did not include Jews in his list of primitives and degenerates (some of his favorite and most loyal clients were, after all, Jewish), Loos's "Ornament and Crime" exposes the unlikely link between two seemingly disparate discourses: that of the modern movement in architecture and that of Zionism in Central Europe at the turn of the century. Coining the term "muscular Judaism" (*Muskeljudentum*) at the second World Zionist Congress in 1903, Nordau stressed that environmental conditions had caused Jewish degeneracy. Once those were changed, Jews would be redeemed from their inauthentic lives in Europe: "All the elements of Aristotelian physics—light, air, water and earth—were measured out to us very sparingly. In the narrow Jewish street our poor limbs soon forgot their gay movements; in the dimness of sunless houses our eyes began to blink shyly; the fear of constant persecution turned our powerful voices into frightened whispers . . . but now, all coercion has become a memory of the past, and at least we are allowed space enough for our bodies to live again. Let us take up our oldest traditions; let us once more become deep-chested, sturdy, sharp-eyed men."[51]

According to Nordau, true emancipation could not be achieved via assimilation; by this time, he no longer shared the Enlightenment belief that Jews would be fully integrated into European society if they became secular and shed their cultural traits. Writing in response to the Dreyfus affair, Nordau warned against the dangerous allure of assimilation, whose effects he interpreted as repression:

> The emancipated Jew is insecure in his relations with his fellow-beings, timid with strangers, suspicious even toward the secret feeling of his friends. His best powers are exhausted in the suppression, or at least in the difficult concealment of his own real character. For he fears that this character might be recognized as Jewish, and *he has never the satisfaction of showing himself as he is in all his thoughts and sentiments [in every tremble of his voice, eyelid, or finger].* He becomes an inner cripple, and externally unreal, and thereby always ridiculous and hateful to all higher feeling men, as is everything that is unreal [fake].[52]

Nordau figures the Jew's fear of exposing his difference "*in every tremble of his voice, eyelid, or finger*": these sites of bodily vulnerability all have both sensorial and expressive functions. Thus the same mouth, eye, and hand that could betray the Jew's Jewishness through his incomplete or excessive mimicry also connect his body's senses with its expressive capacities at the symbolic level. Once the Jew's environment had changed and he no longer needed to conceal the fact of his Jewishness, these are precisely the sites that would mediate the revitalization of his body through its renewed relationship with light, air, water, and land. In this context, the modernist prerequisites of light and air, which in Europe were associated with modern standards of healthy and hygienic living, took on new significance in the Jewish colonial settlement in Palestine.

Nordau's vision of Zionist regeneration was enacted in part through modernist architecture. In the "acclimatization" of the modernist movement in Palestine, the liminal space of the wall received most attention as a boundary and mediator between inside and outside. Loos's bleak white wall came to mark the transformation of Jews from their diasporic condition as degenerate, effeminate, second-class citizens into sovereign subjects with their own nation. This transformation has been canonized in the myth that Tel Aviv, the first "Hebrew City," grew from clear white dunes, undisturbed by the thriving Palestinian community that occupied the area. Both the supposedly clean slate of the territory from which it sprang and the clean, smooth, modernist white wall served as surfaces on which to project the Zionist ideological program. This imaginary was thus inscribed onto the landscape as well as the bodies of its inhabitants.[53] In this reading, I build on Alona Nitzan-Shiftan's discussion of how architectural modernism in Palestine was used to negate the diasporic past in order to emphasize that this negation was embodied: it connected buildings with people in acts of physical and cultural regeneration. As Nitzan-Shiftan writes, referring to architect and theorist Julius Posener, who emigrated from Nazi Germany to Palestine in 1935, "In the context of the Yishuv [the Jewish settlement in Palestine], the stark white house was, for Posener, the proper traceless home for the uprooted Jew, 'an apartment free from past memories.'"[54] Similarly, Aba Elhanani, one of the earliest theorists of Israeli architecture, explained the lack of ornamentation in modernist architecture as the result of "typical traumas of difficult past memories."[55] In a double move of erasure and purification, the white wall served both to heal the degenerate, sick Jewish body and to wipe away memories of past acts by which Jews had been marked as degenerate in the first place. In the Zionist context, the white wall represented the fantasy of liberating the Jewish body from its tortured history in order to imagine Jews anew, in a clean-slate territory, as sovereign subjects.[56]

Given the elevation of function over symbolism in architectural modernism's ideology, the white wall's symbolic functions cannot be divorced from its practical ones. In the context of Zionist settler colonialism, climate presented a particular architectural challenge: while buildings served as protection from the elements, they were concurrently supposed to facilitate the successful acclimatization of the immigrant Jews' bodies. Giving shape to the rejuvenating and regenerating encounter between the New Jew and his old-new environment, architecture mediated the settlers' sensual connection with the territory rather than simply providing protective shelter in the traditional sense.[57] The Labor Zionist challenge was to acclimatize the Jewish body in order to affirm its historic claim to belonging in the territory; Zionists had to naturalize the presence of the Jewish settlers while also maintaining their difference from the Arab population. Contemplating Jewish architectural acclimatization, Posener decisively rejected British colonial architect Edward Lutyens's famous comparison of his architecture in New Delhi to "Englishmen dressed for the weather."[58] Such a position would reenact the Jews' failed attempt at assimilation in Europe by reinstating the divide between a Jew's public and private life, so that he was "a man outside, a Jew within."[59] This split subjectivity characterizes the radical differentiation between interior sensuality and exterior anonymity in the work of Loos, who considered the assimilated Jew his ideal modern man.[60] In Palestine, however, such a split was counterproductive for an architecture of regeneration. Modernism's embrace of the environment instead allowed the blank white wall to be reformulated as a distinct Zionist vernacular. The modernist white wall, which once signified the assimilated Jews' desire for anonymity, desensualization, and transparency, now regained its corporeal expressiveness via reconnection with the national territory.

The main site that signified this transformation was the balcony, which became the most dominant design feature in Tel Aviv's urban landscape in the 1930s and 1940s. In Central and Western Europe in the 1920s and 1930s, the balcony, with its access to light and air, was associated with the healing and emancipatory capacities of modern architecture and the new modes of living it facilitated. Referring to the balcony's "semantic layering" in late colonial and postcolonial architecture, Tom Avermaete shifts from the balcony's biological function in Europe to its symbolic use as a vernacular form in the colonies.[61] Yet as the design for the Ife campus illustrates, the biological function attributed to the balcony in Europe was not lost in this translation from the metropole to non-Western locales; instead, the balco-

**FIGURE 4.11**
"Acrobatics and Architecture." *HaBinyan BaMizrah HaKarov*, 1940s. Reproduced in Nitzan-Shiftan, "Contested Zionism-Alternative Modernism: Erich Mendelsohn and the Tel Aviv Chug in Mandate Palestine," *Architectural History* 39 (1996): 161.

ny's biological and ornamental meanings became inseparable as part of its semantic layering. In Tel Aviv, balconies had decorative value in their play of mass, light and shadow, and curving horizontal lines.⁶² Besides serving as a metonym for the stretching limbs and cheerful movement of the New Jews—as expressed in a caricature in the journal *HaBinyan BaMizrah HaKarov* (Building in the Near East), of which Sharon was a founding editor—balconies provided a stage for the New Jews' performance (fig. 4.11). While balconies faced courtyards in the twenties, in the thirties living rooms and their balconies turned to face the street. In Loos's architecture, the space for theatricality was kept strictly in the interior of the house, but in Tel Aviv, the New Jew moved domestic functions such as evening dining out onto the balcony, where the private sphere met street life.⁶³ In this liminal space, the classic assimilation problem of being a "man outside" and a "Jew within" was supplanted by the blurring of lines between the intimate sphere of petit bourgeois family life and the public life of the nation.

Although Sharon was an active member of the Tel Aviv Chug, a group of prominent architects who were instrumental in importing the International Style into Israel, he was unsatisfied with the various climatic solutions that he and his peers were employing. The main climate adaptation that had been introduced in Palestine was the horizontally elongated balcony that replaced the ribbon window.⁶⁴ Since large glazed apertures were not climatically appropriate for the Middle Eastern sun, window openings were smaller than in Europe and were embedded within protruding concrete frames that limited the light that came in from above.⁶⁵ For the same reason, protruding concrete hoods or thin cast-concrete hanging "aprons" shaded the balconies that replaced the long strips of windows. Along with the aesthetic effect of their streamlined horizontality, the balconies decreased the interior apartments' sun exposure while giving access to airflow.⁶⁶ Notwithstanding these adaptations, in 1940 Sharon claimed that modern architecture in Palestine was "still too European," so much so that it would go unnoticed if placed in Central Europe.⁶⁷ "I am certain," he concluded, "that when our roots have deepened in the country, the climate will be a determinant factor in the building's planning, and will determine its *eretzisraeli* unique character." While the European-looking buildings did incorporate climate control measures to some degree, Sharon argued that these solutions were not radical or satisfactory, since they did not leave "a unique architectural imprint."⁶⁸ At the University of Ife, Sharon articulated this unique imprint in his design for the campus core, in part by rejecting Fry and Drew's excessive use of sun-shading devices.

Nitzan-Shiftan has described the overhangs and concrete frames employed in Palestine as "double screen[s]."⁶⁹ This phrase is an even more apt description of Fry and Drew's parallel screens, which they used systematically in the UCI campus.⁷⁰ When Fry and Drew attempted to incorporate screens into the buildings' mass, the result was a recessed interior space with movable "partitions of air." Following their observation that in both vernacular architecture and British bungalows all activity took place on the verandas that typically surrounded living areas to eliminate sun heat, glare, and rain, Fry and Drew decided to incorporate the veranda into the building's mass.⁷¹ In effect, they transformed the veranda from a lively, semioutdoor space filled with human activity into a device to dissipate the heat stored in the building's outer skin, which rendered it uninhabitable.⁷² Just as the occupants of British bungalows defeated their designers' intentions by moving their activities out onto the verandas, UCI students thwarted Fry and Drew's intentions by closing off their interiorized verandas with Hessian or plastic panels.⁷³ Similarly, many Tel Aviv residents increased the size of their apartments in the 1950s by closing off their balconies with Trisol, a local rendition of the brise-soleil.⁷⁴

At Ife, Sharon narrated his evolving responses to Nigeria's climate as a continuation of experiments in Israel. Despite the fact that sun-shading devices were introduced in Israel in the 1950s, following their success in Latin America, Sharon curiously inverts the timeline, delineating a progression from "louvers and brise-soleil" to a "structural second outer space of terraces and cantilevered ceilings and canopies," which were, in fact, earlier.[75] His story of architectural development thus moves from two-dimensional applied protection to volumetric adaptation of the building's skin. The latter offered Sharon a form that would be both appropriate for the tropical climate and organically connected to the building's mass. By using the term "self-protecting," Sharon did not define the building through an antagonistic relationship with its environment, but rather implied that it could fully participate in the environment without the need for external devices. In his Humanities Faculty buildings, the balconies of the inverted pyramids are neither applied sun protection devices nor secondary outer spaces. It was as if the shaded volumetric openings, interpreted in this narrative as a metaphorical thickening of the wall, were carved out of the staggered, cantilevered stories of the inverted pyramids and thus continued to serve as part of the building's mass in line with modernist principles (see fig. 4.8). To enhance the volumetric presence of the building, the walls and the cantilevers are distinguished by a dramatic play of color: the walls and columns are painted dark grey, while the cantilevers that are exposed to the sun are painted white. This chiaroscuro causes the darkened areas to dematerialize and creates the illusion that the cantilevers float one on top of the other. The inverted pyramid, therefore, contrasted with the UCI campus's design logic of recessed, gnawed-off cubic volume: instead, it maximized the correspondence between the building's usable interior space and its volume. The cantilevered balconies function not only as access galleries to the classrooms but also as shaded spaces that extend classroom activity outdoors. As such, they continue the public function of the traditional veranda.[76]

Sharon was influenced not only by the balconies of apartment buildings in Palestine but equally by developments in the design of public buildings in the early 1960s. The idea for the inverted pyramid most probably derived from the innovative Bat Yam City Hall design that Sharon's son, Eldar; his Technion classmate, Zvi Hecker; and their professor, Alfred Neumann, created in 1960. (Eldar joined his father's office in 1965 and soon became involved in planning the Ife campus.) Like Sharon's Humanities Faculty, although lacking balconies, the staggered floors of Bat Yam City Hall provided shade to its periphery. Its four polyhedral chimneys flooded the building's atrium with light, and their openings enhanced the circulation of air. While Sharon may have been influenced by the inverted pyramid shape for shading, his associate Harold Rubin and the AMY architect Eliezer Schreiber, who were in charge of designing the rest of the faculties in the campus core, further elaborated on the climatic principles that the Bat Yam City Hall project embodied. For example, they used an interior atrium instead of balconies to enable the vertical circulation of warm air.

In addition to the Bat Yam precedent, the recommendations of the Wisconsin team, published in their 1969 report, further shaped the evolution of the campus core's inverted pyramid typology. In his design for the Faculty of Education (1968–72), Harold Rubin, who had emigrated from South Africa to Israel in 1963 and joined Sharon's office soon after, extended the inverted pyramid structure, with two significant revisions. First, Rubin added a raised roof to allow for the vertical evaporation of warm air, as in Bat Yam City Hall. Second, he placed the building on a rise and elevated it above the ground with massive concrete trusses so that a breeze could sweep across the open ground floor (figs. 4.12–4.14, plate 12).

By eliminating the peripheral balconies of the Humanities buildings and replacing them with cool shaded resting areas on the second floor, Rubin in effect reconceptualized Bat Yam City Hall's atrium and transformed it into a roofed hanging garden (plate 13). The Wisconsin team's report was published a year after Rubin had begun working on his design, and his revisions partly overlapped with its recommendations—most significantly in siting the building on a rise, raising it above the ground, and using a double roof.

Schreiber's design for the faculties of administration, law, and social sciences (1972–75), which followed the publication of the Wisconsin team's report, further articulated its recommendations.[77] Schreiber designed the buildings as one ensemble, placing the three elongated buildings parallel to each other and connecting them with bridges that cut through the buildings' masses, like the Humanities and Agriculture Faculties. The Wisconsin report emphasized the roof as the single most important component of a building for thermal insulation in the tropical climate and recommended a double roof for ventilation and a wide overhang for rain protection and reduction of glare.[78] The three buildings followed this suggestion with raised umbrella roofs whose perimeters exceeded those of the rectangular buildings, acting as overhangs that provided shade to the north and south facades and allowed warm air to evaporate (figs. 4.15 and 4.16). With trusses extending diagonally from the roofs to the ground, the buildings' silhouettes created the illusion of inverted pyramids, which connected them visually with the Humanities and Education buildings. Expanding on the vocabulary of the latter, the buildings were raised above

FIGURE 4.12 Harold Rubin, Faculty of Education, southern facade, University of Ife, early 1970s. Courtesy of Amos Spitz.

the ground, creating a shaded courtyard with planters and seating areas at ground level as well as a raised internal mall (plates 14–16). Designed as a hanging garden, the mall is comprised of planters that decorate the concrete roofing of the sunken lecture halls at ground level. With the exception of these sunken halls, the three buildings followed the report's recommendations to the letter by including planters and seating, creating shaded areas, maximizing exterior-interior open space, and using pastel colors to eliminate glare.

FIGURE 4.13 Faculty of Education under construction, University of Ife, early 1970s. Courtesy of Amos Spitz.

FIGURE 4.14  Faculty of Education under construction, University of Ife, early 1970s. Courtesy of Amos Spitz.

Following the Wisconsin team's report, but completely reenvisioning the type of climate-responsive building most suited to the tropics, Rubin's and Schreiber's designs took the veranda's inside-outside ambiguity and transformed it into a courtyard logic of hanging gardens and cool shaded resting areas. The open ground level and raised courtyard replaced the enclosed patio that was used extensively in Israeli university buildings at the time but that the University of Ife administration had rejected despite its use in Yoruba compounds.[79] With the shaded ground level and the hanging gardens of the upper floors, the raised courtyard created dynamic inside-outside relations whose effects far exceeded strictly climatic functions. These relationships were further reinforced by the bridges that cut through Schreiber's buildings and the ramp leading to Rubin's Central Library.

While Fry and Drew's tropical architecture treated students as passive containers of energy that needed to be conserved, the University of Ife's dynamic design increased not only ventilation and evaporation but also the vitality and freedom of movement of the students who inhabited the space. To the Wisconsin team's conception of the human as an active agent, simultaneously affecting and affected by the tropical environment, Sharon's team added the Zionist ideology of regeneration, which they hoped could remedy the inauthentic experience of colonial mimicry just as it aimed to liberate Jews from their failed assimilation in Europe. Frantz Fanon singled out the response of colonial subjects to their native climate on their return home from the metropole as a litmus test to distinguish between "social climbers" and those "who keep their notion of their origin": "If he says: 'I am so happy to be back among you. Good Lord, it's so hot in this place; I'm not sure I can put up with it for long,' they [his friends and family] have been forewarned—it's a European who's come back."[80] If Fry and Drew attempted to accommodate the African elite who preferred to dress in Western suits by creating architectural spaces that would allow this process of alienation, Sharon and his team, in contrast, offered an architecture that invigorated the relationship between postcolonial subjects and their environment.

A comparison of two contrasting images of students in their surroundings vividly demonstrates the difference between Fry and Drew's approach and that of the Israeli team. In an image that appeared in Fry and Drew's *Tropical Architecture in the Humid Zone* and depicts their design for the Wesley Girls' Secondary School in Cape Coast, the Gold Coast (which would become Ghana after independence), three female students are carefully positioned in the photograph's foreground (fig. 4.17).[81] Dressed in

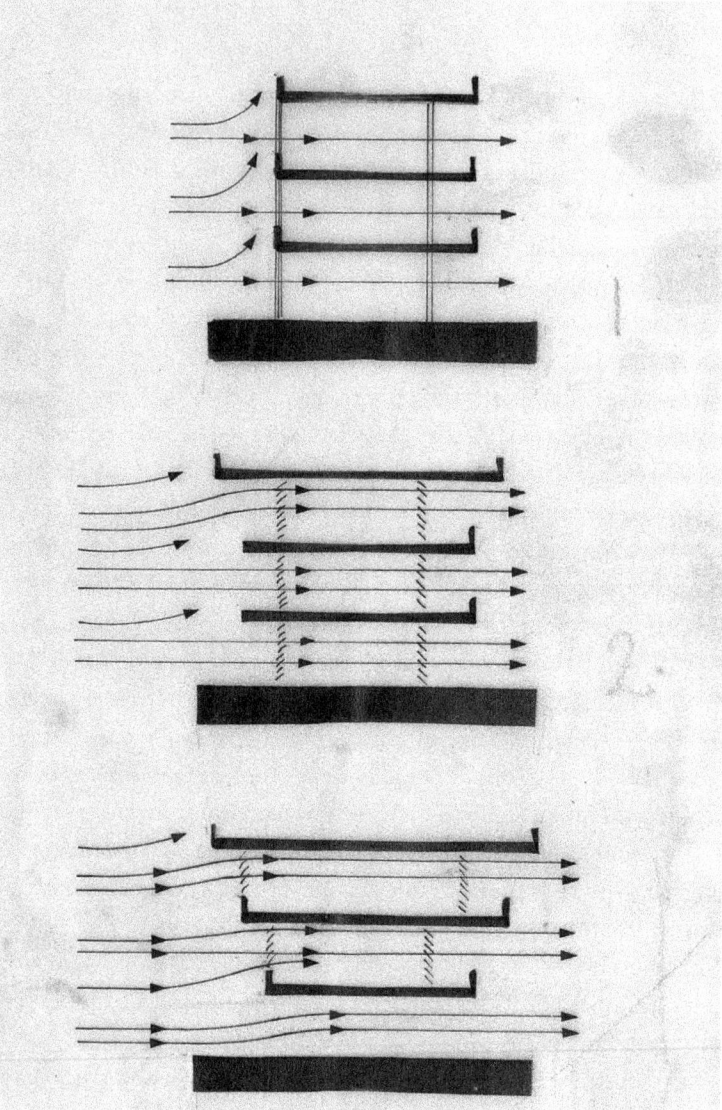

**FIGURE 4.15**
Sketches showing the progression of climatic design considerations from the rectangular design for the Agriculture Faculty and the initial Humanities buildings to the inverted pyramid solution (undated). Courtesy of the Azrieli Architectural Archive; Arieh Sharon collection, AES-1-194 965157789005 06.

**FIGURE 4.16**
*(opposite)* Sketch showing the climatic design of the Faculty of Education, accompanied with original notes. Courtesy of the Azrieli Architectural Archive; Arieh Sharon collection, AES-1-114 965000000322 01.

school uniforms and with matching short haircuts, their posture is rigid. The only elements that soften their pose are the sweaters that rest loosely on their shoulders, which, possibly following neoclassical pictorial representations, capture light and shade in their folds. In the background, the courtyard axis culminates in a church tower that, flanked by the dormitories' and classrooms' gridded facades, serves as the college's focal point. Enclosed by the structure, the young women are sheltered from the ostensibly corrupting environment outside of it. The second image depicts three

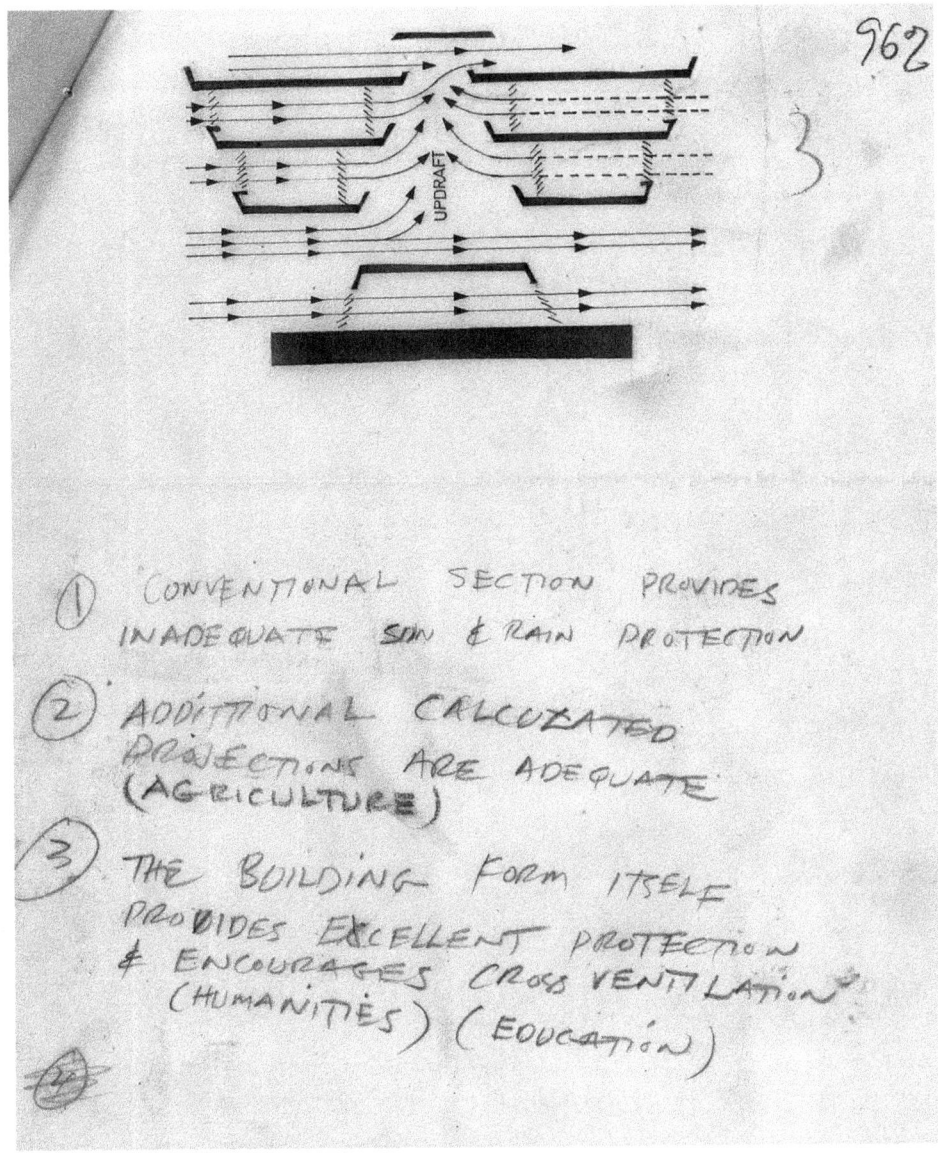

male students wearing short sportswear (one is even topless) and rushing into the Central Library at the University of Ife (fig. 4.18). Taken obliquely from behind as they head up the ramp leading to the library, the photo emphasizes how the architectural complex facilitates the students' dynamic movement. Their liberated, informal manner contrasts with the female students' disciplined one and is reflected in the photographic composition. While the empty architectural complex is at the first image's center and the timid students frame it, the second image places the students at its center,

DESIGNING THE UNIVERSITY OF IFE

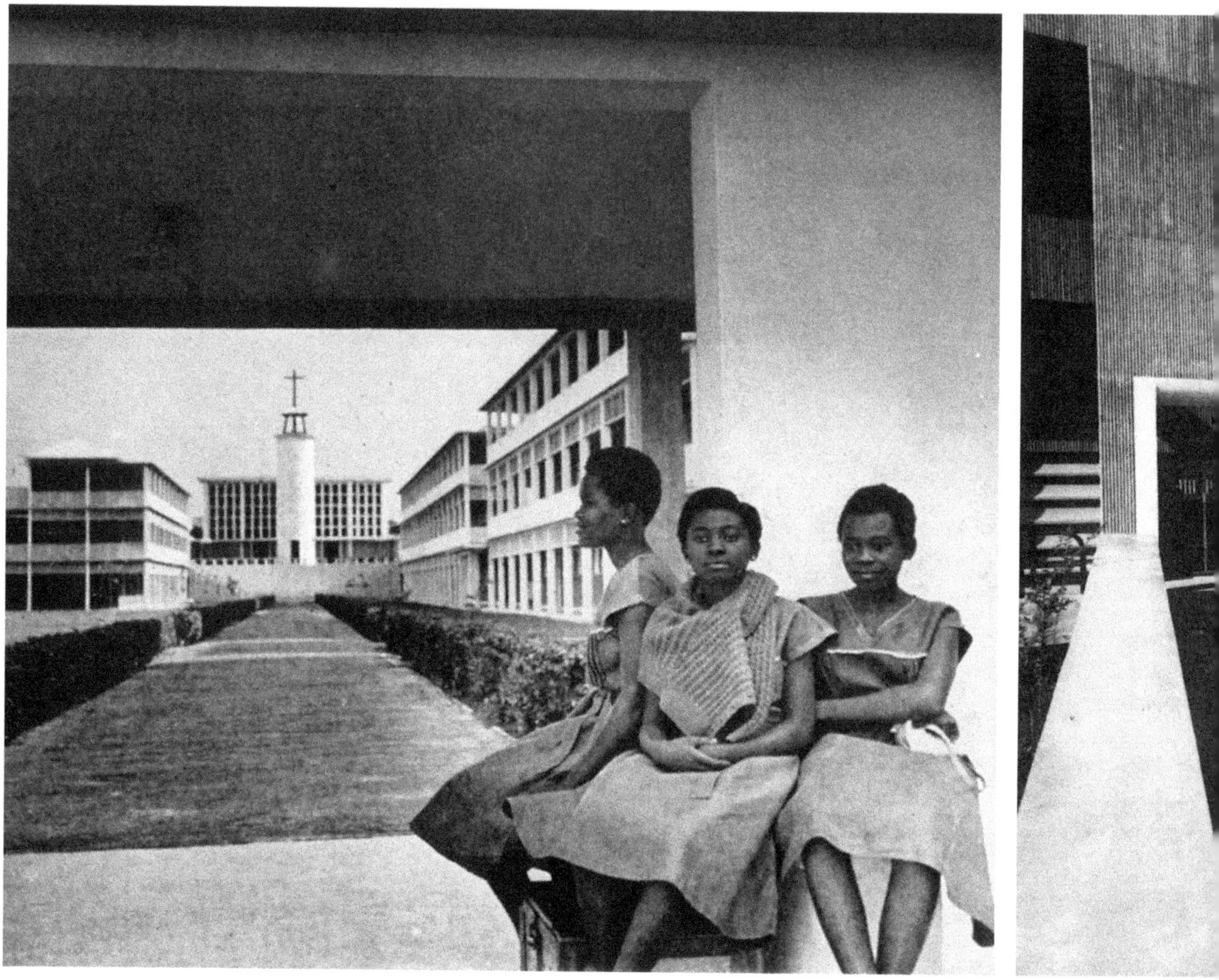

FIGURE 4.17 Maxwell Fry and Jane Drew, Wesley Girls' Secondary School in Cape Coast, early 1950s. Maxwell Fry and Jane Drew, *Tropical Architecture in the Humid Zone* (New York: Reinhold, 1956), 209.

reflecting their new status as postcolonial subjects who feel very much at home in their modern but native environment.

The contrast between these two images of colonial and postcolonial youth is enhanced by their gender difference. Unlike African men, whose perceived physical virility Europeans found threatening, African women were seen as more yielding objects of desire by the colonial gaze and its reformative aspirations. It is not surprising that Fry and Drew later omitted this image, with its quintessential representation of colonial discipline,

FIGURE 4.18 Harold Rubin, Central Library, University of Ife, 1969. Yael Aloni Photo Collection. Courtesy of the Azrieli Architectural Archive; Arieh Sharon collection.

from their publications following Ghana's and Nigeria's independence. Gender and race, however, still play a role in the postcolonial photograph. The image of the male Nigerian athletes demonstrates how Sharon's Zionism rendered able-bodied men the epitome of national productivity in this postcolonial setting. Moreover, the students' exposed black skin conveys their belonging in a way that Israeli observers desired and envied. For example, Anda Amir, an Israeli poet who lived in Kenya with her husband, an agriculture and settlement advisor, wrote a children's poem that recounts an Israeli girl's envy of her doll's black skin. As the doll strolls carelessly under the sun, her skin is not only left unharmed but even beautified by it: "and to her smooth skin / will be added more grace, a shine."[82] The poem fetishizes black skin as an undeniable, empirical marker of nativity whose qualities are enhanced by its unmediated, symbiotic encounter with the environment. From a Zionist perspective, therefore, the biological "fact of blackness" (a term attributed to Fanon) was not an obstacle but a visible sign of belonging and compatibility with the native environment.[83] Fanon's critique targets the white world's reaction to black skin, which locks Africans in their blackness. By celebrating blackness as a sign of nativity, the Zionist gaze bypassed rather than rejected this racial stereotyping. In their encounter with postcolonial African nationalism, Israeli architects perceived blackness as a biological condition for environmental belonging and cultural rejuvenation, which were dependent, in their view, on a return to national territory, as in Zionism. If the European gaze locked Africans in their blackness, the Zionist gaze locked Africans in Africa.

This fantasy of harmony between people and place did not, in fact, entail a relaxed, anxiety-free relationship between postcolonial subjects and their environment. As the term "self-protecting" implies, from this settler colonial perspective feeling at home in one's national territory did not necessarily mean feeling at ease. Sovereignty had to be constantly reaffirmed through the virility that national subjects performed in their exertions to reclaim the environment as their own. While Sharon did not consider the tropical environment an enemy from which students needed protection, he could not completely give his design over to a static, harmonious whole. The territory still had to be conquered, since only such active interventions could shape a new subjectivity. Sharon's postcolonial critique was tinged with Zionist anxieties and thus exchanged the shackles of colonialism for those of settler colonial nationalism.

Coda: The Cultured Skin

In Ife, Sharon emphasized the building's surface as the site on which locality could be literally embodied. The question was how to imbue the campus's modern buildings with local identity without resorting to applied ornamentation. In other words, instead of dressing the modernist buildings up in Yoruba garb, the challenge was to render the modernist building's skin itself Yoruba. While some architectural historians have traced abstracted allusions to local Yoruba architectural motifs in the campus core's sculptured gate, murals, and even layout, the only explicit reference is the replica of Opa Oranmiyan—the Staff of Oranmiya, the successor to Ife's first king, Oduduwa (fig. 4.19).[84] The incorporation of local traditions was highly problematic for several reasons. First, though the university was designed to cater mainly to the western region, it did not wish to present a distinct ethnic identity. Second, any local references would be highly mediated by the influence of European primitivism and its appropriation of African visual languages and could by no means be regarded as direct local expressions.[85] This is especially evident at the University of Ife, where no local artists were involved in the design of the campus core, although it was common to integrate local artists' work into the design of public buildings.[86] Harold Rubin was in charge of the campus core's artistic program because of his own artistic background and his familiarity with African arts in South Africa, though those varied traditions could hardly be considered related to that of the Yoruba. In addition to designing the Faculty of Education, Central Library, and Oduduwa Hall, Rubin designed the murals, sculptural gate, and covered path between the Central Library and the Humanities buildings.

The architects aimed to integrate the artistic program with the buildings organically, rather than having it stand out as applied ornamentation. Modernist architectural projects in Africa incorporated artwork in much the same way as contemporary projects in the West. In Europe, such incorporation became known as "the synthesis of the arts"—a postwar solution to the crisis of representation in modern architecture.[87] Unlike in the European context, however, where the synthesis was assumed to involve only the "major arts"—architecture, painting, and sculpture—and thus reinforced the hierarchy between them and applied art, in the African context such a synthesis often resulted in a paradoxical divorce of structure from art, or of technology from culture, due to the purported continuity between African arts and traditional crafts. Architects employed art as an addition that stood out in its materials and techniques, thus rendering it a superficial marker of local culture and tradition.[88] In contrast, Latin American university campuses—which were among the most celebrated instances of "the synthesis of the arts" at the time and that the University of Ife delegation visited in 1962—exemplified a more assertive integration of local traditions and contemporary technology.[89] According to Sharon's recollections, the delegation was particularly impressed by the frescoes and murals at Mexico City's National Autonomous University of Mexico; designed by Diego Rivera, José Clemente Orozco, and David Alfaro Siqueiros, they espoused racial pride, technological progress, and respect for pre-Columbian ancestors.[90] Singling out the artists who designed relief murals, rather than two-dimensional frescoes such as those Juan O'Gorman famously designed for the library, Sharon specifically referred to their three-dimensionality as the quality that inspired him "to exploit these impressions by proposing sculptural Yoruba elements in the Ife university buildings."[91] Sharon's uneasiness with two-dimensional frescos and his preference for thick, three-dimensional surfaces echo his rejection of additive sun shading devices and the volumetric inverted pyramid solution he proposed in its stead.

In addition to freestanding sculptural objects, such as the gate and the Opa Oranmiyan replica, Sharon and Rubin incorporated sculptural elements into the buildings' masses to emphasize their haptic qualities. This sculptural leitmotif developed gradually in the design and construction of the campus core, first with the controlled plasticity of the Humanities buildings, which found their sculptural outlet in the external staircases on the north side, and bulky semicylinders on the south side. The concrete beams and trusses of Rubin's Education building and the cutouts in his Central Library extended this sculptural tendency, which reached its climax in Oduduwa Hall (see figs. 4.19 and 4.20, and plate 17). A hexagonal mass, the hall comprises an auditorium and an open-air amphitheater connected in the center by a stage tower including both semicircular thrust stages that open up to each of the performance spaces. The interconnected stages allow for flexibility and simultaneous use; they are designed specifically for Yoruba theater.[92] Under the slanting auditorium, the foyer is left completely open to the exterior, as circular and semicircular cutouts pierce the tall walls that frame its concrete stairs and galleries, mirroring the library's cutout and its adjacent arched pergola. The cutouts, grooved texturing of the walls, and white, amorphous murals painted on a grey substrate create a plastic, festive space, as if Louis Kahn's modern monumentality had been rendered free-form. Rather than signaling lightness, the cutouts emphasized the materiality of the wall, which was further accentuated by its grooves.[93]

In *Kibbutz + Bauhaus*, Sharon juxtaposed Oduduwa Hall's grooved mural with one of the famous Ife figurines that dates to the eleventh century, implying that the building's corrugated grooving specifically referred to that sculpture. This juxtaposition could be interpreted as no more than a retroactive "localization" of this design feature. However, Sharon had noted the "special architectural interest" of Yoruba sculptures as early as 1961, in

FIGURE 4.19 View of Oduduwa Hall from the Secretariat, University of Ife, mid-1970s. The Opa Oranmiyan replica is on the right. In the background is the Faculty of Sciences, designed by James Cubitt. Courtesy of Amos Spitz.

one of his draft reports on the town of Ife.[94] It is possible that Sharon's interest was piqued by experiments with textured grooving that had become prevalent in the West in the late 1950s as a form of "repressed" ornamentation.[95] Sharon's instructions for the contractor make evident the double attraction of grooving as both internationally trendy and also undeniably local. While mentioning the walls of the newly built UNESCO building in Paris for reference, Sharon nonetheless suggested the employment of local craftsmen, who, according to him, would execute the grooving much better than Solel Boneh's Israeli workers.[96]

Compared with the abstracted African sculptures and masks known in the West through their modernist appropriation, Yoruba sculptures are

FIGURE 4.20  Obafemi Awolowo University (formerly the University of Ife), Oduduwa Hall, textured murals, contemporary view. Photograph by Ayala Levin.

FIGURE 4.21 Ooni Adesoji Aderemi posing next to Ife figurines, undated. Photographer unknown.

distinctly naturalistic.⁹⁷ Unlike Picasso's rendering of African masks and tattoos as markers and vehicles of abstraction, these sculptures' grooving highlights their three-dimensional naturalism. The grooving is reserved for the representation of Yoruba royalty and chiefs, whose spiritual attributes it signifies (fig. 4.21). Grooving is also reminiscent of tattoo; such bodily inscriptions are practiced in a variety of African cultures and are echoed in textiles and murals. The thickening of the skin in low-relief patterns accentuates its function as boundary between the self and the symbolic realm of society.⁹⁸ These practices underscore the skin's double function of both bounding and expressing the self; they thus complicate Western philosophy's equation of truth with depth and of deceit with surface. As literary theorist Anne Cheng explains in her discussion of the racial aspects of Adolf Loos's architectural bareness, skin is "a medium of transition and doubleness: it is at once surface and yet integrally attached to what it covers. It also serves as a vibrant interface between the hidden and the visually available."⁹⁹ In the case of Yoruba culture, the line is as-

DESIGNING THE UNIVERSITY OF IFE

sociated with civilization, the imposition of human pattern on the disorder of nature. The external marking of lines, whether in sculpture, on the human face, or in the making of roads and boundaries in the forest, allow dialectically for their inner qualities to shine through.[100] The hidden is not solely the domain of the "interior" self, which instead derives from a spiritual world both inside and outside the body and is marked on its surface. Through the social performance of inscription and the traces it leaves, the spiritual is localized and pinned down to an individual in a particular place.[101] More than simply delineating the boundary between private and public, individual and society, the thickening of the skin demonstrates that just as the surface expresses interiority, the interior is inscribed by external sociocultural and religious forces. In this reading, Oduduwa Hall's wall serves both to demarcate a boundary for a specialized activity as well as to imbue it with meaning through grooving and murals. Besides Oduduwa Hall and the concave stand that serves as a backdrop for the Opa Oranmiyan replica, grooving is reserved for only one more building in the campus core, the Central Library. This indicates the campus's hierarchical order and expresses the cultural significance attributed to both buildings as receptacles and disseminators of Yoruba culture and knowledge.

By choosing the grooving on Yoruba head figurines as his primary local reference, Sharon used naturalistic sculpture to link the building's surface with the skin of the human body—and thus added another semantic layer to the Israeli white wall. In Yoruba sculpture and its basis in African metaphysics, Sharon found an intermediary object that mirrored the Zionist dialectic between subject and object—"to build and be built"—that postulates the mutual dependence of society's productive capacities and its natural and built environment. In addition to serving as an anthropomorphic device, the grooved skin of the figures captured the duality of Zionist desires for both acclimatization and national rejuvenation—that is, for both biological and cultural belonging. In this African-Israeli encounter, the skin is neither entirely bare nor a form of inauthentic dressing but instead where the biological and the cultural intertwine and reach their highest synthesis.

PLATE 1  Sierra Leone parliament, interior colonnade, Freetown, 1960. Courtesy of the Azrieli Architectural Archive; Dov and Ram Karmi collection, 8267357058013.

PLATE 2 (TOP) Sierra Leone parliament southern facade, Freetown, 1960. Courtesy of the Azrieli Architectural Archive; Dov and Ram Karmi collection, 8267357058013. PLATE 3 (BOTTOM) Sierra Leone parliament western facade, Freetown, 1960. Courtesy of the Azrieli Architectural Archive; Dov and Ram Karmi collection, 8267357058013.

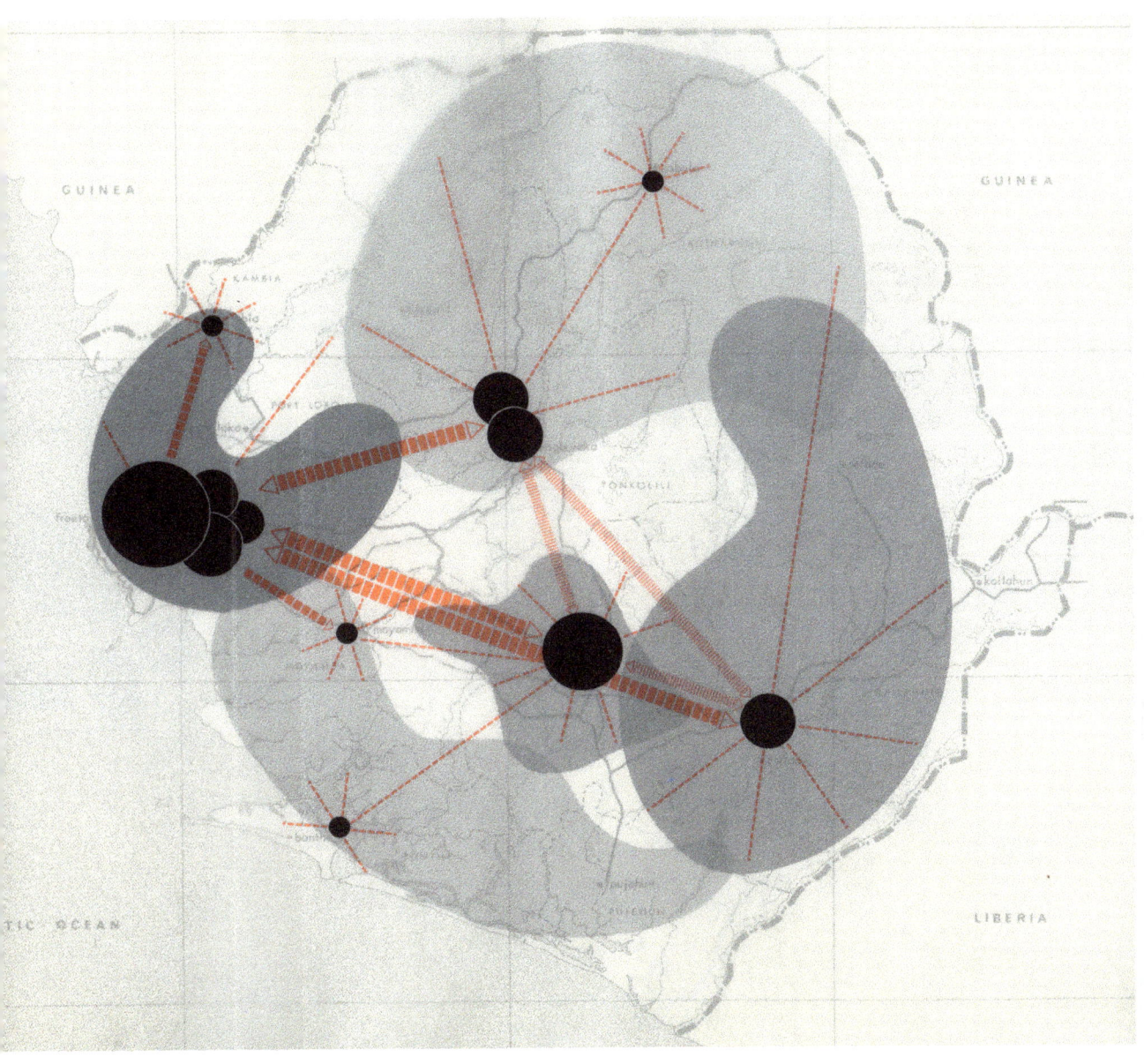

PLATE 4 "Urban Framework." Source: Aryeh Doudai and Ursula Oelsner, *Sierra Leone National Urbanisation Plan* (Tel Aviv: Institute for Planning and Development, 1965).

PLATE 5 (TOP) Arieh Sharon and Egboramy, Campus Core, University of Ife, late 1970s. Courtesy of Eliezer Schreiber's family. PLATE 6 (BOTTOM) Obafemi Awolowo University (formerly University of Ife), faculty housing, contemporary view. Photograph: Ayala Levin.

**PLATE 7 (TOP)** Obafemi Awolowo University (formerly University of Ife), faculty housing, contemporary view. Photograph: Ayala Levin.
**PLATE 8 (BOTTOM)** Obafemi Awolowo University (formerly University of Ife), faculty housing, contemporary view. Photograph: Ayala Levin.

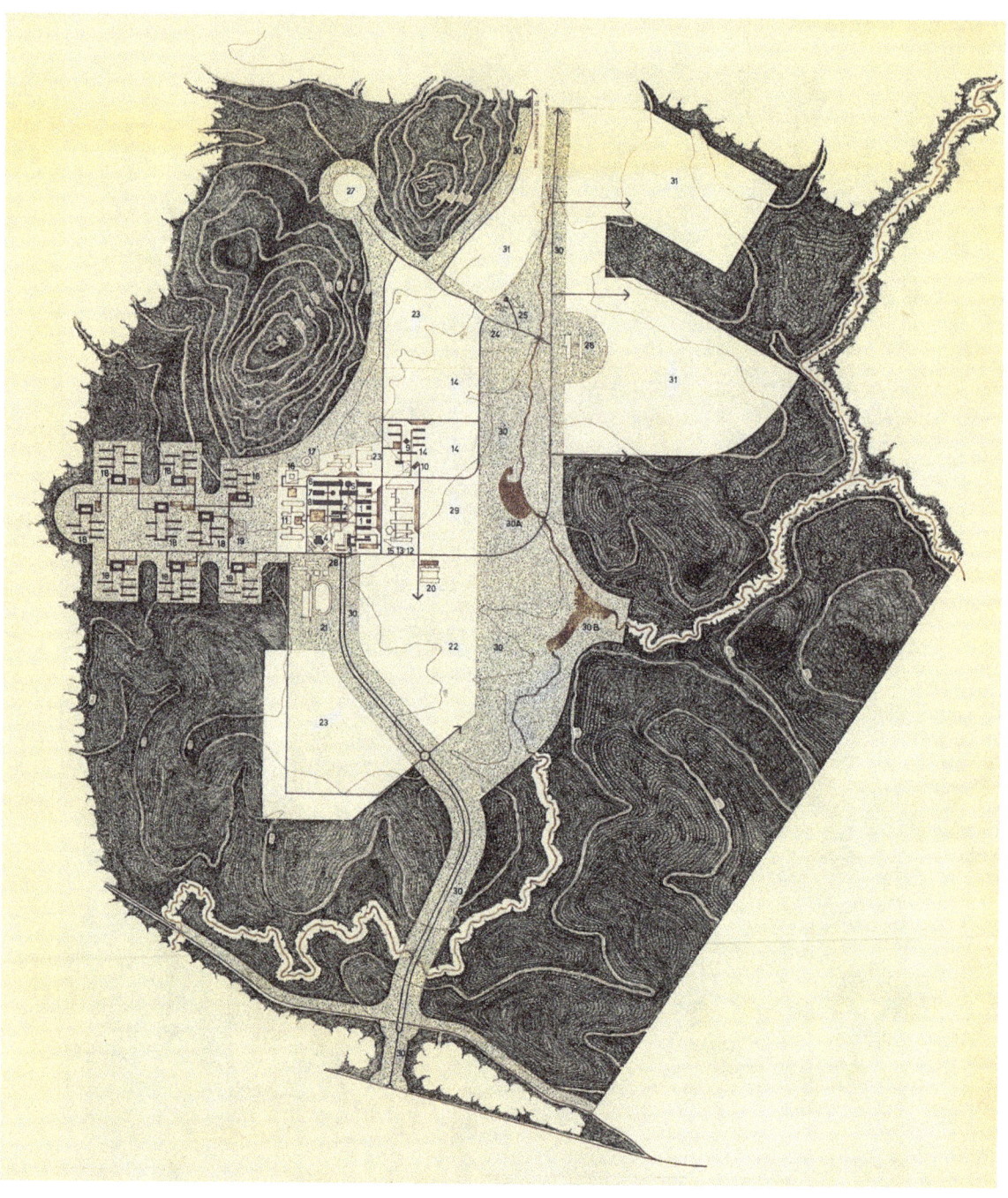

PLATE 9  Arieh Sharon, University of Ife campus plan, 1962. Note the separation between the campus core (center) and the agriculture faculty to the northeast. The groups of buildings to the west are the students' dormitories. In later plans there are fewer dormitories, and they are more dispersed. Faculty housing is located north and east of the agriculture faculty and the campus core. Courtesy of the Azrieli Architectural Archive; Arieh Sharon collection. AES-1-217_965332461001_01_004_135.

PLATE 10  Obafemi Awolowo University (formerly University of Ife), Agriculture Faculty, contemporary view. Photograph: Ayala Levin.

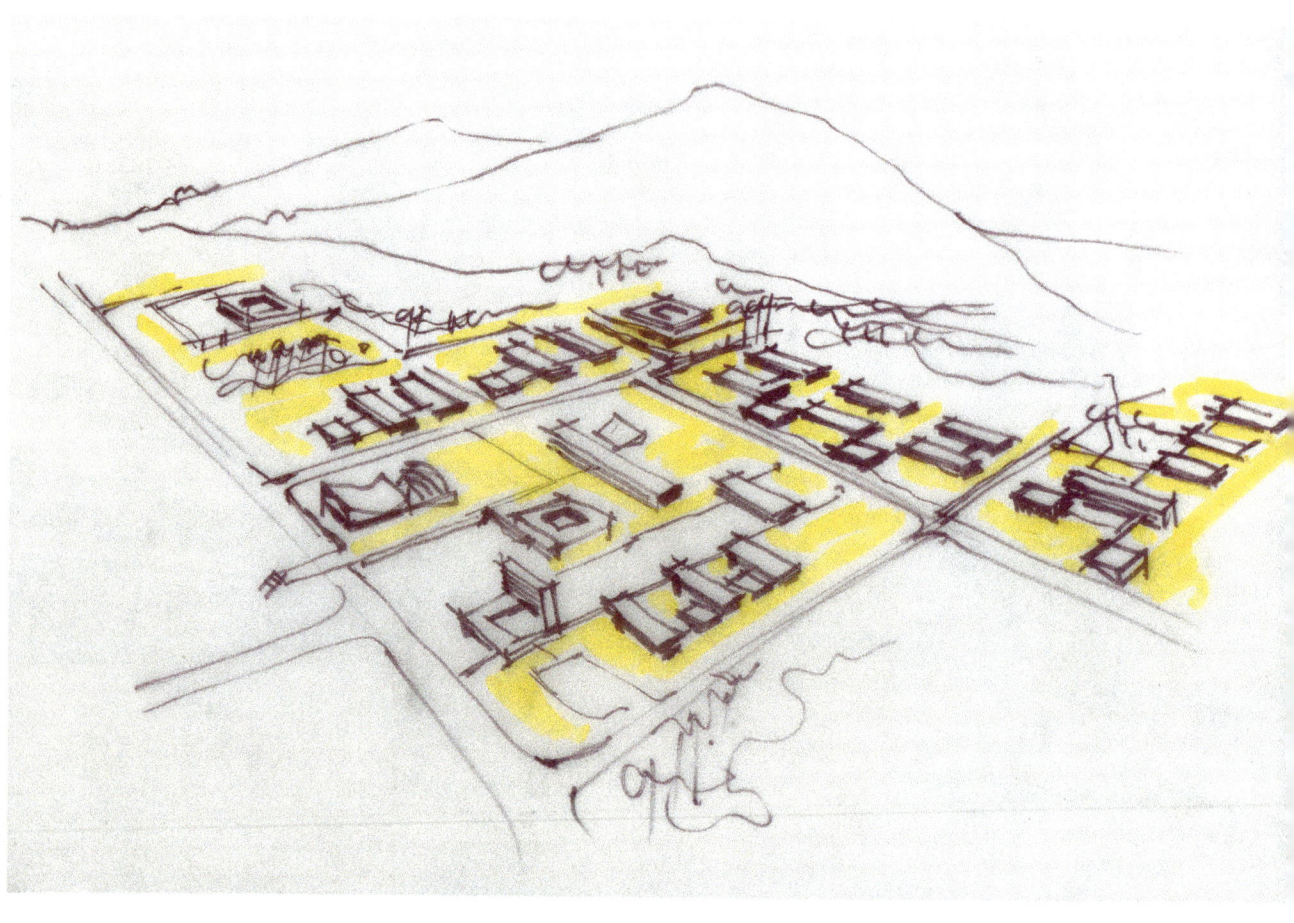

PLATE 11 Arieh Sharon, University of Ife, academic core and surrounding faculties (undated). Courtesy of the Azrieli Architectural Archive; Arieh Sharon collection, AES-1-217.

**PLATE 12 (TOP)** Obafemi Awolowo University (formerly the University of Ife), Faculty of Education, contemporary view from the southeast. Photograph by Ayala Levin.  **PLATE 13 (BOTTOM)** Obafemi Awolowo University (formerly the University of Ife), Faculty of Education, hanging gardens, contemporary view. Photograph by Ayala Levin.

PLATE 14  Obafemi Awolowo University (formerly the University of Ife), Social Sciences and Administration faculty buildings, and the Education Faculty in the background, contemporary view. Photograph by Ayala Levin.

PLATE 15 (TOP) Obafemi Awolowo University (formerly the University of Ife), Faculty of Administration, contemporary view of the open central mall and roof. Photograph by Ayala Levin. PLATE 16 (BOTTOM) Obafemi Awolowo University (formerly the University of Ife), Faculty of Administration, ground level. Photograph by Ayala Levin.

PLATE 17  Obafemi Awolowo University (formerly the University of Ife), Oduduwa Hall, foyer, contemporary view. Photograph by Ayala Levin.

PLATE 18  Zalman Enav and Michael Tedros, Shalom Shelemay Apartment Building, contemporary view. Photograph by Ayala Levin.

PLATE 19  Zalman Enav and Michael Tedros, Filwoha Baths, 1959–64. Courtesy of Zalman Enav.

PLATE 20 (TOP)  Ducor Palace Hotel, Monrovia, date unknown. Courtesy of the Neal Prince Trust Special Archives Collection, New York School of Interior Design, c. 2020.   PLATE 21 (BOTTOM)  Ducor Palace Hotel, Monrovia, undated, as redesigned by Neal Prince, Inter-Continental Hotels' chief designer and architect. Courtesy of the Neal Prince Trust Special Archives Collection, New York School of Interior Design, c. 2020.

PLATE 22  Hotel Ivoire, bird's-eye view, 1970. Source: Mafit Trust Corporation, *The African Riviera: Mafit Project Prepared for the Government of the Republic of Ivory Coast* (Tel Aviv: United Artists, 1970).

# israeli aid, private entrepreneurship, and architectural education in addis ababa

WHEN ZALMAN ENAV, a recent graduate of the Department of Tropical Architecture at the Architectural Association (AA) in London, arrived in Ethiopia in 1959, he had no inkling it would become his prime residence for the next seven years and the site of a rich career adventure that would last for over a decade. Originally planned as a visit to his brothers, who managed a meat factory owned by the Israeli government in Asmara, Eritrea, Enav's trip brought him to Addis Ababa, where he found a growing development industry. That same year, Addis Ababa had experienced a construction boom that was part of emperor Haile Selassie's continuous attempts to modernize the city. The selection of the Ethiopian capital as the seat of the United Nations Economic Commission for Africa in 1958, and as the seat of the Organisation of African Unity in 1963, gave these efforts extra impetus. The construction boom helped position Addis Ababa as a continental capital and assert Selassie's reconsolidation of imperial power; the city sought to become a symbol of African liberation and uninterrupted continuity with tradition for the pan-African world.[1]

Unlike in former colonies where colonial networks continued to dominate construction and architectural markets even after independence, in Ethiopia, which had been formally colonized by Italy for less than six years, architectural production was open to competition among private entrepreneurs. Continuing a long-established tradition of welcoming individual foreign experts as part of modernization efforts that had begun at the end of the nineteenth century, Haile Selassie's regime increasingly promoted private land ownership and created a particularly lucrative setting for developers and architecture firms in the postwar period. At the same time, the regime's diplomatic maneuvers orchestrated development aid from both Cold War blocs as well as from the nonaligned Yugoslavia.[2]

As a private initiative, Enav's practice in Addis Ababa was distinct from those of other Israeli architects who were working in Africa as part of Solel Boneh's joint companies or with the Institute of Planning and Development at that time. Consequently, his effect on the local architectural scene and the development of the city was greater than theirs in both scope and variety. Enav's education at the AA might be taken to imply that his work in Ethiopia was simply an extension of the British-dominated network of tropical architecture to new actors and new geographies.[3] However, by tracing the loyalties and alliances he forged with local elites to sustain his career in Addis Ababa, this chapter demonstrates how Enav worked at the crossroads of varying professional and social networks that challenge narratives of the unidirectional flow of knowledge from the British hegemonic center to the global South. Similarly, free from institutional ties to the Israeli or Ethiopian government, Enav operated in their interstices while taking advantage of strong Israeli trade, military, and diplomatic connections in Ethiopia. He also promoted these whenever he could, in part by commissioning Solel Boneh for his own projects and helping establish an architecture department at the Israeli-run College of Engineering.

In this chapter, I examine Enav's work—which both enabled and was enabled by Israeli connections with Ethiopia—as part of a complex web in which aid, trade, security, diplomacy, and private initiative supported each other. Rather than focusing on specific projects, this chapter presents a mosaic of building-related activities centered on Addis Ababa. This mosaic includes the work of Solel Boneh and Israeli aid personnel, and Enav himself at times recedes into the background as I explore the role that architecture and construction played in both Haile Selassie's and the aid donors' visions for Ethiopian development. In particular, this chapter analyzes how the Ethio-Swedish Building College and the College of Engineering, which Israelis ran provisionally before its management was handed over to German personnel, vied to direct architectural education. As an instance of the theater of development par excellence, this competition over architectural education highlights the challenges of vocational and technical aid in Ethiopia and the differing development aid ideologies that Israel and Sweden offered.

As this chapter will demonstrate, the very definition of an architecture of development was at stake here. While Sweden pushed Haile Selassie's regime to extend development efforts to the rural population and the urban poor, Israeli architectural aid was more in line with Haile Selassie's own vision of accelerated modernization, which centered on highly financed projects in the capital. When an abortive coup d'état dramatically challenged Selassie's approach in 1960, Israeli aid was instrumental in repressing the coup not only via intelligence but also through cultural channels that negotiated the relationship between tradition and modernity. This chapter concludes by examining how Enav and his business partner, Michael Tedros, specifically in their designs for the Ministry of Foreign Affairs building and the Filwoha Baths, addressed these challenges by articulating architectural forms that, through both ornament and structure, could at once tap into traditional repertoires and serve as a basis for change.

The Security-Trade-Diplomacy Complex

Although Enav arrived in Ethiopia on his own initiative and established his practice independently of formal Israeli aid, the increasing strength of Israel's relationship with Ethiopia made his work there possible. Ethiopia accorded Israel de jure recognition in October 1961, which led to the opening of an Israeli embassy in Addis Ababa the following year. Yet relations between the states had been initiated soon after the establishment of Israel. Unlike Israel's diplomatic relations with Nigeria and Sierra Leone, the relationship between Israel and Ethiopia preceded the Bandung Conference and even dated back to the Jewish settlement in Palestine under the British Mandate.[4] Geographical proximity, the establishment of institutions of the Ethiopian Orthodox Tewahedo Church in Jerusalem in the nineteenth century, ancient historical ties between the Israelite King Solomon and the Ethiopian Queen Sheba, and the presence of Beta Israel, a Jewish community in Ethiopia (also named derogatively *falasha,* or invaders, in Amharic) meant that Israel's ties with Ethiopia were considerably more multifaceted and significant than its relations with any other African country. The periphery doctrine, in which Israel established relations with non-Arab states on the periphery of the Middle East in the late 1950s, formalized the strategic component of Israel's relationship with Ethiopia, as well as with Turkey and Iran. Acting as a powerful, US-backed, anti-Arab force in the region, Haile Selassie's imperial regime presented a favored alternative to the growing continental influence of Egyptian leader Gamal Abdel Nasser, who was one of the key leaders to initiate the Non-Aligned Movement.[5]

Zalman Enav's brothers, Azriel and Shmuel Enav, had arrived in Eritrea, then under Ethiopia's control, before Ethiopia's trade relations with Israel were formalized in March 1959.[6] They took over the management of Incode, a canned meat factory in Asmara that was partially owned by the Israeli government and that depended on the Israeli Defense Forces for its product supply.[7] Incode had been established in the early 1950s as part of the informal relations that the Israeli government was cultivating with Ethiopia, despite the Ministry of Foreign Affairs' official policy of conditioning trade on the formalization of diplomatic relations. Perceiving East Africa as an essential economic frontier for developing Israel's Negev Desert and southern port, prime minister David Ben-Gurion sent the head of his recently established Negev Committee to Ethiopia in October 1950 to explore the possibilities for trade between the two countries.[8] The Ethiopian emperor Haile Selassie used Incode as an informal channel for communicating with the Israeli government while he delayed establishing official relations.[9] Israeli security forces embraced this practice and even encouraged it: the plant served for many years, even after the opening of a general consulate in Addis Ababa in 1956, as a cover for the operation of Mossad (Israeli intelligence) agents—among them Azriel Enav, Zalman Enav's brother—in the predominantly Muslim colonial territory of Ethiopia.[10]

Formal and informal or clandestine relationships reached their peak overlap when the diplomatic corps in Addis Ababa was replaced completely with intelligence officers in 1957 and 1958. This merger of intelligence with diplomacy continued until the position as joint head of both Israeli intelligence and the consulate in Ethiopia was split into two separate jobs in December 1960.[11] Since Enav arrived in Addis Ababa before this separation, the contacts he established at the Israeli consulate through his brothers' recommendation should be considered within the framework of this trade-intelligence-diplomacy complex.[12] While detailed evidence about how Israeli intelligence operations in Ethiopia might have shaped the work of

Israeli architects and aid personnel there is not available or accessible, Israel's nonofficial, shadowy military and intelligence presence formed an essential backdrop for their work.

Through the deputy consul who made the introduction, Enav received his first commission from Shalom Shelemay, a prominent Jewish merchant from Aden who, after the 1947 Aden riots, lived in Ethiopia with his family provisionally, having already established trade business in Ethiopia and Eritrea in the 1940s. Shelemay was involved in attempts to rescue members of the Irgun Zvai Leumi Be'Eretz Yisrael (literally, "National Military Organization in the Land of Israel"), an outlawed Zionist paramilitary group whose members were deported and interned in British camps in Eritrea.[13] As an important member of the trade community in Addis Ababa, Shelemay was even offered Ethiopian citizenship at one point.[14] The imperial government acknowledged his prominence by offering him the opportunity to purchase Benin Sefer, a Jewish community compound named after Menahim Messa, known as "Benin," another merchant from Aden who had been a leader of the Jewish community in Addis Ababa.

Taking advantage of the acute housing shortage in the capital and the influx of diplomatic and aid personnel, especially employees of the American embassy, Shalom Shelemay decided to construct a rental apartment building with a commercial ground level and basement for the family's trade business on the site, across the street from another building that the family owned. The commission gave Enav a chance to showcase his originality and improvisatory talent by overcoming an especially narrow and steep site (plate 18 and fig. 5.1) and by addressing the taste and lifestyle of its future occupants. The highly irregular building that resulted consists of four stories on one end and six stories on the other. The regular facade hides a highly diverse combination of apartment types. The largest ones sprawl across two and a half levels, with a spacious living area and dining room separated by a mezzanine for the kitchen. These were designed specifically to accommodate the main leisure activity of expatriate elites in Addis Ababa: hosting and entertaining at lavish dinner parties.

Using sunshade screens, Enav created a dynamic articulation of volumes on the facade that contrasts starkly with the unified mass of the three-story apartment building that still faces it. The Shalom Shelemay Building became a landmark in the city, as patches of modern buildings, besides a few built during the Italian occupation, were very rare and highly visible. Moreover, the emperor himself gave the building special attention because of the high volatility of the site, which was adjacent to one of the most

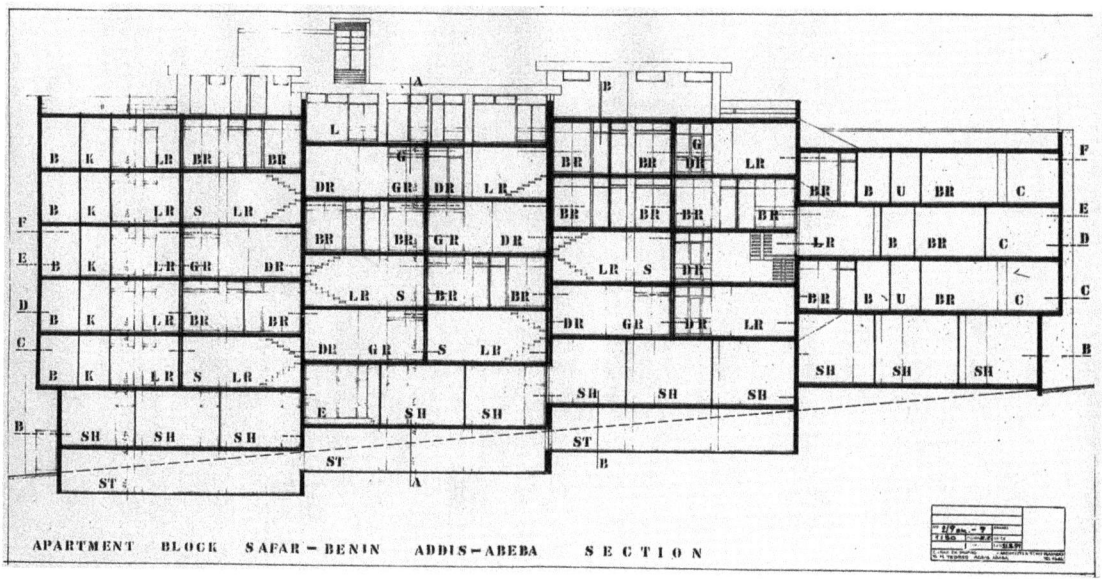

FIGURE 5.1  Zalman Enav and Michael Tedros, Shalom Shelemay Apartment Building, section, 1959. Courtesy of Zalman Enav.

prominent mosques in the city.[15] During the building's construction, the emperor drove past the site every afternoon to make sure that the building would not stir "another Suez crisis" in the neighborhood.[16] This concern was not far-fetched: the Muslim community in Eritrea was crying out against the "second Palestine" they feared was being created by Israeli and non-Israeli Jewish endeavors in the area—especially the commercial farms that the Enav brothers had established following the success of Incode.[17]

What had started out as a business relationship turned into a close family one when Zalman Enav married Shalom Shelemay's daughter Margaret. Through his ties with the Jewish expatriate community, Enav gained access to other local elites, including the royal family. Continuing the tradition of entrusting expatriates with discreet royal affairs, the royal family commissioned Enav to design a house for one of the emperor's grandsons; Enav centered it on an alcohol bar to suit the prince's drinking habits.[18] As the two had grown close, the royal family asked Enav to keep a watchful eye on the prince when they went carousing together. While the prince expressed his appreciation by surprising Enav with the gift of a shiny red Mini Minor, the royal family thanked him by hiring him to design a mausoleum for the emperor and the empress.[19]

### An Israeli-Ethiopian Partnership

In order to deepen his social and professional ties, Enav sought to partner with a local architect. After some inquiries, Enav met Michael Tedros, who at that time was the only Ethiopian with a professional degree in architecture and was working at the Ethiopian Ministry of Education. Born and raised in England, Tedros had acquired some training in the building trades through England's postwar veteran education program. After that training, Tedros was studying architecture at night school when the Ethiopian government asked him to work at the Ministry of Education.[20] The government invited Tedros to follow his brother, an engineer, in apprenticing under the British administration to help fulfill its explicit aim of Ethiopianizing its ministries. The Tedros brothers were among a significant number of Ethiopian returnees who occupied important technical and bureaucratic positions.[21]

The marriage of professionalism and national identity offered Tedros an opportunity for class mobility that he could not enjoy in England, where his skin color made him vulnerable to racial discrimination.[22] By accepting the Ethiopian government's proposal, Tedros could pursue his career aspirations without the hindrances of race and class that he had encountered in England. As a returnee, he benefitted from educational opportunities that far exceeded those accessible to him in England, and from mobility that transgressed both British class divisions and Ethiopia's traditional social hierarchy. Under the American Point Four aid program, which was signed in Ethiopia in 1951, Tedros was granted government scholarships to complete his formal architectural degree at Ohio State University and to go on to graduate study at the University of Pennsylvania under famed architect Louis Kahn.[23]

Enav and Tedros established the first architectural firm in which an Ethiopian was a full partner. Although comparable partnerships between expatriate and local architects proliferated across the postcolonial world, these were often motivated by government regulations, as was the case in Nigeria beginning in the early 1970s. In contrast, Enav's partnership with Tedros was voluntary and unprecedented in Ethiopia. Yet despite Tedros's prestigious training, Enav headed design at the office and acted as Tedros's mentor, while Tedros, with his more agreeable personality, communicated with the workers.[24] These hierarchical work relations were consolidated by their first presentation to the emperor, when Enav discovered, to his utmost embarrassment, that his Ethiopian partner could not speak a word of

Amharic.²⁵ From then on, Enav conversed directly with the emperor, while the intimidated Tedros was instructed to learn the national language if he ever hoped to speak to the emperor again.²⁶

Notwithstanding the mutual respect and friendship between the two, by partnering with a "local" architect, Enav aimed to distinguish himself from his competitors.²⁷ The architectural moguls who dominated the design and construction market in the capital included the Italian-Eritrean Arturo Mezzedimi, the French Henri Chomette, Yugoslav architects Zdravko Kovačević and Ivan Štraus, and firms such as the Norwegian Norconsult.²⁸ As representatives of the first "local" architectural firm, Enav and Tedros—and their image—benefitted from their commitment to developing a local professional community. Enav taught part-time at the College of Engineering, and the two were involved in establishing the Ethiopian Association of Architects and Engineers in 1963 and publishing its journal, *Zede*. As was typical of their strategic alliance, in which Tedros served as the "local face" of their partnership, it was a photo of Tedros helping a student that made it into a university brochure in 1966 and served as a compelling image of the Ethiopianization of the university and of architecture.²⁹ Similarly, Tedros became the first president of the Ethiopian Association of Architects and Engineers, while Enav was active in its formation behind the scenes.

Enav's determination to partner with a local architect can be attributed to his experience studying in the tropical architecture department at the Architectural Association in London after his graduation from the Technion in Israel. The establishment of that department during the critical period of the British Empire's demise served to assert England's continuing global significance in a postcolonial world.³⁰ Architectural historians have emphasized the department's technoscientific research, and yet, in recounting his school days there, Enav emphasized the cosmopolitan variety of its students, who came from such disparate places as Pakistan, Iraq, Trinidad, the Philippines, Ceylon, Vietnam, Jamaica, South Africa, Indonesia, Nigeria, and Thailand.³¹ Describing his schooling experience as eye opening, Enav considered meeting classmates from around the world and learning about each country's social challenges as the most formative aspects of his studies.³²

Despite the highly transnational nature of tropical architecture's body of knowledge, which was meant to be independent of the architect's background, during Enav's schooling there was some correspondence between the students' projects and their countries of origin. In addition to designing a hotel for the Jordanian coast of the Dead Sea, Enav worked on a city plan for Basra. On that project, he collaborated with a student from Iraq, indicating that there was an effort to include someone with intimate knowledge of the specified region on the design team.[33] Practical experience in the department that presupposed a degree of familiarity with a locality thus defied tropical architecture's transnational logic and network, as is evident in Enav's choice to partner with a local, rather than search for a collaborator with expertise in tropical architecture. Furthermore, contrary to the implicit assumption that members of the tropical architecture network would use British contractors and suppliers, Enav preferred to work with the Israeli contractor Solel Boneh and import Israeli products whenever possible.[34] When he needed to expand his office, he turned to Israel to find additional architects. His main perquisite was not familiarity with tropical climates but that the recruits were willing to work under a black man.[35]

The Building Market

While Enav played at best a limited part in strengthening the tropical architecture network, he played a significant role in expanding Israeli involvement in Addis Ababa. His ties with the local political and commercial elite put him in a position to recommend Solel Boneh as a contractor for some of the major projects he designed, both private and public (fig. 5.2). Unlike in many other African countries, Solel Boneh did not establish a local partnership with the Ethiopian government but instead operated as a private enterprise. In Ethiopia, where trade unions became legal only in 1962, Solel Boneh's connection to the Histadrut had no appeal.[36] Before according de jure recognition in October 1962, Ethiopia was reluctant to publicize its relationship with Israel; the Ethiopian government also sought to encourage foreign and local private investment. Moreover, unlike in other decolonizing countries, where the former colonial power's metropolitan firms monopolized the contracting market, in Ethiopia this market was relatively free, with many local Italian, Greek, and Armenian contractors keeping it competitive.[37] Capitalist-minded Haile Selassie was resistant to the idea of a joint venture until late 1963, when the government first attempted to negotiate with Solel Boneh.

By this time, Solel Boneh's eagerness to establish partnerships at any cost had diminished after the losses it experienced due to political instability and mismanagement in Nigeria, Sierra Leone, and other African countries.[38] A year earlier, when the Histadrut pressured Solel Boneh to establish a joint company in Kenya, and the Israeli foreign ministry urged it to enter the markets of Tanganyika, Upper Volta, Niger, and the Central African Republic, its board demanded financial backing and insurance against political risk from the Israeli government.[39] In the midst of its negotiations with the Israeli government, Solel Boneh considered the Ethiopian terms too tough, and the deal fell through.[40]

However, none of this stopped Solel Boneh from offering its services in Ethiopia as a private company, with continuing encouragement from the Israeli government. Sometimes Solel Boneh served as a cover for Israeli military personnel, as it had for intelligence operations by the Haganah (literally, "Defense"), the hegemonic Jewish paramilitary organization that

FIGURE 5.2 Zalman Enav explaining a building plan, 1960. *Foreground, from left to right:* Hannan Bar-On (Israel's consul general in Ethiopia), Zalman Enav, Haile Selassie, Menasse Lemma (director general of the Ministry of Finance), Michael Tedros, Solel Boneh engineer Yehoshua Greunspan, and Solel Boneh project manager Dov Eisenberg. Courtesy of Zalman Enav.

became the basis for the Israel Defense Forces, in the prestate years.[41] Its mode of operation in Ethiopia—opening a private branch rather than partnering with the local government—heralded the company's shift to purely commercial undertakings by the late 1960s. Privatization often enabled Solel Boneh to continue doing business in a country after it broke off diplomatic relations with Israel, as was the case with Nigeria and the design and construction of the University of Ife (see chapters 3 and 4). Solel Boneh also worked under the name Reynolds, a firm it had opened with American partners in order to win American-funded projects.[42] Initially formed in 1959 for work in Turkey, Reynolds also operated in Ethiopia, Iran, Spain, Nigeria, Thailand, and Somalia by the end of 1972.[43] In Ethiopia, Reynolds was involved in building the Bole International Airport, a highly lucrative project funded by American aid; it opened in 1963, just in time for the Organisation of African Unity summit that took place at the end of May that year.[44] The project displayed Ethiopia's modernization, as evidenced by the many photos of Haile Selassie greeting officials and diplomats with the elegant control tower in the background. Together with Africa Hall, designed by Arturo Mezzedimi, Bole airport was a symbol of Ethiopia's new international and continental stature.[45]

Solel Boneh's Ethiopian branch competed with a range of local contractors and international ones such as the Norwegian Norconsult, the Bulgarian Technoexportstroy, and the Yugoslav Centroproject. It managed to win its bid for the Haile Selassie I Stadium, completing construction ahead of schedule for the African Cup.[46] Yet for more architecturally complex projects, Enav's recommendation proved instrumental.[47] Between 1959 and 1965, Enav designed and Solel Boneh constructed the empress-owned apartment building, the Filwoha Baths, the 82 Apartment Building, and the Classroom Building at Haile Selassie I University.[48] Contrary to the Israeli mode of operation examined in previous chapters, in Ethiopia the architect and the construction company switched roles. If, in most African countries, Solel Boneh was responsible for the commissioning of Israeli architects, in this case Enav instead secured jobs for Solel Boneh.[49] In their internationally renowned project, the Filwoha Baths, Enav also involved the engineer Ephraim Spira, the first Israeli dean of Addis Ababa University's College of Engineering.[50]

### Architectural Education and the Competition over Aid

As we saw in chapter 3, higher education was one of the stages on which competition over development aid was performed. In Ethiopia, the single most important undertaking in the field of education was the establishment of Haile Selassie I University. Formally announced in 1961, Haile Selassie I University absorbed the existing University College and other tertiary institutions in Addis Ababa and around the country, including the Technical College and the Ethio-Swedish Institute of Building Technology.[51] Although the emperor first entertained the possibility of affiliating the institution with the University of London out of fear of depending on the United States alone, it was soon decided that the US International Cooperation Administration would take over the whole project, including designing and constructing all major new buildings, purchasing educational materials, paying the wages of senior administrative and teaching personnel, and training an Ethiopian faculty.[52]

For the United States, Haile Selassie I University was to play a strategic role in its cultural diplomacy both locally and on the continental level. Besides shaping a pro-American Ethiopian elite, the university was to serve as a regional center, like the American Universities in Cairo and Beirut. Imagined as a Cold War counterweight to Lumumba University in Moscow, which emphasized the ideological training of African students, Haile Selassie I University was established on African soil in what was going to be the continent's diplomatic capital.[53] Continental centrality was also the Ethiopian administration's aim, as exemplified by the high enrollment of international students in academic year 1963–64. As a university brochure of that year reported, of a total of 1,600 students, 157 were from other countries. Of these, 110 were scholarship students from fifteen African countries, 32 were funded by the Haile Selassie I scholarship program for African students, and the rest by the USAID scholarship program.[54]

The fact that US personnel and funds unequivocally dominated the university did not preclude competition among various countries associated with the Western bloc over the lower tiers of management and administration.[55] Cold War competition over aid took place not only between the blocs and between new (American) and old (British) powers within the Western bloc but also among politically weaker countries that were all supported by the United States to varying degrees. Such was the case with engineering and architectural education, two fields that became the locus of an aid competition among West Germany, Israel, and Sweden, while all three countries were involved in police and military aid in Ethiopia at the same time.[56]

As an exemplary case of the global theater of development, the competition over architectural education aid foregrounds the challenges of vocational and technical aid in Ethiopia as well as the competing development aid ideologies that Israel and Sweden presented. Sweden pushed Haile Selassie's regime to extend development efforts to the rural population and the urban poor by focusing on self-help building techniques. In contrast, Israeli architectural education was focused on high-profile building projects and was attached to engineering education to popularize the profession among students and boost its white-collar image. The foundations of this competition had been laid prior to the establishment of the university. As early as the 1940s, Haile Selassie had instigated a competition between colonial powers France and England over control of education, while preparing the scene for US entry. Selassie eventually turned to a noncolonial party, the French-Canadian Jesuits, who in 1945 took over secondary schools—including the Technical School, the only vocational secondary institution in Ethiopia—and opened the University College in 1950.[57] In 1952, American personnel established the Technical College on the grounds of the existing Technical School. In 1959, the Ethiopian and German governments signed an agreement stating that German personnel would take over the Technical College, and that the German government would provide the college with new facilities so it would not have to share space with the Technical School. In the meantime, Israel sent a dean and staff from the Technion at the Ethiopians' request, as a temporary measure before the Germans were to take over.

Meanwhile, down the road, on Smuts Street, west of the Technical College, a college of building had been established as part of a technical cooperation agreement between the Ethiopian and Swedish governments in October 1954. In the 1950s, Sweden had not yet formalized a foreign aid policy and focused on isolated initiatives in vocational training, continuing its missionary involvement in Ethiopia, which dated back to the nineteenth century.[58] Set up for the triple purpose of education, research, and testing, the Ethio-Swedish Building College opened its research and testing sections in 1956, and by 1960 offered four-year programs that led to a bachelor of science degree in building engineering.[59] Responding to the country's construction needs, the college dedicated itself to training students for a variety of roles in the building trade—such as contractors, foremen, designers, surveyors, and supervisors—that did not all require an engineering degree. As the college's 1960 annual report stated, "The need of trained technicians in the building field is at present great and it is steadily growing. Six years ago the production value in the building trade totaled about Eth.$ 10 million. . . . To-day it is about Eth.$ 25 million."[60] The term "trained technician" was better suited than "engineer" to the variety of roles necessary for the building trade. By 1962, the college's directors intended to reduce the number of students who received engineering degrees in response to an oversaturation of engineers in the local construction industry, which, however, was in dire need of foremen. Students responded by protesting their relegation to more menial jobs and calling for the expulsion of the Swedish administration.[61]

Unlike the cases examined in chapters 1 and 3, the degraded status of the manual worker in Ethiopian society was not the result of a colonial division of labor or educational system. In Ethiopia, slavery was not abolished until the 1940s, and manual labor was traditionally perceived as degrading. For this reason, all work in the entire construction industry was almost exclusively managed and performed by foreigners, particularly Italian, Indian, Arab, Greek, and Armenian masons and artisans. The Italian builder Castagna began making bricks around 1907, and the trade soon expanded to Greek producers. By the late 1920s, Italians also produced tiles.[62] The local class distinction between types of foreigners, expressed in the terms *grik* and *färänj,* also reflected this division of labor. Rather than denoting nationality, "grik" came to designate a class of "manual workers, eating-house proprietors and small traders, irrespective of whether they were really Greek, Armenian or Italian," while "färänj" designated the class of diplomats, government officials, and traders.[63] Reversing the colonial relationship, Europeans' prestige diminished considerably in Ethiopian eyes after Italy's defeat in the Battle of Adwa (1896). The employment of Italian prisoners of war as masons and road builders further relieved Ethiopians from dirtying their hands with manual labor.[64] Consequently, Emperor Menelik II, who ruled Ethiopia from 1889 to 1913, could increasingly afford to be more selective about foreign intervention and even to reject missionaries who trained Ethiopians in trades such as masonry, bricklaying, and carpentry.[65] The reliance on foreign building expertise and labor was not seen as a humiliating subjection but, on the contrary, as a sign of Ethiopian superiority over Europeans and non-Europeans alike.

Reporting the student protest to Jerusalem, the Israeli consulate must have attributed to it a diplomatic significance that could have some bearing on the reorganization of the Technical College. The students' outcry was reminiscent of a similar debate in the Technion's early days, when it too weighed the alternatives of providing university-level education or becoming a vocational school. In the Jewish settlers' case, there was a disproportionally high number of engineers and architects—as opposed to building tradesmen, artisans, and industrial workers—among immigrant Jews. In 1924, the year it was established, Solel Boneh published a booklet deploring the quality of the construction work performed by Jewish laborers.[66] While this ideological pamphlet promoted the New Jew's physiological and psychological transformation through vocational change, it also spoke of architects' dependence on the work of Palestinian artisans and tradesmen to execute their plans. When the matter was presented to the Palestine executive of the Zionist organization that took over the establishment of the Technion following World War I, the general consensus was in favor of creating a middle category of technicians and professional craftsmen, training a "'man of function,' between the European research worker and the Palestinian laborer." Yet soon after the Technion opened, as in the case of the Ethio-Swedish Building College, students demanded that they receive proper diplomas certifying them as engineers and architects. As a list of diplomas for the first graduating class suggests, they succeeded.[67]

Conscious of the need to differentiate the Technical College from the neighboring Ethio-Swedish Building College, its two successive Israeli deans emphasized the college's highly technical and professional training and renamed it the College of Engineering. When Ephraim Spira, the college's first Israeli dean, arrived in 1959, he found poor facilities, a cumbersome bureaucracy, and demoralized students. Spira hoped that the college's expected incorporation into Haile Selassie I University would improve students' conditions and morale. As a student reporter who served as Spira's mouthpiece explained, "Students will now, immaterial of whether they are politicians or technicians[,] enjoy the same rights, facilities and privileges."[68] Yet the college's image problem ran too deep for a university degree to solve, and enrollment continued to be low even after its incorporation into the university.[69] A number of interdependent factors caused this low enrollment: First, the five-year program was longer and more demanding than those in other fields at the university. Second, most students arrived unprepared for this kind of technical education, especially as compared to students from industrialized societies. As Spira explained, the level of secondary education was inadequate, and the college had to compensate for its deficiencies.[70] Third, and most importantly, while the engineer was perceived as the main agent of Ethiopia's modernization, the white-collar image of engineers clashed with the profession's daily practicalities. As another student reporter observed, "Passing back and forth in the compound, were students dressed as if for *real work*, unlike their more academically-looking fellows to be found on the campus of the University College." He specified that "not one of them wore college blazer, scarf, tie or badge," and explained, "Those students, looking like exiles from a modern world made by engineers, remind you strongly of the status of artisans in traditional Ethiopian society. Our old society did not favour such technically productive and constructive men and women."[71] Paradoxically, the reporter linked the engineering students' work attire to a nonmodern world and positioned them as exiles from the modern world they would help to build. The reporter pointed out the discrepancy between the expected "college blazer, scarf, tie or badge"—status symbols and markers of university students' modernity and professional identity—with the unkempt appearance of engineering students who did "real work." According to the reporter, the engineering students' study and work conditions were perceived as demeaning, and even unmodern, since they were associated with the low status of artisans in traditional Ethiopian society.

As a vehicle to boost the white-collar image of the college, an architecture department was set up soon after it was incorporated into Haile Selassie I University. In the first year of his tenure, Spira brought in Enav as a part-time architecture instructor. Spira, a construction engineer, perceived design and planning as essential skills for a successful career in engineering.[72] Yet he had no intention of establishing an independent architecture department; Spira limited his intervention in the school's structure to expanding its curriculum from two departments (civil and industrial engineering) to three (civil, mechanical, and electrical engineering). Technion dean and former Israel Defense Forces (IDF) chief of staff Yaacov Dori suggested founding an architecture department as an attempt to bolster Israel's control over the College of Engineering, which was facing its planned takeover by German staff. In his correspondence with the Israeli foreign ministry's Department of International Cooperation, Spira expressed concerns about the German-Ethiopian agreement, about which he had learned when he arrived in 1959. He was perplexed by Israel's investment in the college, since the Germans would eventually be given credit for all the Israelis' hard work. In what seems to be a counterintuitive response, the ministry in Jerusalem decided to increase Israeli involvement exponentially rather than minimizing it.[73] The ministry encouraged Spira to employ more Israeli faculty to give the college "an Israeli character," and Spira consequently initiated a scholarship master's program at the Technion for leading Ethiopian graduates of the College of Engineering.[74] Heralded in the Ethiopian press as "the MIT of the Middle East,"[75] the Technion was happy to engage in foreign ministry cooperation programs, which gave the institution an opportunity to finally realize an ambition it had harbored since its inception—that of becoming a regional center.[76] An architecture department at the College of Engineering would offer another avenue for increasing Israeli personnel, while also being cheap to set up, as it required no specialized machinery or laboratories.[77]

The German ambassador, who had been working toward the takeover for three years, assumed that by academic year 1961–62, when Spira was scheduled to leave, the German staff could step in.[78] However, Spira's successor, Yehuda Peter, was already on his way when the frustrated German ambassador literally begged his Israeli counterpart to settle this affair with the Ethiopian university administration.[79] The Israeli ambassador politely explained that he was not in a position to intervene in matters subject to the Ethiopians' discretion. Stonewalled, the German ambassador resorted to desperate means, and asked whether it would be possible to have the incoming Israeli dean considered German aid personnel.[80] Absurd as it may have sounded just over a decade after the Holocaust, this hopeless request had some grounding, as Peter had been born and educated in Germany.[81] Instead, the Israeli foreign ministry attempted to make amends by offering a definite deadline for the personnel change at the end of academic year 1962–63, with the option of continuing to hire Israeli faculty on an individual basis.[82]

The Ethiopians, for their part, benefitted from Israeli involvement as a stopgap measure that forced the German government to fulfill its promise to build the college's new facilities. It was in the Ethiopians' interest to delay the arrival of German faculty so that the German government could not enjoy the aura of providing aid without making a considerable monetary investment.[83] Israeli personnel made an excellent "second best" to address the needs of the college in the meantime. When a German delegation arrived to inspect the College of Engineering in 1960, its members were pleased with the structure and curriculum that Spira had set up.[84] This was indeed not surprising, since the Technion, which served as a model for the college, had itself been initially based on the German Technikum.[85] The pedagogic affinity assured a smooth transition, which finally started in 1966 with the arrival of German personnel.[86]

During this period, the Ethio-Swedish Building College also offered some basic architecture classes. In 1959–60, the college's director was an architect, Ingvar Eknor, who had been trained at Chalmers University of Gothenburg and, like his Israeli counterpart at the College of Engineering, taught building construction. Among the full-time teaching personnel was J. Bernhard Lindahl, an architect trained at the KTH Royal Institute of Technology in Stockholm, who taught preliminary courses in drawing and architectural planning.[87] Another Royal Institute graduate, Carl Erik H. Fogelvik, served as chief of the Building Research Institute. The Swedish dominance in Ethiopia's architectural education is also evident in the fact that even the Israeli-run College of Engineering's department of architecture was directed in its initial stages by the Swedish architect and theorist Sven Hesselgren, formerly the associate dean of the Building College, though the department had been initiated by Israeli personnel.[88] In response to the acute housing shortage for lower- and middle-class families, the Building College emphasized traditional Ethiopian building techniques and materials alongside general technical training. A college publication from 1958, "Elementary Planning and Building for Community Leaders," addressed the amateur builder, providing "elementary knowledge . . . based on old, existing traditions in the country."[89] The booklet specified building materials from a mixture of European and local traditions: wood, *chicka* (a mud construction with timber or sticks), stone, bricks, and blocks, and, for roofing, straw, tiles, and galvanized corrugated iron sheets.[90] It concluded with floor plans for a basic school, a community education center, low-cost small and large modern villas, clinic buildings, churches, and countryside dry latrines.[91] Warning that "this book is not, however, to be used for more advanced constructions,"[92] the manual aimed to democratize building for the poor in Addis Ababa and in the countryside, which was systematically denied access to development funds.

The grassroots self-help approach that this manual advocates was so ingrained in the Ethio-Swedish Building College's pedagogy that even the building of its campus became a collaborative educational exercise. Faculty and staff planned and designed it, while students joined them in constructing it in collaboration with Italian contractors. The stone, brick, and concrete buildings of the campus "were designed to accord with methods at the level of development within the country at that time."[93] Staff and students even drilled their own well on campus, freeing the college from dependence on the municipality's poor water infrastructure. Completing this performance of self-help, the Building Research Institute experimented with the construction of housing types on campus grounds.

The eight low-cost villas it built were reused as staff living quarters, and another five traditional Ethiopian houses formed "a picturesque village among the eucalyptus trees."[94]

When the Ethio-Swedish Building College's students went out into rural areas, they not only researched traditional building techniques to bring back to their research institute in the capital but also implemented their studies on-site. By January 1964, the college had set up six brick kilns, at Debra Markos, Bako, Wondo, Gindeberet, Yirgalem, and Wollamo Sodo, to stimulate the growth of brick-making industries in rural areas and to demonstrate techniques for building low-cost housing.[95] Similarly, in 1965 twenty-three students from the college, accompanied by nine Swedish volunteers, fulfilled their duties to the Ethiopian University Service by building low-cost classrooms and schools in the provinces Wollega, Harargh, and Sidamo.[96] This emphasis on rural areas corresponded with Sweden's shift of emphasis to rural development in its assistance programs.[97] Channeled through the Building College and the Elementary School Building Unit, which was attached to the Ministry of Education and Fine Arts, Swedish aid prompted the Ethiopian government to address development beyond the capital. From 1958 to 1968, 109 elementary schools, most in remote regions of Ethiopia, were built with Sweden's encouragement. By 1973, 3,644 classrooms had been constructed and equipped with basic school supplies. Sweden shared expenses equally with the rural communities.[98] In effect, the Ethio-Swedish Building College promoted a cooperative, grassroots attitude that enabled the Ethiopian government to abdicate its responsibilities toward rural communities and leave their improvement up to external aid agencies and their own efforts.

In stark contrast with the Ethio-Swedish Building College's self-help approach, and notwithstanding its initial overlap with the latter's academic leadership, the College of Engineering taught architecture with a capital A. Referring to the profession of engineering, which he knew better, Dean Peter explained that it "is intrinsically international and independent of boundaries" and that prospects were high for students who wished to provide "'consultants' and contractors' service for other developing countries, even before the needs of Ethiopia are fully covered by natives of the country."[99] In this statement, Peter echoed not only the Technion's ambition to become an international center of knowledge production but also the practice of sending Israeli consultants to other countries even before Israel's needs were fully met. The high value placed on professionalization entailed the establishment of the Ethiopian Association of Architects and

Engineers, of which Peter was a founding member; the recognition of the College of Engineering by European counterparts such as the English AA; and the staff's participation in professional organizations.[100] Such ambitions left little room for the study of vernacular architecture or addressing specific local needs.

Even when architecture students at the College of Engineering took field trips to rural areas where development schemes and settlement projects were underway, they focused on their touristic potential rather than the needs of local communities. In a three-day student trip to Wollamo Soddo, where students from the Ethio-Swedish Building College were involved in planning new settlements and building schools, the College of Engineering students surveyed sites chosen by the provincial governor for the construction of hotels. The first site, a hill in the town of Soddo, had originally been intended for a palace for the emperor. The second site was on the shores of Lake Abaya (also known as Lake Margarita), and the third was near a waterfall.[101] Conceived initially as part of "political tourism," these planned hotels would provide accommodation for the emperor and foreign aid delegations on their tours of rural areas.[102] Once a highway connecting Addis Ababa to the area was completed, it was expected that the hotels would also "offer a good week-end resort for safari goers from Addis Ababa," thus promoting middle-class domestic and international tourism.[103] Another College of Engineering study tour in the town of Waliso focused on the construction of modern institutions, such as the Leprosy Hospital buildings, the Blind School at Sebetha, and dormitory buildings for secondary students. That tour concluded with a visit to the newly built Radio Voice of the Gospel station in Addis Ababa.[104] Since Enav, with his professional focus on upper-middle-class apartments and public buildings in Addis Ababa, was one of the few architecture instructors at the college, its emphasis on tourist facilities and modern institutions is not surprising. Although Enav defined his and Tedros's projects as labor-intensive—and although they experimented with vernacular forms, as we shall see later—their designs were based on industrially produced building components. This was also the case with Enav's World Bank commission to design a low-cost school prototype for Ethiopia's rural areas.[105]

The College of Engineering and the Ethio-Swedish Building College thus practiced contrasting architectures of development whose differences can be understood through Israeli and Swedish building traditions as well as through each country's style of aid. First, unlike Israel and many other donor countries, the Swedish government did not condition aid on the purchase of Swedish products.[106] While Swedish industry resented this policy for obvious reasons, it allowed considerably more experimentation with local building techniques and a focus on rural areas. Second, although Israel also promoted economic self-help, its notion of "self-help" emphasized industry over vernacular forms of production. Lacking long-standing building traditions like Sweden's, the Jewish settlement in Palestine had developed a modernized building industry as an alternative to Palestinian domination of the markets for both building expertise and cheap labor. In short, the Israeli idea of "self-help" was the opposite of the Swedish one: it focused on industrial rather than craft-based production. Ironically, despite the fact that Israel championed its experts' active participation in the work of development outside the comforts of the modern office, as discussed in chapter 1, it was the Ethio-Swedish Building College that succeeded in cultivating students who were ready to work in rural areas and actually construct buildings on-site. As the college proudly announced in its report for 1954–71, approximately 35 to 40 percent of its graduates worked outside of Addis Ababa, mostly in rural areas, and 65 to 70 percent engaged in "real construction work" versus office work.[107]

Despite the two colleges' competing approaches to teaching architecture, they were united under the name of the College of Technology in the late 1960s as part of the reorganization of the university and the arrival of German personnel. Though the separate campuses were kept, the former College of Engineering's architecture department was relocated to the campus of the Ethio-Swedish Building College, which was renamed the Ethio-Swedish Institute of Building Technology (or ESIBT, now the Ethiopian Institute of Architecture, Building Construction, and City Development).[108] Although the German-run College of Technology (as the College of Engineering was later renamed) eventually conceded the Israeli-established Department of Architecture to the Ethio-Swedish Institute, architecture played an important performative role in the German takeover. It was only after a German architect, called "Professor Nebel" in students' accounts, presented a model of the college's future German-funded facilities that the much-anticipated transfer of the college to German aid was finally set in motion. The College of Technology campus was completed in 1971 and constituted the college's northern campus.[109]

The reorganization did not resolve the problem of overlapping responsibilities that resulted from technical aid competition. In May 1968, the associate dean of ESIBT proposed a degree course in municipal engineering to address town-planning needs across the country. While the university rejected his proposal on the grounds of lack of funds, the municipality of Addis Ababa itself offered such a course in academic year 1970–71 with the support of French aid.[110] Since Sweden had by then considerably reduced its funding for the college, the Ethiopian administration reasonably sought new avenues to solicit foreign aid. What the associate dean interpreted as "a typical duplication of resources which should be avoided" was simply the usual modus operandi of Haile Selassie's administration, which deliberately instigated competition over aid.[111] What seemed like duplication and waste to the associate dean was, from the Ethiopian point of view, a way to increase national revenue.

Constructing an Ethiopian Modernity

Of the two contrasting architectures of development offered by the Ethio-Swedish Building College and the Israeli-run College of Engineering, the latter conformed more to Haile Selassie's vision of modernization, which focused on heavily capitalized projects in Addis Ababa.[112] For Selassie, who initiated many of these projects, they had a dual objective: to modernize the city so it could successfully represent Ethiopia's continental leadership to international dignitaries and to encourage investment in the building market by setting an example for the land-owning class.[113] The Ethio-Swedish Building College's practical focus on building technology and low-cost construction not only had little to offer for such international and upper-middle-class domestic audiences, but its conventional differentiation between "European-style" and traditional Ethiopian houses also left little room for questions of form. As we shall see, form was central to negotiating the relationship between Ethiopian traditions and modern technology, a matter with which Haile Selassie's regime was highly concerned.

Reconciling the hierarchical structure of traditional Ethiopian society, from which the imperial regime drew its legitimacy, with the emperor's desire for accelerated modernization was the central task of Haile Selassie's administration, particularly following the abortive 1960 coup instigated by Germame Neway and his brother, Brigadier General Mengistu Neway.[114] In the prewar years, both Menelik and Selassie had been inspired by Japanese modernization as a model for keeping society intact while adopting Western technoscience, but the coup attempt proved that it was no longer viable to separate traditional culture from modern technology.[115] As a result of the coup, the emperor turned to a gradual, reformist approach, as is manifested in the government's 1962 review of the *First Five-Year Devel-*

*opment Plan* (1957–61). The review stressed that although the development plan aimed to accelerate Ethiopia's social and economic progress, it was only transitional and demanded patience—modernization involves more than setting up a few factories and institutions. Since Ethiopia "comprises its own traditional patterns of economic and social life, as well as new ones," the governmental review explained, "the path of development and the planning approach and techniques employed should reflect Ethiopian traits which link together national traditions and scientific, cultural, and technological achievements of the modern world."[116]

Linking "national traditions" with the "achievements of the modern world" was the crux of Haile Selassie's reformist approach: modernization, including social progress, could take place only if it was based on traditional Ethiopian social and political structures. "We believe in a progress that builds on a sound foundation and not on shifting sands," the emperor announced in 1962. "We believe in the adaptation of modern economic and social theories to local conditions and customs rather than in the imposition on Ethiopia's social and economic structure of systems which are largely alien to it and which [it] is not equipped to absorb or cope with."[117] To absorb the shocks of modernization successfully, Ethiopian society needed a sound yet malleable traditional basis. With such a basis, modernization would not only serve the traditional social system but would also serve as a means of sustained development.

Israeli aid was instrumental both in repressing the coup via intelligence channels and in mitigating revolutionary forces at the cultural level.[118] Although not in an official capacity, unlike most of his compatriots, Enav was part of a group of Israelis who—by following the Israeli model—attempted to create a modern approach to Ethiopian culture, which, in turn, would serve the basis for forging an Ethiopian modernity. For example, Zvi Yavetz, the Israeli dean of the arts faculty at Haile Selassie I University, established the Institute of Ethiopian Studies (IES), the most important institution in the country for the study of national history and culture.[119] As Ben-Gurion put it, "The English and American cultures are too distant from theirs, and they [the Ethiopians] would like to learn from us."[120]

For the Ministry of Foreign Affairs, their most important commission, Enav and Tedros envisioned an "Ethiopian building." The stakes were particularly high because the plot slated for the building was situated in the emperor's new triangle of power, next to the Jubilee Palace, Selassie's prime residence in the wake of the coup, and across the street from Africa Hall, which hosted the first summit of the Organization of African Unity in 1963.¹²¹ Resisting the minister of finance's urgings to erect a curtain wall high-rise in the spirit of the UN headquarters in New York, Enav and Tedros convinced the emperor that their diamond-shaped, four-story courtyard design conveyed a particularly Ethiopian character. Their reluctance to build in the late modern idiom of the New York UN headquarters stemmed from the incongruity between its corporate modernity and Ethiopia's modernity as they understood it. In fact, in the first issue of *Zede*, the journal of the Association of Ethiopian Architects and Engineers, Enav questioned the very modernity of the modern-style buildings that had sprung up in Addis Ababa's cityscape: "Aesthetically many of the commercial buildings one sees around suffer from a basic fault. They are what is supposed to be modern without being so in the true sense. The true sense of modern buildings I have in mind are buildings which convey, with contemporary methods and materials, a country's cultural heritage. They should be designed to be at the service of the people and to conform with the country's economic and social progress and capacity."¹²²

This statement might seem to recall the Ethio-Swedish Building College faculty's decision to design campus buildings "to accord with methods at the level of development within the country at that time."¹²³ However, Enav and Tedros's vision of an Ethiopian modernity was much more ambitious: it involved investigating form as the bearer of cultural heritage and as a dynamic force that cannot be entirely determined by technological capacities.

The two architects imbued the Ministry of Foreign Affairs building with an "Ethiopian character" through a pentagonal concrete lattice facade, which, when lit at night, transformed into a pattern composed of the emblem in the badge of the Order of the Queen of Sheba (figs. 5.3 and 5.4), denoting the ancient and Christian origins of the monarchy. Misidentifying it as the Star of Solomon, Enav chose this image following the selection of its Jewish equivalent, the Star of David, for the Israeli flag. In a similar way, Enav turned the ruling Amhara lineage's cross-bearing Seal of Sheba into a national secular motif. The form was so abstracted that at first even the emperor found it unfamiliar.¹²⁴ And yet its grammar was meant to speak to all Ethiopians. In his article in *Zede*, Enav borrowed freely from the terminology that anthropologist Ruth Benedict had developed in her seminal *Patterns of Culture*. Enav argued that if architecture were to express society, the architect had to study man's "intellectual, emotional and physical pattern of behavior" as "an essential background for design."¹²⁵ Merging patterns of behavior with those of physical shape and situating them in the *longue durée* of Benedict's "cultural processes," Enav consid-

FIGURE 5.3  Zalman Enav and Michael Tedros, Ministry of Foreign Affairs, 1962–65. Courtesy of Zalman Enav.

FIGURE 5.4  Zalman Enav and Michael Tedros, Ministry of Foreign Affairs, night view, 1962–65. Courtesy of Zalman Enav.

ered forms such as the pentagon irreducible kernels of Ethiopian culture, disregarding the country's multiple ethnicities and religions. As part of an extended cultural process, the pentagon was not limited by tradition, but on the contrary opened up the possibility for further experimentation. For Enav, the pentagon's structural capacities took on prime significance because they allowed for further elaborations of form.[126]

A dispute between Israeli and English experts about the modernization of Amharic script sheds some light on Enav's approach to forging a symbol that could reconcile modernity and cultural heritage. Ze'ev Ras, an Israeli expert who led the Ministry of Education's Extra-Curricular Department, introduced a quicker-to-write cursive to supplement the existing system of printed letters. While this project was generally approved, the English IES librarian Stephen Wright commented that "the Ethiopian script is attractive and beautiful as it is"; he preferred to protect the traditional script from change rather than to adapt it to Ethiopian society's growing literacy.[127] For Enav, as for Ras, tradition had no intrinsic value if it could not be communicated and disseminated on a national level. Enav and Tedros's search for an Ethiopian symbol that could be used in various configurations and patterns was similar to the transformation of letters from fixed symbols into everyday tools of communication.

While the pentagon motif merely decorated the facade of the Ministry of Foreign Affairs, it now, extended into a hexagon, became the dominant spatial element in Enav and Tedros's design for the Filwoha Baths (1959–64), a public mineral springs bathing facility located in the heart of Addis Ababa. Conceived as a series of domed hexagonal pavilions connected by covered walkways, the complex formed a semi-enclosed compound similar to those of indigenous villages in Ethiopia (plate 19 and fig. 5.5).[128] Its structural and spatial qualities differentiated the pentagonal or hexagonal ornament from two-dimensional, literal references to Ethiopia's ancient tradition. Examples of the latter include the two vertical strips covered with a geometric pattern that adorn the center of the Africa Hall's facade as well as the literal references to Ethiopia's historical sites incorporated freely into the facade, interior decoration, and even the pool of the Hilton hotel that was built across the street from the Ministry of Foreign Affairs in the late 1960s.[129]

The progress from ornament to structure in Enav and Tedros's work in Addis Ababa suggests continuity across different scales, from a single unit through the structure of a building to the city at large. Enav developed his sensitivity to scale through his work as a student at the AA, where he

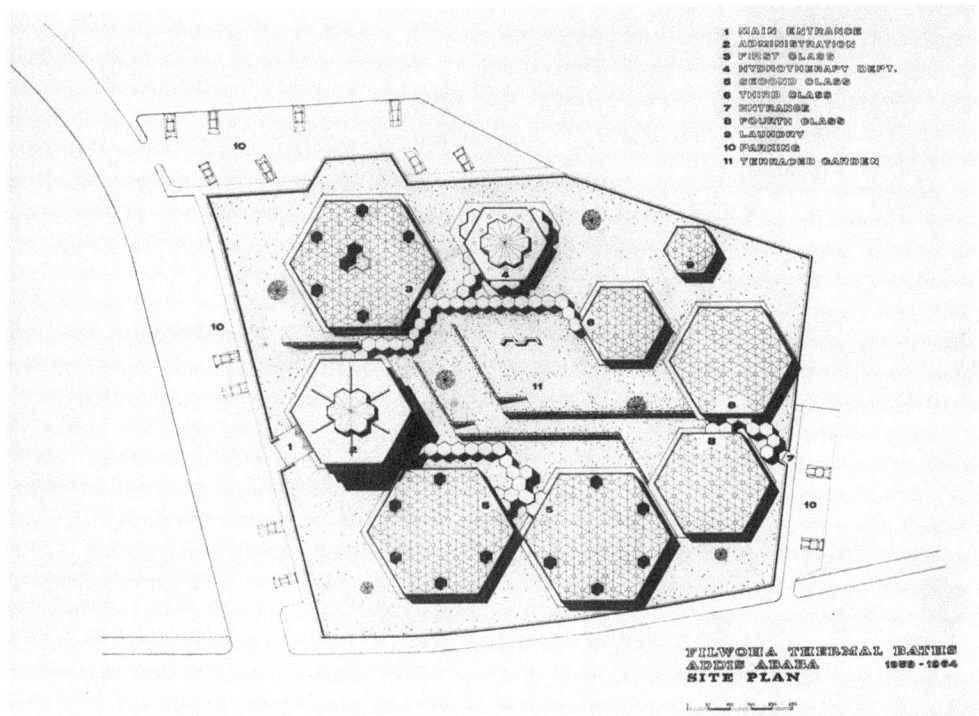

FIGURE 5.5  Zalman Enav and Michael Tedros, Filwoha Baths, site plan, 1959–64. Courtesy of Zalman Enav.

FIGURE 5.6  Zalman Enav and Michael Tedros, Filwoha Baths, under construction, 1959–64. Courtesy of Zalman Enav.

designed a project for Basra using his concept of modular continuity "from the mud brick to the city."[130] As the reference to the "brick" suggests, scalar interconnectedness was based on repetitive use of the smallest building component. This student work evolved into Enav's mature approach to design on the human scale. By "human scale," he meant not the scale of the user's body, as in architectural thought since the Renaissance, but instead that of the construction worker's body. By choosing prefabricated building components that corresponded to the physical capacities of unskilled workers, Enav and Tedros favored using readily available, cheap unskilled labor over importing heavy machinery (fig. 5.6). In this regard, their approach is reminiscent of that of their French contemporary Henri Chomette, who began his African career in Ethiopia before embarking on multiple projects in Francophone West Africa. According to Chomette, an architect could intervene in a building market by shaping local labor.[131] For Chomette, this meant modernizing vernacular building traditions by employing local carpenters and craftsmen. However, perhaps because such artisans were mostly of non-Ethiopian descent and therefore could not represent an authentic continuity with tradition, Enav and Tedros instead emphasized providing as many jobs as possible to unskilled workers by taking advantage of industrial techniques. These differing approaches to labor were reflected in the architects' differing design methods. Unlike Chomette, who drew references for his ornamental programs freely and associatively, Enav and Tedros hardly used ornaments that required craftsmanship, while their structures were based on repetitive form to streamline construction and use the large reserve of cheap, unskilled labor most efficiently, even if they thereby ossified the exploitative labor conditions that this "humanistic" approach ultimately legitimates.[132]

Coda

Zalman Enav's experience in Ethiopia demonstrates how private and public, professional and geopolitical interests were entangled and mutually beneficial. Enav's ability to navigate complicated layers of loyalty to the local elite—including the Jewish community, the royal family, and the Israeli embassy in Addis Ababa—proved no less important to his success than his professional training in Israel and England. Enav never perceived his loyalty to Israel or to the emperor as being in conflict with his loyalty to the Ethiopian people. Just as official representatives of Israel complied with the regime, overlooked its shortcomings, and even helped to sustain it, so

Enav offered a version of development and modernization that ultimately buttressed the Ethiopian status quo. Any reforms Enav and other educated elites may have contemplated would have been impeded by their own professional interests, just as local elites were impeded by their own privileges.

Not acting as an official representative of Israel but maintaining strong ties to it proved very profitable for Enav. On the one hand, acting independently of the Israeli government afforded Enav more professional opportunities than his Israeli counterparts who gained access to African markets via Solel Boneh or IPD. For example, Enav won the World Bank commission for rural schools because he was considered a "local."[133] On the other hand, Enav's persistent ties with Israel allowed him to extend his reach globally after his return to Israel in 1966, when growing student unrest in Addis Ababa foreshadowed the bloody revolution to come in 1974. Enav's return to Israel did not mean the end of his partnership with Tedros, which lasted until 1971 and even expanded to Zambia. In Israel, Enav continued to cultivate private commissions via institutional connections in the highest echelons of politics and the military, just as nonofficial ties that circled around military intelligence operations were key to his work in Ethiopia. In the aftermath of the 1973 war, Enav drafted the lines for the Israeli withdrawal from Sinai and subsequently participated in the Camp David peace talks in 1978, which led to a planning project in Egypt.[134] Since the 1970s, Enav and his second wife, Ruth, with whom he established a professional partnership, have been enjoying the fruits of his long-lasting relationships with political and military personnel in Israel: they have received commissions for IDF military bases, Jewish settlements in the occupied Palestinian territories, and private villas for prominent officials, including former prime minister Ariel Sharon.[135] Capitalizing on Enav's "security expertise," they named their office "SAFE": "Security, Architecture, Foreplanning [sic], Engineering." This choice of name indicates their ambition to participate in the homeland security industry that has become one of Israel's most profitable exports.[136] Enav even took a leading role in promoting Israeli exports. Since the 1980s, in addition to cultivating partnerships in the United States and China, Enav served as the Head of the Israel Export Institute's delegations to Thailand and Singapore in 1989, China in 1993, and the United Nations and World Bank in 2004.[137]

Similarly, Tedros's reputation in Ethiopia earned him opportunities abroad, first in Tanzania, where he was invited to participate in the planning of the new capital, Dodoma, in the late 1970s. (This opportunity allowed him to leave the country, which the Derg regime had governed since the revolution.) Tedros was later invited to work in the European headquarters of an international development agency, but declined because of his expressed loyalty to Africa, and chose to settle in Eritrea instead.[138] Far from their playing the role of detached foreign experts, as in the prevalent image of development technocrats, it was instead Enav's and Tedros's strong identification with the local that afforded them opportunities to expand their practices elsewhere in Africa and, in Enav's case, globally.

# postscript

Ghosts of Modernity

A BOOK THAT DISCUSSES Israeli architectural and planning production in Africa in the framework of settler colonialism cannot but raise certain expectations among its readers. Readers might wonder whether such development aid represented an expansion of Israeli colonialism to Africa, or whether Israeli architecture in Africa correlated with planning and construction in the occupied Palestinian territories. Yet Israel did not colonize territories in Africa, and the relationship between Israeli architectural production in Africa and the occupied Palestinian territories does not lend itself to any clear-cut formulation, as their historical contexts differ considerably. Reading Israeli architectural production in Africa vis-à-vis the occupied Palestinian territories would not only risk anachronism but would also predetermine the analysis by assuming colonial power relations between Israel and African states. To move away from such predetermined readings, this book posits Israeli attempts at solidarity with African nations as performative acts in the global theater of development. It argues that architectural expertise based on Israeli settler colonial experience was ironically performed as postcolonial, and thereby played a role in defining and articulating a variant of southern developmentalist modernism.

Modernization theory, as conceived and practiced by Western technocrats, did not and could not account for the multiple and contradictory temporalities that postcolonial societies experienced. This is the gap Israeli diplomats, construction managers, and architects tried to fill with their settler colonial modus operandi in design and building. With their extreme emphasis on producing results fast, Israeli projects were stopgap mechanisms rather than long-term solutions. Their focus was not so much on creating a sustainable future but also, and primarily, on securing a precarious present amid the urgencies and anxieties that characterized the ambiguous transitional period of decolonization that African states faced in parallel with Israeli society's transformation from voluntary settlement into statehood.

In terms of form, to reiterate a claim made in the introduction, it was not an "Israeli architecture" that was exported to Africa, but rather Israeli expertise in adapting architectural modernism to non-Western locales. In the hands of Israeli architects, International Style modernism proved to be adaptive but not derivative, in the sense that a double remove from the hegemonic center—first to the Middle East and then from the Middle East to Africa—did not compromise the principles of modernist architecture but instead enhanced its capacity to expand globally. Adding to the locales where architectural knowledge was produced, Israeli architects perceived their work as reinforcing the discipline's internationalism—showing its adaptability, relevance, and validity for new societies in other parts of the world.

This postscript discusses the aesthetics that emerged from the Israeli-African encounter. After a synthetic account of its characteristics and major themes, the postscript considers the contemporaneous case of the private tourist industry enterprises that the entrepreneur brothers Moshe and Mordechai Mayer set up in Liberia and the Ivory Coast. These "outliers" are introduced as a counterexample to further tease out the aesthetic and political differences between Labor Zionist modes of Israeli-African architectural partnerships and private ventures in the continent. The postscript then turns to shifts in Israeli involvement in Africa, primarily since the breaking off of relations in 1973 but also earlier, starting in the mid-1960s, and presents some ways in which Israeli architects and planners have been involved in Africa more recently, particularly through building housing for resettled veterans in Angola. I argue that many contemporary projects reproduce the modernist aesthetics of earlier partnerships to cynically capitalize on the aura of Labor Zionist ideology that was once invested in them. Since contemporary projects no longer assume "development," they do not emphasize the transfer of knowledge or state-building processes. Instead, these are "turnkey" projects that assume underdevelopment as fact and further cement it beyond repair. In other words, I argue that even if such contemporary projects look similar to earlier ones, their logic of operation is completely different. Devoid of the developmentalist hope once instilled in them, they nonetheless continue to haunt the continent with the broken promises of modernity their predecessors embodied. The postscript then concludes with some reflections on the endurance of this aesthetic and offers a theoretical framework for future study of the social afterlives of their historic counterparts.

## The "Golden Age" of Israeli Aid in Africa: Aesthetics, Labor, and National Becoming

The projects discussed in this book articulate a departure from preceding local colonial experiences, even if paradoxically they were based on settler colonial expertise. My analysis has located such departures in the aesthetics of these building and planning objects, which marked a change of course from colonial to postcolonial governmentality. The local media that covered these processes did not portray such buildings and plans as foreign impositions but used them to engage literate citizens and create a nationally or regionally shared public sphere. Unlike the colonial "not yet," whose tantalizing targets kept moving away with every step taken in their direction, these objects acted as tangible agents of becoming and change. By mobilizing actors and resources, they anchored the future they heralded in concrete forms in the present, even while these produced temporal disjunctions and asynchronicities.

Notwithstanding the differences among the projects discussed in this book and among the African countries in which they took place, the following interrelated themes recur: (1) the modernist building's skin is reimagined to create distinct local aesthetics; (2) the relations between surface and depth, or skin and mass, respond to local labor conditions and building practices; and (3) the deployment of aesthetics in mobilizing resources, whether human or natural, aims to facilitate an economic and cultural national becoming.

The emphasis on the relationship between aesthetics and labor produces a multifaceted and at times disjointed temporality in most of the projects discussed. In the Sierra Leone parliament, the crushed laterite stone attached to the surface signified an autochthonous identity that ostensibly transcended ethnic differences. Through it, Ram Karmi communicated

Zionist second-generation settler colonialism's fantasy of nativism that paradoxically legitimized claims for Jewish primordial belonging based on technological modernity. Zionism was to overcome Jews' lack of continuity on the land and the loss of vernacular building techniques by modernizing the building industry in Palestine, with the result that unskilled Hebrew laborers supplanted skilled Arab builders. In Sierra Leone, Solel Boneh managers and the architects involved engaged in a similar process of de-skilling, as they did not actively seek Krio or any other vernacular building techniques. Instead, the architects reverted to a labor-intensive technique of manually embedding gravel within concrete plates. Offering an aesthetic alternative to British neoclassical designs as well as to vernacular building techniques identified with specific ethnic groups, the unifying aesthetic that "grows from the ground" also seemingly unified the workers, as unskilled laborers could work side by side with skilled ones—a fact celebrated by the national press.

Through this mutual Israeli-African interpellation in the media, Israeli architectural aid aimed to transform citizens into human material, understood both physically and culturally, in the process of becoming new men and a new nation. The employment of labor-intensive practices involved a spectacle of national becoming that divested workers of their ethnic loyalties and traditional hierarchies. As in the Jewish settlement in Palestine and in Israel during the early state period, where construction sites were used to train workers, the parliament site served as a training ground. Unlike in the Israeli case, however, this site was not supported by a building industry that produced prefabricated building components but instead relied on some meager workshops Solel Boneh set up on-site. In this spectacle, modern construction was performed by a mixture of imported heavy machinery, abundant and cheap unskilled laborers, and on-site prefabrication, with no industrial infrastructure to support it.[1]

Ram Karmi's fantasy of nativism had its limits: it could not transcend the sociocultural and historical schism between the Krio population and the former protectorate population, as revealed in a parliament clerk's critical comment about the rough appearance of the building, which to him seemed incomplete without a marble coating. We could disregard this critique as expressing the disgruntlement of Sierra Leone's settler colonial minority, who unlike Karmi had no desire for nativism, as they wished to maintain a boundary between themselves as "civilized" Krio and the growing majority of hinterland parliament members. But we can also read it as a factual statement, since the building was indeed incomplete at the time of independence. Following the "facts-on-the-ground" approach of Labor Zionist settler colonialism, in which concrete action and quick results were more valued than careful planning and measured execution, the parliament building was inaugurated before its completion. Rather than interpreting this as a failure of the Israeli–Sierra Leonean joint construction company or the architects involved, the Sierra Leone government used its incompleteness to send a message to the nation about the path ahead following independence. Similarly, while the laterite stone on the parliament's facade presented an empirical signifier of autochthonous belonging, it was also subject to change. Gradually taking on a unified corroded color and becoming one with the ground surface, it directed attention to the historicity and teleology of nation building, undermining the architect's fantasy of representing an immediate and irrefutable nativity. Neither a priori nor a fait accompli, the building represented the Sierra Leone nation as undergoing a gradual process of becoming, while the Sierra Leonean media and the speaker of its House of Representatives invoked this logic to extend a sense of civic commitment from the construction site to the Sierra Leone citizenry more broadly, in line with David Ben-Gurion's attempt to instill a sense of "pioneering" commitment among all citizens.

At the University of Ife's campus in Nigeria, the wall gained cultural meaning beyond the issues of climate that dominated the discourse of late colonial British architecture. While designing microclimatic environments remained a concern, Arieh Sharon and his team, instead of adding layers of architectural skin in the form of imported brise-soleil as protection against the climate, created a volumetric skin that blurs the boundary between indoors and outdoors. Moreover, the architects invested this "thickening" of the architectural skin with a specifically African cultural significance, referring to Yoruba sculpture engraving. This solution was based on another variant of the Zionist desire for nativism, namely climatic or environmental belonging. Unlike British imperialists, who sought to insulate themselves from the tropics with protective gear, Zionism aimed to regenerate the Jewish body by means of exposure to the elements that would reverse what were considered the degenerating effects of living in diaspora. To the Israelis, unlike the Jewish body that needed to prove belonging via acclimatization, the African body presented an ideal of inherent belonging that expressed itself via the empirical fact of skin pigmentation; this allowed for an incorporation of Yoruba sculptural and mural traditions in continuum with scarring techniques, in contrast with the initial Jewish rejection of Palestinian vernacular forms. In terms of the labor employed, however, while Sharon insisted on hiring local artisans for the grooving, he did not consider seeking local artists, such as the prominent painter and sculptor Ben Enwonwu, who joined the University of Ife in 1971 as its first professor of fine arts, to design the murals or sculptural gates.

Unlike the British colonial tropical architecture approach, which aimed to conserve students' productive capacity by shielding them from the tropical climate, the university's Israeli architects and their American consultants encouraged a dynamic relationship in which "human capital" was developed in tandem with, and depended on, natural resources. Drawing on kibbutz planning and land grant universities, the planners mobilized land for agricultural experimentation and the creation of a salubrious environment that would cater to the bodies and minds of the students. The university's plan also offered a competing vision of rural modernity to attract faculty and discourage students from migrating to urban centers upon graduation. The emphasis, therefore, was not simply on producing human capital but also on anchoring it in nonurban centers, where it would help elevate the entire population's standards of living. Despite the University of Ife's attempt to benefit the region in a more democratic way than the elitist, urban, former colonial University College Ibadan, by the late 1970s, after the federal state had taken over all regional universities, and with state development lagging behind, the university ended up reproducing the history of kibbutzim. With the establishment of the Israeli state, they had changed position from spearheading Jewish frontier settlements to becoming elitist enclaves that sought to preserve their autonomy in the face of state-led rural development. Similarly, following the federalization of the university, the University of Ife turned from being the prime vehicle for the state's development to an increasingly self-sustaining entity.

Anchoring human resources in the hinterland was also the aim of the Sierra Leone national urbanization plan, which sought to mitigate emigration from the countryside to the port city of Freetown by creating regional urban centers throughout the country. This shift in attitude by which the rural environment came to be perceived as a resource for development rather than an impediment to it was linked to a broader trend in postcolonial governance also evident at the University of Ife: reemphasizing the role of agricultural production in national economies. Unlike at the University of Ife, however, the population in question did not consist of educated professionals and academics, but rather youth in general, who were perceived as a reserve labor force for seasonal agricultural production. As on the University of Ife campus, attempts to modernize the agricultural sector were not introduced as radical reforms of the traditional hierarchies and land tenure that had been formalized by indirect rule under British colonialism. Quite the opposite: through these projects, the government harnessed chiefs' support and in return buttressed their authority in a period when it was increasingly undermined. As Israeli regional planning exploited mass immigration from the North African countries to Jewify the hinterland against dispossessed Palestinians' claims of return according to the sacrificial logic of *halutziut mamlakhtit*, so Sierra Leonean youth were expected to stay under the purview of their tribal chiefs in their now compromised pursuit of economic and social independence.

In Ethiopia, a country that was colonized only briefly and that pursued its own colonial ambitions in neighboring Eritrea and Somalia, the contradictions of the Israeli ethos of egalitarianism and pioneering as it was exported in development aid are cast in sharp relief. Negotiations between surface and depth as they relate to national unification and labor reached their peak in the work of Zalman Enav and Michael Tedros, who transformed the hexagon ornament in their design for the Ministry of Foreign Affairs in Addis Ababa into a structural and spatial principal in their design for the Filwoha Baths. Conceived as a method of three-dimensional patterning, the continuity between surface and structure imbued architectural form with a dialectic role, so that it acted as an agent of both social transformation and cultural preservation, in line with Haile Selassie's attempt to contain expectations for rapid social and economic modernization after the abortive 1960 coup. Moreover, the implicit assumption that the Star of Solomon that formed the hexagon could unite the various ethnic groups and religions in Ethiopia into a single national-imperial culture was based on the fact that Enav purposefully overlooked the star as a religious symbol of the Amhara rulers' Christian lineage—not unlike the nationalist abstraction of the Star of David of its religious meaning on the Israeli flag.

In terms of labor, the architects emphasized how the scale of the prefabricated elements used in construction corresponded with workers' bodies and how much they could carry, so that the building could be assembled on-site without the use of heavy machinery. While this method sought to balance industrial production with providing jobs to the unemployed, it also reinforced the exploitative relations embedded in labor-intensive work. The maintenance of a clear hierarchy of skilled, semiskilled, and unskilled laborers, and a clear separation of the design office from the factory and the construction site, mirrors the economy of degree and certificate programs in the competition over architectural education in Addis Ababa. In contrast with Solel Boneh's egalitarian ethos, according to which construction managers would roll up their sleeves and get down with the people to get the job done, the department of architecture set up by the Israeli-run College of Engineering served to do the exact opposite: it dissociated the engineer from the "dirty work" of manual technical labor. This department contrasted with the certificate program offered by the Ethio-Swedish Building College, where teaching and research were geared to producing manuals for laymen and reworking vernacular building techniques to help the building industry manufacture cheap housing. Sweden's and Israel's competing approaches to architectural education aid in Ethiopia demonstrate that, while Israel was promoting "self-help" in terms of economic independence, its experts had in mind an exclusively industrial "self-help." Blinded by their industrial bias, which originated in the prestate sidelining of Palestinian builders, the Israelis took an approach very different from that of the Swedes, who incorporated vernacular techniques and materials into an architecture that could be made available to laymen and the poor in the capital and remote corners of the country alike. Thus while Israeli experts helped African countries curb rural-urban migration by rebranding the countryside, as in the case of the University of Ife and the Sierra Leone national urbanization plan, they did not consider the countryside and its culture, agriculture, or crafts as significant sources or reference points for architectural modernization.

The Outliers: The Mayers' Tourism Industry

While the contradictions in Israeli architectural development aid were rooted in its settler colonial history and the Labor Zionist ideology that undergirded both, private Israeli entrepreneurship in Africa differed. The history of the Mayer brothers' involvement in the tourism industry in Liberia and the Ivory Coast offers an alternative to the Labor Zionist model, and points at the concurrent entanglement of private entrepreneurship in Africa with the liberalization of the Israeli economy and built environment. Here, internal contradictions emanated from the clash between business objectives and the Israeli government's stipulations about aid. This case also complicates any attempt to delineate a linear causal relationship between Israeli involvement in Africa and its architectural and planning work in the occupied Palestinian territories by shifting the focus from military concerns—the lens through which settlements in the West

Bank are usually considered—to the American-influenced suburban tastes that informed them.² As this outlier instance showcases, the decline of Labor Zionist hegemony in Israel and the growing influence of liberalism in the Israeli economy played out in architectural and urban planning projects in Israel and Africa in tandem before the latter also went on to shape construction in the West Bank.

The Mayers found their first business opportunity in Africa when the Liberia Construction Corporation (LCC), established in 1955 by another Israeli businessman, Shlomo Muriel, got into financial trouble.³ At that time, Liberian president William Tubman was enacting reforms to unite the divided country, which, like Sierra Leone, had been established by repatriated westernized slaves, but which, unlike Sierra Leone, had remained independent of European colonial rule while maintaining close ties with the United States. To boost the country's economy and bring it up to par with those of decolonizing African countries, President Tubman declared an open-door policy for foreign investors. Ties with Israel were also welcomed on ideological grounds. Given the wave of decolonization sweeping the British and French colonies, Liberia had to radically refashion its politics, which until the 1950s had maintained a strict political, economic, and cultural boundary between the Americo-Liberians and the indigenous population. Ironically, Liberia needed Israel, just as Israel needed African countries, to revamp its diplomatic standing.⁴ In 1955, the same year Israel was excluded from the Bandung Conference, Muriel, together with Simon Simonovitch, a prominent local Jewish businessman who facilitated Muriel's ties with the local government, were made Israel's honorary consuls in Monrovia, and in 1957 an Israeli ambassador was assigned to Liberia.⁵

The entanglement of business entrepreneurship and diplomacy did not end with the formalization of relations. As early as 1956, the LCC faced a financial crisis due to mismanagement, and the Mayers, who at that time were looking to expand their export business, took over the company. Like Solel Boneh projects that received Israeli governmental backing, so the LCC—which was responsible for constructing many new governmental buildings in Monrovia in the late 1950s and 1960s, including the Department of Public Works, the Ministry of Information, City Hall, and the Executive Mansion (the president's private residence)—enjoyed direct Israeli loans that reached two million dollars at their peak.⁶ Relations with the Israeli government were beneficial in other regards as well, since the Mayers, who registered their export company in Lichtenstein, depended on governmental permission to export capital from Israel. It can be assumed that the Israeli government turned a blind eye to the extent of the Mayers' financial activity overseas in exchange for the diplomatic work the LCC did for Israel in Monrovia.

The Mayer Brothers' crownpiece in Liberia was the Ducor Palace Hotel (plates 20 and 21). Recognizing the growing need for a luxury hotel that would facilitate President William Tubman's diplomatic and economic ambitions, the Mayers envisioned a five-star hotel comparable in standards to European and American ones. For the site—inspired perhaps by the Hilton hotel that was concurrently being planned for a hill hovering over the shores of Tel Aviv—they chose a prominent hill overlooking the Atlantic and the Mesurado River. As in Israel, where the government initiated the Hilton hotel project and provided loans for it, the construction of the Ducor Palace Hotel had economic and diplomatic significance.[7] Governments of decolonizing African countries saw building luxury hotels as a necessary step in their economic development, and one that went far beyond attracting tourists: such hotels enabled countries to host African and international dignitaries for diplomatic conventions and facilitated the arrival of business investors. Furthermore, with their pools and high standards of living, these hotels provided getaways for employees of foreign companies working in the country and calibrated the aspirations of the emerging African middle and upper classes.

Unlike Solel Boneh, which often commissioned Israeli architects for their projects if they were at liberty to do so, the Mayers hired the Viennese architect Adolf Hoch as well as an Austrian construction engineer to design the Ducor. For the interior, they commissioned Heinz Fenchel, a German-born Israeli architect who at the time was working on the design for the Dan Hotel in Tel Aviv, the crown jewel of what was then the most high-end Israeli hotel chain. By hiring European professionals and importing materials and products from Europe, the Mayers transgressed the patriotic codes of Israeli work in Africa. As a reporter for *Davar*, the Labor party's newspaper, argued, under their leadership the company had lost its "Israeli imprint." Warning of the negative effects this could have on Israel's status in Africa, he claimed that such internationalization could fuel campaigns against importing Israeli technical expertise. If Israel did not contribute its own original skills and equipment, but merely facilitated the entry of European ones, he argued, why shouldn't African countries reach out directly to the (European) source?[8] Backed by their trusted friend, Hanan Yavor, the Israeli ambassador to Liberia, the Mayers denied this accusation. Yet in private correspondence with the ambassador, they disclosed their difficulty in relying on Israeli suppliers, personnel, and shipment services without compromising their business operations. As Mordechai Mayer complained, use of Israeli suppliers and the Israeli shipping company Zim entailed financial losses and slowed down construction. Israeli manufacturers did not hold supply reserves in the same quantities as their European counterparts; Zim stopped in Monrovia irregularly, compared with other shipping companies that set and communicated their schedules months in advance; and Israeli personnel demanded higher compensation for working in Monrovia than Italians, for example.[9] The Mayers were thus caught between their desire to maximize profit by operating a successful business enterprise and their commitments to the government of Israel, whose loans often stipulated the use of Israeli products and personnel.[10]

Even with the Israeli government's backing, the magnitude and luxury of the Ducor Palace Hotel project required a capital investment that the Israeli financial market was unable to support. Seeing this as an opportunity to attract American investors, the Mayers approached Chase National Bank, which was already involved in finance in Liberia, and consequently Pan Am's InterContinental Hotels Company took over the management of the Ducor Palace Hotel.[11] (The Rockefellers, who were major Chase shareholders, controlled Pan Am.) Liberia, then, served the Mayers as an entrée into the US financial market: although they had already collaborated with American investors on projects in Israel, these were not comparable in magnitude.

Similarly, the Ducor Palace in Liberia was the Mayers' key to expanding their operation to the Ivory Coast, then the most economically viable country in former French West Africa. Following his visit to the Ducor in Monrovia, Ivory Coast's president, Félix Houphouët-Boigny, approached the Mayers in July 1960, via the Israeli embassy in Paris, to build a similar hotel in Abidjan. The Mayers, who were looking to expand their activities in West Africa, welcomed the opportunity. In March 1961, the contract for the Hotel Ivoire, a two-hundred-room hotel that would be financed by the Ivorian government with a loan from the Israeli government, was signed. French, German, and Swiss companies provided the supplies, interior finishing, furniture, and air conditioning, while the hotel's design was entrusted to the Israeli Fenchel, who had designed the interiors of the Ducor (plate 22). As in Monrovia, InterContinental Hotels was responsible for managing the hotel, control of which the Mayers and the Ivorian government shared.[12]

When reporting on the Mayers' activities in the Ivory Coast, the Israeli daily *Ma'ariv* gave its news story the telling subtitle "With no French Mediation."[13] Establishing direct business relations with the economically successful former French colony was indeed a feat worthy of recognition. More forcibly than the British Commonwealth system, France continued to monopolize postcolonial development markets via its extensive technical aid. Resisting France's grip, the Ivory Coast asserted its independence by soliciting and accepting aid from other countries, such as the United States and Israel. Yet while France objected vehemently to Ivorian use of American aid, it accepted Israeli aid and trade due to the latter's dependency on French arms, which ensured that Israeli loyalty lay with France first. In this theater of development, Israeli involvement ultimately served both French and Ivorian interests, as it helped the Ivory Coast to perform its independence from France while not actually threatening French interests in the area.[14]

Identifying West Africa as an untapped destination for mass tourism, Moshe Mayer thought that Abidjan's lagoons could become an international attraction that would draw visitors from all tiers of the jet-age generation. In his vision, Western taste and Ivorian culture could coexist and complement each other. For the hotel's inauguration festivities, he suggested that "Ivory [Coast] be a state of culture and festival . . . like the Salzburger Festspiele (the famous Salzburg festival that occurs every summer) and Olympic sports games." The plan for the festivities also included water games, opportunities to stroll beside elephants, and a "romantic beautiful village" of arts and crafts, which was to exhibit the Ivory Coast's handicrafts and ivory products for sale.[15] To compensate for a lack of wildlife attractions like the safaris in Kenya, the ultimate reference point for tourism development in Africa, Moshe Mayer and the architects involved—first Fenchel and, starting in the mid-1960s, the American William Pereira and his Israeli intern, Tommy Leitersdorf, who worked on expanding the resort into an African Riviera—instead created a fantastic blend of local cultures and animals with Western amenities, such as an ice-skating rink, golf course, and casino.[16]

Fenchel's design comprised a spectacular language of African-inspired motifs and forms, detached and abstracted from their original contexts. An architect and stage designer by training, Fenchel had begun his career in the late 1920s as an art director at the famed UFA film studios in Berlin; in Israel, his practice articulated a distinct luxury bourgeois lifestyle through his designs for cafes, shops, housing interiors, and the Dan Hotels.[17] While his designs in Israel added scenic compositions with restrained use of colors, materials, light, and vegetation to the prevailing modernist aesthetic, in the Hotel Ivoire and its conference center, Fenchel experimented with bold shapes and forms reminiscent of the expressionist aesthetic that had dominated German film production. The interiors of the hotel towers feature rich geometric patterns and textures, while the pavilions simulate African huts (fig. 6.1). These expressive forms and exterior ornamental patterns reflect Fenchel's work method: he first sketched the building facades, prioritizing form and ornament over function and program, before turning the design and planning over to other members of his office.[18] This method, deriving perhaps from his cinematic production design past in Germany, substantially diverged from the design principles that guided the architects whom Solel Boneh commissioned for its projects. Fenchel did not shy away from exuberance, which is expressed in his method—from facade to interior—and in his preference for expensive materials and fantastic forms.

These differences cannot be explained strictly as a result of hiring architects associated with the labor movement, like Sharon, versus architects

FIGURE 6.1 Hotel Ivoire, contemporary view of one of the pavilions, 2017. Photograph by Abdallahh from Montréal, Canada—Sofitel Abidjan Hôtel Ivoire, CC BY 2.0, accessed Dec. 10, 2018, https://commons.wikimedia.org/w/index.php?curid=65688172.

FIGURE 6.2  Premier Hotel, Ibadan, early 1970s. Courtesy of Amos Spitz.

like Fenchel, whose client base was primarily private and bourgeois. For example, for its Premier Hotel in Ibadan, Nigeria, Solel Boneh commissioned Shmuel Rosoff, who catered mostly to the tastes of the upper middle class in Israel (fig. 6.2). Yet the hotel employed restrained functionalist aesthetics and modest building materials, such as the locally available timber that served to clad the reception hall's wall or was made into partitions to divide up the open space of the lobby. Unlike Fenchel's patterned ornamentation that defined the architectural spaces, the Premier's walls remained blank, both in the interior and on the exterior, and were punctuated by a few artworks by local artists. As this case demonstrates, the shift from a Labor Zionist program in Solel Boneh's projects to a liberal one in private US-funded projects also entailed an aesthetic shift, in which ornamentation through the abstraction of pseudo-African motifs was pushed to its limits, privileging spectacle over function. Unlike the other projects discussed in this book, Fenchel designed the Hotel Ivoire with apparent disregard for the structure or the builders. Disconnected from the material conditions of the country, its rich ornamental patterns created a one-of-a-kind extravaganza rather than forms or building techniques that could potentially be of use in future projects or have a lasting effect on the country's building industry.

The Ducor and Hotel Ivoire demonstrate the Mayers' gradual shift from European tastes and standards to American ones, and reflect a concurrent process of Americanization in Israel exemplified by Tel Aviv's urban renewal projects, in which the Mayers played a leading role.[19] In 1961, as they were planning the Hotel Ivoire, they commissioned famed Chinese-American architect I. M. Pei to submit proposals for two commercial projects in Tel Aviv.[20] While these proposals never materialized, the Mayers successfully constructed Tel Aviv's first skyscraper, which was then the tallest building in the Middle East, the Shalom Meir Tower (commonly known as Migdal Shalom, 1959–65). Like the Hotel Ivoire, which was meant to be a tourist destination in its own right, the Shalom Meir Tower included an observatory, Israel's only wax museum, and, on its rooftop, an amusement park called "Mayerland."[21] Constructed on the grounds of the demolished Herzliya Hebrew Gymnasium—Tel Aviv's first high school and an architectural landmark that denoted the historical limit of Ahuzat Bayit, Tel Aviv's first neighborhood—the Shalom Meir Tower signified the beginning of urban renewal and the liberalization of the Tel Aviv cityscape.[22]

Tommy Leitersdorf, Moshe Mayer's son-in-law, who had interned in Pereira's office in Los Angeles and planned Abidjan's African Riviera, would expand the importation of American-inspired planning techniques, including Walt Disney's theme park ideas, to Israel and the West Bank, first via Israel's tourism master plan, and in the late 1970s, through planning for Ma'ale Edumim, the largest Jewish settlement in the West Bank at the time, and then for Emmanuel in the 1980s. While discussing what this translation entailed is beyond the scope of this postscript, it is interesting to note that it is in his plan for Emmanuel—a town in the West Bank that was slated for an ultraorthodox population—that Leitersdorf incorporated one of the most Disneyesque elements of the African Riviera. Like the Riviera plan, in which an aerial tramway and a monorail connected a set of attractions to be consumed by tourists and commuters alike, Emmanuel was to include a tram that would form part of an interactive closed-circuit network controlled by personal computers.[23] As this example, like other projects in this book, demonstrates quite vividly, there is nothing self-evident about the itineraries architecture takes in processes of globalization, and as such, even the study of projects Israeli architects undertook in the West Bank should take into consideration the multidirectional translations at work, which in this case include a double translation from the United States to the Ivory Coast, and then from the Ivory Coast to the settlement of Emmanuel.

### From Development to Humanitarianism, from Governmental Aid to Private Entrepreneurship

Private Israeli businesses in Africa, like that of the Mayers', heralded a shift to pragmatism in Israeli-African relations that intensified with the breaking off of diplomatic relations in 1973.[24] One of this shift's best-known manifestations was the Israel Defense Forces' (IDF) 1976 raid on Entebbe International Airport, in which the president of Uganda, Idi Amin—not long before an IDF protégé—exhibited to the world his alliance with the Popular Front for the Liberation of Palestine (PFLP). Amin invited members of the PFLP, who were collaborating with the Red Army Faction, to land the Air France plane they had hijacked en route to Paris from Tel Aviv at the airport in Entebbe.[25] Built by Solel Boneh during the "golden age" of Israeli-African relations, the airport now became the site of a military operation. The advantage of IDF in this well-known rescue operation was its ability to access to Solel Boneh's plans for the airport. In this case, architectural development aid became an actual military tool.

This and other more covert military involvement in the continent, as well as Israel's strengthening of relations with apartheid South Africa beginning in 1973, did not mark the end of all civilian contact. Relationships continued informally through the private sector, with trade in both civilian and military products comprising commodities and expertise.[26] It was not so much that these private relationships supplanted governmental aid as that they grew out of it, since such aid laid both the diplomatic and financial foundations for Israeli entry into African (and other) foreign markets. As we have seen, private entrepreneurship had been growing in parallel with aid since the 1960s, with semipublic companies such as Solel Boneh shifting to commercial activities in 1964 and with the entrance of private figures such as Zalman Enav and the Mayer brothers. By the 1980s, this transition to the pragmatic logic of the free market was complete.

This shift in emphasis from governmental aid to private business also entailed a gradual shift in discourse from development to humanitarian aid. While the history of the former cannot be neatly separated from that of the latter, the occupation of the West Bank and the Gaza Strip marked a definitive, if somewhat confused, change in Israeli discourse.[27] Writing in the early 1970s, high-ranking foreign ministry officer Shimeon Amir could move seamlessly from discussing Israeli aid in Africa to its "administration" of the occupied Palestinian territories, and then back to Africa.[28] Indeed, in the early years of Israeli occupation, development was debated as a governing policy in the Palestinian territories. The Israeli government considered economic development—including projects that focused on agriculture, industry, water supply, and housing—as a means of integrating Palestinians in occupied areas into the Israeli economy. This strategy aimed to suppress political demands by raising standards of living, even while also strengthening the Israeli economy.[29] As we have seen, Leitersdorf and Enav turned to projects in the occupied Palestinian territories after their return to Israel, as many of their generation did. Yet questions about whether and how any of their experiences in Africa informed debates about "development" in the Palestinian territories still require further research.

After the 1967 occupation, Israel found it harder and harder to fashion itself as moral and just internationally and even domestically, as Palestinian subjects who crossed the border daily replaced the now too-contented Hebrew laborers as construction workers. By the end of the decade, Israeli experts had become more reluctant to undertake pioneering sacrifice, and expected better incentives for working in Africa.[30] A study conducted in the early 1970s (and concealed by the government that commissioned it) shows no correlation between ideological zeal and aid experts' satisfaction with their experience abroad.[31] Just as pioneering lost its appeal in Israel, work in Africa likewise became no more than a paying job. After the occupation, the Palestinian territories would offer new scope for "pioneering." Before that, it was hoped that Africa would rejuvenate Israelis' "pioneering spirit" and lure it off "the beaten paths" of Israel's limited land and opportunity.[32] Yet the reenactment of pioneering could only go so far in the face of the country's changing economic, social, and political conditions. When pioneering in Africa turned into a business enterprise, opportunities for exploitation became more apparent—and with them came cynicism and greed.[33]

By the 1980s, as development turned into humanitarianism, aid became "just business," since any pretense of solidarity was obliterated.[34] With this shift in discourse, imbalanced relations between developed and developing nations became fixed as an ahistorical fact. This change in terminology cemented the binary between the two types of nations, locking in a new difference between developed and never-to-be-developed nations and serving to conceal the continuous—and even intensifying—process of the latter's underdevelopment. In the shift from development aid to humanitarian aid, the trade in hope became no more than a provisional effort to deal with present crises—a system that keeps feeding on itself with the cyclical production of crises, famously defined by Naomi Klein as "disaster capitalism."[35] There is no trace left of the belief that "developing countries" will ever "catch up" with the West.

To be sure, diplomacy was never short on interests to pursue, and its rhetoric was always challenged by practice. Even during the height of the "golden age" of diplomatic relations, Israeli diplomacy faced many such challenges, since Israel's involvement in the African continent comprised a plethora of civilian and military institutions, each with its own interests, including, in addition to the foreign ministry, the Histadrut, private businesses, and the military and intelligence apparatuses that ultimately held the upper hand.[36] Israeli diplomats aimed to contain the "disruptions" that potentially undermined their efforts. While diplomats had little power over Israeli military activity in Africa, they at least tried to control the behavior of Israeli envoys and experts.[37] This tension unfolded on a day-to-day basis: for example, one delegate reported not only that a Solel Boneh manager abused the company's Nigerian employees but also that Solel Boneh managers' housewives too quickly became accustomed to living in luxury estates and ordering their "boys" around.[38] However, most threatening of all was the rise of the Israeli businessman or middleman as experts first sent as representatives of the state transitioned to the private sector. Resorting to the most radical measures they had at their disposal, some diplomats in Nigeria even considered not renewing these businessmen's passports or stamping them "except for Nigeria" or any country in which they had served as representatives of Israel.[39]

The turn to exclusively private economic activities in 1973 did not end the state's involvement. As Haim Yacobi explains, private entrepreneurship has helped boost Israel's economy and undergirded the revival of diplomatic relations in the last two decades. These business transactions tend to shift seamlessly from military training and arms dealing, often paid for with raw materials such as oil and diamonds, to civilian enterprises such as communications, agriculture, and construction. Unlike in the 1960s, when every Israeli working in Africa was perceived as an "emissary" of the state and the men who turned to private business were seen as potential liabilities, now the private character of these transactions shields the state, which can deny its involvement and refuse responsibility. Employing this "plausible deniability" tactic, Israel continues to grow its hypermilitaristic and neoliberal economy while maintaining the image of a democratic regime operating according to an ethical code.[40] Thus the space vacated by the Histadrut as one of the forces behind Israel's diplomatic relations in the Third World is now filled by a private sector that expands Israel's diplomatic reach.

One such company, the LR Group, known in Angola as a construction company,[41] was established by three IDF air force veterans in the late 1980s and specialized initially in security technology. A vast project for securing the Portuguese coast led to a similar project in Portugal's former colony, Angola, before Israel renewed its ties with the latter in 1993. Since then, the group has constructed six airports in the country, followed by another contract to refurbish an international airport in the Republic of the Congo. The Angolan Civil War, which lasted for almost three decades, from Angola's independence in 1975 to 2002, served as a backdrop for these transactions, which also included arms dealing.

Other Israeli companies also participated in planning and reconstruction in Angola, such as the Tahal Group, a former governmental water engineering company that, like Solel Boneh, began its operations on the continent in the 1960s and was privatized in the mid-1990s. In 2010, Tahal helped draft a new master plan for Angola's entire coastal area, which had been densely populated with migrants from the country's interior since the civil war.[42] Tahal's planning involvement followed a thirty-four-million-euro agreement it signed in 2008 to supply water to seven neighborhoods in the capital, Luanda.[43] This sequence is similar to that of Israeli aid in Sierra Leone in the 1960s, as analyzed in chapters 1 and 2: in Angola as well, specific construction and infrastructure projects led to comprehensive planning. However, unlike earlier projects discussed in the book, current ones do not involve passing on professional knowledge and skills to local personnel.

## Labor Zionist Hauntology, or the Afterlives of Israeli Architectural Aid in Africa

Residential projects that Israeli architects and planners have undertaken in Angola and Nigeria in recent decades show how modernist aesthetics and Labor Zionist social ideology continue to haunt Israeli architectural work in Africa. In concluding here, I discuss the persistence of modernist aesthetics in relation to the ontology of the "not-yet" that these historical projects embodied. In societies where the "incompletion" of modernity is felt most strongly, the specter of its promises often lingers in premature modern ruins. Yet a strange reversal occurs when historical projects that marked independence outlive more recent ones—as is the case with the buildings discussed in this book, all of which survived radical changes in their respective countries' political regimes and still house the institutions they were originally designed for.[44] Moreover, most of them have been recently refurbished. This fact cannot be underestimated in a context where constructing new buildings is often easier, and provides more opportunities for the mobilization of funds, than maintaining existing ones. This final section, therefore, ruminates on the tensions between current and historical projects in order to offer some directions for further study of the latter's social afterlives and the futures they still might entail.

In 2010, as part of Angola's postwar reconstruction, the LR Group announced that it would construct "100,000 social houses."[45] After securing the coastal territory, which was the only area the government could control during the civil war, the LR Group ventured into an ambitious experimental agricultural project seventy kilometers inland, east of Luanda. Named Aldeia Nova ("New Village"), the project's first stage included the construction of six villages to house six hundred villagers.[46] In Kimina, a similar 208-million-dollar veteran resettlement project funded by the Angolan government and executed by Tahal, includes 310 houses with thirty *dunam* (7.4 acres) of farmland each. Kimina has irrigation systems and agricultural training; a logistical center for processing, preserving, and marketing products; and 10,000 dunam (2,471 acres) of shared agricultural land.[47] The provision of each household, regardless of its size, with the same starting point—a standard brick house, basic furnishings, a garden and a chicken coop, as well as cooperative training and facilities for processing and marketing—is reminiscent of the Lakhish project discussed in chapter 2. However, while it is the same model in outlook, it does not adhere to the same premises. As LR CEO Gabi Nahum explains, "In the fifties, they sold people an ideology of mutual guarantee; that the system will solve all of their problems. In practice, the sooner they realized that the system does not solve their problems, and can become parasitic, the sooner the moshav [cooperative village] became successful." "In this project," he concluded, "we exposed the family to this economic logic right from the start."[48] Clearly, the Angolan project explicitly builds on the neoliberalization of the agricultural sector in Israel. Similarly, when asked whether the project was a mixture of socialism and capitalism, economist José Cerqueira, the director of Aldeia Nova, retorted, "This isn't kibbutz spirit."[49] The social ethics that once undergirded the project are now supplanted by a new focus on global environmental concerns.[50]

But perhaps the differences are not so great after all. Angolan veterans, who must go through interviews in order to be selected for the settlements, are required to sign a contract in which they agree not to have more than one wife, to refrain from alcohol consumption, to sell their produce only through the co-op, to send their children to school, and to refrain from domestic violence.[51] This neoliberal contract, an example of the so-called new contractualism, replaces the state's supervision of welfare, which was especially heavy-handed in the case of Arab-Jewish immigrants in Israel.[52] At the same time, however, it is reminiscent of the contracts some Moroccan Jewish immigrants had to sign before embarking on their journey to Israel in the 1950s, which stated they had agreed to settle the Lakhish region.[53] Like the immigrants who settled in Lakhish, the Angolan families too are subject to supervision and evaluation. In the present case, however, it is only their work ethic and productivity that are considered as criteria, not their degree of cooperation and self-management, as was the case in Lakhish. In fact, in contrast to earlier projects that aimed to train local managers and workers, there is no real expectation that the Angolans will ever take over management of the projects, since "they don't want us to leave," as one manager remarked haughtily.[54]

An important component of such "turnkey" projects is the aura of social ideology that once justified their logic.[55] David Hacohen, Israel's first diplomatic representative in a Third World country and a graduate of the London School of Economics, had already figured this out in the early 1960s, when discussing demonstration farms that Israelis set up in African countries: "In our economic attempts we should not take the conventional direct business approach. We cannot, for example, sell fertilizers unless we establish farms on thousands of dunams, and improve them with our fertilizers, build an on-site research station, and prove that fertilizing is desirable . . . if our economic activity were run according to the norm of world trade diplomacy, we would be weak compared to our more experienced and wealthier competitors."[56]

What differentiated Israeli farms from other demonstration farm projects were the socialist values that undergirded them. In the 1960s, it was not just fertilizers, sprinklers, and agricultural training that were transported from Israel to African farmland. As we saw in the case of the University of Ife, agriculture was promoted as part of a new way of life, and therefore the demonstration farms that Hacohen described exhibited, in addition to agricultural production, the system of living that facilitated them. It was important to send the "best people"—in other words, the "right people" in terms of their socialization and party affiliation[57]—in order to show not only that fertilization works but also that the entire system that sustains it works. "If only we could transfer 1,000 Africans with their families and children to moshavim and kibbutzim for two years, to learn and be compelled by our exemplary life," Hacohen mused out loud.[58] Israeli expertise and products could not be dissociated from the Labor Zionist project, and depended on it. As we saw above, even today, this past aura of Labor Zionist social ideology continues to haunt neoliberal ventures such as Aldeia Nova, which cynically exploit it. If, in the 1960s, the "best people" and equipment even better than that used in Israel were deployed to Africa, now Israeli companies engage in cheap construction, often with reused equipment.[59]

The Aldeia Nova and Kimina projects thus veil government-sponsored yet privately managed entrepreneurial endeavors with a socialist-cooperative cloak. Similarly, the modernist aesthetics of the Israeli public housing that was constructed rapidly in the 1950s and 1960s continues to inform such projects as the Dolphin housing estate in Ikoyi, Lagos. Constructed in the 1990s by the Israeli-owned company HFP Engineering,[60] this vast project addressed the acute shortage of housing for Lagos's growing middle class. In order to lower costs and expedite construction, the company used prefabricated frames and left most of the filling to local contractors. As a result of the cheap materials used, the estate is currently in very poor condition. The exposed prefabricated frame that still dominates its image, together no doubt with its ruinous condition overall, have led a couple of architects who have recently studied the city to mistakenly date the project to the 1950s or 1960s and thus to rewrite it as part of the city's modernist heritage.[61] In their cynical exploitation of earlier models, the Aldeia Nova, Kimina, and Dolphin Estate projects function as empty shells that are not only drained of but also occlude the promise they once held.

In closing, I would like to consider the ghostly persistence of the Labor Zionist ethos as an affirmation of the hopes that the projects discussed in this book embodied and continue to endure. As a prelude to a future study of the social afterlives of these projects, I suggest reading them as vehicles for what Okwui Enwezor has called the "yet-to-come-modernity" of the African "aftermodern."⁶² Enwezor's phrasing and disjunctive temporality, which attempt to dialectically capture the dreams of independence in the ruins of colonial modernity, recall Ernst Bloch's politics of hope with which I began this book. Following Bloch, the hope inscribed aesthetically and institutionally in the buildings was ultimately open-ended. These architectural objects did not necessarily act in a temporally immediate way; they were not legible causes of direct effects. More like triggers of a spillover effect, these objects and the institutions they facilitate have the potential to shape future outcomes beyond their original trajectories. If, once set in motion, buildings and plans were "unlikely instruments of an unplotted strategy," as James Ferguson puts it, their "success" cannot be assessed fully from the perspective of international development institutions and their grim outlook on the "failed state" in Africa.⁶³ Just as their effects cannot be foreseen, neither can their symbolic content be fully scripted by either international or local stakeholders, since, as Bloch explains, "Its space (of the utopian imagination) is the objectively real possibility within process, along the path of the Object [*Objekt*] itself, in which what is radically intended by man is not delivered anywhere but not thwarted anywhere either. Its concern, to which all its energies must be devoted, remains what is truly hoping in the subject, truly hoped for in the object [*Gegenstand*]: our task is to research the function and content of this central Thing For Us."⁶⁴

This temporal open-endedness allows the object to act beyond immediate interests and opens up space for alterity. Furthermore, the significance of an object is not determined by its creators' original intentions because its addressee—"Us"—is both heterogeneous and changes over time. Even if the projects discussed in this book were only stopgap mechanisms, they offered placeholders amid the great aspirations and anxiety of postcolonial African states' transition to independence. Their endurance in their respective landscapes, at once isolated as monuments to a bygone era filled with hope and possibility, and surrounded by new developments themselves in various stages of ruin, speaks to the tension between the promises of the past and their occluded future. A full consideration of these projects' uses and afterlives, therefore, will move beyond questions of state or institutional failure and success, and beyond neocolonial or elite imposition and users' resistance, to consider them in their full complexity as vehicles signaling and carrying forward other, undreamt-of futures yet to come.

# notes

**INTRODUCTION**

1. For a survey of Israeli construction in the continent, see Efrat, *Israeli Project*, 607–30.

2. The Histadrut consolidated Labor Zionism's hegemony by providing an infrastructure and services for the Jewish population, acting as a de facto state-within-a-state under the British Mandate and as the breeding ground for the future state's political leadership. In the state period, due to its intimate relationship with the ruling party, with which many of its actors overlapped (e.g., David Ben-Gurion, Israel's first prime minister, served as its first elected secretary), the Histadrut helped the foreign ministry establish initial contacts with Third World leaders, sometimes even before their countries' independence. See Gorni, Bareli, and Greenberg, *Workers' Society to Trade Union*.

3. This view, for example, is expressed in James Ferguson's seminal book *The Anti-Politics Machine*, 8. International historians have started to broaden the categories of "development" and "modernization" by tracing the multiple north-south alliances that gave rise to various regional modernities. See Engerman and Unger, "Introduction."

4. As Frederick Cooper has noted, even among Western countries, "the world of development has offered a variety of approaches and a variety of linkages to scholars and practitioners in ex-colonial polities; development orthodoxies have been far less orthodox than images suggest." Cooper, "Writing," 16.

5. There is ample international relations literature on the subject. The most recent and comprehensive study is Levey, *Israel in Africa, 1956–76*. The UN recommended the "Five Year Development Plan" model in 1951, and subsequently it was widely adopted among decolonizing African countries regardless of their Cold War ideological affinity. See McVety, *Enlightened Aid*, 119.

6. Other players might include Brazil and the Gulf states, especially after 1973. This list is informed by nascent scholarship on architectural development aid in Africa and is in no way conclusive. See Łukasz Stanek, ed., "Cold War Transfer: Architecture and Planning from Socialist Countries in the 'Third World'" special issue, *Journal of Architecture* 17, no. 3 (2012); Stanek, *Architecture in Global Socialism*; Roskam, "Non-Aligned Architecture." On the role Egypt assumed in the production of knowledge on Third World housing, see Elshahed, "Revolutionary Modernism?," 401–5. Other sources include exhibitions such as the Nordic pavilion, "Forms of Freedom: African Independence and Nordic Models," at the Venice Architecture Biennale in 2014, and art projects such as Che Onejoon's video documentation of North Korean architecture and art, *Mansudae Master Class* (South Korea, 2013–15), DVD, which was exhibited at the New Museum Triennial: *Surround Audience* (February 25 to May 24, 2015).

7. Arturo Escobar's influential analysis of development discourse, to take one notable example, ignores issues of social, cultural, and geopolitical positionality in the performance of development expertise. See Escobar, *Encountering Development*. As historian Nick Cullather has observed, "The real stakes were measured in prestige, state power, and international alignments" rather than in purely economic terms. See Cullather, "Third Race," 508. The third category that Israel occupied between north and south is akin to that of "semi-periphery countries" in world-systems theory.

8. John Tettegah and Tom Mboya quoted in Peters, *Israel and Africa*, 3.

9. Chakrabarty, *Provincializing Europe*, 7–9. I refer here and throughout the text to decolonization in historical rather than epistemological terms, indicating the final years of colonial rule leading to independence.

10. Watts, "New Deal in Emotions," 49–50.

11. Adas, "Modernization Theory," 35–36.

12. Cooper, "Writing," 15.

13. Lamptey, "Ghana Experience," 12–13.

14. Although trade was an important part of these relations, its sum was negligible compared to the resources Israel invested in its aid. Israel's goal was diplomatic; trade was perceived as a way to establish these relationships rather than their end result. Similarly, aid was not tied to how African countries voted at the UN; they did not consistently favor Israeli objectives. For Israel's security interests, see Bergman, "Israel and Africa."

15. Bergman, "Israel and Africa," 283.

16. For the term "contractual dependency," see Mafeje, "Neo-Colonialism," 412.

17. Golda Meir quoted in Levey, *Israel in Africa*, 31.

18. Oded, *Africa and Israel*, 30.

19. Levey, "Israel's Entry to Africa," 104. Peters, *Israel and Africa*, 4. Only Mauritania and Somalia refused to establish relations with Israel.

20. N. Pundak, "I Was a Guinea Pig for the Jungle," *Davar*, July 26, 1963, 3. On the pejorative use of the term "jungle" in Israeli political and cultural discourse, see Bar-Yosef, *Villa in the Jungle*, 10. Here and throughout the text, I use the term "Third World" in its historical sense as a political position and not as a category of economic standing.

21. ISA, MFA 226/5 (93). See also Avimor, *Relations*, 138.

22. For Solel Boneh's history, see Biletzky, *Solel Boneh*; Dan, *On the Unpaved Road*.

23. Biletzky, *Solel Boneh*, 403–6; Dan, *On the Unpaved Road*, 170–80. Solel Boneh often used these jobs as cover for clandestine intelligence gathering for the Jewish settlement and Zionist recruiting in the Middle East. See Dan, *On the Unpaved Road*, 170–80; Svorai, "Solel Bone," 129–30.

24. Biletzky, *Solel Boneh*, 249–51, 286–94, 319–42. Greenberg, "Labor's Expanding Economy."

25. In 1963, due to financial losses, Overseas and Harbour Works was merged with Building and Public Works.

26. See Neuberger, "Early African Nationalism"; Echeruo, "Jewish Question"; Hill, "Black Zionism: Marcus Garvey and the Jewish Question." For a critique of the comparison, see Williams, "Pan-Africanism and Zionism: The Delusion of Comparability."

27. Meir, *My Life*, 325.

28. "Head of Ceremony to the President's office," April 20, 1955, ISA, Pres 53/19.

29. Oded, *Africa and Israel*, 30. Likewise, while the Histadrut Afro-Asian Training Center in Tel Aviv enjoyed funding from the American Federation of Labor and Congress of Industrial Organizations, it denied any interference in its operations. Gillis, "Developing Identity," 96.

30. Bergman, "Israel and Africa," 279–83, 288–92, 306–7.

31. Ajayi, "Expectations of Independence," 4.

32. Zeleza, "Historic and Humanistic Agendas," 40, 47.

33. Givoni, "Who Cares?"

34. Developed into a doctrine in the 1950s and 1960s, *mamlakhtiut* has no adequate translation in English, and has usually been referred to as "statism" or "republicanism." See Bareli and Kedar, *Israeli Republicanism*.

35. David Ben-Gurion, *Knesset Minutes* 22 (March 16–31, 1959). Quoted in Levey, *Israel in Africa*, 33.

36. Veracini, "Other Shift," 28. Veracini distinguishes between pre- and post-1967 Zionist settler colonialism, since the latter, according to him, has not succeeded in superseding itself. For a review of studies of Israel in a settler colonial studies framework from a Palestinian perspective, see Sabbagh-Khoury, "Settler Colonialism."

37. Kemp, "Borders, Space, and Collective Identity."

38. Mooreville, "Eyeing Africa," 46. During the sixties, Israel had more experts working abroad in proportion to its population than many advanced industrialized countries. Nearly two-thirds of those sent to the Third World worked in Africa. According to Joel Peters, "In 1964 the Israeli ratio of experts to total population (0.028 per cent) was almost twice that of all the OECD countries combined (0.015 per cent)." Peters, *Israel and Africa*, 4.

39. Bar-Yosef, *Villa in the Jungle*, 33–34; Yacobi, *Israel and Africa*, 25–26.

40. Theodor Herzl, *Old New Land*, trans. Lotta Levensohn (Princeton, NJ: Markus Wierner Publishers, 2000 [1941]), 169–70.

Netanel Lorch, the head of the Africa desk in the foreign ministry, ordered Israeli embassies around the world to quote this paragraph in conversations and publications. See Yacobi, *Israel and Africa*, 26. Subsequently, this quote opened a traveling exhibition that toured British and French West Africa. Dan Avni to Israeli Representatives in Africa, August 28, 1964, LA IV-277-189; "Israeli Exhibition Due in Freetown Soon," *Daily Mail*, February 17, 1962, 12. As part of Israeli book donations, *Altneuland* was distributed to Nigerian universities and categorized with the history books, thus effacing its utopian and fictive character. See M. Artsieli to David Ben Dov, January 19, 1965, ISA, MFA 1932/6.

41. It is assumed that this character was based on Alexander Marmorek (1865–1923), an Austrian-Jewish physician and assistant at the Pasteur Institute. See "Alexander Marmorek," *Herzl Museum*, accessed December 30, 2014, http://www.herzl.org/english/Article.aspx?Item=532. Botanist Otto Warburg, who advised Herzl in writing the book, may be another possible influence. Warburg gained his expertise through his service in the German colonization of Cameroon and Togoland, and across the Ottoman Empire. See Troen, "Higher Education," 47–48; Otto Warburg: A Biographical Note, *The Otto Warburg Minerva Center for Agricultural Biotechnology, The Hebrew University of Jerusalem*, accessed December 30, 2014, http://departments.agri.huji.ac.il/biotech/otto3.htm.

42. Kahane, "Dominant Ideology's Stances"; Penslar, *Israel in History*, 150–66.

43. Sufian, *Healing*, 34–38.

44. These "ideal" characteristics implied a distinct racial hierarchy. In the selection criteria for Israeli aid experts, there was a clear preference for men of European descent who were kibbutz or moshav members or Israel Defense Forces veterans, although Mizrahi Jews were also included once their knowledge of French was recognized as beneficial, especially in former French colonies. See Bar-Yosef, *Villa in the Jungle*, 167–73.

45. See Kreinin, *Israel and Africa*; Goldberg, *Israel, Africa, and Asia:*

*Partners in Progress*; Laufer, *Israel and the Developing Countries*; Amir, *Israel's Development Cooperation*; Curtis and Gitelson, *Israel in the Third World*.

46. Hever and Gensler, "Minority Discourse"; Massad, "'Post-Colonial' Colony."

47. These numbers are approximate.

48. Black, "Interior's Exterior," 86.

49. Westad, *Global Cold War*, 5–6.

50. On the work of Israeli architects in the Middle East and the Mediterranean region, see, for example, Feniger and Kallus, "Expertise"; Kallus, "Crete Development Plan." A notable exception is Feniger's study of landscape design in rural Iran, which traces the roots of Israeli design to prestate colonization practices. See Feniger, "From Nahalal to Danesfahan."

51. Yacobi, *Israel and Africa*, 31; Gillis, "Developing Identity," 74–76; Bar-Yosef, *Villa in the Jungle*, 123–84.

52. Shafir, *Land, Labor, and the Origins of the Israeli-Palestinian Conflict, 1882–1914*.

53. Yacobi, *Israel and Africa*, 21.

54. Yacobi, *Israel and Africa*, 3, 5.

55. Framed this way, any attempt to evaluate the altruism of individual actors and the authenticity of their intentions is limited at best. For examples of such efforts, see De Raedt, "Between 'True Believers'"; Beeckmans, "Adventures." For a critique of limiting analysis to the "interests" and "intentions" of actors, whether they be states, international institutions, or individual experts, see Ferguson, *Anti-Politics Machine*, 16–21.

56. Bayart, *State in Africa*, 24.

57. Bayart, *State in Africa*, 6.

58. Bayart, *State in Africa*, 27.

59. The term should not be confused with the theater practice known as "theater of development" or "theater for development" that took shape in Africa in the early 1960s. My usage of the term shares with this more literal application the disruption of a colonial binary between creator and consumer that it assumed, as theorized by French Martinique poet and politician Aimé Césaire. Curto, *Inter-tech(s)*, 28–30.

60. Miescher, Bloom, and Manuh, *Modernization as Spectacle in Africa*.

61. Quoted in Levey, *Israel in Africa*, 37.

62. As Ferguson explains, arguments that see African modernity as an inauthentic shadow or copy of Western modernity ignore "the fact that a shadow is not only a dim and empty likeness.... Likeness here implies not only resemblance but also a connection, a proximity, an equivalence, even an identity. A shadow, in this sense, is not simply a negative space, a space of absence; it is a likeness, an inseparable other-who-is-also-oneself to whom one is bound." Ferguson, *Global Shadows*, 16–17. Nkrumah's Ghana comes closest

to formulating an iconic language that bends the international style to the task of forging and representing an "African personality." See Hess, *Art and Architecture*, 70–90.

63. Very often, the conditions of aid specified the use of architects and construction materials from the donor country.

64. Kellner, "Ernst Bloch," 91.

65. Appadurai, *Modernity at Large*, 7

66. For Bloch, this hope derives its power from basic human needs, such as physical or metaphorical hunger. Kellner, "Ernst Bloch," 87–88. This discourse of needs presents an alternative to Achille Mbembe's bleak portrayal of the "vulgar aesthetics" of African politics, in a study that draws mainly from the 1990s. Mbembe, *On the Postcolony*, 102–41.

67. Daniel, "Reclaiming the 'Terrain of Fantasy,'" 55. Bloch's sensitive understanding of the significance of consumer desires also presents an alternative to the prevailing critique of development as the creation of false needs. See, for example, Watts, "New Deal in Emotions," 50. The best source to counter the development critics' cynicism regarding Africans' desire for development is Ferguson's account of modernity as a broken promise for equal status in the world and equal standards of living. See Ferguson, *Global Shadows*, especially 186–87.

68. Bayart, *State in Africa*, especially 70–83.

69. Diouf, "Modernity," 1478.

70. Enwezor, "Modernity and Postcolonial Ambivalence," n.p.

71. Roskam, "Non-Aligned Architecture," 267.

72. Stanek, "Architects from Socialist Countries."

73. Prakash, "Epilogue."

74. It is rarely acknowledged that Jewish architects' studies in major centers of knowledge production, such as the Bauhaus, often followed their immigration to Palestine and were therefore colored by this experience. I suggest that their professional and personal objectives in Palestine should be taken into consideration when examining their studies and the professional knowledge they brought back with them.

75. Tilley, *Africa as a Living Laboratory*, 10.

76. For the spelling of their names in English, I follow their publications.

77. For the most authoritative study of the campus to date, see Ben-Asher Gitler, "Campus Architecture as Nation Building."

### ONE. FAST-TRACKING THE NATION-STATE

1. "Buildings and Projects."

2. Massad, "'Post-Colonial' Colony," 311–46.

3. The key text that expresses the search for new monumentality is Sieg-

fried Gideon's 1944 lecture "The Need for a New Monumentality." One of the voices most critical of the UN building was Lewis Mumford. See Vale, "Designing Global Harmony."

4. Literary theorist Aamir Mufti foregrounds the "Jewish problem" in Europe as the discourse that set in motion postcolonial partitions based on ethnicity and religion. Yet it appears that the very idea of a Jewish "return" as the paradigmatic displacement of racialized populations in the name of enlightenment was preceded by another "return," namely that of freed slaves to Africa. Mufti, *Enlightenment in the Colony*, 96.

5. For a comprehensive history of Freetown's establishment, including its physical growth, see Fyfe and Jones, *Freetown*.

6. The Krio language developed from a mix of English and African languages. From this point on I will refer to the Creoles of Sierra Leone as Krio. See Wyse, *Krio of Sierra Leone*, 96–97.

7. The act of August 20, 1853, conferred the rights of natural-born British subjects on liberated Africans, namely the right to hold land and property within the colony. See Porter, *Creoledom*, 97.

8. Mamdani, *Citizen and Subject*, 18.

9. From the 1840s onward, Freetown Krio traveled in Africa, particularly Nigeria and the former Gold Coast, serving as accountants, clerks, teachers, ministers, and administrators, either independently or as agents of the government, the church, or trading companies. Porter, *Creoledom*, 57.

10. See Neuberger, "Early African Nationalism"; Echeruo, "Jewish Question."

11. Porter, *Creoledom*, 58.

12. As in the historiography of the Jewish settler society in Palestine, historians do not agree about the extent to which the Krio society was complicit with British colonialism. According to one historian, "Colony people regarded natives of the Protectorate as unredeemed savages"; the Creoles "spoke of the natives as 'aborigines,' taking the name of the Government Aborigines Department" even after the British changed the department's name in 1891. See Banton, *West African City*, 9. See Wyse, *Krio of Sierra Leone*; and Porter, *Creoledom*, for a more nuanced history of the Krios' relations with the protectorate natives.

13. Wyse, *Krio of Sierra Leone*, 104–6.

14. Everil, "Material Culture."

15. Ferme, "Staging Politisi," 120.

16. "Have You Any Idea for Our National Costume?," *Daily Mail*, December 9, 1960, 4.

17. This tradition of civic pride goes back to the early British philanthropists, who emphasized the appearance of the settlers' gardens even over the provision of food. See Peterson, "Enlightenment," 15–16.

18. On Israel's first diplomatic steps in Africa, see Levey, "Rise and Decline," 155–77. While in Nigeria the largely Muslim northern region presented Israel with a continuous diplomatic challenge, in Sierra Leone this was never an issue. On the contrary, Israel was presented in the media as an example of cooperation and tolerance. For example, Freetown's Muslim mayor, Alderman Abdul Fattah Rahman, participated in the congress of the International Union of Local Authorities held in Israel, where he was photographed conversing with Arab mayors of Israeli cities. "Mayor of Freetown at Israel Talks," *Daily Mail*, November 30, 1960, 4.

19. Quoted in *Daily Mail*, March 3, 1961, 1.

20. "Who Will Represent SA. Leone Abroad?," *Daily Mail*, May 27, 1960, 1.

21. Golda Meir visited Freetown in January 1960. Israel Representative in Monrovia to Foreign Ministry, January 15, 1960, ISA, MFA 2033/20.

22. The loan was in the sum of 193,801 British pounds (BP). Israel Bank to Israel Ministry of Treasury, August 2, 1963, ISA, MFA 3142/11. The total estimate for the parliament building's construction was 400,000 BP, of which 90,000–100,000 BP was the planned cost of stage one. The estimate, however, had already proven naïve by December 1960, and had more than doubled by March 1961. The Director of Public Works to the Permanent Secretary, Ministry of Works, December 2, 1960; Permanent Secretary's Minute Paper, January 3, 1961; the Director of Public Works to the Ministry of Works, March 14, 1961, Sierra Leone National Archive RG 4/1B/186.

23. Greenberg, "Labor's Expanding Economy," 334–35, 339.

24. Dov Karmi designed the Histadrut Headquarters in Tel Aviv (1949–53) and, in collaboration with Arieh Sharon, the Solel Boneh Tel Aviv Headquarters (mid- to late 1950s).

25. "Plans for the New House of Reps. Afoot," *Daily Mail*, August 16, 1960, 1; "Plans for the New House Submitted," *Daily Mail*, August 30, 1960, 3.

26. Karmi interview, in Yagid-Haimovich, *Dov Karmi*.

27. Tower Hill was the location of the British barracks until January 1959, when the responsibility for the administration of the Sierra Leone military forces was transferred to the government of Sierra Leone.

28. More specifically, where "the Parcel post and Telegraph Sections are and across the road including the 'Big Market' at Oxford Street," as reported by the *Daily Mail* on July 23, 1960.

29. "Market Women Object to Site for New House," *Daily Mail*, July 28, 1960, 1.

30. Kroyanker, *Jerusalem Architecture*, 94–103. Until the opening of the parliament the Israeli government convened in Fromin House on King George Street at Jerusalem's city center. The decision to allocate separate grounds away from the city center for the government facilities and national institu-

tions had to do with security and traffic considerations in addition to issues of representation.

31. Fry and Farms, *Town Planning Scheme for Freetown*, 6.

32. Fry and Farms, *Town Planning Scheme for Freetown*, 16–17.

33. Kenny, "Climate, Race, and Imperial Authority." For the Sierra Leone context, see Frenkel and Western, "Pretext or Prophylaxis?"

34. "The committee notes with regret the use of the phrase 'European and Better Class African Areas' at paragraph 3 (e) and 4 (c) of the report, and suggests that a more appropriate expression would be 'Better Class Areas.'" *Sierra Leone Interim Town Planning Committee Report* (Lagos, Nigeria: Government Printer, 1948), 7. On a list of members of the Interim Town Planning Committee, at least one name was that of a Krio. In addition to Fry's reluctance to adapt to changes in postwar colonial rhetoric, his anachronism reflected the degradation of Freetown's proud Krio society. Up to the end of the nineteenth century, there were no areas reserved exclusively for English residents in Freetown. Only at the beginning of the twentieth century was a hill station built exclusively for the white population; in the 1940s and 1950s, it admitted senior African civil servants as part of postwar colonial development policy. See Wyse, *Krio of Sierra Leone*, 95; Porter, *Creoledom*, 98–99.

35. Efrat, *Israeli Project*, 734.

36. See, for example, the case of the Hebrew University campus on Mount Scopus. A. Levin, "Mountain and Fortress," 21.

37. "Ancient Tower Declared a Relic," *Daily Mail*, October 2, 1961, 3. The water tank was part of the first plan for a piped water supply drawn in 1872. See Olu-Wright, "The Physical Growth of Freetown," 36.

38. Yonatan Amir, "Owner of Plan no. 13," *Ma'ariv*, July 26, 1957, 2 (in Hebrew).

39. "The House of Representatives," *Davar*, August 2, 1957, 23 (in Hebrew).

40. Amir, "Owner of Plan no. 13."

41. Fuchs and Herbert, "Representing Mandatory Palestine," 284–85.

42. Hattis-Rolef, "Knesset Building," 140; Kroyanker, *Jerusalem Architecture*, 106–8. See also Nitzan-Shiftan, "Contested Zionism," 154–55. Even the fact that Walter Gropius, the highly regarded pioneer of modern architecture, designed a modern Greek temple for the American embassy in Athens that same year did not attenuate the outrage. The difference between his design and that of the Knesset, however, lies in the materials used, a subject I address later in the chapter.

43. Shaul Ben-Haim, "On the Delay in Implementing the Plan," *Ma'ariv*, February 11, 1960, 3 (in Hebrew). Hattis-Rolef, "Knesset Planning."

44. "House of Representatives," 23. Hattis-Rolef, "Knesset Building," 145. The terraces were completed in 1991. Intended to accommodate growth and

change, this horizontal expansion logic was influenced by Dutch architect Aldo van Eyck's structuralism, exemplified in his Amsterdam Orphanage (1955–60), and by American architect Louis Kahn's contemporaneous design for the Jewish Community Center in Trenton, New Jersey (1954–59).

45. Karmi interview, in Yagid-Haimovich, *Dov Karmi.*

46. Elhanani et al., "Monumental Construction," 14–22. Bill Gillit, a British architect who had been Ram Karmi's classmate at the AA and joined the Knesset design team in its latter stages, also expressed this criticism. See Hattis-Rolef, "Knesset Planning," 174.

47. Hattis-Rolef, "Knesset Building," 147; Karmi interview, in Yagid-Haimovich, *Dov Karmi.*

48. Nitzan-Shiftan, "Seizing Locality."

49. Manor, *Art in Zion,* 128–65; Nitzan-Shiftan, "Contested Zionism," 163–71.

50. Eyal, *Disenchantment,* 152–84. For a periodization of the Arab village as an architectural source of inspiration in Israel/Palestine, see Yacobi and Shadar, "Arab Village."

51. Peffer, *Art,* 21.

52. Hever, *Nativism,* 3–4.

53. Karmi, *Lyric Architecture,* 46; translation mine.

54. The tension between these two temporalities is similar to what postcolonial theorist Homi K. Bhabha identifies as the nation's conflict between "the accumulative temporality of the pedagogical, and the repetitious, recursive strategy of the performative." See Bhabha, *Location of Culture,* 209.

55. Karmi's formulation is reminiscent of Frank Lloyd Wright's statement: "I knew well that no house should ever be on a hill or on anything. It should be of the hill." Quoted in Sabatino, "Spaces of Criticism," 49.

56. As in the Knesset, the sunken library draws from Alver Aalto's Viipuri Library, and the separate circulation according to audience is reminiscent of Le Corbusier's assembly hall in Chandigarh.

57. The "traditional" house in Sierra Leone is a clay and earth structure topped with a thatch roof. These houses tend to be constructed either of "wattle and daub" (in which a "wattle," or frame of poles secured by intertwined twigs and vines, is "daubed," or plastered with soft earth to cover it) or of clay and earth blocks that have been dried and hardened in the sun.

58. The very category of "laterite" is a nineteenth-century invention. According to Lucia Allais, it describes "such a wide variety of materials that it points more to the desire to unify the tropics conceptually than to their morphological coherence." Allais, *Designs of Destruction,* 284.

59. Allais, *Designs of Destruction,* 284.

60. Karmi interview.

61. Curtis, "Authenticity."

62. Karmi interview.

63. S. Shehori, "The Sierra Leone Parliament Opened on Time: Solel Boneh's Israeli Engineers Won the Race against the Clock," *Davar*, May 11, 1961.

64. Extract no. 94: Government/Israeli Construction Company (extracted from the minutes of Executive Council Meeting no. 9 of 1960, held at the Government House on Tuesday the 22nd of March, 1960), NASL RG 4/1B/142. This was not a Solel Boneh company but the Israeli-owned Liberia Construction Corporation. See the postscript for a brief history of the company.

65. The Government of Sierra Leone: Minute Paper, January 3, 1961, NASL RG 4/1B/186.

66. N. Pundak, "I Was a Guinea Pig for the Jungle," *Davar*, July 26, 1963, 3 (in Hebrew).

67. For Solel Boneh's history, see Biletzky, *Solel Boneh*.

68. Avriel, "Some Minute Circumstances," 31. As in Solel Boneh's agreement with the government of Sierra Leone, Zim owned only 40 percent of Black Star, and its management was limited to a period of five years.

69. "Israeli Trade Delegation," *Sierra Leonean*, no. 1, February 2, 1961, 4.

70. Inbal and Zahavi, *Rise and Fall*, 32.

71. The colonial administration turned to "import substitution industries" in the 1950s to preserve the local market for British transnational corporations against the importation of cheaper manufactured goods from Japan and the United States. See Dibua, *Modernization*, 156.

72. "Israeli Trade Delegation," 4. Like Solel Boneh's model of cooperation, this industrial model of cooperation was piloted in Burma. See ISA, MFA 226/5 (93); ISA, MFA 229/7 (93).

73. Chakrabarty, *Provincializing Europe*, 8.

74. Correspondence between J.C. Mitchell and Mr. Pearl, November 2, 1959–January 28, 1960, NASL RG 4/1B/142; Acting Permanent Secretary, Ministry of Works and Housing to M. Boren, March 8, 1960, NASL RG 4/1B/142.

75. Haim Darin-Drabkin, "Economic and Social Aspects of Israeli Housing," in *Public Housing in Israel* (Tel Aviv: Gadish, 1959), 78. Quoted in Kozlovsky, "Necessity by Design," 16.

76. As a 1961 survey indicates, there were approximately fifty thousand industrial employees in Sierra Leone, representing about 12 percent of the labor force, and the government was their largest employer. The total composition of employment was: public administration (including health and education) 34 percent; construction 20 percent; mining 13 percent; transportation 13 percent; commerce and private business 10 percent; waterfront 3 percent; agriculture and forestry 6 percent; defense services 1 percent. See Doudai and Oelsner, *Sierra Leone*, 64.

77. Political scientists interpret Sierra Leone's relatively peaceful transition to independence as a symptom of an ideological lethargy. According to Jimmy D.

Kandeh, Ricardo René Larémont, and Rachel Cremona, "Anticolonial nationalism in Sierra Leone never assumed the form of a transformative ideology nor did it rise above the minimum requirements of an independence movement . . . independence was neither preceded nor followed by any serious attempt to mobilize the population on the basis of a common national imaginary." Kandeh, Larémont, and Cremona, "Ethnicity and National Identity," 195. Less concerned with questions of ideology, political scientist Jeffrey Herbst claims that this peacefulness presented concrete state-building challenges. Comparing the formation of African states to that of European ones, Herbst argues that boundary disputes, war, and crisis were key to the creation of "important symbols around which a disparate population could unify and bond with the state in a manner that legitimized the capital's authority." Furthermore, war not only justified taxation but also forced leaders to become more efficient in collecting taxes. In accepting colonial boundaries that in turn are recognized and defended internationally, Herbst contends, African states lacked a sense of a "productive" crisis in their formative years. Herbst, *States and Power in Africa*, 113.

78. "The New House Will Be Ready in Time!," *Daily Mail*, September 28, 1960, 1.

79. Larkin, *Signal and Noise*, 16–47.

80. Nye, *American Technological Sublime*, 60, quoted in Larkin, *Signal and Noise*, 39.

81. Larkin, *Signal and Noise*, 39.

82. Nye, *American Technological Sublime*, 103.

83. "The New House Will Be Ready in Time!," *Daily Mail*, September 28, 1960, 1; emphasis mine.

84. Althusser, *Essays on Ideology*. Brian Larkin alludes to Althusser's concept of interpellation when he refers to technology's "ideological mode of address, hailing people as new sorts of political subjects." See Larkin, *Signal and Noise*, 43.

85. Bhabha, *Location of Culture*, 208–9. Roy Kozlovsky makes a similar argument regarding this vocational transformation via construction as a mechanism for transforming a heterogeneous group of immigrants into a proletariat, which in turn will become the "building blocks" for nation building. See Kozlovsky, "Necessity by Design," 10–27.

86. Headrick, *Tentacles of Progress*, 304–51.

87. Banton, *West African City*, 10–22, 56–58. Another important factor that added to this sense of freedom was that the hierarchical relation between Freetown the colony and the protectorate also entailed unequal taxation. Residents of Freetown, unlike their counterparts in the protectorate, were free from direct taxation during colonial times.

88. Larkin, *Signal and Noise*, 21.

89. Fanon, *Wretched of the Earth*, 141.

90. Chakrabarty, "Legacies of Bandung," 53.

91. Richard Wright, *The Color Curtain: A Report on the Bandung Conference* (New York: World, 1956), 132. Quoted in Chakrabarty, "Legacies of Bandung," 53.

92. Chakrabarty, "Legacies of Bandung," 53.

93. Fanon, *Wretched of the Earth*, 138.

94. Chakrabarty, "Legacies of Bandung," 54–55.

95. Roberts, *Anguish*, 92; emphasis mine. This attitude, however, was not limited to aid from socialist or social democratic regimes. Even the American Point Four Program employed a "grassroots" approach, according to Amanda Kay McVety, who characterized American aid in Ethiopia under Truman's administration as "intimate, farmer-by-farmer extension activities." See McVety, "Pursuing Progress," 388.

96. Laufer, *Israel*, 55–56; emphasis mine.

97. "Activities of the N.C.C.," *Daily Mail*, September 16, 1961, 6–7. A *Daily Mail* caption even referred to an Israeli photographed with a group of Sierra Leoneans as the one without a jacket. *Daily Mail*, October 5, 1960, 1.

98. *Daily Mail*, December 5, 1961, 1. The performance of African youth as Israeli pioneers extended far beyond clothing. An agriculture course in Asawa, Eritrea, opened in 1963 with the singing of "Shalom Aleichem." On top of professional literature, the Israeli staff ordered Hebrew song records for "rikudey am" (Israeli folk dance), a gramophone, tembel hats, a contoured map of Israel, and copies of "The Kibbutz Album" as gifts for the director and top students; ISA, MFA 1921/7. For an extended analysis of this multifaceted phenomenon, see Bar-Yosef, *Villa in the Jungle*, 123–84.

99. Hess, *Art and Architecture*, 141.

100. This image was hard to sustain. Israeli diplomats would often criticize Solel Boneh managers' work relations, and what they deemed was a too comfortable lifestyle. The most radical case was a strike that took place in the East Nigerian company, in protest against one Mr. Teichman, who beat the workers and called them stupid. See January 3, 1962, ISA, MFA 1908/7; January 31, 1962, ISA, MFA 1908/7. See also Bar-Yosef, *Villa in the Jungle*, 174–75. As a professional organization, Solel Boneh had its own interests that did not always correspond with the foreign ministry representative ones. This is demonstrated most clearly in a comparison of Solel Boneh and Mashav promotional films, in which the first emphasizes the machinery employed, and is reminiscent of what Nye calls the "American technological sublime," while the latter focuses on African and Israeli youth working side by side, constructing a school in an African village. See *Solel Boneh Overseas* (place unknown, c. 1964), DVD, SSJFA; David Eldan, *Shalom Africa* (place and date unknown), DVD, SSJFA.

101. Banton, *West African City*, 9.

102. Wyse, *Krio of Sierra Leone*, 109.

103. Cooper, *Decolonization and African Society*, 422.

104. Reuven Barkatt, opening address of the First Afro-Asian Seminar, Tel Aviv, November 20, 1958, LA IV-104-38-104. Reprinted in Aynor, Avimor, and Kaminer, *Role of the Israel Labour Movement*, 2; translation mine.

105. Aynor, Avimor, and Kaminer, *Role of the Israel Labour Movement*, 2; translation mine.

106. Aynor, Avimor, and Kaminer, *Role of the Israel Labour Movement*, 4; emphasis and translation mine. However, this zeal derived most of its ethos and raison d'être from the prestate period. Even Mapai's most zealous members admitted that importing its model to young African countries would be anachronistic.

107. Frenkel, Shenhav, and Herzog, "Political Embeddedness," 138. This "affective concept of productivity" should be distinguished from the concept of "Affective Labor" that Michael Hardt uses to describe industries, such as those of service and care, that produce affects rather than concrete products. See Hardt, "Affective Labor." While Hardt locates the affect in the product, Frenkel, Shenhav, and Hertzog locate it at the level of the producers.

108. Frenkel, Shenhav, and Herzog, "Political Embeddedness," 130, 132–33. On the figure of the Jewish pioneer, see Near, "Pioneers and Pioneering in the State of Israel," and Near, "Like All Nations? Zionist Pioneering in Intercultural Perspective."

109. Frenkel, Shenhav, and Herzog, "Political Embeddedness," 7.

110. Svorai, "Solel Bone," 126–27.

111. Meltzer interview.

112. Chibber, *Postcolonial Theory*, 112, 140–42.

113. Meltzer interview.

114. Chakrabarty, *Provincializing Europe*, 56.

115. The Director of Public Works, House of Representatives, February 1, 1961, NASL RG 4/1B/186.

116. Greenberg, "Labor's Expanding Economy," 338–40.

117. "New House Will Be Ready," 1.

118. Meltzer interview.

119. Hashimshony, "Architecture," 205–6.

120. Hattis-Rolef, "Knesset Building," 142.

121. Eli Eyal, "Shlomo Gur's Building Methods," *Ha'aretz*, March 4, 1960 (in Hebrew). See also Hattis-Rolef, "Knesset Planning," 173.

122. Rotbard, "Wall and Tower," 46.

123. See Svorai, "Solel Bone," 63; Biletzky, *Solel Boneh*, 235; Dan, *On the Unpaved Road*, 125.

124. Rotbard, "Wall and Tower," 51. Rotbard characterizes this performance of production as a masterful hyperactivity: the forceful changing of the face of

the land in order to claim it as their own. This characterization is comparable to what Sarah Hinsky has described as the fetish of work in Israeli art. See Hinsky, "Silence of the Fish," 110.

125. Rotbard, "Wall and Tower," 53.

126. Efrat, *Israeli Project*, 372.

127. The fact that the nickname was in Arabic demonstrates the pervasiveness of the Arab ruins that dotted the state as a result of the 1948 war. The term *hirbe*, which derives from *al-kharab* in Arabic, is close to the Hebrew *hurva*, and became common parlance.

128. Efrat, *Israeli Project*, 733–34.

129. Meltzer interview.

130. Meltzer interview; "Freetown Gets New Road," *Daily Mail*, January 19, 1961.

131. Bar-Yosef, *Villa in the Jungle*, 163.

132. Similarly, the failures of Nahal (youth frontier settlement) projects were explained by the aid personnel's enthusiasm, overexcitement, and eagerness for action. See Bar-Yosef, *Villa in the Jungle*, 166–67.

133. In its visibility and provisional but unsustainable success, Solel Boneh's mode of operation was similar to that of Israeli aid agricultural projects that focused on demonstration farms that had limited implications beyond their boundaries. See Schwartz and Hare, *Foreign Experts*.

134. Aryeh Levin to Asia-Africa Division, Foreign Ministry, July 29, 1963, ISA, MFA 1903/12 A.

135. Minister of Finance to Prime Minister, November 23, 1960, NASL RG 4/1B/142.

136. The Quantity Surveyors' Report, January 7, 1961, NASL RG 4/1B/186; A. P. Atkinson to the Ministry of Finance, March 1, 1961, NASL RG 4/1B/186.

137. D. F. Pearl to the Ministry of Finance, November 14, 1960, NASL RG 4/1B/186.

138. Svorai, "Solel Bone"; Greenberg, "Labor's Expanding Economy," 331.

139. Greenberg, "Labor's Expanding Economy," 340. Armstrong, March 3, 1961, NASL RG 4/1B/186.

140. Armstrong, March 3, 1961, NASL RG 4/1B/186.

141. Foreign Ministry correspondence, ISA, MFA 1763/6. Such oversights and failures were also part and parcel of the process of the Knesset construction in Israel. In 1960, while also orchestrating the construction of the Hadassah Hospital and the Hebrew University campus in Givat Ram, Shlomo Gur was accused of mistakenly paving a road in the wrong place and of budget irregularities. See Ben-Haim, "On the Delay."

142. Davidson, *Black Man's Burden*, 185.

143. H. J. Lightfoot Boston, "Parliament Building Will Inspire Deliberations towards Good Government," *Sierra Leonean*, May 4, 1961, 9; emphasis mine.

144. Ministry of Works to Ministry of Finance, March 9, 1961, NASL RG 4/1B/186.

145. Karmi interview.

146. Kulagbanda interview.

147. Kulagbanda interview. See also Rama Musa, "The Al-Aqsa of Africa," *Tablet Magazine,* January 3, 2013.

148. Appel, "Walls and White Elephants."

## TWO. ROOTEDNESS AND OPEN-ENDED PLANNING

1. Meeting at the Tel Aviv Engineering Club, December 27, 1963, ISA, MFA 1898/16.

2. The planning projects the IPD had been involved in by the time Doudai received the Sierra Leone national urbanization plan commission included preliminary reports for three regions and a study of housing problems in Cote d'Ivoire; an overall survey of land, urban centers, and their surroundings in the Republic of Chad and the Central African Republic; a national plan and master plans for a few principal towns in Nyasaland; and an agriculture school and farm in Upper Volta. In addition, the institute was negotiating the drafting of a national plan and master plans for towns based on preliminary studies it had already conducted in Uganda and Ethiopia, the planning of agricultural regions in Tanganyika, pilot projects for low-cost housing in Uganda's capital, Kampala, and consulting on housing problems in Latin America through the Centre of Regional Planning in Venezuela. In Sierra Leone, the institute had already conducted a reconnaissance survey, with particular emphasis on town planning and housing problems in Freetown, and submitted preliminary master plans for Freetown and several provincial towns. See "The Aim of the Institute for Planning and Development LTD and Its Current Activities," n.d. [December 1965], ISA, MFA 496/8. The IPD had very little ability to control architects who left to take private commissions. For example, Shmuel Giron, who planned agricultural settlements in East Nigeria for the IPD, later returned to Nigeria as a private planner, despite attempts to stop him. See Israel Embassy in Lagos to Foreign Ministry, December 31, 1963, ISA, MFA 1932/14; A. Shlush to Foreign Ministry, March 16, 1965, ISA, MFA 3569/22. This was no longer a problem after 1967, when the IPD reorganized and began offering its services in the private market.

3. IPD AMY Agreement, undated, ISA, MFA 496/8. (Though undated, this document appears to be from sometime around May 16, 1963.)

4. "Aim of the Institute."

5. The same is true of negotiations with East African countries, which were mostly based on a self-initiated study tour that an IPD representative took.

6. See, for example, IPD Board Meeting no. 11, October 24, 1963, ISA, MFA 1898/16.

7. UN Department of Economic and Social Affairs, "Report of the Ad Hoc Group of Experts on Housing and Urban Development" (New York: United Nations, February 7–21, 1962).

8. Despite Doudai's prominence as planner, very little is known about him. Even less is known about Ursula Oelsner, his collaborator on this and other projects. A recent article sheds some light on their biographies. See Yacobi and Misgav, "Geo-Biographies," 1388–90. For convenience's sake, I will refer henceforth to Doudai as the plan's primary author.

9. Yehuda Tamir to Aryeh Doudai and Nelly Levin, November 12, 1963, ISA, MFA 1898/16.

10. Sierra Leone Government, *Ten-Year Plan*; Sierra Leone Government, *Draft, Five-Year Plan of Economic and Social Development, July 1, 1966–June 30, 1971*.

11. Rina Gutman to Yehuda Tamir, November 21, 1965, ISA, MFA 469/8; Review of IPD Activities no. 3, updated to April 1, 1965, ISA, MFA 469/8; Report on Doudai's West Africa Tour, March 3–27, 1964, ISA, MFA 469/7 (130).

12. Scott, *Seeing Like a State*.

13. Lévi-Strauss, *Savage Mind*, 1–22.

14. I borrow the definition of the region as a flexible spatial-temporal unit from Ijlal Muzaffar's analysis of the joint Venezuelan-American planning of Ciudad Guayana in Venezuela. See Muzaffar, "Fuzzy Images," 315.

15. Harris and Parnell, "Turning Point," 131.

16. Harris and Parnell, "Turning Point," 132, 139–40.

17. Dutta, "Linguistics," 10; Muzaffar, "Periphery Within," 286.

18. Doudai and Oelsner, *Sierra Leone*, 4.

19. Doudai and Oelsner, *Sierra Leone*, 4.

20. Herbst, *States and Power*, 78.

21. See chapter 1.

22. Njoh and Akiwumi, "Colonial Legacies," 214.

23. Njoh, "Urban Planning," 312. Doudai and Oelsner, *Sierra Leone*, 38, 40.

24. Bo, the second largest city in Sierra Leone, is located in the geographical center of the country. See Michael A. O. Johnson, "An Assessment of Physical Planning and Planning in Freetown and the Regional Towns," June 14, 2011, first draft, prepared as part of the current Urban Planning Project funded by the European Union Commission Delegation to Sierra Leone. There is no mention of any plans made for Bo in a 1969 UN report that reviewed planning in the country for the purposes of planning water supply. See Yagale, "Report."

25. Reichman, *From an Outpost*, 91.

26. A. Sharon, *Physical Planning in Israel*, 6.

27. A. Sharon, *Physical Planning in Israel*, 6; translation mine. This preference for European precedents may date back to the period from 1880 to 1930 and the early, prestate model of colonization that Ilan Troen characterizes as antihistoric and romantic. See Troen, *Imagining Zion*, 15–41.

28. At the turn of the century, the withdrawal of Baron de Rothschild's funding, which had financed the first immigrant waves and settlements, entailed a shift to a system of independent agents and institutions in the region. While this transition from centralized European control to local management "was initially conceived in purely economic terms, the reformulation of settlement policy and administration quickly devolved into a cultural project of reframing land as the product of Jewish work." Zakim, *To Build*, 59.

29. Troen, *Imagining Zion*, 73.

30. See chapter 1. Troen, *Imagining Zion*, 62–63.

31. Reichman, *From an Outpost*, 240–41.

32. Quoted in S. Sharon, "Not Settlers but Settled," 92; translation mine.

33. A. Sharon, *Physical Planning in Israel*, 6. For a critique of the coerced settlement that the plan assumed, and its prioritization of defense over economic concerns, see Efrat, *Israeli Project*, 456.

34. A. Sharon, *Physical Planning in Israel*, 6.

35. Mabogunje, "Urban Planning," 129–31. Alongside Christaller's "Central Place Theory," Mabogunje mentions theories from the 1950s by the German August Lösch and the "growth pole strategy" of the French economist François Perroux. On Christaller's influence in Israel despite his association with the Nazi regime, see Golan, "Central Place Theory"; Efrat, *Israeli Project*, 998–1000.

36. Rössler, "Applied Geography," 419–31.

37. Barnes and Minca, "Nazi Spatial Theory," 674.

38. Bassin, "Race contra Space," 123.

39. Barnes and Minca, "Nazi Spatial Theory," 672–74.

40. Schwartz and Hare, *Foreign Experts*, 13.

41. Raanan Weitz studied agricultural economics at the University of Florence during the fascist regime and was influenced by contemporary Italian agricultural settlement schemes. He was particularly influenced by the internal colonization scheme in the Pontine Marshes that was conceived and implemented by his professor, Arrigo Serpieri. See Forester, Fischler, and Shmueli, *Israeli Planners and Designers*, 320; S. Sharon, "Importing and Translating"; S. Sharon, "Not Settlers but Settled," 80–88. On the Pontine Marshes, see Caprotti, *Mussolini's Cities*; Caprotti, "Destructive Creation"; Caprotti, "Internal Colonisation"; Caprotti and Kaïka, "Producing the Ideal Fascist Landscape."

42. S. Sharon, "Not Settlers but Settled," 54–55.

43. S. Sharon, "Not Settlers but Settled," 43–44; on the Israel Defense Forces' involvement in civilian planning, see 56–59.

44. Abreek-Zubiedat, "Architecture in Conflict," 79–82.

45. S. Sharon, "Not Settlers but Settled," 43, 45, 88–90, 142–45.

46. Escobar, *Encountering Development*, 79.

47. Yacobi, *Israel and Africa*, 28–35; Bar-Yosef, *Villa in the Jungle*, 123–84.

48. IPD Board Meeting no. 15, October 26, 1964, ISA, MFA 469/7 (130).

49. Doudai and Oelsner, *Sierra Leone*, 32.

50. Otto Koenigsberger to Aharon Remez, July 6, 1962, ISA, MFA 1908/18. In this letter, addressed from Lagos after his second visit to Israel in April and May 1962, Koenigsberger explains that, because he found Israel's experience in the settlement of newcomers valuable to other countries, he wanted to extend his research in Israel to include settlements in cities and to publish a study addressed to administrators and politicians as well as an academic audience. For more on this visit, see ISA, MFA 1900/5. The date of Koenigsberger's first visit to Israel is unknown. He may have informally attended the International Housing Seminar held in Kefar Vitkin, Israel, from May 4 to June 15, 1960; its program included Ernest Weissmann and Oscar Niemeyer. For details of the conference, see ISA, MFA 2025/18.

51. A. Sharon, *Physical Planning in Israel*, 5. Time is the third element after "the country" and "the people."

52. S. Sharon, "Planners," 31–57.

53. Forester, Fischler, and Shmueli, *Israeli Planners and Designers*, 325.

54. Weitz, interview by Shimeon Amir, 25.

55. S. Sharon, "Not Settlers but Settled," 113–14.

56. S. Sharon, "Not Settlers but Settled," 113–14. Immigrants were accommodated in provisional housing, and jobs were created for them haphazardly. See S. Sharon, "Not Settlers but Settled," 127, 141.

57. Forester, Fischler, and Shmueli, *Israeli Planners and Designers*, 323.

58. S. Sharon, "Not Settlers but Settled," 113.

59. Meeting at the Tel Aviv Engineering Club.

60. Abrams, Kobe, and Koenigsberger, "Growth and Urban Renewal," 94.

61. Avermaete, "Framing the Afropolis," 97.

62. Olaiya, "Systemic Shifts," 190; Beeckmans, "French Planning," 63, 69.

63. Doudai, "Relationship," 3; emphasis mine.

64. Meeting at the Tel Aviv Engineering Club. Raanan Weitz, too, attributed his planning experience to the fact that by the age of thirty-six he had experienced two wars. See Forester, Fischler, and Shmueli, *Israeli Planners and Designers*, 319.

65. Meeting at the Tel Aviv Engineering Club.

66. Doudai and Oelsner, *Sierra Leone*, 5.

67. Meeting at the Tel Aviv Engineering Club; translation mine.

68. Horowitz and Lissak, *Origins of the Israeli Polity*, 149. On the tension between pioneering and professional, technical expertise, see also Kahane, "Dominant Ideology's Stances," 181–236; Penslar, *Israel in History*, 150–66.

69. Meeting at the Tel Aviv Engineering Club.

70. Scott, *Seeing Like a State*, 310; emphasis mine.

71. Scott, *Seeing Like a State*, 311, 313–15.

72. Scott, *Seeing Like a State*, 323, 331–32. While criticizing the binary opposition created between these two forms of knowledge, Scott nonetheless still retains the distinction between scientific and practical knowledge, or "the art of the locality." See Scott, *Seeing Like a State*, 316–17.

73. Scott, *Seeing Like a State*, 311.

74. Schwartz and Hare, *Foreign Experts*, 19.

75. Lévi-Strauss, *Savage Mind*, 19–21.

76. Malkhin and Goldberg, *Israel's Relations*, 46.

77. Paraphrased by Doudai. Meeting at the Tel Aviv Engineering Club.

78. Schwartz and Hare, *Foreign Experts*, 13; S. Sharon, "Not Settlers but Settled," 155–87.

79. Doudai and Oelsner, *Sierra Leone*, 60, 62.

80. Ekbladh, "Mr. TVA," 345.

81. Doudai and Oelsner, *Sierra Leone*, 4–5; emphasis mine.

82. Lindblom, "Muddling Through," 81.

83. Sierra Leone Government, *Ten-Year Plan*, 5; emphasis mine.

84. IPD Board Meeting no. 23, November 24, 1966, ISA, MFA 2899/19.

85. Lévi-Strauss, *Savage Mind*, 19–21.

86. Porter, "The Homesickness of Development Discourse," 72.

87. For the complete itinerary of Mead's visit to Israel, see Lev, "Mission in Israel," 232–34.

88. "Margaret Mead Did Not Understand . . . ," *Ma'ariv*, June 14, 1965, 4 (in Hebrew). Another version of this story can be found in Eliyahu Agers, "Staying on Top of It," *Davar*, March 6, 1970, 8 (in Hebrew).

89. Muzaffar, "Periphery Within," 297–99, 301–2.

90. Arieh Doudai to Nelly Levin, May 10, 1964, ISA, MFA 469/7.

91. For the board's discussion of the plan's circulation, see IPD Board Meeting no. 12, November 26, 1963, ISA, MFA 1898/16; IPD Board Meeting no. 23.

92. Matless, "Regional Surveys," 469.

93. Apthorpe, "Development Policy Discourse," 381–82.

94. Njoh and Akiwumi, "Colonial Legacies," 211–13.

95. Mabogunje and Faniran, *Regional Planning*, xi.

96. Weitz, interview by Shimeon Amir, 25.

97. These organic shapes are reminiscent of Arieh Sharon's "neighborhood units" in development towns. See A. Sharon, *Physical Planning in Israel*. The organic form allowed future changes to the shape of the region following shifts

in the Lakhish region's boundaries that were caused by the challenges of municipal administrative zones. See S. Sharon, "Not Settlers but Settled," 100–107.

98. Doudai identified urban potentialities in four towns besides Freetown: adjacent Magburaka and Makeni as centers of the northeast region, Kenema in the southeast, and Bo at the center of the southern region. Doudai and Oelsner, *Sierra Leone*, 82. Bonthe and Moyamba, administrative towns in the thinly populated southwest, are indicated on the map as secondary centers, as are Kambia in the northwest and Kabala, which was the administrative headquarters of its district, in the far northeast. The fact that the five regions do not cover the whole territory and leave blank areas in their midst further suggests that population concentration and planning flexibility were determining factors in the delineation of the regions.

99. Cupers, "*Géographie Volontaire*," 9

100. Doudai and Oelsner, *Sierra Leone*, 90.

101. Sharon, "Not Settlers but Settled," 103.

102. Doudai and Oelsner, *Sierra Leone*, 80.

103. Doudai and Oelsner, *Sierra Leone*, 82.

104. Doudai and Oelsner, *Sierra Leone*, 88; emphasis mine.

105. Doudai and Oelsner, *Sierra Leone*, 90.

106. Ajayi, "Expectations of Independence," 4.

107. At this point the prime minister was Albert Margai, Milton Margai's brother. The other powerful ethnic group in Sierra Leone is the Temne.

108. Doudai and Oelsner, *Sierra Leone*, 42.

109. Foucault, *Security, Territory, Population*.

110. Weitz, interview by Shimeon Amir, 25. See also S. Sharon, "Not Settlers but Settled," 103.

111. Phokaides, "Rural Networks," 471–97.

112. IPD Board Meeting no. 22, June 23, 1966, ISA, MFA 2899/19; IPD Board Meeting no. 23.

113. For the bitter correspondence between IPD managers and the government, see ISA, MFA 2899/19.

114. ISA, MFA 2899/19. This decision was made at the government level. Starting in 1967, the IPD expanded its relationships with American public and private companies extensively. Victor Gruen Associated offered it a partnership for works outside of Canada and the United States, beginning with a project in Bangkok. These negotiations started in October 1967 via USAID and the Israeli embassy in Washington. Israeli embassy in Washington to Jerusalem, Cable 54, October 1967, ISA, MFA 2899/19; Mordechai Lador to S. Dror, May 28, 1967, ISA, MFA 2899/19.

115. Y. Horowitz to M. Lador, August 22, 1971, ISA, MFA 4380/10. There is no evidence that the new plan was ever drafted. Architect Tommy Leitersdorf, who was involved in the 1960s in the planning of Abidjan's Riviera and was

invited to participate in this project according to the correspondence, has no recollection of it. Leitersdorf interview.

116. Retired planners in Sierra Leone still hold the IPD in high esteem. Mouna interview.

### THREE. PLANNING A POSTCOLONIAL UNIVERSITY CAMPUS

1. Niyi Egbe, "Memoirs of Times at 50 Year Old Great Ife," *Nigeria Village Square* (February 24, 2012), accessed July 17, 2014, http://www.nigeriavillagesquare.com/ojukwu-memoirs-of-times-at-50-year-old-great-ife.html.

2. In addition to the Israeli team, which was in charge of the master plan and many of the buildings in the representative core, as well as the agriculture faculty and the students' halls, other firms were commissioned for specific projects, including the English firms Fry, Drew, and Atkinson and James Cubitt, as well as the local Design Group. In the 1970s, following the government's introduction of policies to Nigerianize all foreign companies, Solel Boneh's planning and design subcompany, AMY, partnered with architect Augustine Akhuemokhan Egbor (1924–2011), who headed the Public Works Department in the 1950s and was the president of the Nigerian Association of Architects from 1968 to 1970.

3. Omosini and Adediran, *Great Ife*, 14. See also Oluwasanmi, "Preservation," 11.

4. De Kiewiet, *Emergent African University*, 3.

5. Omosini and Adediran, *Great Ife*, 6–10.

6. Hannan Yavor to the Division of International Aid, November 18, 1960, ISA, MFA 2031/12.

7. Chief Obafemi Awolowo was committed to public education even prior to independence, starting free primary education in the region in the 1950s. Omosini and Adediran, *Great Ife*, 4.

8. Akintoye, *Ten Years*, 13–14.

9. Akintoye, *Ten Years*, 21–25.

10. Omosini and Adediran, *Great Ife*, 11–12.

11. Israel's loan was 3 million BP (8.4 million USD), repayable in seven years at ½ percent above the UK Bank Rate, which, at the time of the agreement, was 5 percent. The commonwealth's loan was 12 million BP, repayable in twenty years at ¾ percent above the rate, and the International Bank's loan was 10 million BP, repayable in sixteen years at ¼ percent above rate. Federal Government Dabates [sic], Overseas Loans, April 2 1962, ISA, MFA 3142/11.

12. UCI admitted, at best, a third of the qualified students from the western region by the mid-1950s. By the 1960s, the pressure on enrollment became more acute due to the rapid expansion of secondary education in the western region. Omosini and Adediran, *Great Ife*, 4–6.

13. Omosini and Adediran, *Great Ife*, 7.

14. Omosini and Adediran, *Great Ife*, 9.
15. Omosini and Adediran, *Great Ife*, 4.
16. Omosini and Adediran, *Great Ife*, 10.
17. When the University Planning Committee was established on October 21, 1960, it comprised Chief Awolowo, D. S. Onabamiro, S. G. Ikoku, and H. A. Oluwasanmi—all members of the Action Group. By January 1961, the committee expanded to include other interest groups. The committee met four times and took far-reaching decisions on the university's siting, physical development, academic programs, and finance. In addition, Premier Chief Akintola set up an unofficial committee of intellectuals, regardless of party affiliation. See Omosini and Adediran, *Great Ife*, 10–12; and *White Paper on the Establishment of a University in Western Nigeria*, NAN PR/D17. According to Omosini and Adediran, the white paper was published in July 1960. However, other evidence suggests that it was published in November 1960.
18. In lieu of an official representative, and due to increased activity around negotiations and the establishment of the joint company, an Israeli foreign ministry representative was stationed undercover in Lagos, posing as a Dizengoff West Africa employee. See Ehud Avriel to Asia-Africa Division, Foreign Ministry, August 27, 1958, ISA, MFA 1951/5. This close relationship would later become a source of embarrassment, as Dizengoff was condemned for operating as "a second embassy" and interfering with diplomacy.
19. The volume of Israel's trade with British West Africa from 1955 to 1957 reached $3.7 million, and by early 1958 nearly $670,000 of that sum was in the form of commerce with the western region of Nigeria. Levey, *Israel in Africa*, 91.
20. Solel Boneh Board Meeting no. 4/62, May 2, 1962, LA IV-204-4-536.
21. Levey, *Israel in Africa*, 91.
22. Levey, *Israel in Africa*, 91.
23. Ehud Avriel to the Foreign Ministry, Jerusalem, October 15, 1958, ISA, MFA 1951/6.
24. "Memorandum and Articles of Association," article RR, September 29, 1959, Ministry of Works, Ibadan; Solel Boneh Board Meeting no. 1/63, June 1, 1963, LA IV-204-4-536.
25. Ehud Avriel to Simkha Golan, November 27, 1958, ISA, MFA 3114/16.
26. Solel Boneh Overseas: End of the Year 1960 Review, LA IV-204-4-536. Compare the number of Solel Boneh personnel in the western region of Nigeria to those in Cyprus (14), Turkey (75), Ghana (45), East Nigeria (20), Sierra Leone (17), Burma (10), Ethiopia (32), and Iran (45).
27. Young, *Ideology*, 227.
28. Quoted in Akinsanya, "Former Western Nigeria Development Corporation," 30.
29. Osaghae, *Crippled Giant*, 48–49. In 1965, there were 115 joint ventures, in 73 of which expatriate interests held controlling shares.

30. In 1964, 62 percent of foreign- and state-owned industry was situated in these areas. See Young, *Ideology,* 229; Osaghae, *Crippled Giant,* 49.

31. A. Tzur to the Foreign Ministry, Jerusalem, December 29, 1958, ISA, MFA 1951/6.

32. The Eastern Nigeria Construction and Furniture Company was established in November 1959, with 51 percent of the company shares held by the government of East Nigeria, and the remaining 49 percent by Solel Boneh. Its projects included East Nigeria's parliament, two hotels, and glass and beer factories. Israeli Embassy in Nigeria Weekly Report, August 3, 1964, ISA, MFA 3569/23. The company was dissolved following the Nigerian Civil War (1967–70).

33. Young, *Ideology,* 226–27.

34. A. Tzur to the Foreign Ministry; translation mine.

35. Solel Boneh Board Meeting no. 13/61, November 20, 1961, LA IV-204-4-536.

36. Following the military coup in 1966, Solel Boneh sold its shares in Nigersol to the Nigerian government; the company went bankrupt in 1971. Solel Boneh continued to work on the university's construction as a private company. Solel Boneh Overseas: Review 1973, LA IV-104-38-104.

37. "Memorandum and Articles of Association," article RR. The document states the company's commitment to expand to various markets and serve as a marketing agent for various products. There is even very little evidence that the prime activity of the company was construction.

38. Avriel to Golan, November 27, 1958; translation mine.

39. Hannan Yavor to the Foreign Ministry, Jerusalem, January 7, 1959, ISA, MFA 3114/12.

40. Aide Memoire, July 13, 1960, ISA, MFA 3142/11.

41. Chief Festus Sam Okotie-Eboh, July 20, 1962, ISA, MFA 3142/11.

42. Hannan Yavor to the Foreign Ministry, Jerusalem, ISA, MFA 2031/12.

43. This was not without objection. Nigersol began clearing the bush based on a noncommittal meeting in Jerusalem, held during a visit from the Nigerian minister of labor and minister of education, who were finishing a tour that included the United States, Mexico, and Brazil. It seems that the minister of education, Dr. S. D. Onabamiro, wished to start preparing the site, while the minister of labor was not ready to turn the entire operation over to Nigersol and Solel Boneh's planning team (AMY). S. Y. Momoh to S. D. Onabamiro, January 20, 1961, AAAC, ASE.

44. Yeruham Cohen to Ehud Avriel, September 9, 1959, ISA, MFA 1951/5; Solel Boneh Board Meeting no. 13/61, November 20, 1961, LA IV-204-4-536.

45. Solel Boneh Board Meeting no. 13/61.

46. Rosoff was also commissioned for a hotel in the eastern region; he arrived there on November 22, 1960, according to the *Daily Express.*

47. Occasionally, Solel Boneh in-house architects were assigned to such jobs; for example, Stephen Dunsky designed the extension for the Presidential Hotel in East Nigeria, and Mordechai Mone designed a hotel in Yaoundé, Cameroon, and the Teheran Hilton. Solel Boneh Bulletin no. 44 (1/70), May 1970, LA IV-104-38-104.

48. Hannan Yavor to the Division of International Aid, Foreign Ministry, Jerusalem, November 28, 1960. The eastern region's government had already promised the construction work to local contractors. Al Mansfeld's model accompanied the University of Nigeria's publications, but eventually English architect James Cubitt was awarded the project. Perhaps in order to compensate him, he was included initially, and only briefly, in the team of architects for the Ife campus. See the University of Nigeria: Plan of Work, Official Document no. 1 of 1960, NAN, UNIV 2/6; Al Mansfeld to Nnamdi Azikiwe, December 1, 1960, ISA, MFA 2031/12; Anna Teut, *Al Mansfeld, an Architect in Israel* (Berlin: Ernst and Sohn, 1999), 93–94; M. Spitz to A. Sharon and B. Idelson, September 7, 1961, AAAC, ASE; "University of Nigeria."

49. Hannan Yavor to the Division of International Aid, Foreign Ministry, Jerusalem, November 28, 1960. Planning was perceived as a way to boost a project's net worth. See Yaakov Shor, "Israeli Contractorship Overseas," paper given in the Israeli Center for Management on June 27, 1968, LA, IV-204-4-1603 (in Hebrew).

50. Omosini and Adediran, *Great Ife*, 10.

51. Mabogunje, *Urbanization in Nigeria*, 200.

52. *White Paper*, article 3, 3, NAN PR/D17.

53. Arieh Sharon to Dr. D. S. Onabamiro, November 22, 1960, AAAC, ASE. Sharon's visit coincided with a petition signed in October 14, 1960, by a group of university professors in the western region that called to locate the university in Ife. See Akintoye, *Ten Years*, 3.

54. This focus had already been decided in October 1960. See Extracts from the 1st Meeting of the Western Region University Planning Committee, October 21, 1960, AAAC, ASE.

55. Arieh Sharon to Chief S. L. Akintola, February 12, 1961, AAAC, ASE. As Sharon explained in a private conversation, the decision was political as much as professional and was made by a local chief. Harold Rubin and Miriam Keini interview. According to Omosini and Adediran, a parcel of land of about 13,850 hectares had been acquired by October 1960, prior to Sharon's first and second reports.

See Omosini and Adediran, *Great Ife*, 13.

56. Following this tour, Sharon repeated his previous conclusions with only slight modulations in the figures for expected student enrollment, which rose from 3,000 to 3,000–5,000; for the expected growth of the town, which rose from 150,000 people to 150,000–152,000 people; and for the distance between

the university and the town, which was reduced from two or three miles to one or two miles, thus giving up on the idea of urban development around the university. Going beyond Sharon's previous conclusions, however, this report went on to suggest specific sites around the town of Ife, including the area to the northwest that was eventually selected, as most recommended for the campus.

57. Sharon to Akintola.

58. Sharon to Akintola.

59. Arieh Sharon to Dr. D. S. Onabamiro, November 22, 1960, AAAC, ASE.

60. Sharon to Akintola.

61. In handwritten notes added to the printed report, date unknown.

62. Mabogunje, *Urbanization in Nigeria*, 115.

63. Omosini and Adediran, *Great Ife*, 12–13.

64. On Southern Nigeria land tenure systems, see Oluwasanmi, *Agriculture*, 23–31, 37–47.

65. Notable examples include the first vice-chancellor of the University of Ife, professor Oladele Ajose, who had been the first African professor at UCI and also acted as head of its Department of Preventive and Social Medicine; Dr. S. O. Biobaku, who had been UCI's registrar and became the pro-vice-chancellor (deputy vice-chancellor) at the University of Ife. Professor Ajose was succeeded by vice-chancellor Hezekiah Oluwasanmi, who was a lecturer at UCI when he was appointed to the planning committee for the western regional university. See Ajayi and Tamuno, *University of Ibadan*, 40. Omosini and Adediran, *Great Ife*, 14.

66. Livsey, "Suitable Lodgings for Students," 664–65; Ajayi and Tamuno, *University of Ibadan*, 20.

67. Ajayi and Tamuno, *University of Ibadan*, 14–16.

68. Ajayi and Tamuno, *University of Ibadan*, 24–25. A testament to the chiefs' involvement in promoting and sponsoring education is the fact that they did not sell the land but rented it for 999 years for a nominal fee.

69. Ajayi and Tamuno, *University of Ibadan*, 13–14. The authors attribute the high rate of failure at the college to the limited positions available in the government departments. See also Livsey, "Suitable Lodgings for Students," 671.

70. Ajayi and Tamuno, *University of Ibadan*, 18–19.

71. Ajayi and Tamuno, *University of Ibadan*, 29.

72. Various sources disagree on the precise number, which varies from 2,550 to 2,982 acres. The original desired number was 3,230 acres. See Mellanby, *Birth of Nigeria's University*, 70.

73. Ajayi and Tamuno, *University of Ibadan*, 28.

74. Omosini and Adediran, *Great Ife*, 4.

75. Ajayi and Tamuno, *University of Ibadan*, 24.

76. These points are demonstrated in a film produced by the British

Petroleum Company that depicts the arrival of three Nigerian students from each of the three administrative regions, the northern, western, and eastern, respectively. In this film, the modernized campus facilitates the students' carefree lifestyle, which is free of ethnic and regional distinction. This lifestyle was carefully enabled by UCI's facilities; the film shows a university club that minimizes the students' need to go to town. "Three Roads to Tomorrow" (1958), Colonial Film, accessed October 13, 2014, http://www.colonialfilm.org.uk/node/475.

77. Ajayi and Tamuno, *University of Ibadan*, 25.

78. Ajayi and Tamuno, *University of Ibadan*, 38; Livsey, "Suitable Lodgings for Students," 672.

79. Turner, *Campus*, 10.

80. Ajayi and Tamuno, *University of Ibadan*, 25; Livsey, "Suitable Lodgings for Students," 665.

81. Quoted in Ajayi and Tamuno, *University of Ibadan*, 27.

82. Ajayi and Tamuno, *University of Ibadan*, 28.

83. Ajayi and Tamuno, *University of Ibadan*, 24–26.

84. Sharon to Onabamiro.

85. Egboramy, Arieh Sharon, and Eldar Sharon, *The 1980–85 Master Plan* Vol. 1; *University Brief: A Survey Report*, 10, Obafemi Awolowo University, Planning Department Archive (hereafter cited as *Master Plan 1980–85*).

86. Sharon to Onabamiro.

87. *Master Plan 1980–85*, 10. Currently there are more than twenty thousand undergraduate students and six thousand graduate students.

88. Dr. M. S. Randhawa, "Agricultural Universities in India—Progress and Problems," The Agricultural Division of the National Association of State Universities and Land Grant Colleges, Washington, November 12, 1968, accessed December 28, 2014, http://pdf.usaid.gov/pdf_docs/PNABJ266.pdf. See also Goldsmith, "Management of Institutional Innovation," 317–30.

89. An important distinction, however, is that in Nigeria the appropriated land was not meant to be sold for capital, as in the United States, but was to be used directly as a site for agricultural experimentation.

90. Agency for International Development, "Three Nigerian Universities," AID Project Impact Evaluation Report no. 66, Washington, March 1988. In addition to USAID, American involvement included the Ford Foundation, the Rockefeller Foundation, and the African-American Institute. See Oluwasanmi, *March Forward*, 8; Oluwasanmi, *Address*, 6.

91. However, as at UCI, the University of Nigeria's degrees were conferred by the University of London and Michigan State University, and most of its faculty was foreign. According to Israeli Foreign Ministry correspondence, the university requested Israeli faculty since its leadership did not want all staff to be from Western countries but also wanted to limit Indian personnel. See the

University of Nigeria: Plan of Work; Gideon Yarden to the Division of International Cooperation, the Foreign Ministry, July 30, 1962, ISA, MFA 1912/1.

92. Ajayi and Tamuno, *University of Ibadan*, 16.

93. British involvement was mediated through the Inter-University Council of England, established in March 1946 on the recommendation of the Asquith Commission. American involvement was mediated through the International Co-operation Administration of the United States, which was incorporated into USAID in 1961. See Ajayi and Tamuno, *University of Ibadan*, 20. The team of advisors included J. W. Cook of the University of Exeter, John A. Hannah of Michigan State University, and Glen L. Taggart of Michigan State University. University of Nigeria: Eastern Region Official Document no. 4 of 1958, NAN RG/C16.

94. Ajayi and Tamuno, *University of Ibadan*, 20, 4–5.

95. *White Paper*, article 5. The delegation included Dr. Onabamiro, Dr. Biobaku, Dr. Oluwasanmi, Dr. V. A. Oyenuga, Mr. Kesington Mommoth, Mr. S. G. Ikoku, and G. N. I. Enobakhare. In addition to Sharon, Mr. Babatunde Sobowale, an architect of the Regional Ministry of Works and Transport, joined the team. Western Nigeria University Project: Itinerary for Overseas Team, November–December 1960, AAAC, ASE.

96. Schedule: Nigerian Study Commission, November 3, 1960, AAAC, ASE.

97. See Arieh Sharon's correspondence with Zvi Cohen, July–September 1960, AAAC, ASE; Wera Meyer-Waldeck to Arieh Sharon, July 4, 1960, AAAC, ASE.

98. At a certain point, it was also suggested that the trip to Israel be canceled, but pressure from the Israeli embassy prevented that. Hannan Yavor to the Division of International Aid, the Foreign Ministry, November 18, 1960.

99. On the possible discrepancy between the impressions of Sharon and those of the West Nigerian delegation, see A. Levin, "Exporting Architectural National Expertise," 58–59.

100. A. Sharon, *Kibbutz + Bauhaus*, 126–27; Omosini and Adediran, *Great Ife*, 13.

101. Thomas, "Colonising the Land," 109–23.

102. Quoted in Omosini and Adediran, *Great Ife*, 13.

103. Omosini and Adediran, *Great Ife*, 5.

104. For Latin American reformed universities, see Arocena and Sutz, "Latin American Universities," 575.

105. Omosini and Adediran, *Great Ife*, 14. See also Oluwasanmi, "Preservation," 11.

106. Omosini and Adediran, *Great Ife*, 14.

107. Omosini and Adediran, *Great Ife*, 13.

108. Extracts from the 1st Meeting of the Western Region University

Planning Committee. According to Omosini and Adediran, "The diversity of courses reflected the intention of government to produce the much-needed personnel in the Science-related professions. The bias for the Sciences was further buttressed by the committee's recommendation that the ratio of intake should be 65:35 at the expense of the humanities." Omosini and Adediran, *Great Ife*, 13.

109. *Three Nigeria Universities and Their Role in Agricultural Development*, AID Project Impact Evaluation Report no. 66, 4–6. Cooperation between Michigan State University and the University of Nigeria was abruptly terminated after only six or seven years because of the Nigerian Civil War (1967–70). Before that, Michigan State University had assisted in the founding and launching of the entire university. The Kansas State University cooperation project with Ahmadu Bello University lasted from 1962 to 1978 and involved the establishment of the faculties of agriculture and veterinary medicine as well as several off-campus agricultural training schools. Similarly, the University of Wisconsin was involved from 1962 to 1975 in the establishment of the University of Ife's Faculty of Agriculture.

110. For example, regional governments acquired land for farm settlements operated by Israeli personnel in East and West Nigeria. For a study of one such farm in East Nigeria, see Nwana, "Ohaji Farm Settlement," 109–28.

111. Oluwasanmi, *Agriculture*, 23–31.

112. In response to UCI's limited capacity, the vice-chancellor insisted on acquiring a large expanse of land. Omosini and Adediran, *Great Ife*, 15.

113. "Ife—Permanent Site of the University," *Nigerian Daily Sketch*, February 8, 1967, 7.

114. Larkin, *Signal and Noise*, 21.

115. Oluwasanmi, *March Forward*, 10–11.

116. Akinola Agboola, "Thought on Nigerian Agriculture," *Nigerian Daily Sketch*, March 18, 1967, 5.

117. According to Agboola, "There is a great psychological effect. Pupils always think that only important subjects are taught in schools and since farming is not taught in school, therefore, it is not important." Agboola, "Thought on Nigerian Agriculture," 5.

118. Jeremiah I. Dibua cites the preference for educated farmers in Israeli farm settlements in West Nigeria as one of the causes for their failure. Dibua, *Modernization*, 182–83. It should be noted that Israeli experts preferred educated settlers not only for their technical literacy, as explained by Agboola, but also for "ideological literacy."

119. *Master Plan 1980–85*, 80–81.

120. For example, agricultural experiment stations and model villages in the Philippines displayed the spectacle of the Green Revolution. Cullather, "Miracles of Modernization," 227–38.

121. "A Young Institution with a Bright Future," *Nigerian Daily Sketch*, February 8, 1967, 9.

122. Mabogunje, *Urbanization in Nigeria*, 232–33.

123. The Bodija Estate was supposed to attract households of diverse incomes but failed to attract low-income residents.

124. *Master Plan 1980–85*, 45.

125. Oluwasanmi, *Challenge*, 1.

126. *Master Plan 1980–85*, 48–49.

127. *Master Plan 1980–85*, 21.

128. Omosini and Adediran, *Great Ife*, 15.

129. Former faculty member A. M. A. Imevbore specifically mentions white staff. Imevbore, *Science and Spirituality*, 14.

130. Beier, "Moment of Hope," 47–48.

131. *Master Plan 1980–85*, 45.

132. Ogbogbo interview.

133. This principle was followed throughout all stages of planning, even when the siting was different.

134. For the history of the Faculty of Agriculture, see Katz and Ben-David, "Scientific Research," 152–81; Troen, "Higher Education in Israel," 45–63.

135. Chyutin and Chyutin, *Architecture and Utopia*, 100; Bar-Or, "Initial Phases," 20.

136. Chyutin and Chyutin, *Architecture and Utopia*, 114–15.

137. Bar-Or, "Initial Phases," 21.

138. Bar-Or, "Initial Phases," 26–27, 32.

139. A. Sharon, *Kibbutz + Bauhaus*, 63.

140. Akintoye, *Ten Years*, 12; Amole, "*Cité Universitaire*," 59–60. Amole draws from the pathos expressed in Bruno Zevi's foreword to Sharon's monograph *Kibbutz + Bauhaus*. For a discussion of Zevi's foreword, see A. Levin, "Exporting Architectural National Expertise," 54–55.

141. Chyutin and Chyutin, *Architecture and Utopia*, 1–49.

142. Turner, *Campus*, 4.

143. Niemann and Tishler, *Physical Development Plan*, 78.

144. This is following the tradition of a domed building as focal point in many American campuses, including, for example, those of the University of Virginia and Columbia University.

145. A. Sharon, *Kibbutz + Bauhaus*, 63.

146. Cars are typically shared in a kibbutz, and the access paths to residential areas are mainly pedestrian.

147. Agency for International Development, "Three Nigerian Universities," 4. The next chapter will examine some of the university's buildings in greater detail.

148. See, for example, in Appel, "Walls and White Elephants," 439–65.

149. *Master Plan 1980–85*, 45–46.
150. *Master Plan 1980–85*, 20–22.
151. *Master Plan 1980–85*, 21; emphasis mine.
152. Oluwasanmi, *March Forward*, 12.
153. See S. Sharon, "Not Settlers but Settled," 72–73, 104–5.
154. A. Shapira, "Kibbutz and the State," 204.
155. Osayimwese and Iyare, "Economics of Nigerian Federalism," 89–92.

## FOUR. DESIGNING THE UNIVERSITY OF IFE

1. Oluwasanmi, *The Technological Gap*, 3.
2. For an early Marxist critique of the concept, see Berner, "Human Capital."
3. Adas, "Modernization Theory," 35–36.
4. Bar-Yosef, *Villa in the Jungle*, 167–73.
5. Summaries and Conclusions, LA IV-320-6, November 24 (no year) Meeting; A Conversation with Haim Glogamor who Returned from Abadan, August 8, 1943; The Managers of Work Meeting with the Administration, April 10, 1945 LA IV-320-7; translation mine.
6. Hart, *Social Science*, 7–49; Abu El-Haj, *Genealogical Science*, 67–78; According to Sandar Gilman, in nineteenth-century Europe, Jews were considered black. See Gilman, *Jew's Body*, 171–78.
7. Neumann, *Land and Desire*, 157.
8. Arieh Sharon to Dr. Ajose, December 20, 1961, AAAC, ASE.
9. Le Roux, "Networks of Tropical Architecture;" le Roux, "Building on the Boundary;" le Roux, "Modern Architecture;" Baweja, "Pre-history," 107–35. See also Stanek, "Architects from Socialist Countries." The following anecdote underscores the prevalence of tropical architecture discourses: the first question the Hungarian architect Charles Polónyi was asked at a press conference in the city of Calabar in southeast Nigeria was how he could design a master plan for the city, as the Hungarians did not have a "tropical experience." See Moravánsky, "Peripheral Modernism," 351.
10. J.-H. Chang, "Colonial Technoscientific Network." "Form Follows Climate" is the title of a talk Indian architect Charles Correa gave in 1980. Correa, *Form Follows Climate*, recording. Arieh Sharon also scribbled this saying on the pages of a talk on hospitals that he gave in Nairobi in 1971; he was probably inspired by one of the other presentations. See Yacobi, "Architecture of Foreign Policy," 43.
11. Fry and Drew, *Tropical Architecture in the Humid Zone*, 27.
12. Crush, "Introduction," 10.
13. Crush, "Introduction," 10.

14. See Jackson, "Tropical Architecture and the West Indies;" Chang and King, "Genealogy of Tropical Architecture."

15. Arnold, "'Illusory Riches,'" 7; Arnold, *Problem of Nature*.

16. Harrison, *Climates and Constitutions*, especially 17–21, 205.

17. Le Roux, "Networks of Tropical Architecture"; J.-H. Chang, "Colonial Technoscientific Network."

18. Crinson, *Modern Architecture*, 127–49.

19. Fry and Drew, *Tropical Architecture in the Humid Zone*, 31.

20. Fry and Drew, *Tropical Architecture in the Dry and Humid Zones*, 17–20, 31.

21. Presner, *Muscular Judaism*, 4.

22. Sufian, *Healing the Land*, 124.

23. Niemann and Tishler, "Cool Planning," 216.

24. Fry and Drew, *Tropical Architecture in the Dry and Humid Zones*, 23.

25. Schultz, "Investment in Human Capital," 9.

26. Alexandrowicz, "Appearance and Performance," 1–11.

27. Alexandrowicz, "Architecture's Unwanted Child," 103–4.

28. A. Sharon, *Kibbutz + Bauhaus*, 188. See also A. Levin, "Exporting Architectural National Expertise," 55–57.

29. Arieh Sharon to Dr. D. S. Onabamiro, November 22, 1960, AAAC, ASE.

30. Here is how Sharon describes the difficult environment of his early years in Palestine: "For a year we worked under very hard conditions—making roads, clearing swamps and working as farmhands to gain some agricultural experience. In the following year, we took over a small kibbutz named Gan Shmuel in the swamp area of Wadi Hedera. Our small group consisted of eighteen boys and girls, eking out an existence under incredibly bad living conditions, with insufficient food, and with all of us afflicted by recurring bouts of malaria." A. Sharon, *Kibbutz + Bauhaus*, 14–15.

31. On the work of Lipa Yahalom and Dan Tzur, see Lissovsky and Dolev, *Arcadia*.

32. Lipa Yahalom to Arieh Sharon, April 16, 1961, AAAC, ASE.

33. A. Sharon, "Public Construction in the Country," 116; translation mine.

34. Sharon to Onabamiro, November 22, 1960. The broad, long entry road that leads to the campus contradicts this early vision.

35. "Madam Goldameir [sic] Speaks to Students," *Busi-Body* 1, no. 6 (December 26, 1963): 5, IES, University of Addis Ababa; emphasis mine.

36. Such arguments displaced the problem from the natural realm to human capacity in order to insist that Jewish immigration to Palestine was feasible. Following the 1929 Palestinian revolts, the British Mandate imposed limitations on Jewish immigration based on the country's limited capacity to absorb the settlers economically. As a response, the Zionist Organization commissioned various experts, Jewish and non-Jewish, to prove the economic

potential of the land, which, they argued, was once one "of milk and honey." Zionists also held that Jewish immigration and modernization of agriculture would benefit not only the Jews but also the Arabs and the region at large.

37. In Ife, Sharon not only found the perfect scenery in which to work out his vision for rural public buildings but also had the backing of Vice-Chancellor Oluwasanmi, who was criticized for spending more on the university's lawns than on staff housing. See Imevbore, *Science and Spirituality*, 44.

38. Fry and Drew, *Tropical Architecture in the Dry and Humid Zones*, 23.

39. A. Sharon, *Kibbutz + Bauhaus*, 128.

40. Sufian, *Healing the Land*, 9.

41. Sufian, *Healing the Land*, 36–38.

42. Quoted in Sufian, *Healing the Land*, 37.

43. A. Sharon, *Kibbutz + Bauhaus*, 15. Sharon's group refused to leave their settlement following the death of some members, despite the fact that the Jewish authorities urged them to do so.

44. Omosini and Adediran, *Great Ife*, 35–36.

45. A. Sharon, *Kibbutz + Bauhaus*, 128; emphasis mine.

46. Quoted in Alexandrowicz, "Appearance and Performance," 6.

47. Le Corbusier had once proclaimed that "the task of the architect is to vitalize the surfaces which clothe these masses, but in such a way that these surfaces do not become parasitical, eating up the mass and absorbing it to their own advantage." By the 1940s, however, he prided himself on having "invented" the brise-soleil as the building's clothing: "You have given it a skeleton (independent structure), its vital organs (the communal services of the building); a fresh shining skin (the curtain wall); you have stood it on its legs (the pilotis). And now you have given it magnificent clothes adaptable to all climates!" Whereas the curtain wall once stood for clothing, with the invention of the brise-soleil it was naturalized and rendered as skin, while the brise-soleil was rendered as clothing. This naturalization masks the redundancy of the doubling of the building's envelope. Quoted in Wigley, *White Walls*, 114; quoted in le Roux, "Building on the Boundary," 443. See also Barber, "Le Corbusier," 21–32.

48. Payne, *From Ornament to Object*, 9–11.

49. The essay represents the culmination of ideas that Loos began to develop as early as 1898, when he wrote an article on the occasion of the Vienna Jubilee exhibition. See Canales and Herscher, "Criminal Skins," 236.

50. Mosse, "Max Nordau," 565–81.

51. Nordau, "Jewry of Muscle," 547.

52. Nordau, "Address"; emphasis mine. I added in brackets parts that were omitted from the English translation of the German original but appear in the Hebrew translation. In the Hebrew translation, the last sentence reads, "He has never the joyful feeling of showing himself as he is, to be himself in

every thought and sentiment. In his interiority he becomes crippled, in his exteriority—fake." Quoted in Neumann, *Land and Desire*, 156; translation mine.

53. Azaryahu, *Tel Aviv*, 55–61.

54. Nitzan-Shiftan, "Contested Zionism," 158.

55. Elhanani, "Our Contribution," 133; translation mine. Curiously, according to the "Afterword" that appeared in the *Frankfurter Zeitung*, where the essay was published in German in 1929, Loos's "Ornament and Crime" had been already translated into Hebrew in the 1920s. See Loos, *Ornament and Crime*, 175. I could not find corroboration that this translation ever existed.

56. For the role of the white wall as a cleansing agent in the modernist movement, see Wigley, *White Walls*, 8. As architectural critic Sharon Rotbard stresses, far from marking a clean break with history, the white wall was used as a tool for violent erasure and exclusion in Tel Aviv, which was first built as an ethnically pure suburb of Jaffa and later reconstructed as a Hebrew and Israeli city. See Rotbard, *White City*.

57. Like the hoe and the rifle, which Neumann argued were prostheses that connected the pioneer's body with the territory, I consider architecture, and specifically the architectural envelope, as another such prosthetic device.

58. Nitzan-Shiftan, "Contested Zionism," 157. Posener (1904–1996) immigrated to England after World War II. In the late 1950s, he served as head of the architecture department at the Technical College in Kuala Lumpur, Malaysia, before returning to Germany.

59. This sentence can also be translated as "Be a man in the street and a Jew at home." This much-cited saying first appeared in a 1862 poem by Russian-Jewish poet Judah Leib Gordon. See Stanislawski, *For Whom Do I Toil?*, 51.

60. E. Shapira, "Adolf Loos."

61. Avermaete, "Impossibility."

62. Metzger-Szmuk, *Houses from the Sand*, 24; translation mine.

63. Metzger-Szmuk, *Houses from the Sand*, 29. On the theatricality of Loos's domestic spaces, see Colomina, "Split Wall," 72–98.

64. Nitzan-Shiftan, "Contested Zionism," 158–59; Metzger-Szmuk, *Houses from the Sand*, 26; M. Levin, "Regional Aspects," 253.

65. Metzger-Szmuk, *Houses from the Sand*, 25–26; M. Levin, "Regional Aspects," 244.

66. Metzger-Szmuk, *Houses from the Sand*, 28–29. In addition, Alexandrowicz lists roller shutters and northwestern orientation as other adaptations to the climate. Alexandrowicz, "Appearance and Performance," 2. The recessed balcony, which was carved out of the building's mass and created the most convincing ribbon window allusion, was also the least climatically functional since it captured a pocket of hot air behind its shading "apron."

67. A. Sharon, "Public Construction in the Country," 116.

68. A. Sharon, "Public Construction in the Country," 116.

69. Nitzan-Shiftan, "Contested Zionism," 161.

70. Le Roux, "Building on the Boundary," 448.

71. Fry and Drew, *Tropical Architecture in the Dry and Humid Zones*, 31–32.

72. Le Roux, "Building on the Boundary," 448–49.

73. Le Roux, "Building on the Boundary," 449.

74. Efrat, *Israeli Project*, 868–70.

75. A. Sharon, *Kibbutz + Bauhaus*, 188.

76. The elevation of the verandah above the street level recalls British architects and Team 10 members Alison and Peter Smithson's "street in the air," a term they coined in the 1950s for a feature that was similarly inspired by the traditional verandah found in the colonies. Crinson, "Rainforest."

77. Eliezer Schreiber's archive includes the translation of entire sections of the Wisconsin report into Hebrew, compiled alongside the original images as a manual. Parts of these drawings are also found in Arieh Sharon's papers.

78. *Master Plan 1980–85*, 51.

79. The enclosed patio was at the center of the Israeli team's initial designs for the Central Library and Secretariat Buildings. It was perceived as a traditional climatic solution in Mediterranean architecture that also had a parallel in Yoruba compounds. See Beier, *Art in Nigeria 1960*, 19. From the archival record, it is not clear why the university administration rejected this model, but it might be because the Wisconsin team advised them against it.

80. Fanon, *Black Skin*, 20.

81. Fry and Drew, *Tropical Architecture in the Humid Zone*, plate 249: the caption reads, "View from entrance. Chapel and bell tower in centre, dormitories to right and left." That Fry and Drew removed the image from the 1964 revised edition of the book demonstrates that they too felt uncomfortable with its colonial undertones.

82. Quoted in Bar-Yosef, *Villa in the Jungle*, 53; translation mine. Another of Amir's poems praises the black skin of the female peasant: it shines from sweat and sun and is taut just like the skin of a drum. This poem expresses a mature woman's envy of her African counterpart, whose skin does not wrinkle as a result of exposure to the elements. Quoted in Bar-Yosef, *Villa in the Jungle*, 80.

83. As Teresa de Lauretis notes, this phrase, which is usually attributed to Franz Fanon, is in fact a mistranslation of his chapter title "L'expérience vécue du Noir" (The lived experience of the Black) in *Black Skin, White Masks*. De Lauretis, "Difference Embodied," 58.

84. Both Nnamdi Elleh and Inbal Ben-Asher Gitler consider the loose courtyard layout to be reminiscent of Yoruba compound or palace architecture. See Ben-Asher Gitler, "Campus Architecture," 122–23; Elleh, *African*

*Architecture*, 309. However, considering both the university administration's rejection of the patio design and the planning considerations detailed in the previous chapter, it is highly unlikely that these references were intentional. It should also be noted that these local references, besides the literal replica of the Opa Oranmiyan, were lost on local architectural historians. See Osasona, Ogunshakin, and Jiboye, "Ile-Ife," 151–52; Amole, "*Cité Universitaire*."

85. Okeke-Agulu, "Nationalism."

86. Beier, *Art in Nigeria 1960*, 20. See also Carroll, *Architectures of Nigeria*, 116.

87. Ockman, "Plastic Epic," 37–39.

88. See, for example, the case of Eugène Palumbo in 1960s Congo. Lagae and De Raedt, "Building for 'l'Authenticité.'"

89. See the previous chapter for a detailed itinerary of the tour.

90. A. Sharon, *Kibbutz + Bauhaus*, 127. For a study of the murals, see Burian, "Modernity and Nationalism," 211–23. The National Autonomous University of Mexico campus planners, who had envisioned an International Style image for the campus, rejected the pre-Columbian pyramid in O'Gorman's original scheme for the building.

91. A. Sharon, *Kibbutz + Bauhaus*, 127.

92. Ben-Asher Gitler, "Campus Architecture," 128.

93. Similarly, the traditionally thick walls of the Ooni's palace (sometimes over three feet thick) make visible the boundary between the market and the ceremonial space of the Ooni's courtyard, as well as the Ooni's residence inside the civil courtyard. This is especially true in Ife, where the Ooni's palace used to have an unusually thick gate. See Ojo, "Traditional Yoruba Architecture," 15, 17, 70.

94. Arieh Sharon, n.d., AAAC, ASE.

95. See Rohan, "Rendering the Surface."

96. Arieh Sharon to Harold Rubin, February 14, 1975, AAAC, ASE; Arieh Sharon to Eldar Sharon, February 12, 1975, AAAC, ASE.

97. For the German ethnologist Leo Frobenius, who is famous for the "discovery" of Yoruba art, these sculptures' ideal naturalism linked Yoruba and Hellenic traditions, thereby legitimating Yoruba's entry into world history as an ancient civilization.

98. Schildkrout, "Inscribing the Body."

99. A. Cheng, *Second Skin*, 28. See also Mark Wigley's discussion of Gottfried Semper: "The body is only defined by being covered in the face of language, the surrogate skin of the building. The evolution of skin, the surface with which spatiality is produced, is the evolution of the social. The social subject, like the body with which it is associated, is a product of decorative surfaces. The idea of the individual can only emerge within language. Interior-

ity is not simply physical. It is a social effect marked on the newly constituted body of the individual. Culture does not precede its masks. It is no more than masking." Wigley, *White Walls*, 13. Semper's theory is particularly appropriate for the African context where there is a formal and symbolic continuity among body paint, textiles, and murals.

100. Thompson, "Yoruba Artistic Criticism," 35–36.

101. Clastres, *Society against the State*, 177–88. Clastres links inscription and torture as prerequisites for entry into society, but does not deal with the aesthetic aspects of this process.

### FIVE. AID, ENTREPRENEURSHIP, AND EDUCATION

1. Historian Shimelis Bonsa Gulema dubs the 1960s the "golden age" of the city of Addis Ababa. See Gulema, "Urbanizing a Nation," 584–95. He notes that the importance attributed to the capital as a national symbol is evident in the emperor's speeches and the urban elite's writings even before the Italian occupation, but increased after the 1940s. See Gulema, "Urbanizing a Nation," 388.

2. For a detailed history of American and Soviet aid in Ethiopia, see McVety, *Enlightened Aid*. The Israeli embassy in Addis Ababa reported frequently on the development work of Yugoslav technical experts in Ethiopia in the early sixties. Another indication of the importance Ethiopia attributed to this diplomatic relationship was the fact that the street leading to the Yugoslav embassy was named after Josip Tito.

3. Yacobi suggests this in "The Architecture of Foreign Policy," 47.

4. Erlich, *Alliance and Alienation*, 35–58.

5. Erlich, *Alliance and Alienation*, 35–58, 77–85, 88–91, 124–26; Erlich, *Ethiopia and the Middle East*, especially 127–40. The competition between these two leaders split African countries into the Monrovia and Casablanca blocs. For a history of the polarization of the Pan-African movement, see Esedebe, *Pan-Africanism*, 165–89.

6. Erlich, *Alliance and Alienation*, 90. The following month, on April 18, Israel gave Ethiopia fifty tons of cement, as announced in the *Ethiopia Observer* no. 78 (July 1959): 268.

7. The factory was originally set up by Israeli parliament member Ya'akov Meridor, who had been deported from Palestine and incarcerated in Eritrea by the British Army in the 1940s. In the wake of diplomatic negotiations with Ethiopia in the 1950s, Meridor returned to Eritrea and, together with some local Jews, established a canned-meat factory named Incode (sometimes spelled Inkoda). The Israeli government stepped in and purchased his part of the company when it was in financial trouble, before the plant was handed

over to the Enav brothers. By 1960, Incode had become the largest industrial enterprise and the largest single employer in Eritrea. See Erlich, *Alliance and Alienation*, 72–73; Carol, *Jerusalem*, 58. Years later, Azriel Enav supplied canned meat to American soldiers fighting in Vietnam. Elazar Levin, "Azriel Enav Yuval Obituary," *Globes*, December 10, 1996 (in Hebrew). http://www.globes.co.il/news/article.aspx?did=140736 (accessed January 1, 2015).

8. Erlich, *Alliance and Alienation*, 72.

9. Erlich, *Alliance and Alienation*, 71.

10. Erlich, *Alliance and Alienation*, 85, 89. See also Bergman, "Israel and Africa," 57.

11. Erlich, *Alliance and Alienation*, 89.

12. It is unclear to what extent, if at all, Enav contributed his professional expertise to security personnel. The latter had prepared a strategic map of Addis Ababa that, to their embarrassment, was used by the abortive coup's conspirators in December 1960. See Erlich, *Alliance and Alienation*, 93. By then, Enav had developed a keen interest in security planning in his work in the Lakhish region. Enav interview.

13. Erlich, *Alliance and Alienation*, 58.

14. Shelemay, *Song of Longing*, 63. As holders of British passports granted to Adenite Jews, the family declined the offer.

15. Shelemay interview. The great mosque was originally commissioned by Benin himself, who imported Muslim builders from Yemen for his compound's construction. The mosque has continued to bear his name, even though its recent reconstruction was financed by Saudi donors.

16. Shelemay interview.

17. A. Levin to Africa-Asia Division, Foreign Ministry, July 29, 1963, ISA, MFA 1903/12 A.

18. On the tradition of entrusting foreigners with royal affairs, see Pankhurst, "Menilek." Foreigners were sometimes perceived as more trustworthy than locals since they did not have a stake in local affairs. This was especially true in an environment as filled with intrigue and suspicion as Haile Selassie's court, which is depicted, perhaps with some exaggeration, in Ryszard Kapuściński's documentary novel *The Emperor: Downfall of an Autocrat*.

19. Enav interview. The mausoleum did not get built.

20. From 1941 to 1945, a British official advised the minister and the director general of education on policies and the organization of the educational system. The principals of all the main schools in Addis Ababa were British. A shift from British to US control started in 1945 when two American officials were appointed as superintendents of Ethiopian schools. However, the ties with Britain were not severed; in fact, Haile Selassie sought to affiliate the University College of Addis Ababa with the University of London before he decided to accept US aid. See Milkias, *Haile Selassie*, 79–81.

21. Milkias, *Haile Selassie*, 43. Tedros was not from a privileged background; his family had blood ties with neither the royal family nor the aristocracy. His father was an adventurer who left the family a donkey as a farewell gift to compensate for abandoning them and pursued jobs in the hotel industry in Europe, starting in Italy and eventually ending up in London. However, the Tedros family gained the imperial government's special recognition during the Italian occupation, when the Ethiopian government was exiled in Bath. Michael's brother, who served as an engineer in the British Army, would come occasionally to the exiled ministers' house to help them operate and repair mechanical appliances. After this, the Tedros family's house in London served as a trustworthy destination for the Ethiopian elite, where, for example, their children could stay on their way to boarding schools. Tedros interview.

22. Tedros interview.

23. Tedros interview.

24. Tedros interview.

25. Although English had become the language of instruction in secondary and university education by the early 1950s, and French was the emperor's preferred language, Amharic was the national language. Amharization began under Emperor Menelik, but Selassie implemented the policy "with apparent ruthlessness"; during his regime, all books, periodicals, and magazines were published in Amharic or a few European languages, such as English and French. See Milkias, *Haile Selassie*, 56, 81.

26. Tedros interview. However, he never did learn Amharic, even after years of residence in the country.

27. This cultural capital has not attenuated even today. See Gulema, "Urbanizing a Nation," 549.

28. For a comprehensive overview, see Mariam, "Architecture in Addis Ababa;" Gulema, "Urbanizing a Nation," 549–55.

29. College Day Science and Engineering, May 14, 1966, List 6, IES.

30. As I demonstrated earlier in this book, Israeli, Polish, and Hungarian architects all claimed to have "tropical knowledge."

31. See, for example, the student body for the year 1957/8. 1957/8 Year Summary, Council Minute Book, 1955–61, Architectural Association Archives, London, 2007:66.

32. Enav interview.

33. Enav interview.

34. Enav interview. Hannan Bar-On to the Division of International Aid, Foreign Ministry, November 1, 1960, ISA, MFA 2027/18. In a newspaper interview, Enav encouraged more trade relations with Israel and complained about Israeli products. Yehuda Hagderati, "The Sabra Who Led New Construction in Addis Ababa," April 4, 1964, ISA, MFA 1922/12 A (in Hebrew).

35. Zalman Enav to Hannan Bar-On, October 31, 1960, ISA, MFA 2027/18.

36. Zewde, *History of Modern Ethiopia*, 200.

37. For a comprehensive list of Italian-owned building industries in Eritrea in 1959, see "Italian Industrial Enterprises in Eritrea—Year 1959," accessed May 27, 2014, http://www.dankalia.com/archive/1000/1111.htm.

38. Solel Boneh Board Meeting no. 6/62, June 17, 1962, LA IV-204-4-536.

39. Solel Boneh Board Meeting no. 4/62, February 5, 1962, LA IV-204-4-536.

40. Solel Boneh Overseas: Review 1973, LA IV-104-38-104.

41. Erlich, *Alliance and Alienation*, 91.

42. Beginning in 1960, Solel Boneh operated in three different capacities in Ethiopia: (1) as a local branch of Solel Boneh; (2) in partnership with the two Israeli companies Harish and National Engineers, which each held 17.5 percent of the shares, mainly on road construction; and (3) under the name Reynolds, a company Solel Boneh had opened with American partners and registered in the United States. Until 1964, the American Theo Ben Nahum Group acted as a silent partner. In 1964, the American Paul Schulman replaced it as general manager and partner. This partnership lasted until 1969; in 1972, Solel Boneh signed a new agreement with another American entrepreneur, Leon Marantz. Ya'akov Shor, "Israeli Contractorship Overseas" (a talk given in the Israeli Center for Management on June 27, 1968), LA IV-204-4-1603 (in Hebrew); Solel Boneh Overseas Annual Meeting, March 7, 1962. LA IV-204-4-536; Solel Boneh Overseas: Review 1973.

43. Reynolds's work constituted 16 percent of Solel Boneh's operations abroad during this period.

44. Ethiopian Air Lines had been established in 1946 with American aid. For its history and coverage of the opening of the airport, see Rampone, "Haile Selassie."

45. Reynolds built the terminal building, hangar, control tower, office buildings, food service, and stores. Rampone, "Ethiopia Enters the Jet Era." In addition, Reynolds constructed other terminals in Asmara, Jimma, and Dir Dawa. Solel Boneh Overseas *Company Bulletin*, no. 18, May 14, 1962, LA IV-204-4-536.

46. Certificate signed by Dr. Haile Giorgis Workneh, March 10, 1962, attached to S. Golan to Golda Meir, April 4, 1962, ISA, MFA 1903/10 A.

47. Hannan Bar-On to the Division of International Aid, Foreign Ministry, November 1, 1960, ISA, MFA 2027/18.

48. The Solel Boneh projects that did not involve Enav included the Haile Selassie I Stadium, the Harar water supply scheme, and 120 kilometers of roads, including 60 kilometers near Baher Dar. By 1973, Solel Boneh undertook its largest enterprise in East Africa, building a 125-mile road connecting Ethiopia and Kenya. See Carol, *Jerusalem*, 80–81.

49. Enav probably did this with some, but not substantial, encouragement

in the form of loans from the Israeli embassy. According to Carol, "By 1969, some forty Israeli firms in Ethiopia were registered as Ethiopian enterprises, and during this period (1950–69) Ethiopia received some $114,000 in Israeli loans and credits." Carol, *Jerusalem*, 6.

50. "Thermal Baths: Addis Ababa," *Architectural Design* 135 (Oct. 1965): 522.

51. Milkias, *Haile Selassie,* 46–47.

52. Milkias, *Haile Selassie,* 49, 81, 91. In 1972, the list of international institutions providing financing included USAID, UNESCO, the United Nations Development Program, the Ford Foundation, the Swedish International Development Agency, and the British Inter-University Council. Bilateral agreements with the Federal Republic of Germany and with Israel are also mentioned. See The President's Report 1969–70, 1970–71, January 1972, Haile Selassie I University Miscellanea 4, IES.

53. Milkias, *Haile Selassie,* 89–90.

54. Haile Selassie I University, Office of Public Relations, *This Is Haile Selassie I University* (Addis Ababa: Artistic Printing Press, 1964), 62–63, IES. The breakdown of international students by nationality was as follows: Kenya (29), Nigeria (17), Uganda (13), India (12), Nyasaland (11), USA (10), Cameroon (8), Liberia (7), Tanganyika (7), Zanzibar (6), Greece (6), Sudan (4), Southern Rhodesia (3), Israel (3), Northern Rhodesia (2), Gambia (2), Armenia (2), China (2), Colombia (2), France (1), Germany (1), Ghana (1), Canada (1), Italy (1), Lebanon (1), Mozambique (1), Norway (1), Philippines (1), Poland (1).

55. The breakdown of academic staff by nationality in academic year 1963–64 was as follows: Ethiopian, 88; American, 75; British, 26; Swedish, 13; Israeli, 12; Indian, 10; Canadian and German, less than 10. Haile Selassie I University, Office of Public Relations, *This Is Haile Selassie I University*, 29–30.

56. Zewde, *History of Modern Ethiopia,* 207. For a history of earlier Swedish aid in Ethiopia, see Norberg, "Swedes."

57. Milkias, *Haile Selassie,* 82.

58. Sisaye, "Swedish Development Aid Policy," 147–48.

59. The Ethio-Swedish Institute of Building Technology, Addis Ababa: Annual Report 1959–60, 9, IES.

60. Ethio-Swedish Institute of Building Technology, Addis Ababa: Annual Report, 26.

61. H. Goma to Middle East Division, Foreign Ministry, May 31, 1962, ISA, MFA 1903/10 A.

62. Pankhurst, "Menilek," 74–75.

63. Pankhurst, "Menilek," 85.

64. Pankhurst, "Menilek," 44.

65. Pankhurst, "Menilek," 51.

66. *Solel Boneh: A Collection,* 65–68, 100.

67. Alpert, *Technion*, 95–96, 98, 123–24, 141. The first class of graduates included ten engineers and seven architects, among them one woman, Zipporah Neufeld. They received their diplomas in February 1929.

68. "College of Engineering," *Ethio-Engineer* (July 1960): 8, IES.

69. Yehuda Peter, "Engineering Education in Ethiopia," paper given at a conference in Kumasi, Ghana, July 1967, IES 67-5252.

70. Ephraim Spira to Ato Million Neqniq, Ethiopia Ministry of Education, October 28, 1959, ISA, MFA 2031/10.

71. "College of Engineering," 6; emphasis mine.

72. Spira to Neqniq.

73. Israeli Embassy in Addis Ababa to the Division of International Cooperation, Foreign Ministry, December 12, 1961, ISA, MFA 2031/10.

74. Hannan Bar-On to Hannan Aynor, November 2, 1959, ISA, MFA 2031/10; Hannan Bar-On to Division of International Aid, Foreign Ministry, November 8, 1960, ISA, MFA 2031/10.

75. Quoted in Erlich, *Alliance and Alienation*, 106.

76. See Alpert, *Technion*, 96–98, 319–21. Zewde Berhane and Alemayehu Teferra are two notable examples of students who graduated from the College of Engineering and continued to graduate degrees at the Technion. Berhane completed his master's and doctorate in civil engineering at the Technion; Teferra received his MSc from the Technion and his doctorate from the Technical University in Aachen and went on to become dean of the Faculty of Technology at Addis Ababa University. Another case in point is architect Beda Jonathan Amuli from Tanganyika, who enrolled in a full-time degree course in architecture—in Hebrew!—at the Technion in 1960. After 1961, the Technion created a special agricultural engineering program in English for nearly thirty students from twelve Afro-Asian countries, Cyprus, and the West Indies. This program was discontinued in 1967, but trainees continued to arrive on an individual or group basis for special courses. At the same time, Ethiopian students and students of other African nationalities studied at the Hebrew University of Jerusalem, pursuing degrees in fields such as medicine, agriculture, and political science. See Technical Cooperation with Ethiopia, n.d., ISA, MFA 1903/10 A.

77. Yaacov Dori to Ehud Avriel, August 25, 1962, ISA, MFA 1903/11.

78. Rahamim Timor to Division of International Cooperation, the Foreign Ministry, September 20, 1962, ISA, MFA 2031/11.

79. Timor to Division of International Cooperation.

80. Rahamim Timor to the Foreign Ministry, July 27, 1962, ISA, MFA 2031/11.

81. Yehuda Peter graduated from the Berlin Technological Institute in 1926. R. Timor to Lij Kassa Wolde Mariam, President of Haile Selassie I University, September 14, 1962, ISA, MFA 2031/11.

82. Jerusalem to Bonn, November 28, 1962, ISA, MFA 2031/11.

83. Timor to Division of International Cooperation.

84. Ephraim Spira to Division of International Cooperation, the Foreign Ministry, November 6, 1961, ISA, MFA 2031/10.

85. Even the Technion's original language of instruction was German, leading to what is known as "the war of the languages." See Alpert, *Technion*, 5–9, 19–20, 36–75.

86. This was the result of a new cooperation agreement the German and Ethiopian governments signed in 1964. *Ethiopia Information Bulletin* no. 13, July 1964, 23, IES.

87. The only architecture course that the Ethio-Swedish Institute offered was "Introduction to Architectural Planning," which was taught in the first and third terms. The first term focused on "dwelling: functional requirements, living rooms, bedrooms, kitchens, toilets and bathrooms," and the third term on "general planning—town planning, fact finding and space programs, building shapes in relation to cost, space grouping, development in stages, sketching a specialized building." Ethio-Swedish Institute of Building Technology, Addis Ababa: Annual Report, 20, 58.

88. Sven Hesselgren chaired the university committee that was convened in October 1962 to study a proposal to establish a department of architecture in the College of Engineering. He headed the department until 1965, when the Israeli Hannan Pavel took over until his departure the following year. Pavel was then succeeded by the American Jan Reiner. Tedros, "Department of Architecture," 37.

89. Ethio-Swedish Institute of Building Technology, Addis Ababa: Annual Report, 11.

90. Ethio-Swedish Institute of Building Technology, Addis Ababa: Annual Report, 13, 28.

91. Ethio-Swedish Institute of Building Technology, Addis Ababa: Annual Report, 70.

92. Ethio-Swedish Institute of Building Technology, Addis Ababa: Annual Report, 11.

93. Ostensson, *Report*, 7.

94. Ostensson, *Report*, 51–52. More European-type houses ("low cost villas") were erected on the grounds of secondary schools in Addis Ababa, to be used for training students in home economics.

95. *Ethiopia Information Bulletin* no. 7, January 1964, IES.

96. The Ethiopian University Service was a literacy campaign through which students volunteered across the countryside. According to Paulos Milkias, this university program was a response to the National Ethiopian Student Union's independent initiative to radicalize the peasantry. To thwart the student union's politically subversive agenda, the university diverted their efforts into a literacy campaign in regular elementary and high schools, thus

severing students' direct contacts with peasants and addressing the regime's shortage of teachers. See Milkias, *Haile Selassie*, 117–18.

97. Sisaye, "Swedish Development Aid Policy," 148.

98. Milkias, *Haile Selassie*, 44–45.

99. Peter, "Engineering Education in Ethiopia."

100. Yehuda Peter, "From the Dean's Desk," *Ethio-Engineer* 6 (June 1964): 7–10, IES.

101. "Architects' Study Tour to Wollamo-Soddo," ACME *Perspective* 5, no. 2, (December 3, 1964): 7, IES.

102. Tourist facilities were located in developing areas for the purpose of "political tourism"—in other words, to facilitate the visits of diplomats who could thereby observe these sites of development first-hand. Mezzedimi, "Haile Selassie."

103. Ashwin R. Kamani, "A Trip to Wolamo-Sodo," ACME *Perspective* 5, no. 2 (December 3, 1964): 8–9, IES.

104. "Architects' Study Trip," ACME *Perspective* 4, no. 6 (Jan. 31, 1964): 2, IES.

105. Efrat, *Israeli Project*, 616.

106. Ohlin, "Swedish Aid," 56–57.

107. Ostensson, *Report*, 37.

108. The institutional history of these intertwined entities is confusing. The Ethio-Swedish Institute of Building Technology seems to have become the southern campus of the College of Technology while retaining some autonomy, as expressed in its different name.

109. "Inaguration [*sic*] Evening," ACME *Perspective* 5, no. 1 (Nov. 18, 1964): 2, IES; "Model for the New College of Engineering Building," ACME *Perspective* 4, no. 5 (Jan. 13, 1964): 2–3, IES; the President's Report 1969–70.

110. Ostensson, *Report*, 60–62.

111. Ostensson, *Report*, 62.

112. Gulema, "Urbanizing a Nation."

113. A. Levin, "Haile Selassie's Imperial Modernity."

114. For the history of the coup, see Zewde, *History of Modern Ethiopia*, 211–15.

115. For an analysis of debates on the relationship between culture and technology in the Ethiopian intellectual tradition, see Giorgis, "Charting Out Ethiopian Modernity and Modernism." On the analogy with Japan, see Kebede, "Japan and Ethiopia."

116. *Second Five-Year Development Plan* (Addis Ababa: Imperial Ethiopian Government, October 1962), 33–34.

117. Quoted in McVety, *Enlightened Aid*, 176.

118. For a discussion of Israeli involvement in suppressing the coup, see Erlich, *Alliance and Alienation*, 91–94.

119. Erlich, *Alliance and Alienation*, 141–42.

120. Quoted in Erlich, *Alliance and Alienation*, 73; translation mine.
121. A. Levin, "Haile Selassie's Imperial Modernity," 450.
122. Enav, "Architecture in Ethiopia Today," 23.
123. Ostensson, *Report*, 7.
124. Enav interview.
125. Enav, "Architecture in Ethiopia," 17–18.
126. Enav interview.
127. *Ethiopia Information Bulletin* no. 10, April 1964, 23.
128. Enav incorporated an aerial view of these settlement patterns into his *Zede* article. As was typical of this ahistorical structuralist approach, there is no mention of the village's name, its geographical location, or the date on which the photo was taken.
129. A. Levin, "Haile Selassie's Imperial Modernity," 459–62.
130. Enav interview.
131. Noyer-Duplaix, "Henri Chomette."
132. See the comparable case of the labor-intensive "humanism" of Félix Candela's work in Mexico. Pendas, "Fifty Cents."
133. Although World Bank tenders were published internationally according to its protocol, the bank generally preferred architects who lived in the local area, since experience showed that they could pursue projects more efficiently. Furthermore, World Bank projects entailed the active involvement of local governments if they so wished, while other international agencies were assigned to various ministries of the national government to oversee the entire process. Of the thirteen firms that applied from Japan, Italy, Norway, Sweden, Australia, the United States, the United Kingdom, Israel, Germany, and Ethiopia, the Ethiopian government retained four. All four were prominent architectural firms operating at the time in Addis Ababa: Studio Arturo Mezzedimi, Studio Henri Chomette, the Norwegian Norconsult, and Enav, Tedros and Associates. The entire design and building process was supervised by architects provided by the Swedish International Development Cooperation, the Norwegian Agency for Development Cooperation, UNESCO, and so on, who were assigned to different ministries in the Ethiopian government. While Enav was in charge of the design work, the follow-up process was in the hands of external experts. The first prototype school was built in Debra Marcos. See De Raedt, "Architecture as Development Aid," 413–18.
134. Enav acted as Head of the Deployment, Mapping, and Infrastructure Unit of the IDF Planning Branch for the Israeli-Egyptian talks from 1973 to 1979, and he was a member of the Israeli military's delegations to the Israeli-Egyptian talks in Egypt in 1973–74, in Geneva in 1975, and in Washington in 1978–79. The planning project in Egypt was an urban design for Hilouan, a satellite town with sixty thousand residents. See Enav Planning Group company profile brochure, 2007. See also "Zalman Enav: Drawing the Lines

in Sinai," *Israel's Documented Story, the English-language blog of the Israel State Archive*, accessed October 2, 2014, http://israelsdocuments.blogspot.com/2014/04/zalman-enav-drawing-lines-in-sinai.html.

135. Haim Yacobi attributes the design of Ariel Sharon's villa to the tradition of colonial bungalow-style hill station houses. See Yacobi, "Architecture of Foreign Policy," 49. While Enav may have been familiar with the type from his education at the AA, he did not design anything of this kind in Ethiopia.

136. On Israel's security export, see Gordon, "Political Economy." See also Feldman, *Lab*.

137. Enav Planning Group company profile brochure.

138. Tedros interview.

## POSTSCRIPT

1. In 1965, the Israeli commercial firm Dizengoff West Africa set up a cement factory in Sierra Leone, using raw material imported from Poland. Before then the firm imported the Israeli Nesher cement to the country. IPD Board Meeting no. 18, 11 March 1965, ISA, MFA 469/8.

2. On the settlements as suburbs, see Allegra et al., *Normalizing Occupation*.

3. Mayer, *The Mayer Brothers' Story*, 102.

4. Gershoni, "Liberia and Israel," 37–38. See also Gershoni, "Liberia and the Decolonization."

5. Born in Russia to a wealthy family, Simon Simonovitch fled the country after the Soviet revolution. During World War II, Simonovitch arrived in Liberia as a war refugee and established close contacts with heads of the local government. Simonovitch and Muriel met at an International Labor Organization meeting at which the former was representing the Liberian government.

6. Mayer, *Mayer Brothers' Story*, 102–9, 117; Gershoni, "Liberia and Israel," 39. In 1959, Israeli loans to the Liberian government reached thirteen million dollars. Levey, "Israel's Entry to Africa, 1956–61," 91.

7. Wharton, *Building the Cold War*, 117–18.

8. A. Roger, "Today Liberia Celebrates," *Davar*, July 26, 1959 (in Hebrew).

9. Mordechai Mayer to Hanan Yavor, November 6, 1958, ISA, MFA 54/3.

10. On the loan agreement, see Mordechai Mayer to Hanan Yavor, February 26, 1959, ISA, MFA 54/3.

11. Mayer, *Mayer Brothers' Story*, 113. InterContinental Hotels' chief architect and interior designer, Neal Prince, redesigned the hotel's interiors.

12. Mayer, *Mayer Brothers' Story*, 124–28, 142.

13. "Ghana is already ready to buy with credit," *Ma'ariv*, February 28, 1961, 5 (in Hebrew).

14. Heimann, "Diplomatic Symbiosis."

15. Mayer, *Mayer Brothers' Story*, 127–28; translation mine.

16. Herz, "Project of a Nation," 386–90.

17. Berkowitz and Rubin, *Haim Heinz Fenchel*.

18. Leitersdorf interview.

19. Klein and Kark, "Demolition."

20. Mayer, *Mayer Brothers' Story*, 130.

21. Mayer, *Mayer Brothers' Story*, 207, 210.

22. These transformations included massive tourist developments on the city's beachfront and a plan, only partially realized, for its business center, "The City," on the ruins of the mixed Arab-Jewish neighborhood Manshiya, which connected Tel Aviv with Jaffa. Elhyani, "Seafront Holdings."

23. I thank Noam Shoked for this information about the tram. For an interview on the planning of Ma'ale Edumim, see Tamir-Tawil, "To Start a City." For the planning history of Emmanuel, see Shoked, "Rabbis."

24. By mid-November 1973, twenty-one African states had broken off relations with Israel, leaving only four countries that continued relations: Malawi, Swaziland, Lesotho, and Mauritius. Peters, *Israel and Africa*, 38.

25. On Israel's relationship with Idi Amin, see Bar-Yosef, *Villa in the Jungle*, 215–32.

26. Chazan, "Israel and Africa," 7–12.

27. The confluence of humanitarian aid and development in the region began as early as the late 1950s, when the United Nations Relief and Works Agency changed course from immediate humanitarian relief to development in refugee camps for Palestinians who were displaced from 1947 to 1949. The agency's turn to long-term planning has been interpreted as a betrayal of the refugees' claims to the right of return, as it undermines their refugee status.

28. Amir, "Traditional Leadership," 39–41. For another example, see Bar-Yosef, *Villa in the Jungle*, 181.

29. Abreek-Zubiedat, "Architecture in Conflict."

30. Bar-Yosef, *Villa in the Jungle*, 174–77. In a letter to a friend, Ephraim Spira, the first Israeli dean at the Ethiopian Technical College (later the College of Engineering), ridiculed the foreign ministry's emphasis on "pioneering." "Who in Israel nowadays," he asked rhetorically, "believes in that anymore?" Ephraim Spira to Prof. D. Yitzkhaki, October 29, 1959, ISA, MFA 2031/10; translation mine. Similarly, an Israeli head of the surgical department at a hospital in Kumasi, Ghana, complained to the embassy about his living arrangements and was furious to get "nationalist lectures about pioneering" in response. He wrote, "Never in my life have I heard so much about pioneering. If I wished to be a pioneer, I would have travelled to the Negev or to Eilat." Dr. Pe'er to Ysaskhar Ben-Yaacov, January 30, 1961, ISA, MFA 2029/14; translation mine.

31. Chazan, *Roles of Preliminary Training*. According to Chazan, the study was concealed upon completion.

32. Malkhin and Goldberg, *Israel's Relations*, 50–51.

33. Bar-Yosef, *Villa in the Jungle*, 238–39.

34. See, for example, the current discourse of IsraAID, the Israeli forum for international humanitarian aid that consists of Israeli and American Jewish organizations, in Yacobi, *Israel and Africa*, 112–13.

35. Klein, *Shock Doctrine*.

36. Bergman, "Israel and Africa," 265.

37. Diplomats were not always informed of Israeli military actions in Africa. See Bar-Yosef, *Villa in the Jungle*, 221n47.

38. Report to Aharon Remez, undated (c. December 1961 or January 1962), ISA, MFA 1908/17.

39. Yaacov Doron, undated (c. April 1965), ISA, MFA 3569/22.

40. Yacobi, *Israel and Africa*, 117–18.

41. "Israeli Group Proposes to Build 100,000 Houses in Angola," *MachauHub*, March 24, 2010, accessed January 5, 2015, http://www.macauhub.com.mo/en/2010/03/24/8802/.

42. Esther Zandberg, "After the Arms Trade, the Israelis Also Sell to Angola National Planning," *City Mouse*, March 25, 2010, accessed January 5, 2015, http://www.mouse.co.il/cm.articles_item,1042,209,47524,aspx (in Hebrew).

43. Yoram Gabizon, "Tahal Signed a 200 Million Dollar Project in Angola," *The Marker*, August 29, 2011 (in Hebrew).

44. For examples of more recent buildings falling into ruin, see Hoffman, *Monrovia Modern*.

45. Their relatively large size makes it doubtful that these homes were indeed offered to low income families (100 square meters for three-bedroom apartments and 120 square meters for four-bedroom apartments).

46. Yacobi, *Israel and Africa*, 122.

47. Gabizon, "Tahal."

48. Quoted in Yotam Feldman, "Black Business: The Fantastic Life of the Arms' Dealers in Angola," *The Marker*, December 26, 2008, accessed January 5, 2015, http://www.themarker.com/law/1.501267 (in Hebrew).

49. Quoted in "A New Angolan Model," *Foreign Policy*, September–October 2010, 15.

50. Pelleg Architects, the firm in charge of the Kimina village planning, describes the project in ecological terms.

51. Feldman, "Black Business."

52. See, for example, Rozin, "Terms of Disgust."

53. S. Sharon, "Not Settlers but Settled," 125. On the Lakhish settlers' selection process, economic and social management, and resistance, see 121–54.

54. Quoted in Feldman, "Black Business."

55. Yacobi, *Israel and Africa*, 122.

56. Malkhin and Goldberg, *Israel's Relations*, 40–41; translation mine.

57. Malkhin and Goldberg, *Israel's Relations*, 36; Bar-Yosef, *Villa in the Jungle*, 170–71.

58. Malkhin and Goldberg, *Israel's Relations*, 40; translation mine.

59. Zandberg, "After the Arms Trade."

60. Established in Nigeria in 1979 and specializing in housing and shopping mall construction, the company has since expanded its operations to the Eastern European market under the name Globe International Holdings.

61. Sabine Bitter and Helmut Weber, "Project Global Prayers: Lagos, Rio de Janeiro, Beirut," January 2011, accessed December 12, 2014, http://globalprayers.info/uploads/media/Bitter_Weber_Project_02.pdf.

62. Enwezor, "Modernity." For the first study of the afterlife of an Israeli project in Africa, see Schler and Gez, "Development Shadows." For video documentation of the contemporary state and usage of the University of Ife campus, see Efrat, *Most Beautiful Campus*.

63. Ferguson, *Anti-Politics Machine*, 20.

64. Bloch, *Principle of Hope*, 1:7.

# bibliography

ARCHIVES CONSULTED AND THEIR ABBREVIATIONS

AAAC, ASE   Azrieli Architectural Archive Collection, Arieh Sharon Estate, Tel Aviv Museum of Art
IES   Institute of Ethiopian Studies, Addis Ababa University, Addis Ababa
ISA   Israel State Archives, Jerusalem
LA   Labour Movement Archives, Lavon Institute for Labour Research, Tel Aviv
MFA   Ministry of Foreign Affairs
NAN   National Archive Nigeria, Ibadan
NASL   National Archives of Sierra Leone, Fourah Bay College, Mount Aureol, Freetown
SSJFA   Steven Spielberg Jewish Film Archive, The Hebrew University of Jerusalem

INTERVIEWS

Zalman Enav. Interview by the author. July 15, 2009, Tel Aviv.
Ram Karmi. Interview by the author. August 4, 2011, Herzliya Pituach, Israel.
Peter J. Kulagbanda (principal clerk of committees at Sierra Leone's House of Representatives). Interview by the author. February 20, 2013, Freetown, Sierra Leone.
Tommy Leitersdorf. Interview by the author. June 7, 2016, Tel Aviv, Israel.
Zvi Meltzer. Interview by the author. August 16, 2011, Rishon LeZion, Israel.
Joseph Mouna (former town planning director at Freetown City Council, 1971–2011). Interview by the author. February 20, 2013, Freetown, Sierra Leone.

Christopher Bankole Ndubisi Ogbogbo (professor in the Department of History at the University of Ibadan). Interview by the author. January 14, 2013, Ibadan, Nigeria.

Harold Rubin. Interview by the author. July 31, 2011, Jaffa, Israel.

Harold Rubin and Miriam Keini. Interview by the author. June 27, 2012, Jaffa, Israel.

Jack Shelemay. Interview by the author. December 16, 2011, Cambridge, MA.

Amos Spitz. Interviews by the author. December 20, 2012, Ramat Hasharon, Israel; January 17–18, 2013, Lagos, Nigeria.

Zvi Szkolnik. Interview by the author. August 3, 2011, Haifa, Israel.

Michael Tedros. Interview by the author. October 20, 2011, Burke, VA.

## OTHER SOURCES

Abrams, Charles, Susumu Kobe, and Otto Koenigsberger. "Growth and Urban Renewal in Singapore." *Habitat INTL* 5, no. 1/2 (1980): 85–127.

Abreek-Zubiedat, Fatina. "Architecture in Conflict beyond the Green Line: Gaza and Yamit Cities, 1967–1982." PhD diss., Technion Israel Institute of Technology, 2018 (in Hebrew).

Abu El-Haj, Nadia. *The Genealogical Science: The Search for Jewish Origins and the Politics of Epistemology*. Chicago: Chicago University Press, 2012.

Adas, Michael. "Modernization Theory and the American Revival of the Scientific and Technological Standards of Social Achievements and Human Worth." In *Staging Growth: Modernization, Development, and the Global Cold War*, edited by David C. Engerman et al., 25–45. Amherst, MA: University of Massachusetts Press, 2003.

Agency for International Development. "Three Nigerian Universities and Their Role in Agricultural Development." AID Project Impact Evaluation Report No. 66, Washington, DC, March 1988.

Ajayi, J. F. Ade. "Expectations of Independence." *Daedalus* 111, no. 2 (Spring 1982): 1–9.

Ajayi, J. F. Ade, and Tekena N. Tamuno, eds. *The University of Ibadan, 1948–73: A History of the First Twenty-Five Years*. Ibadan, Nigeria: Ibadan University Press, 1973.

Akinsanya, A. "The Former Western Nigeria Development Corporation: A Framework for Performance Evaluation." *Public Administration and Development* 1 (1981): 25–33.

Akintoye, Stephen Adebanji. *Ten Years of the University of Ife, 1962–1972*. Ile Ife, Nigeria: University of Ife Press, 1973.

Alexandrowicz, Or. "Appearance and Performance: Israeli Building Climatology and Its Effect on Local Architectural Practice (1940–1977)." *Architectural Science Review* (2017): 1–11.

Alexandrowicz, Or. "Architecture's Unwanted Child: Building Climatology in Israel, 1940–1977." PhD diss., Vienna University of Technology, 2015.

Allais, Lucia. *Designs of Destruction: The Making of Monuments in the Twentieth Century.* Chicago: Chicago University Press, 2018.

Allegra, Marco, et al., eds. *Normalizing Occupation: The Politics of Everyday Life in the West Bank Settlements.* Bloomington, IN: Indiana University Press, 2017.

Alpert, Carl. *Technion: The Story of Israel's Institute of Technology.* New York: American Technion Society, 1982.

Althusser, Louis. *Essays on Ideology.* London: Verso, 1984.

Amir, Shimeon. *Israel's Development Cooperation with Africa, Asia, and Latin America.* New York: Praeger, 1974.

Amir, Shimeon. "Traditional Leadership and Modern Administration in Developing Countries." In *Israel in the Third World*, edited by Michael Curtis and Susan Aurelia Gitelson, 37–44. New Brunswick, NJ: Transaction Books, 1976.

Amole, Bayo. "The *Cité Universitaire* in Ile-Ife: An Architectural Critique." In *Architects and Architecture in Nigeria: A Book of Reading in Honour of Professor Ekundayo Adeyinka Adeyemi*, edited by Uche Obisike Nkwogu and Ekundayo Adeyinka Adeyemi, 57–76. Akure, Nigeria: Association of Architectural Educators in Nigeria, 2001.

Anderson, Warwick. *Colonial Pathologies: American Tropical Medicine, Race, and Hygiene in the Philippines.* Durham, NC: Duke University Press, 2006.

Anderson, Warwick. *Cultivation of Whiteness: Science, Health, and Racial Destiny in Australia.* Durham, NC: Duke University Press, 2006.

Appadurai, Arjun. *Modernity at Large: Cultural Dimensions of Globalization.* Minneapolis, MN: University of Minnesota Press, 2008.

Appel, Hannah C. "Walls and White Elephants: Oil Extraction, Responsibility, and Infrastructural Violence in Equatorial Guinea." *Ethnography* 13, no. 4 (December 2012): 439–65.

Apthorpe, Raymond. "Development Policy Discourse." *Public Administration and Development* 6, no. 4 (1986): 377–89.

Arnold, David. "'Illusory Riches': Representations of the Tropical World, 1840–1950." *Singapore Journal of Tropical Geography* 21, no. 1 (2000): 6–18.

Arnold, David. *The Problem of Nature: Environment, Culture, and European Expansion.* Cambridge, MA: Blackwell, 1996.

Arocena, Rodrigo, and Judith Sutz. "Latin American Universities: From an Original Revolution to an Uncertain Transition." *Higher Education* 50 (2005): 573–92.

Avermaete, Tom. "Framing the Afropolis: Michel Ecochard and the African City for the Greatest Number." *OASE* 82 (2010): 77–100.

Avermaete, Tom. "The Impossibility of a Universal Balcony: Mutations of a Modern Element across the Mediterranean." In *Elements of Architecture—Balcony*, edited by Tom Avermaete, Rem Koolhaas, and Irma Boom, 910–27. Venice, Italy: Marsilio, 2014.

Avimor, Shimon, ed. *Relations between Israel and Asian and African States: A Guide to Selected Documentation No. 5; Union of Burma*. Jerusalem: Hebrew University of Jerusalem, Harry S. Truman Research Institute for the Advancement of Peace, Leonard Davis Institute for International Relations, 1989 (in Hebrew).

Avriel, Ehud. "Some Minute Circumstances." *Jerusalem Quarterly*, no. 14 (Winter 1980): 28–40.

Aynor, Hannan S., Shimon Avimor, and Noam Kaminer, eds. *The Role of the Israel Labour Movement in Establishing Relations with States in Africa and Asia: Documents, 1948–1975*. Tel Aviv: Lavon Institute for Labour Movement Research / Jerusalem: The Hebrew University in Jerusalem, Harry Truman Institute for the Advancement of Peace, 1989 (in Hebrew).

Azaryahu, Maoz. *Tel Aviv—The Real City*. Beer Sheva, Israel: Ben-Gurion Research Institute, Ben-Gurion University, 2005 (in Hebrew).

Banton, Michael. *West African City: A Study of Tribal Life in Freetown*. London: Oxford University Press, 1957.

Barber, Daniel A. "Le Corbusier, the Brise-Soleil, and the Socio-Climatic Project of Modern Architecture, 1929–1963." *Thresholds* 40 (2012): 21–32.

Bareli, Avi, and Nir Kedar. *Israeli Republicanism*. Jerusalem: The Israel Democracy Institute, 2011 (in Hebrew).

Barnes, Trevor J., and Claudio Minca. "Nazi Spatial Theory: The Dark Geographies of Carl Schmitt and Walter Christaller." *Annals of the Association of American Geographers* (2012): 669–87.

Bar-Or, Galia. "The Initial Phases: A Test Case." In *Kibbutz: Architecture without Precedents; Israeli Pavilion, 12th International Architecture Exhibition, The Venice Biennial*, edited by Galia Bar-Or and Yuval Yaski, 17–50. Tel Aviv: Top Print, 2010.

Bar-Yosef, Eitan. *A Villa in the Jungle: Africa in Israeli Culture*. Jerusalem: Van Leer Jerusalem Institute and Hakibbutz Hameuchad, 2013 (in Hebrew).

Bassin, Mark. "Race contra Space: German Geopolitik and National Socialism." *Political Geography Quarterly* 6, no. 2 (April 1987): 115–34.

Baweja, Vandana. "A Pre-History of Green Architecture: Otto Koenigsberger and Tropical Architecture, from Princely Mysore to Post-Colonial London." PhD diss., University of Michigan, 2008.

Bayart, Jean-François. *The State in Africa: The Politics of the Belly*. Translated by Mary Harper, Christopher Harrison, and Elizabeth Harrison. Cambridge, UK; Malden: MA: Polity Press 2010.

Beeckmans, Luce. "The Adventures of the French Architect Michel Ecochard in Post-Independence Dakar: A Transnational Development Expert Drifting between Commitment and Expediency." *Journal of Architecture* 19, no. 6 (2014): 849–71.

Beeckmans, Luce. "French Planning in a Former Belgian Colony: A Critical Analysis of the French Urban Planning Missions in Post-Independence Kinshasa." *OASE* 82 (2010): 55–76.

Beier, Ulli. *Art in Nigeria 1960*. Cambridge, UK: University Press, 1960.

Beier, Ulli. "A Moment of Hope: Cultural Developments in Nigeria before the First Military Coup." In *The Short Century: Independence and Liberation Movements in Africa, 1945–1994*, edited by Okwui Enwezor, 45–49. Munich: Prestel, 2001.

Ben-Asher Gitler, Inbal. "Campus Architecture as Nation Building: Israeli Architect Arieh Sharon's Obafemi Awolowo University Campus, Ile-Ife, Nigeria." In *Third World Modernism: Architecture, Development, and Identity*, edited by Duanfang Lu, 112–40. New York: Routledge, 2011.

Benedict, Ruth. *Patterns of Culture*. Boston: Houghton Mifflin, 2005.

Bergman, Ronen. "Israel and Africa: Military and Intelligence Liaisons." PhD diss., University of Cambridge, 2007.

Berkowitz, Arie, and Carmela Rubin, eds. *Haim Heinz Fenchel: A Complex Puzzle*. Tel Aviv: Fenchel and Federman Families, 2012.

Berner, Boel. "'Human Capital,' Manpower Planning and Economic Theory: Some Critical Remarks." *Acta Sociologica* 17, no. 3 (1974): 236–55.

Bhabha, Homi K. *The Location of Culture*. London: Routledge, 1994.

Biletzky, Eliyahu. *Solel Boneh, 1924–1974*. Tel Aviv: Am Oved, 1974 (in Hebrew).

Black, Megan. "Interior's Exterior: The State, Mining Companies, and Resource Ideologies in the Point Four Program." *Diplomatic History* 40, no. 1 (January 2016): 81–110.

Bloch, Ernst. *The Principle of Hope*. Vol. 1. Translated by Neville Plaice, Stephen Plaice, and Paul Knight. Cambridge, MA: MIT Press, 1986.

"Buildings and Projects." *Journal of the Association of Architects, Engineers, and Town Planning* 4 (1963): B2–B37.

Burian, Edward R. "Modernity and Nationalism: Juan O'Gorman and Post-Revolutionary Architecture in Mexico, 1920–1960." In *Cruelty and Utopia: Cities and Landscapes of Latin America*, edited by Jean-François Lejeune, 211–23. New York: Princeton University Press, 2005.

Campbell, Bolaji. *Painting for the Gods: The Arts and Aesthetics of Yoruba Religious Murals*. Trenton, NJ: Africa World Press, 2008.

Canales, Jimena, and Andrew Herscher. "Criminal Skins: Tattoos and Modern Architecture in the Work of Adolf Loos." *Architectural History* 48 (2005): 235–56.

Caprotti, Federico. "Destructive Creation: Fascist Urban Planning, Architecture, and New Towns in the Pontine Marshes." *Journal of Historical Geography* 33 (2007): 651–79.

Caprotti, Federico. "Internal Colonisation, Hegemony and Coercion: Investigating Migration to Southern Lazio, Italy, in the 1930s." *Geoforum* 39 (2008): 942–57.

Caprotti, Federico. *Mussolini's Cities: Internal Colonisation in Italy, 1930–1939*. Youngstown, NY: Cambria Press, 2007.

Caprotti, Federico, and Maria Kaïka. "Producing the Ideal Fascist Landscape: Nature, Materiality and the Cinematic Representation of Land Reclamation in the Pontine Marshes." *Social and Cultural Geography* 9, no. 6 (September 2008): 613–34.

Carol, Steven S. *From Jerusalem to the Lion of Judah and Beyond: Israel's Foreign Policy in East Africa*. Bloomington, IN: iUniverse, 2012.

Carroll, Kevin. *Architectures of Nigeria: Architectures of the Hausa and Yoruba Peoples and of the Many Peoples between Tradition and Modernization*. London: Ethnographica / Lester Crook Academic Publishing, 1992.

Chakrabarty, Dipesh. "The Legacies of Bandung: Decolonization and the Politics of Culture." In *Making a World after Empire: The Bandung Moment and Its Political Alternatives*, edited by Christopher J. Lee, 45–68. Athens, OH: Ohio University Press, 2010.

Chakrabarty, Dipesh. *Provincializing Europe: Postcolonial Thought and Historical Difference*. Princeton, NJ: Princeton University Press, 2000.

Chang, Jiat-Hwee. "Building a Colonial Technoscientific Network: Tropical Architecture, Building Science and the Politics of Decolonization." In *Third World Modernism*, edited by Duanfang Lu, 211–35. London: Routledge, 2011.

Chang, Jiat-Hwee. *A Genealogy of Tropical Architecture: Colonialism, Ecology, and Technology*. London: Routledge, 2016.

Chang, Jiat-Hwee, and Anthony D. King. "Toward a Genealogy of Tropical Architecture: Historical Fragments of Power-Knowledge, Built Environment and Climate in the British Colonial Territories." *Singapore Journal of Tropical Geography* 32 (2011): 283–300.

Chazan, Naomi. "Israel and Africa: Dynamics of Relationships in the Seventies." *Kidma: Israel Journal of Development* no. 2 (1973): 7–12.

Chazan, Naomi. *The Roles of Preliminary Training in Israeli Aid: Evaluation and Prediction.* Jerusalem: The Truman Institute, The Hebrew University, 1972. Unpublished report (in Hebrew).

Cheng, Anne Anlin. *Second Skin: Josephine Baker and the Modern Surface.* New York: Oxford University Press, 2011.

Chibber, Vivek. *Postcolonial Theory and the Specter of Capital.* London: Verso, 2013.

Chyutin, Bracha, and Michael Chyutin. *Architecture and Utopia: Kibbutz and Moshav.* Jerusalem: Magness Press, 2010 (in Hebrew).

Clastres, Pierre. *Society against the State.* Translated by Robert Hurley. New York: Zone, 1998.

Colomina, Beatriz. "The Split Wall: Domestic Voyeurism." In *Sexuality and Space*, edited by Beatriz Colomina, 72–128. New York: Princeton Architectural Press, 1992.

Cooper, Frederick. *Decolonization and African Society: The Labor Question in French and British Africa.* Cambridge, UK: Cambridge University Press, 1996.

Cooper, Frederick. "Writing the History of Development." In "Modernizing Missions: Approaches to 'Developing' the Non-Western World after 1945," special issue, *Journal of Modern European History* 8, no. 1 (2010): 5–23.

Correa, Charles. *Form Follows Climate.* London: Pidgeon Digital, 2009. Recording.

Crinson, Mark. "From the Rainforest to the Streets." In *Colonial Modern: Aesthetics of the Past Rebellions for the Future*, edited by Tom Avermaete, Serhat Karakayali, and Marion von Osten, 98–111. London: Black Dog, 2010.

Crinson, Mark. *Modern Architecture and the End of Empire.* Aldershot, UK: Ashgate, 2003.

Crush, Jonathan. "Introduction: Imagining Development." In *The Power of Development*, edited by Jonathan Crush, 1–23. London: Routledge, 1995.

Cullather, Nick. "Miracles of Modernization: The Green Revolution and the Apotheosis of Technology." *Diplomatic History* 28, no. 2 (April 2004): 227–54.

Cullather, Nick. "The Third Race." *Diplomatic History* 33, no. 3 (June 1, 2009): 507–12.

Cupers, Kenny. "*Géographie Volontaire* and the Territorial Logic of Architecture." *Architectural Histories* 4, no. 1 (2016): 1–13.

Curtis, Michael, and Susan Aurelia Gitelson, eds., *Israel in the Third World.* New Brunswick, NJ: Transaction, 1976.

Curtis, William J. R. "Authenticity, Abstraction and the Ancient Sense: Le

Corbusier's and Louis Kahn's Ideas of Parliament." *Perspecta* 20 (1983): 181–94.

Curto, Roxanna Nydia. *Inter-tech(s): Colonialism and the Question of Technology in Francophone Literature*. Charlottesville, VA: University of Virginia Press, 2016.

Dan, Hillel. *On the Unpaved Road: The Story of Solel Boneh*. Jerusalem: Schocken, 1963 (in Hebrew).

Daniel, Jamie Owen. "Reclaiming the 'Terrain of Fantasy': Speculations on Ernst Bloch, Memory, and the Resurgence of Nationalism." In *Not Yet: Reconsidering Ernst Bloch*, edited by Jamie Owen Daniel and Tom Moylan, 53–62. London: Verso, 1997.

Dash, Jacob, and Elisha Efrat. *The Israel Physical Master Plan*. Jerusalem: The Israel Government Ministry of the Interior, Planning Department, 1964.

Davidson, Basil. *Black Man's Burden: Africa and the Curse of the Nation-State*. London: James Curry, 1992.

de Kiewiet, Cornelius. *The Emergent African University: An Interpretation*. Washington, DC: Overseas Liaison Committee, American Council on Education, 1971.

de Lauretis, Teresa. "Difference Embodied: Reflections on Black Skin, White Masks." *Parallax* 8, no. 2 (2002): 54–68.

De Raedt, Kim. "Architecture as Development Aid." PhD diss., University of Ghent, 2017.

De Raedt, Kim. "Between 'True Believers' and Operational Experts: UNESCO Architects and School Building in Postcolonial Africa." *Journal of Architecture* 19, no. 1 (2014): 19–42.

Dibua, Jeremiah I. *Modernization and the Crisis of Development in Africa: The Nigerian Experience*. Aldershot, UK: Ashgate, 2006.

Diouf, Mamadou. "Modernity: Africa." In *New Dictionary of the History of Ideas*, vol. 4, edited by Maryanne Cline Horowitz, 1475–79. New York: Charles Scribner's Sons, 2005.

Doudai, Aryeh. "Regional Planning and Development." Paper presented at the *International Seminar on Rural Planning*, October–November 1961, Ministry of Foreign Affairs, Department for International Cooperation, Jerusalem.

Doudai, Aryeh. "The Relationship between Physical and Social Aspects in Urban Communities." Paper presented at the *International Seminar on Social and Cultural Integration in Urban Areas*, November 1964, Mount Carmel International Training Centre for Community Service, Haifa, Israel.

Doudai, Aryeh, and Ursula Oelsner. *Sierra Leone National Urbanisation Plan*. Tel Aviv: Institute for Planning and Development, 1965.

Dutta, Arindam. "Linguistics, Not Grammatology: Architecture's *A Prioris* and Architecture's Priorities." In *A Second Modernism: MIT, Architecture, and the "Techno-Social" Moment,* edited by Arindam Dutta, 1–69. Cambridge, MA: SA+P Press, MIT Press, 2013.

Echeruo, Michael J. C. "'The Jewish Question,' and the Diaspora: Theory and Practice." *Journal of Black Studies* 40, no. 4 (March 2010): 544–65.

Efrat, Zvi. *The Israeli Project: Building and Architecture, 1948–1973.* Tel Aviv: Tel Aviv Museum of Art, 2004 (in Hebrew).

Efrat, Zvi. *The Most Beautiful Campus in Africa.* Israel and Nigeria, 2019. DVD.

Ekbladh, David. "'Mr. TVA': Grass-Roots Development, David Lilienthal, and the Rise and Fall of the Tennessee Valley Authority as a Symbol for U.S. Overseas Development, 1933–1973." *Diplomatic History* 26, no. 3 (Summer 2002): 335–74.

Elhanani, Abba, Abraham Erlik, Shlomo Gilad, Nahum Zolotov, Yitzhak Yashar, Michael Nadler, Emanuel Friedman, Moshe Rosetti, and David Reznik. "Monumental Construction in This Century: A Symposium." *Tvai* (1967): 14–22 (in Hebrew).

Elhanani, Abba, Abraham Erlik, Shlomo Gilad, Nahum Zolotov, Yitzhak Yashar, Michael Nadler, Emanuel Friedman, Moshe Rosetti, and David Reznik. "Our Contribution to Modern Architecture." *Handasa VeAdrikhalut* 19, no. 5–6 (May–June 1961): 133–36 (in Hebrew).

Elhyani, Zvi. "Seashore Holdings." In *Back to the Sea: Israeli Pavilion, 9th International Architecture Exhibition, the Venice Biennial,* edited by Sigal Barnir and Yael Moria-Klain, 104–16. Jersualem: Keter, 2004.

Elleh, Nnamdi. *African Architecture: Evolution and Transformation.* New York: McGraw-Hill, 1996.

Elshahed, Mohamed. "Revolutionary Modernism? Architecture and the Politics of Transition in Egypt, 1936–1976." PhD diss., New York University, 2015.

Enav, Zalman. "Architecture in Ethiopia Today." *Zede* 1, no. 1 (November 1965): 17–25.

Engerman, David C., and Corrina R. Unger. "Introduction: Toward a Global History of Modernization." *Diplomatic History* 33, no. 3 (June 2009): 375–85.

Enwezor, Okwui. "Modernity and Its Postcolonial Ambivalence." In *Altermodern: Tate Triennial,* edited by Nicolas Bourriaud, n.p. London: Tate, 2009.

Erlich, Haggai. *Alliance and Alienation: Ethiopia and Israel in the Days of Haile Selassie.* Tel Aviv: Moshe Dayan Center for Middle Eastern and African Studies, Tel Aviv University, 2013 (in Hebrew).

Erlich, Haggai. *Ethiopia and the Middle East.* Boulder, CO: Lynne Rienner, 1994.

Escobar, Arturo. *Encountering Development: The Making and Unmaking of the Third World*. Princeton, NJ: Princeton University Press, 2011.

Esedebe, Peter Olisanwuche. *Pan-Africanism: The Idea and Movement, 1776–1963*. Washington, DC: Howard University Press, 1994.

Everil, Bronwen. "Material Culture and Sierra Leone's Civilising Mission in the Nineteenth Century." In *The Cultural Construction of the British World*, edited by Barry Crosbie and Mark Hampton, 198–218. Manchester, UK: Manchester University Press, 2016.

Eyal, Gil. *The Disenchantment of the Orient: Expertise in Arab Affairs and the Israeli State*. Stanford, CA: Stanford University Press, 2006.

Fanon, Frantz. *Black Skin, White Masks*. Translated by Richard Philcox. New York: Grove, 2008.

Fanon, Frantz. *The Wretched of the Earth*. Translated by Richard Philcox. New York: Grove, 2004.

Feldman, Yotam. *The Lab*. Israel; Belgium; France: Gun Films, 2013. DVD.

Feniger, Neta. "From Nahalal to Danesfahan: The Transfer of Israeli Modern Rurality to Village Planning in Iran." In "The Modern Village," special issue, *Journal of Architecture* 23, no. 3 (2018): 367–91.

Feniger, Neta, and Rachel Kallus. "Expertise in the Name of Diplomacy: The Israeli Plan for Rebuilding the Qazvin Region, Iran." *International Journal of Islamic Architecture* 5, no. 1 (2016): 106–34.

Ferguson, James. *The Anti-Politics Machine: "Development," Depoliticization, and Bureaucratic Power in Lesotho*. 1994. Minneapolis, MN: University of Minnesota Press, 2009.

Ferguson, James. *Global Shadows: Africa in the Neoliberal World Order*. Durham, NC: Duke University Press, 2006.

Ferme, Mariane. "Staging Politisi: The Dialogics of Publicity and Secrecy in Sierra Leone." In *Readings in Modernity in Africa*, edited by Peter Geschiere, Brigit Meyer, and Peter Pels, 111–23. London: The International African Institute, School of Oriental and African Studies, 2008.

Forester, John, Raphael Fischler, and Deborah Shmueli, eds. *Israeli Planners and Designers: Profiles of Community Builders*. Albany, NY: State University New York Press, 2001.

Foucault, Michel. *Security, Territory, Population: Lectures at the Collège de France, 1977–1978*. Translated by Graham Burchell. New York: Picador, 2007.

Frenkel, Michal, Yehouda Shenhav, and Hanna Herzog. "The Political Embeddedness of Managerial Ideologies in Pre-State Israel: The Case of PPL 1920–1948." *Journal of Management History* 3, no. 2 (1997): 120–44.

Frenkel, Stephen, and John Western. "Pretext or Prophylaxis? Racial Segregation and Malarial Mosquitoes in a British Tropical Colony: Sierra Leone."

*Annals of the Association of American Geographers* 78, no. 2 (January 1988): 211–28.

Fry, E. Maxwell, and K. W. Farms. *Town Planning Scheme for Freetown*. Lagos: Government Printer, 1945.

Fry, Maxwell, and Jane Drew. *Tropical Architecture in the Dry and Humid Zones*. New York: Reinhold, 1964.

Fry, Maxwell, and Jane Drew. *Tropical Architecture in the Humid Zone*. New York: Reinhold, 1956.

Fuchs, Ron, and Gilbert Herbert. "Representing Mandatory Palestine: Austen St. Barbe Harrison and the Representational Buildings of the British Mandate in Palestine, 1922–37." *Architectural History* 43 (2000): 281–333.

Fyfe, Christopher, and Eldred Jones, eds. *Freetown: A Symposium*. Freetown: Sierra Leone University Press, 1968.

Gershoni, Yekutiel. "Liberia and Israel: The Evolution of a Relationship." *Liberian Studies Journal* 14, no. 1 (1989): 34–50.

Gershoni, Yekutiel. "Liberia and the Decolonization." Paper presented at the Seventh Annual African Studies Conference, May 2, 1987, Stanford-Berkeley Joint Center for African Studies.

Gideon, Siegfried. "The Need for a New Monumentality." In *New Architecture and City Planning: A Symposium*, edited by Paul Zucker, 549–68. New York: Philosophical Library, 1944.

Gillis, Rivi. "Developing Identity: Israeli Training of Africans, 1958–1980." PhD diss., Tel Aviv University, 2018 (in Hebrew).

Gilman, Sandar. *The Jew's Body*. New York: Routledge, 1991.

Giorgis, Elizabeth Wolde. "Charting Out Ethiopian Modernity and Modernism." *Callaloo* 22, no. 1 (Winter 2010): 82–99.

Givoni, Michal. "Who Cares (What's to Be Done)? Israeli Responses to Biafra." *Theory and Criticism* 23 (Fall 2003): 57–81 (in Hebrew).

Golan, Arnon. "Central Place Theory and Israeli Geography: Space, the Holocaust, Modernism, and Silence." *Ofakim BeGografia* 74–76 (1997): 39–52 (in Hebrew).

Goldberg, Sidney. *Israel, Africa, and Asia: Partners in Progress*. London: Labour Friends of Israel, 1968.

Goldsmith, Arthur A. "The Management of Institutional Innovation: Lessons from Transferring the Land Grant Model to India." *Public Administration and Development* 8 (1988): 317–30.

Gordon, Neve. "The Political Economy of Israel's Homeland Security/Surveillance Industry." *The New Transparency: Surveillance and Social Sorting; Working Papers III*. Accessed December 12, 2014. http://www.sscqueens.org/sites/default/files/The%20Political%20Economy%20of%20Israel%E2%80%99s%20Homeland%20Security.pdf.

Gorni, Yosef, Avi Bareli, and Yitzhak Greenberg, eds. *The Histadrut from*

Workers' Society to Trade Union: Selected Essays on Histadrut, 1920–1994.* Sede Boqer, Israel: Ben-Gurion University of the Negev Press, 2000 (in Hebrew).

Greenberg, Itzhak. "Labor's Expanding Economy, 1948–1988." In *Society and Economy in Israel: Historical and Contemporary Perspectives,* edited by Tuvia Friling and Daniel Gutwein, 332–42. Sede Boqer, Israel: The Ben-Gurion Research Institute, 2005 (in Hebrew).

Gulema, Shimelis Bonsa. "Urbanizing a Nation: Addis Ababa and the Shaping of the Modern Ethiopian State, 1941–1975." PhD diss., UCLA, 2011.

Hardt, Michael. "Affective Labor." *Boundary 2* 26, no. 2 (Summer 1999): 89–100.

Harris, Richard, and Susan Parnell. "The Turning Point in Urban Policy for British Colonial Africa, 1939–1945." In *Colonial Architecture and Urbanism in Africa,* edited by Fassil Demissie, 127–51. Farnham, UK: Ashgate, 2012.

Harrison, Mark. *Climates and Constitutions: Health, Race, Environment, and British Imperialism in India, 1600–1850.* New Delhi: Oxford University Press, 1999.

Hart, Mitchell B. *Social Science and the Politics of Modern Jewish Identity.* Stanford, CA: Stanford University Press, 2000.

Hashimshony, Avia. "Architecture." In *Art in Israel,* edited by Benjamin Tammuz and Max Wykes-Joyce, 199–284. London: W. H. Allen, 1966.

Hattis-Rolef, Sheila. "The Knesset Building in Giv'at Ram: Planning and Construction." *Katedra* 96 (2000): 131–70 (in Hebrew).

Hattis-Rolef, Sheila. "The Knesset Planning: Additions and Corrections." *Katedra* 105 (2002): 171–80 (in Hebrew).

Headrick, Daniel R. *The Tentacles of Progress: Technology Transfer in the Age of Imperialism, 1850–1940.* New York: Oxford University Press, 1988.

Heimann, Gadi. "A Case of Diplomatic Symbiosis: France, Israel and the Former French Colonies in Africa, 1958–62." *Journal of Contemporary History* 51, no. 1 (2016): 145–64.

Herbst, Jeffrey. *States and Power in Africa: Comparative Lessons in Authority and Control.* Princeton, NJ: Princeton University Press, 2000.

Herz, Manuel. "Project of a Nation: The African Riviera and The Hôtel Ivoire." In *African Modernism: The Architecture of Independence: Ghana, Senegal, Côte d'Ivoire, Kenya, Zambia,* edited by Manuel Hertz, 382–97. Zürich: Park Books, 2015.

Hess, Janet Berry. *Art and Architecture in Postcolonial Africa.* Jefferson, NC: McFarland, 2006.

Hever, Hannan. *Nativism, Zionism, and Beyond.* Syracuse, NY: Syracuse University Press, 2014.

Hever, Hannan, and Orin D. Gensler. "Minority Discourse of a National

Majority: Israeli Fiction of the Early Sixties." *Prooftexts* 10, no. 1 (January 1990): 129–47.

Hill, Robert A. "Black Zionism: Marcus Garvey and the Jewish Question." In *African Americans and Jews in the Twentieth Century: Studies in Convergence and Conflict,* edited by Vincent P. Franklin, 40–53. Columbia, MO: Missouri University Press, 1998.

Hinsky, Sarah. "The Silence of the Fish: The Local and the Universal in the Israeli Art Discourse." *Theory and Criticism* 4 (Fall 1993): 105–22 (in Hebrew).

Hoffman, Danny. *Monrovia Modern: Urban Form and Political Imagination in Liberia.* Durham, NC: Duke University Press, 2017.

Horowitz, Dan, and Moshe Lissak. *Origins of the Israeli Polity: Palestine under the Mandate.* Tel Aviv: Am Oved, 1977 (in Hebrew).

Imevbore, A. M. A. *Science and Spirituality: The Autobiography of an African Scientist.* Ile-Ife, Nigeria: Christ Apostolic Church, 2005.

Inbal, Aliza Belman, and Shachar Zahavi. *The Rise and Fall of Israel's Bilateral Aid Budget 1958–2008.* Tel Aviv: Harlod Hartog School of Government and Policy, Tel Aviv University / Pearce Foundation, 2009. Accessed January 8, 2015. http://socsci.tau.ac.il/government/images/PDFs/riseandfall.pdf.

Jackson, Iain. "Tropical Architecture and the West Indies: From Military Advances and Tropical Medicine to Robert Gardner-Medwin and the Networks of Tropical Modernism." *Journal of Architecture* 18, no. 2 (2013): 167–95.

Jackson, Iain, and Jessica Holland. *The Architecture of Edwin Maxwell Fry and Jane Drew: Twentieth Century Architecture, Pioneer Modernism, and the Tropics.* Farnham, UK: Ashgate, 2014.

Kahane, Reuven. "The Dominant Ideology's Stances on Science, Scientists and Professionalism in the Yishuv Era." In *Social Classes in Israel: A Reader,* edited by Shmuel Noah Eisenstadt, Rivka Bar-Yosef, Reuven Kahane, and A. Shelach, 181–236. Jerusalem: Akademon, 1968 (in Hebrew).

Kallus, Rachel. "The Crete Development Plan: A Post–Second World War Israeli Experience of Transnational Professional Exchange." *Planning Perspectives* 30, no. 3 (2015): 339–65.

Kandeh, Jimmy D., Ricardo René Larémont, and Rachel Cremona. "Ethnicity and National Identity in Sierra Leone." In *Borders, Nationalism, and the African State,* edited by Ricardo René Larémont, 210–65. Boulder, CO: Lynne Rienner, 2005.

Kapuściński, Ryszard. *The Emperor: Downfall of an Autocrat.* Translated by William R. Brand and Katarzyna Mroczkowska-Brand. 1978. New York: Vintage Books, 1989.

Karmi, Ram. Interview. In Meira Yagid-Haimovich, *Dov Karmi: Architect-*

*Engineer Public Domestica*. Tel Aviv: Tel Aviv Museum of Art, 2011. DVD and booklet (in Hebrew).

Karmi, Ram. *Lyric Architecture*. Tel Aviv: Israeli Ministry of Defense, 2001 (in Hebrew).

Katz, Shaul, and Joseph Ben-David. "Scientific Research and Agricultural Innovation in Israel." *Minerva* 13, no. 2 (Summer 1975): 152–81.

Kebede, Massay. "Japan and Ethiopia: An Appraisal of Similarities and Divergent Courses." *Ethiopia in Broader Perspective: Papers of the XIIIth International Conference of Ethiopian Studies, Kyoto, 12–17 December 1997*, edited by Katsuyoshi Fukui, Eisei Kurimoto, and Masayoshi Shigeta, 639–51. Kyoto, Japan: Shokado, 1997.

Kellner, Douglas. "Ernst Bloch, Utopia, and Ideology Critique." In *Not Yet: Reconsidering Ernst Bloch*, edited by Jamie Owen Daniel and Tom Moylan, 80–95. London: Verso, 1997.

Kemp, Adriana. "Borders, Space, and Collective Identity." In *Space, Land, Home*, edited by Yehouda Shenhav, 52–83. Tel Aviv: The Van Leer Jerusalem Institute and Hakibbutz Hameuchad, 2003 (in Hebrew).

Kenny, Judith T. "Climate, Race, and Imperial Authority: The Symbolic Landscape of the British Hill Stations in India." *Annals of the Association of American Geographers* 85, no. 4 (1995): 694–714.

Kilson, Martin. *Political Change in a West African State: A Study of the Modernization Process in Sierra Leone*. Cambridge, MA: Harvard University Press, 1966.

Klein, Naomi. *The Shock Doctrine: The Rise of Disaster Capitalism*. New York: Picador, 2008.

Klein, Yossi, and Ruth Kark. "The Demolition of Herzliya Gymnasium and the Construction of the Shalom Meir Tower as the Beginning of Tel Aviv's Americanization." In *Tel Aviv-Yafo, from a Garden Suburb to World City: The First Hundred Years*, edited by Baruch Kipnis, 103–28. Haifa, Israel: Pardes, 2009 (in Hebrew).

Kozlovsky, Roy. "Necessity by Design." *Perspecta* 34 (June 2003): 10–27.

Kreinin, Mordechai E. *Israel and Africa: A Study in Technical Cooperation*. New York: Praeger, 1964.

Kroyanker, David. *Jerusalem Architecture, Periods, and Styles: Modern Architecture outside the Old City Walls, 1948–1990*. Jerusalem: Keter, 1991 (in Hebrew).

Kroyanker, David. *Jerusalem: The Knesset Residence in Fromin House, 1950–66*. Jerusalem: Society of the Old Knesset Residence, 2003 (in Hebrew).

Lagae, Johan, and Kim De Raedt. "Building for 'l'Authenticité': Eugène Palumbo and the Architecture of Mobutu's Congo." In "Building Modern Africa," special issue, *Journal of Architectural Education* 68, no. 2 (2014): 178–89.

Lamptey, G. Odartey. "The Ghana Experience." In *Conference on Free World*

*Cooperation with Africa: American and Israeli Approaches*, Duquesne University, 1964. New York: American Histadrut Cultural Exchange Institute, 1964.

Larkin, Brian. *Signal and Noise: Media, Infrastructure, and Urban Culture in Nigeria*. Durham, NC: Duke University Press, 2008.

Laufer, Leopold. *Israel and the Developing Countries: New Approaches to Cooperation*. New York: Twentieth Century Fund, 1967.

Lee, Christopher J., ed. "Introduction: Between a Moment and an Era: The Origins and Afterlives of Bandung." In *Making a World after Empire: The Bandung Moment and Its Political Afterlives*, edited by Christopher J. Lee, 1–42. Athens, OH: Ohio University Press, 2010.

le Roux, Hannah. "Building on the Boundary: Modern Architecture in the Tropics." *Social Identities* 10, no. 4 (2004): 439–53.

le Roux, Hannah. "Modern Architecture in Post-colonial Ghana and Nigeria." *Architectural History* 47 (2004): 361–92.

le Roux, Hannah. "The Networks of Tropical Architecture." *Journal of Architecture* 8 (Autumn 2003): 337–54.

Lev, Tali. "A Mission in Israel: Margaret Mead's Visit in Israel in Summer 1956." *Theory and Criticism* 36 (2010): 231–39 (in Hebrew).

Levey, Zach. *Israel in Africa, 1956–76*. Dordrecht, The Netherlands: Martinus-Nijhoff, 2012.

Levey, Zach. "Israel's Entry to Africa, 1956–61." *Diplomacy and Statecraft* 12, no. 3 (2007): 87–114.

Levey, Zach. "The Rise and Decline of a Special Relationship: Israel and Ghana, 1957–1966." *African Studies Review* 46, no. 1 (April 2003): 155–77.

Levin, Ayala. "Exporting Architectural National Expertise: Arieh Sharon's Ile-Ife University Campus in West Nigeria (1962–1976)." In *Nationalism and Architecture*, edited by Raymond Quek and Darren Deane, 53–66. Aldershot, UK: Ashgate, 2012.

Levin, Ayala. "Haile Selassie's Imperial Modernity: Expatriate Architects and the Shaping of Addis Ababa." *Journal of the Society of Architectural Historians* 75, no. 4 (December 2016): 447–68.

Levin, Ayala. "The Mountain and the Fortress: The Location of the Hebrew University Campus on Mount Scopus in the Israeli Imaginary of National Space." *Theory and Criticism* 38–39 (Winter 2011): 11–34 (in Hebrew).

Levin, Michael. "Regional Aspects of the International Style in Tel Aviv and Jerusalem." In *Critical Regionalism: The Pomona Meeting Proceedings*, edited by Spyros Amourgis, 240–57. Pomona, CA: College of Environmental Design, California State Polytechnic University, 1991.

Lévi-Strauss, Claude. *The Savage Mind*. Translated by George Weidenfeld and Nicholson. 1962. Chicago: University of Chicago Press, 1966.

Lindblom, Charles E. "The Science of 'Muddling Through.'" *Public Administration Review* 19 (1959): 79–88.

Lissovsky, Nurit, and Diana Dolev. *Arcadia: The Gardens of Lipa Yahalom and Dan Zur*. Tel Aviv: Babel, 2012 (in Hebrew).

Livsey, Tim. "'Suitable Lodgings for Students': Modern Spaces, Colonial Development and Decolonization in Nigeria." *Urban History* 41, no. 4 (November 2014): 664–85.

Loos, Adolf. *Ornament and Crime: Selected Essays*. Translated by Michael Mitchell. Riverside, CA: Ariadne, 1998.

Mabogunje, Akin L. *Urbanization in Nigeria*. New York: Africana, 1969.

Mabogunje, Akin L. "Urban Planning and the Post-Colonial State in Africa: A Research Overview." *African Studies Review* 33, no. 2 (September 1990): 121–203.

Mabogunje, Akin L., and Adetoye Faniran, eds. *Regional Planning and National Development in Tropical Africa*. Ibadan, Nigeria: Ibadan University Press, 1977.

Mafeje, Archie. "Neo-Colonialism, State Capitalism or Revolution?" In *African Social Studies: A Radical Reader*, edited by Peter C. W. Gutkin and Peter Waterman, 412–22. New York: Monthly Review, 1977.

Mafit Trust Corporation. *The African Riviera: Mafit Project Prepared for the Government of the Republic of Ivory Coast*. Tel Aviv: United Artists, 1970.

Malkhin, Ahuvia, and Ze'ev Goldberg, eds. *Israel's Relations with the Developing Countries: A Discussion*. Tsofit, Israel: Berl Katznelson Institute, 1962 (in Hebrew).

Mamdani, Mahmood. "Beyond Settler and Native as Political Identities: Overcoming the Political Legacy of Colonialism." In *The Short Century: Independence and Liberation Movements in Africa, 1945–1994*, edited by Okwui Enwezor, 21–28. Munich: Prestel, 2001.

Mamdani, Mahmood. *Citizen and Subject: Contemporary Africa and the Legacy of Late Colonialism*. Princeton, NJ: Princeton University Press, 1996.

Manor, Dalia. *Art in Zion: The Genesis of Modern National Art in Jewish Palestine*. London: Routledge, 2005.

Mariam, Dejene H. "Architecture in Addis Ababa." In *Proceedings of the International Symposium on the Centenary of Addis Ababa, November 24–25, 1986*, edited by Ahmed Zekaria, Bahru Zewde, and Taddese Beyene, 199–215. Addis Ababa: Addis Ababa City Council, 1987.

Massad, Joseph. "The 'Post-Colonial' Colony: Time, Space, and Bodies in Palestine/Israel." In *The Pre-Occupation of Postcolonial Studies*, edited by Fawzia Afzal-Khan and Kalpana Seshadri-Crooks, 311–46. Durham, NC: Duke University Press, 2000.

Matless, David. "Regional Surveys and Local Knowledges: The Geographic

Imagination in Britain, 1918–39." *Transactions of the Institute of British Geographers* 17, no. 4 (1992): 464–80.

Mayer, Shay. *The Mayer Brothers' Story*. Tel Aviv: Kavim, 2009 (in Hebrew).

Mbembe, Achille. *On the Postcolony*. Berkeley, CA: University of California Press, 2001.

McVety, Amanda Kay. *Enlightened Aid: US Development as Foreign Policy in Ethiopia*. Oxford: Oxford University Press, 2012.

McVety, Amanda Kay. "Pursuing Progress: Point Four in Ethiopia." *Diplomatic History* 32, no. 3 (June 2008): 371–403.

Meir, Golda. *My Life*. New York: Putnam, 1975.

Mellanby, Kenneth. *The Birth of Nigeria's University*. London: Methuen, 1958.

Metzger-Szmuk, Nitza. *Houses from the Sand: International Style Architecture in Tel Aviv*. Tel Aviv: Tel Aviv Foundation and the Israeli Ministry of Defense, 1994 (in Hebrew).

Mezzedimi, Arturo. "Haile Selassie: A Testimony for Reappraisal (1992)." Arturo Mezzedimi Architetto. Accessed November 20, 2014. http://www.arturomezzedimi.it/en/home.swf.

Miescher, Stephan, Peter J. Bloom, and Takyiwaa Manuh, eds. *Modernization as Spectacle in Africa*. Bloomington, IN: Indiana University Press, 2014.

Milkias, Paulos. *Haile Selassie, Western Education, and Political Revolution in Ethiopia*. Youngstown, NY: Cambria Press, 2006.

Mooreville, Anat. "Eyeing Africa: The Politics of Israeli Ocular Expertise and International Aid, 1959–1973." *Jewish Social Studies* 21, no. 3 (Spring/Summer 2016): 31–71.

Moravánsky, Ákos. "Peripheral Modernism: Charles Polónyi and the Lessons of the Village." *Journal of Architecture* 17, no. 3 (2012): 333–59.

Mosse, George L. "Max Nordau, Liberalism and the New Jew." *Journal of Contemporary History* 27, no. 4 (October 1992): 565–81.

Mufti, Aamir R. *Enlightenment in the Colony: The Jewish Question and the Crisis of Postcolonial Culture*. Princeton, NJ: Princeton University Press, 2007.

Muzaffar, M. Ijlal. "Fuzzy Images: The Problem of Third World Development and the New Ethics of Open-Ended Planning at the MIT-Harvard Joint Center for Urban Studies." In *A Second Modernism: MIT, Architecture, and the "Techno-Social" Moment*, edited by Arindam Dutta, 310–41. Cambridge, MA: SA+P Press, MIT Press, 2013.

Muzaffar, M. Ijlal. "The Periphery Within: Modern Architecture and the Making of the Third World." PhD diss., Massachusetts Institute of Technology, 2007.

Near, Henry. "Like All Nations? Zionist Pioneering in Intercultural Perspective." In *The Age of Zionism*, edited by Anita Shapira, Yehuda Reinhartz, and Ya'akov Haris, 109–26. Jerusalem: Zalman Shazar Center, 2000.

Near, Henry. "Pioneers and Pioneering in the State of Israel: Semantic and Historical Aspects, 1948–1956." *Iyunim Bitkumat Israel* 2 (1992): 116–40.

Neuberger, Benyamin. "Black Nationalism, Jews, and Zionism." *Avar Ve'Atid: A Journal for Jewish Education, Culture, and Discourse* (April 1996): 18–22. Accessed December 30, 2014. http://www.bjpa.org/Publications/details.cfm?PublicationID=12840.

Neuberger, Benyamin. "Early African Nationalism, Judaism and Zionism: Edward Wilmot Blyden." *Jewish Social Studies* 47, no. 2 (Spring 1985): 151–66.

Neumann, Boaz. *Land and Desire in Early Zionism*. Tel Aviv: Am Oved, 2009 (in Hebrew).

Niemann, Bernard J., and William H. Tishler. "Cool Planning for a Hot Campus in Ife, Nigeria." *Landscape Architecture* 61, no. 3 (April 1971): 216–26.

Niemann, Bernard J., and William H. Tishler. *University of Ife Physical Development Plan, Ife, Nigeria*. Madison, WI: Dept. of Landscape Architecture, School of Natural Resources, College of Agricultural and Life Sciences, University of Wisconsin, 1969.

Nitzan-Shiftan, Alona. "Contested Zionism—Alternative Modernism: Erich Mendelsohn and the Tel Aviv Chug in Mandate Palestine." *Architectural History* 39 (1996): 147–80.

Nitzan-Shiftan, Alona. "Seizing Locality in Jerusalem." In *The End of Tradition?*, edited by Nezar AlSayyad, 231–55. London: Routledge, 2004.

Njoh, Ambe J. "Urban Planning as a Tool of Power and Social Control in Colonial Africa." *Planning Perspectives* 24, no. 3 (2009): 301–17.

Njoh, Ambe J., and Fenda Akiwumi. "Colonial Legacies, Land Policies and the Millennium Development Goals: Lessons from Cameroon and Sierra Leone." *Habitat International* 36, no. 2 (2012): 210–18.

Norberg, Viveca Halldin. "Swedes in Haile Selassie's Ethiopia, 1924–1952: A Study in Early Development Co-Operation." PhD diss., University of Stockholm, 1977.

Nordau, Max. "Address at the First Zionist Congress, August 29, 1897." *Jewish Virtual Library*. Accessed January 8, 2015. http://www.jewishvirtuallibrary.org/jsource/Zionism/nordau1.html.

Nordau, Max. "Jewry of Muscle (June 1903)." In *The Jew in the Modern World*, edited by Paul Mendes-Flohr and Jehuda Reinharz, 547–48. New York: Oxford University Press, 1995.

Noyer-Duplaix, Léo. "Henri Chomette: Africa as a Terrain of Architectural Freedom." In *African Modernism: The Architecture of Independence: Ghana, Senegal, Côte d'Ivoire, Kenya, Zambia*, edited by Manuel Herz, 271–82. Zürich: Park Books, 2015.

Nwana, Eugene. "Ohaji Farm Settlement: A Flash in the Pan." In *Foreign Experts and Unsustainable Development: Transferring Israeli Technology to Zambia, Nigeria, and Nepal*, edited by Moshe Schwartz and A. Paul Hare, 109–28. Aldershot, UK: Ashgate, 2000.

Nye, David. *American Technological Sublime*. 1994. Cambridge, MA: MIT Press, 1996.

Ockman, Joan. "A Plastic Epic: The Synthesis of the Arts Discourse in France in the Mid-Twentieth Century." In *Architecture + Art: New Visions, New Strategies*, edited by Eeva-Liisa Pelkonen and Esa Laaksonen, 30–61. Helsinki: Alvar Aalto Academy, 2007.

Oded, Aryeh. *Africa and Israel*. Jerusalem: Magness Press, 2011.

Ohlin, Göran. "Swedish Aid Performance and Development Policy." *Development Policy Review* A6, no. 1 (November 1973): 50–62.

Ojo, G. J. Afolabi. "Traditional Yoruba Architecture." *African Arts* 1, no. 3 (Spring 1968): 14–72.

Okeke-Agulu, Chika. "Nationalism and the Rhetoric of Modernism in Nigeria: The Art of Uche Okeke and Demas Nwoko, 1960–1968." *African Arts* 39, no. 1 (2006): 26–93.

Olaiya, Yetunde. "Systemic Shifts: The Case of Abidjan's Urban Planning, 1945–60." *Journal of Architectural Education* 68, no. 2 (2014): 190–98.

Olgyay, Victor. *Design with Climate: Bioclimatic Approach to Architectural Regionalism*. Princeton, NJ: Princeton University Press, 1963.

Oluwasanmi, Hezekiah. *Address by the Vice-Chancellor Professor H. A. Oluwasanmi at the University of Ife Graduation Ceremony, 1969*. Ile-Ife, Nigeria: University of Ife / Ibadan, Nigeria: Ibadan University Press, 1969.

Oluwasanmi, Hezekiah. *Agriculture and Nigerian Economic Development*. Ibadan, Nigeria: Oxford University Press, 1966.

Oluwasanmi, Hezekiah. *The Challenge of the Technological Gap: Being a Text from an Address of the Vice Chancellor to the Convocation of the University of Ife, October 10, 1970*. Ile-Ife, Nigeria: University of Ife, 1970.

Oluwasanmi, Hezekiah. *The March Forward: An Address to the Convocation of the University, July 3, 1971*. Ile-Ife, Nigeria: University of Ife, 1971.

Oluwasanmi, Hezekiah. "The Preservation of Intellectual Freedom and Cultural Integrity." Paper presented at the symposium "The Role of the University in a Post-Colonial World," 1975, Duke University Center for International Studies, Durham, NC.

Olu-Wright, R. J. "The Physical Growth of Freetown." In *Freetown: A Symposium*, edited by Christopher Fyfe and Eldred Jones, 24–37. Freetown: Sierra Leone University Press, 1968.

Omosini, Olufemi, and 'Biodun Adediran, eds. *Great Ife: A History of Obafemi Awolowo University, Ile-Ife, 1962–1987*. Ile-Ife, Nigeria: Obafemi Awolowo University Press, 1989.

Osaghae, Eghosa E. *The Crippled Giant: Nigeria after Independence.* Bloomington, IN: Indiana University Press, 1998.

Osasona, Cordelia, Lee O. Ogunshakin, and David A. Jiboye. "Ile-Ife: A Cultural Phenomenon in the Throes of Transformation." In *Proceedings of African Perspectives 2009, The African Inner City: [Re]sourced*, ed. Karel A. Bakker, 147–55. Pretoria: University of Pretoria, 2009.

Osayimwese, Izevbuwa, and Sunday Iyare. "The Economics of Nigerian Federalism: Selected Issues in Economic Management." In "Federalism in Nigeria: Toward Federal Democracy," special issue, *Publius* 21, no. 4, (Autumn 1991): 89–101.

Ostensson, David. *Report on ESBIT for 1954–1971.* Addis Ababa: Ethio-Swedish Institute of Building Technology, 1971.

Pankhurst, Richard. "Menilek and the Utilisation of Foreign Skills in Ethiopia." *Journal of Ethiopian Studies* 5, no. 1 (January 1967): 29–86.

Payne, Alina. *From Ornament to Object: Genealogies of Architectural Modernism.* New Haven, CT: Yale University Press, 2012.

Peffer, John. *Art and the End of Apartheid.* Minneapolis, MN: University of Minnesota Press, 2009.

Pendas, Maria. "Fifty Cents a Foot, 14,500 Buckets: Concrete and the Illusory Shells of Mexican Economy." *Grey Room* 71 (Spring 2018): 14–39.

Penslar, Derek J. *Israel in History: The Jewish State in Comparative Perspective.* London, 2007.

Peters, Joel. *Israel and Africa: The Problematic Friendship.* London: British Academic Press, 1992.

Peterson, John. "The Enlightenment and the Funding of Freetown." In *Freetown: A Symposium*, edited by Christopher Fyfe and Eldred Jones, 9–23. Freetown: Sierra Leone University Press, 1968.

Phokaides, Petros. "Rural Networks and Planned Communities: Doxiadis Associates' Plans for Rural Settlements in Post-Independence Zambia." In "The Modern Village," special issue, *Journal of Architecture* 23, no. 3 (2018): 471–97.

Porter, Arthur T. *Creoledom: A Study of the Development of Freetown Society.* London: Oxford University Press, 1963.

Porter, Doug J. "Scenes from Childhood: The Homesickness of Development Discourse." In *The Power of Development*, edited by Jonathan Crush, 63–86. London and New York: Routledge, 1995.

Prakash, Vikramaditya. "Epilogue: Third World Modernism, or Just Modernism: Toward a Cosmopolitan Reading of Modernism." In *Third World Modernism: Architecture, Development and Identity*, edited by Duanfang Lu, 255–70. New York: Routledge, 2011.

Presner, Todd Samuel. *Muscular Judaism: The Jewish Body and the Politics of Regeneration.* London: Routledge, 2007.

Rampone, Oscar. "Ethiopia Enters the Jet Era." *Ethiopia Mirror* 1, no. 4 (July–Sept. 1962): 6–14.

Rampone, Oscar. "Haile Selassie 1st National Airport." *Ethiopia Mirror* 3, no. 2 (April–June 1964): 6–13.

Randhawa, M. S. "Agricultural Universities in India—Progress and Problems." The Agricultural Division of the National Association of State Universities and Land Grant Colleges, Washington, November 12, 1968. Accessed December 28, 2014. http://pdf.usaid.gov/pdf_docs/PNABJ266.pdf.

Reichman, Shalom. *From an Outpost to a Country of Residence*. Jerusalem: Yad Ben-Zvi, 1979 (in Hebrew).

Roberts, George. *The Anguish of Third World Independence: The Sierra Leone Experience*. Washington, DC: University Press of America, 1982.

Rohan, Timothy M. "Rendering the Surface: Paul Rudolph's Art and Architecture Building at Yale." *Grey Room* 1 (Fall 2000): 84–107.

Roskam, Cole. "Non-Aligned Architecture: China's Designs on and in Ghana and Guinea, 1955–92." *Architectural History* 58 (January 2015): 261–91.

Rössler, Mechtild. "Applied Geography and Area Research in Nazi Society: Central Place Theory and Planning, 1933–1945." *Environment and Planning D: Society and Space* 7 (1989): 419–31.

Rotbard, Sharon. "Wall and Tower: The Mold of Israeli Architecture." In *A Civilian Occupation*, edited by Rafi Segal and Eyal Weizman, 39–56. Tel Aviv: Babel / New York: Verso, 2003.

Rotbard, Sharon. *White City, Black City*. Tel Aviv: Babel, 2005 (in Hebrew).

Rozin, Orit. "'Terms of Disgust': Hygiene and Parenthood of Immigrants from Muslim Countries as Viewed by Veteran Israelis in the 1950s." *Iyunim Bitkumat Yisrael* 12 (2002): 195–238 (in Hebrew).

Sabatino, Michelangelo. "Spaces of Criticism: Exhibitions and the Vernacular in Italian Modernism." *Journal of Architectural Education* (2009): 35–52.

Sabbagh-Khoury, Areej. "Settler Colonialism, the Indigenous Perspective, and the Sociology of Knowledge Production in Israel." *Theory and Criticism* 50 (Winter 2018): 391–418 (in Hebrew).

Schildkrout, Enid. "Inscribing the Body." *Annual Review Anthropology* 33 (2004): 319–44.

Schler, Lynn, and Yonatan N. Gez. "Development Shadows: The Afterlives of Collapsed Development Projects in the Zambia Copper Belt." *Africa Spectrum* 53, no. 3 (December 2018): 3–31.

Schultz, Theodore W. "Investment in Human Capital." *American Economic Review* 51, no. 1 (March 1961): 1–17.

Schwartz, Moshe, and A. Paul Hare. *Foreign Experts and Unsustainable Development: Transferring Israeli Technology to Zambia, Nigeria, and Nepal*. Aldershot, UK: Ashgate, 2000.

Scott, James C. *Seeing like a State: How Certain Schemes to Improve the Human Conditions Have Failed.* New Haven, CT: Yale University Press, 1998.

Segre, D. V. "The Philosophy and Practice of Israel's International Cooperation." In *Israel in the Third World*, edited by Michael Curtis and Susan Aurelia Gitelson, 7–26. New Brunswick, NJ: Transaction Books, 1976.

Shafir, Gershon. *Land, Labor, and the Origins of the Israeli-Palestinian Conflict, 1882–1914.* Cambridge, UK: Cambridge University Press, 1991.

Shapira, Anita. "The Kibbutz and the State." *Iyunim Bitkumat Israel* 20 (2010): 193–207.

Shapira, Elena. "Adolf Loos and the Fashioning of 'the Other': Memory, Fashion, and Interiors." *Interiors* 2, no. 2 (2011): 213–38.

Sharon, Arieh. *Kibbutz + Bauhaus: An Architect's Way in a New Land.* Stuttgart: Kramer Verlag, 1976.

Sharon, Arieh. *Physical Planning in Israel.* Jerusalem: Ministry of Housing, 1952 (in Hebrew).

Sharon, Arieh. "Public Construction in the Country." In *Twenty Years of Building: Settlement, Housing, and the Workers' Institutions*, 115–17. Tel Aviv: General Federation of Jewish Labour in Palestine / Engineers,' Architects' and Surveyors' Union, 1940 (in Hebrew).

Sharon, Smadar. "Importing and Translating the Italian Colonial Model to the Lakhish Region." In *Zionism and Empires*, edited by Yehouda Shenhav, 301–26. Jerusalem: Van Leer Institute Press and Hakibbutz Hameuchad, 2015 (in Hebrew).

Sharon, Smadar. "Not Settlers but Settled: Immigration, Planning and Settlement Patterns in the Lakhish Region in the 1950s." PhD diss., Tel Aviv University, 2012 (in Hebrew).

Sharon, Smadar. "The Planners, the State, and the Planning of National Space." *Theory and Criticism* 29 (Fall 2006): 31–57 (in Hebrew).

Shelemay, Kay Kaufman. *A Song of Longing: An Ethiopian Journey.* 1991. Urbana, IL: University of Illinois, 1994.

Shoked, Noam. "Rabbis, Architects, and the Design of Ultra-Orthodox City-Settlements." In *Social Housing in the Middle East: Architecture, Urban Development, and Transnational Modernity*, edited by Kıvanç Kılınç and Mohammad Gharipour, 241–66. Indiana University Press, 2019.

Sierra Leone Government. *Ten-Year Plan of Economic and Social Development for Sierra Leone 1962/3–1971/2.* Freetown: Government Printer, 1962.

Sisaye, Seleshi. "Swedish Development Aid Policy: A Discussion with Reference to Ethiopia." *Public Administration and Development* 2, no. 2 (1982): 147–67.

*Solel Boneh: A Collection to Note the Founding of the Company.* Jerusalem: Dfus Hapoalim, 1924 (in Hebrew).

Stanek, Łukasz. "Architects from Socialist Countries in Ghana (1957–1967): Modern Architecture and *Mondialisation*." *Journal of the Society of Architectural Historians* 74, no. 4 (December 2015): 416–42.

Stanek, Łukasz. *Architecture in Global Socialism: Eastern Europe, West Africa, and the Middle East in the Cold War.* Princeton, NJ: Princeton University Press, 2020.

Stanek, Łukasz. "Introduction: The Second World's Architecture and Planning in the Third World." In "Cold War Transfer: Architecture and Planning from Socialist Countries in the 'Third World,'" special issue, *Journal of Architecture* 17, no. 3 (2012): 299–307.

Stanislawski, Michael. *For Whom Do I Toil? Judah Leib Gordon and the Crisis of Russian Jewry.* New York: Oxford University Press, 1988.

Sufian, Sandra M. *Healing the Land and the Nation: Malaria and the Zionist Project in Palestine, 1920–1947.* Chicago: University of Chicago Press, 2007.

Svorai, Dan. "'Solel Bone'—An Economical Civil Organization in the Service of and Recruited by the Authorities, during the Transition from Mandate to a Status of a Sovereign State." PhD diss., Tel Aviv University, 2008 (in Hebrew).

Tamir-Tawil, Eran. "To Start a City from Scratch." In *A Civilian Occupation: The Politics of Israeli Architecture*, edited by Rafi Segal and Eyal Weizman, 161–61. Tel Aviv: Babel / New York: Verso, 2003.

Tedros, Michael. "The Department of Architecture." *Zede* (1966): 37–38.

"Thermal Baths: Addis Ababa." *Architectural Design* 135 (October 1965): 522.

Thomas, Helen. "Colonising the Land: Heimat and the Constructed Landscapes of Mexico's Ciudad Universitaria (1943–1953)." In *Transculturation: Cities, Spaces, and Architectures in Latin America*, edited by Felipe Hernández, Mark Millington, and Iain Borden, 109–23. Amsterdam: Rodopi, 2005.

Thompson, Robert Farris. "Yoruba Artistic Criticism." In *The Traditional Artist in African Societies*, edited by Warren L. d'Azevedo, 19–61. Bloomington, IN: Indiana University Press, 1973.

"Three Roads to Tomorrow." 1958. *Colonial Film.* DVD. Accessed October 13, 2014. http://www.colonialfilm.org.uk/node/475.

Tilley, Helen. *Africa as a Living Laboratory: Empire, Development, and the Problem of Scientific Knowledge, 1870–1950.* Chicago: University of Chicago Press, 2011.

Troen, Ilan S. "Higher Education in Israel: An Historical Perspective." *Higher Education* 23, no. 1 (January 1992): 45–63.

Troen, Ilan S. *Imagining Zion: Dreams, Designs, and Realities in a Century of Jewish Settlement.* New Haven, CT: Yale University Press, 2003.

Turner, Paul Venable. *Campus: An American Planning Tradition.* New York: Architectural History Foundation / Cambridge, MA: MIT Press, 1984.

UN Department of Economic and Social Affairs. "Report of the Ad Hoc Group of Experts on Housing and Urban Development." New York: United Nations, February 7–21, 1962.

"University of Nigeria." *Architectural Review* 125, no. 745 (February 1959): 132–36.

UN Technical Assistance Administration. "Metropolitan Lagos: Prepared for the Government of Nigeria." New York: United Nations, Commissioner for Technical Assistance, Department of Economic and Social Affairs, 1964.

Vale, Lawrence J. "Designing Global Harmony: Lewis Mumford and the United Nations Headquarters." In *Lewis Mumford: Public Intellectual,* edited by Thomas P. Hughes and Agatha C. Hughes, 252–82. New York: Oxford University Press, 1990.

Veracini, Lorenzo. "The Other Shift: Settler Colonialism, Israel, and the Occupation." *Journal of Palestine Studies* 42, no. 2 (Winter 2013): 26–42.

Watts, Michael. "'A New Deal in Emotions': Theory and Practice and the Crisis of Development." In *Power of Development,* edited by Jonathan Crush, 44–62. London: Routledge, 1995.

Weitz, Raanan. Interview by Shimeon Amir. *Kidma* 33, 9, no. 1 (1986): 25.

Westad, Odd Arne. *The Global Cold War: Third World Interventions and the Making of Our Times.* New York: Cambridge University Press, 2005.

Wharton, Annabel Jane. *Building the Cold War: Hilton International Hotels and Modern Architecture.* Chicago: University of Chicago, 2001.

Wigley, Mark. *White Walls, Designer Dresses: The Fashioning of Modern Architecture.* Cambridge, MA: MIT Press, 1995.

Williams, Michael W. "Pan-Africanism and Zionism: The Delusion of Comparability." *Journal of Black Studies* 21, no. 3 (1991): 348–71.

Wyse, Akintola. *The Krio of Sierra Leone: An Interpretative History.* London: C. Hurst, 1989.

Yacobi, Haim. "The Architecture of Foreign Policy: Israeli Architects in Africa." *OASE* 82 (2010): 35–54.

Yacobi, Haim. *Israel and Africa: A Genealogy of Moral Geography.* Abingdon, UK: Routledge, 2016.

Yacobi, Haim. "The Moral Geopolitics of Exported Spatial Development: Revisiting Israeli Involvement in Africa." *Geopolitics* 15 (2010): 441–61.

Yacobi, Haim, and Chen Misgav. "The Geo-Biographies of Spatial Knowledge: Regional Planning from Israel to Sierra Leone and Back." *GeoJournal* 84 (2019): 1383–401.

Yacobi, Haim, and Hadas Shadar. "The Arab Village: A Genealogy of (Post) Colonial Imagination." *Journal of Architecture* 19, no. 6 (2014): 975–97.

Yagale, L. R. "Report on Physical Planning Aspects." United Nations Special Fund, Freetown, December 1969.

Young, Crawford. *Ideology and Development in Africa*. New Haven, CT: Yale University Press, 1982.

Zeleza, Paul Tiyambe. "The Historic and Humanistic Agendas of African Nationalism: A Reassessment." In *Power and Nationalism in Modern Africa: Essays in Honor of Don Ohadike*, edited by Toyin Falola and Salah M. Hassan, 37–53. Durham, NC: Carolina Academic Press, 2008.

Zewde, Bahru. *A History of Modern Ethiopia, 1855–1991*. Oxford, UK: James Curry; Athens: Ohio University Press / Addis Ababa: Addis Ababa University Press, 2001.

# index

*Note:* Photoplate images are indicated by page as *p1, p2, p3*, respectively.

AA. *See* Architectural Association School of Architecture
Aalto, Alver, 228n56
Action Group, 99, 109
Adas, Michael, 5
Addis Ababa, 22; architectural education in, 176–86, 256n20; building market in, 173–75; colonialism and, 165–66; construction in, 165–66, 172–75, 178; development aid for, 165–94; Enav and, 165–70, 174, 187–94, 201; Ethiopian modernity in, 186–92; Haile Selassie I University in, 136, 175–80, 187, 259n54; Israeli-Ethiopian relations and, 171–94; Technical College, 170–79; Tedros and, 167–74, 184, 187–94, 201
Adediran, 'Biodun, 98, 110, 241n17
Aderemi, Oba Sir Titus Martins Adesoji Tadeniawo, 109, 115, 163
aesthetics: architectural design, climate, and, 128–35, 145–54; architectural objects and, 17; debate about, 20–23; Israeli-African relations and, 196–202; labor and, 197–202; nativism and, 68–69, 158, 161, 198–99
affective labor, 232n107
Africa: German colonization of, 222n41; independence in, 3, 217; Israeli architecture in, 7–8, 21–23; Soviet Union and, 72, 166, 255n2. *See also specific countries; specific topics*
Africa Hall, Addis Ababa, 175
African elites, 2
African masks, 161–64
African modernity: in Ethiopia, 186–92, 201–2; Western modernity and, 5, 223n62, 224n67
Afro-Asian Training Center, Tel Aviv, 221n29
Agboola, Akintola, 116, 247n117
agricultural projects, 78–79, 215–16, 233n133
agricultural settlement, 21, 74–75, 78–82
agriculture: fertilizer and, 215; *kibbutzim* and, 21, 74–75, 82, 119–24, 136; labor and, 78–79, 200–201, 214–16; in Nigeria, 101–2, 106–7, 114–23, 247n118; rural rebranding and, 116–18; University of Ife and, 118–24, 200–201
Ajayi, J. F. Ade, 93
Ajose, Oladele Adebayo, 115, 128, 138–39, 244n65
Akintola, Samuel Ladoke, 114, 241n17
Akran, C. D., 102
Aldeia Nova, 216
Allais, Lucia, 228n58
All People's Congress, 96
*Altneuland* (Herzl), 12, 222nn40–41

295

American Embassy, Athens, Greece, 227n42
Amharic script, 190, 257n25
Amir, Anda, 157–58
Amole, Bayo, 120
Amuli, Beda Jonathan, 260n76
Angkor Wat temple, Cambodia, 42
Angola, 213–15, 266n45
anthropology, 88, 142–43
anti-Semitism, 131–34
Appadurai, Arjun, 17
appropriation, 35–36, 39, 53–54, 84, 161–63
Arab architecture, 39–40
Arab-Israeli War, 13, 38–39, 75, 233n127
Arab village, 39, 228n50
Architectural Association School of Architecture (AA), 37–39, 184
architectural design: balconies in, 145–50, 153, 252n66; climate and, 128–35, 145–54; color and, 148, 252n56; construction and, 58–66, 71; cultural preservation and, 187–90; environment and, 128–35; human capital and, 128–35; ornamentation and, 127–28, 142–44, 158–61, 208–9; regeneration and, 139–58; of Sierra Leone parliament building, 33–43, 58–66; for University of Ife, 125–64. *See also* tropical architecture
architectural education, 176–86, 256n20
architectural modernism: nativist modernism and, 38–42; performing expertise and, 19–23; regeneration and, 142–47; representation and, 28; revising, 38–39; Sierra Leone parliament building and, 27–28; theater of development and, 15–18; Western modernity and, 19
architectural objects, 17–18
architecture, 17–18; temporality and, 27, 228n54. *See also* British colonial architecture; Israeli architecture; *specific topics*
Argentina, 74
Armstrong, R. L., 58
Ashby Committee, 99, 101–2
Atkinson, J. Robin, 118
Australia, 74
Avni, Dan, 222n40

Awolowo, Obafemi, 103, 113, 240n7, 241n17
Azikiwe, Nnamdi (Zik), 111–13
Aztec towns, 114

balconies, 145–50, 153, 252n66
Bandung Conference, 9, 26, 53, 167, 203
Banton, Michael, 55
Barkatt, Reuven, 56
Bar-On, Hannan, 174
Bar-Yosef, Eitan, 14, 265n30
Bat Yam City Hall building, 148–49
Bayart, Jean-François, 15–18
Beit Alpha, 121
belonging, national, 37–38
Benedict, Ruth, 188
Ben-Gurion, David, 11–12, 187
Berhane, Zewde, 260n76
Bhabha, Homi K., 228n54
biblical abundance, 135–37
Binyanei Ha'Uma (Nation Buildings), Jerusalem, 60–63
Black, Megan, 13–14
Black skin, 157–58, 253n82
Black Star, 46–47, 229n68
Bloch, Ernst, 17, 217, 224nn66–67
Blyden, Edward, 9, 29–30
Bodija Estate, Ibadan, 116–17, 248n123
body, 254n99; environment and, 131–35; human face and, 163–64; human scale and, 192; Jewish, 143–46; skin and, 157–58, 197–202, 253n82; Zionism and, 127–28, 131–34, 145
Bole International Airport, Addis Ababa, 175
border crossings, 12
Brasília, 114
bricoleurs, 71, 84–85, 89
brise-soleil, 142, 147–48, 160, 199, 251n47
British colonial architecture, 20–22, 36; tropical architecture and, 128–35, 200
British colonialism, 2–3, 7, 20–21, 29–35, 39, 72–74, 225n12, 225n17. *See also* colonialism; decolonization
Building Research Station, Garston, England, 128
building's skin: aesthetics and, 197–202; brise-soleil and, 142, 147–48, 160, 199, 251n47; "cultured skin" and, 158–64;

"self-protecting" building and, 139–42, 158
Burma, 7, 46

Cambodia, 42
capitalism, 9–10, 17, 103, 212–15
Capitol building, Liberia, 40
Center for the Study of Rural and Urban Settlements, Rehovot, Israel, 94
central place theory, 76
Cerqueira, José, 215
Césaire, Aimé, 223n59
Chakrabarty, Dipesh, 53–54
Chekhov's gun, 17
Cheng, Anne, 163
Chinese construction companies, 18, 67
Chomette, Henri, 172, 192
Christaller, Walter, 76
Christianity, 29–30, 188
civic pride, 225n17
classicism, 36–37
class solidarity, 55–56
class struggles, 65
climate: architectural design and, 128–35, 145–54; environment and, 108–9, 125–26, 250n30; "self-protecting" building and, 139–42, 158; tropical, 125–36; University of Ife and, 108–9, 125–26
clothing, 130–31, 153, 180
cocoa, 47
Cold War politics, 3, 9–10, 176–77
College of Engineering, Ethiopia, 166, 172, 175–86, 260n76
colonial economy, 47
colonial hierarchies, 2, 4, 30
colonialism: Addis Ababa and, 165–66; African territories and, 73–74; British, 2–3, 20–21, 29–35, 39, 72–74, 225n12, 225n17; development aid and, 2–3, 11–15; education and, 50, 109–10, 116; gender and, 157–58; in Germany, 76, 222n41; internal colonization and, 21, 70–71, 76–77, 236n41; Israeli-African relations and, 8–9, 195–97; knowledge and, 50–53, 84–85; land tenure and, 73–74; manufacturing and, 47, 229n71; race and, 153–58; science and, 13; settler, 4, 11–15, 21–22, 30, 197, 221n36; symbolism and, 36; technology and, 50–53; urbanization and, 72–74; Wesley Girls' Secondary School and, 153–58, 253n81
Colonial Welfare and Development Act (1946), 73
color, 148, 252n56
communism, 9–10
concrete, 40–42, 139, 146–47, 149–50, 160, 182, 188
Congrès Internationaux d'Architecture Moderne (International Congress of Modern Architecture), 28
conquest of labor (kibush ha'avoda), 13–14, 46
"conquest of wasteland" (kibush hashmama), 14
The Conquest of Wasteland exhibition (Kibush HaShmama), 60–63
construction: in Addis Ababa, 165–66, 172–75, 178; architectural design and, 58–66, 71; by Chinese construction companies, 18, 67; "de-skilling" in, 42; of Empire State Building, 51; fast-tracking, 59; in Ghana, 18, 102; Jewish workforce in, 48–49; of Knesset, 38, 60; labor, immigration, and, 48–49, 230n85; labor and, 42, 48–49, 178–81, 192; by Liberia Construction Corporation, 203–4; manual labor and, 50–57, 178; nation building and, 50–52, 57–58, 230n85; in Nigeria, 100–106; postcolonial development and, 46–54; prefabrication and, 20, 51, 59–60, 111, 192, 198–201, 216; private aid and, 213; road building and, 61, 233n141; self-help approach to, 182–83, 202; of Sierra Leone parliament building, 43–67; of Sierra Leone "traditional" houses, 41–42, 228n57; SLNCC and, 51, 58, 60–65, 106; speed, patience, and, 46, 49–50, 62–65; of University of Ife, 99–100; wattle and daub, 228n57
constructive socialism, 10, 56
contractual dependency, 6
Cooper, Frederick, 5, 219n4
Cremona, Rachel, 229n77
criminal anthropology, 142–43
Crush, Jonathan, 129
Cubitt, James, 161, 243n48
Cullather, Nick, 220n7
cultivation of sameness, 50

cultural capital, 117–18
cultural hierarchies, 29–30
cultural preservation, 72, 92–93, 187–90
cultural products, 17
"cultured skin," 158–64
customary law, 73–74, 93

*Daily Mail* (newspaper), 31–32, 49–51, 66, 231nn97–98
data, 87–92
*Davar* (newspaper), 43
decolonization, 5, 11, 30, 196; labor force and, 48; of Nigeria, 98–99; term usage, 220n9
degeneration, 127–34, 142–44
*Degeneration* (Nordau), 127, 142–43
Department of Interior, US, 13–14
Department of International Cooperation (Mashav), 6
Department of Tropical Architecture at the Architectural Association (AA), 130, 165–66, 172–73, 190–92
*Design with Climate* (Olgyay), 132, 134
"de-skilling," 42
"developed world," 3
"developing world," 3, 50–56, 71, 72–73, 84–85
development: discourse, 2–3, 219n4, 220n7; industry, 16, 223n59; of Israel, 4–6; modernization theory and, 5, 195–96; of Nigeria, 98–99; resource mobilization and, 18, 124; of Sierra Leone, 32–33; social welfare and, 18. *See also* postcolonial development; *specific topics*
development aid: for Addis Ababa, 165–94; colonialism and, 2–3, 11–15; education and, 176–86; entrepreneurship and shift to private aid, 210–13; in Ghana, 4–6; "golden age" of Israeli aid, 197–202; humanitarianism and, 210–13, 265n27; IPD and, 70; Israeli-African relations and, 5–15, 84–85; Labor Zionism and, 197–200, 213–17; morality and, 11–12; outliers in, 202–10; performing expertise and, 19–23; politics and, 3, 5–6, 11–13, 210–12; postcolonial development and, 54–55; University of Ife and, 100–106; US and, 9, 13–14, 21

"Development Decade," 3
diaspora, 8–10, 13, 22, 199
Dickson-Thomas, G., 70
Diouf, Mamadou, 18
Dizengoff West Africa, 102, 241n18, 264n1
Dolphin Estate, Lagos, 216
Dome of the Rock mosque, Jerusalem, 40
Dori, Yaacov, 180
Doudai, Aryeh, 20–22, 235n8; Sierra Leone national urbanization plan and, 68–74, 79–96, 239n98, *p4*
Doxiadis, Constantinos, 95
Drew, Jane, 21–22, 111, 118, 125–35, 147, 153–58, 253n81
drilling equipment, 84
Ducor Palace Hotel, Monrovia, 204–5, 209, *p20–p21*
Dukuly, Momolu, 9

Eastern Nigeria Construction and Furniture Company, 103–5, 242n32
Écochard, Michel, 82
economy, 47, 72–73, 103–5
education: architectural, in Addis Ababa, 176–86, 256n20; colonialism and, 50, 109–10, 116; development aid and, 176–86; *kibbutzim* and, 120–24; in Latin America, 113–14; models for, 109–15; in Nigeria, 99, 109–16; science and, 246n108; in US, 115, 121. *See also* University of Ife
Edward, Prince, Duke of Kent, 43, 45
egalitarianism, 55
Egbor, Augustine Akhuemokhan, 240n2
Eisenberg, Dov, 174
Eknor, Ingvar, 181–82
Elizabeth II, Queen, 1–2
Emmanuel (settlement), 209–10
Empire State Building, 51
Enav, Zalman, 22–23, 165–70, 174, 187–94, 201, 210, 256n12, 263n128, 263n134, *p18–p19*
engineering, 53, 82–84; College of Engineering and, 166, 172, 175–86, 260n76
Enlightenment, 28–32, 143, 225n4
entrepreneurship, 103–4, 202–3, 210–13
environment: architectural design and, 128–35; body and, 131–35; climate and, 108–9, 125–26, 250n30; health and, 129–31, 137–39, 250n30; University of

Ife and, 107–9, 121–22, 128–36; Zionism and, 135–39, 199–200
Enwezor, Okwui, 18, 216–17
Enwonwu, Ben, 200
Escobar, Arturo, 220n7
Ethiopia, 255n2; College of Engineering in, 166, 172, 175–86, 260n76; cultural preservation in, 187–90; decolonization of, 11; Filwoha Baths in, 4, 22–23, 190–92, 201, *p19*; *First Five-Year Development Plan* in, 186–87; geopolitics and, 167–70, 192–94; Germany and, 181, 185; governance in, 10; higher education in, 176–86; housing in, 169; Israeli-African relations and, 11, 167–94, 255n7; Italy and, 11; Jews in, 167–69, 188; labor force in, 178–81, 185, 201–2; Labor Zionism in, 179–80; loans in, 258n49; military coup in, 167, 186–87; modernity in, 186–92, 201–2; security-trade-diplomacy complex in, 167–70; slavery and, 178; Solel Boneh in, 173–75, 179, 193, 258n42, 258n48; Sweden and, 177–86, 202; US and, 175, 176, 231n95. *See also* Addis Ababa
Ethiopian Association of Architects and Engineers, 172, 183–84
Ethiopian Ministry of Foreign Affairs, 4, 187–90, 201
Ethiopian University Service, 183, 261n96
Ethio-Swedish Building College, 166, 177–88, 261n87
ethnic favoritism, 93
ethnicity, 30, 91–92, 197–202, 225n4
Europe, 29, 35, 147, 153; urban planning in, 74–75, 236n27
expertise, performing, 19–23
Eyal, Gil, 39

Fallingwater, 40–41
Fanon, Frantz, 52–53, 153, 158
fascism, 28
fast-tracking, 59
feedback mechanism, 85–91
Fenchel, Heinz, 204–9
Ferguson, James, 16, 217, 223n62, 224n67
Filwoha Baths, 4, 22–23, 190–92, 201, *p19*
"Five Year Development Plan" (UN), 219n5
flooding, 60–61
flow maps, 89–92

Fogelvik, Carl Erik H., 182
"folk communities," German, 76
food production, 78
Ford Foundation, 9, 245n90
Foucault, Michel, 94
France, 82, 177, 206
Freetown, 29–35, 73, 92, 96, 227n34, 230n87
Frenkel, Michal, 232nn107–8
Fridan, Moshe, 38
Frobenius, Leo, 254n97
Fry, E. Maxwell, 21–22, 35, 111, 118, 125–35, 147, 153–58, 253n81

Gandhi, Mahatma, 25–26
Gan Shmuel, 74, 250n30
Garvey, Marcus, 9
Gaza Strip, 13
gender, 157–58
geopolitics, 2–4; African territories and, 73–74; Enlightenment colony and, 28–32; Ethiopia and, 167–70, 192–94; Israeli-African relations and, 6, 9–10, 14–15, 79–85; in Nigeria, 99–101; race and, 9, 26, 225n4; urbanization and, 73–78
German colonization, of Africa, 222n41
German "folk communities," 76
Germany, 23, 121, 181, 185; colonialism in, 76, 222n41; Holocaust and, 9–10, 181; Nazi, 144
Ghana, 4–6, 47; construction in, 18, 102; Wesley Girls' Secondary School in, 153–58, 253n81
Gillis, Rivi, 14
Gillit, Bill, 228n46
Giron, Shmuel, 234n2
Givat Ram, 35–36
"golden age" of Israeli aid, 197–202
Greece, 36, 178, 227n42
Green Revolution, 85
Greunspan, Yehoshua, 174
Gropius, Walter, 121, 227n42
Guinea, 18
Gulema, Shimelis Bonsa, 255n1
Gur, Shlomo, 59–60, 233n141

*HaBinyan BaMizrah HaKarov* (journal), 146
Hacohen, David, 7, 46, 215–16

Hadassah Hospital, 233n141
Haganah, 59
Haile Selassie I University, 23, 136, 175–80, 187, 259n54
*halutz* (Zionist pioneer), 55, 57, 139
Hardt, Michael, 232n107
Hare, A. Paul, 84
Harrison, Austen St. Barbe, 36
health, 12–13, 129–31, 137–39, 250n30
heat exchange, 132–35
Hebrew labor, 46, 48–49
Hebrew songs, 231n98
Hebrew University campus in Givat Ram, 106, 233n141
Herbst, Jeffrey, 229n77
Herzl, Theodor, 12, 142, 222nn40–41
Herzog, Hanna, 232nn107–8
Hesselgren, Sven, 182, 261n88
"He tells *me* this" cartoon, 61, 64
Hezekiah Oluwasanmi Library (University of Ife Central Library), 97, 157; design for, 160, 164
higher education: in Ethiopia, 176–86; in Nigeria, 99, 109–16
high modernism, 71, 83–86, 94–95, 137
Hilton hotel: Addis Ababa, 190; Tel Aviv, 204
Himmler, Heinrich, 76
Hinsky, Sarah, 232n124
Histadrut, 2, 7–8, 46–47, 56, 173–74, 219n2, 221n29, 226n24
Hoch, Adolf, 204
Holocaust, 9–10, 181
horizontal expansion logic, 227n44
Hotel Ivoire, Abidjan, 205–9, *p22*
housing: in Angola, 214, 266n45; Bodija Estate, Ibadan, 116–17, 248n123; in Ethiopia, 169; projects, 216; in Sierra Leone, 49, 70; at University of Ife, 98, 117, *p5–p9*; urban planning and, 70
human basic needs, 224n66
human capital, 126, 128–35
humanitarianism, 210–13, 265n27
human scale, 192

Idelson, Benjamin, 119
identity, national, 10, 30–32, 57, 171
Ife, Nigeria, 106–9. *See also* University of Ife
immigration: construction, labor, and, 48–49, 230n85; in Israel, 69; Jews and, 48–49, 77–78, 250n36; population distribution and, 69; settlement patterns and, 76–80, 236n28; Sierra Leone national urbanization plan and, 79; urban planning and, 69
"imperial scientific knowledge," 84–85
Incode, 168, 255n7
independence: in Africa, 3, 217; of Nigeria, 10, 98–103, 156–57; of Sierra Leone, 10, 43, 229n77
India, 36, 145
Indigenous Americans, 13–14
indirect rule, 29
industrialization, 78
infrastructure, 2, 61, 84, 117, 233n141
Institute for Planning and Development (IPD), 68–70, 95–96, 234n2
Institute of African Studies, University of Ife, 118
Interim Town Planning Committee, Sierra Leone, 35, 227n34
internal colonization, 21, 70–71, 76–77, 236n41
International Congress of Modern Architecture (Congrès Internationaux d'Architecture Moderne), 28
International Style, 18, 196
inverted pyramid, 139–42, 148–53, 154
IPD (Institute for Planning and Development), 68–70, 95–96, 234n2
Irgun Zvai Leumi Be'Eretz Yisrael (National Military Organization in the Land of Israel), 169
Israel: Arab-Israeli War and, 13, 38–39, 75, 233n127; Department of International Cooperation in, 6; development of, 4–6; Gaza Strip and, 13; Givat Ram and, 35–36; government facility locations in, 226n30; Hebrew songs and, 231n98; immigration in, 69; infrastructure in, 2; IPD in, 68–70, 95–96, 234n2; Jerusalem, 20, 33–38, 40–41; Lakhish Region settlement project in, 76–82, 92–93; *mamlakhtiut* in, 11–12, 221n34; military and Defense Forces in, 75; national identity of, 10; nation building in, 28; as "postcolonial colony," 25–26; Sierra Leone and, 2, 226n18; sun-shading devices in, 147–48; Tel Aviv, 144, 145–47, 203,

209, 226n24; UN and, 6; urban planning in, 69, 74, 76–78; US and, 14–15, 78, 239n114; West Bank in, 209–10
*Israel and Africa* (Yacobi), 14
Israeli-African relations: Addis Ababa and, 165–94; aesthetics and, 196–202; Cold War politics and, 9–10, 176–77; colonialism and, 8–9, 195–97; contractual dependency in, 6; cooperation in, 4–11; development aid and, 5–15, 84–85; entrepreneurship and, 210–13; Ethiopia and, 11, 167–94, 255n7; as "experiment," 79–85; geopolitics and, 6, 9–10, 14–15, 79–85; "golden age" of, 3; "golden age" of Israeli aid and, 197–202; Hacohen and, 7; Israelis working abroad and, 6, 222n38; Labor Zionism and, 7–15, 22–23; in Nigeria, 10–11, 102–6, 113–14; performing expertise and, 19–23; postcolonial development and, 5, 25–26; repatriation narrative and, 8–9; in Sierra Leone, 10, 25–33, 66–67; Sierra Leone parliament building and, 25–32; Solel Boneh and, 7–8, 12; theater of development and architectural modernism in, 15–18; tourism and, 202–10; trade and, 10, 102, 105, 220n14, 241n19; US and, 6, 9; youth and, 78–79, 231nn98–100
Israeli architecture, 195–96, 223n50; in Africa, 7–8, 21–23; Hacohen and, 7; Klarwein and, 36–37; locality in, 38–40; urban planning and, 14; Zionism and, 15, 19, 21–22, 37, 40
Israeli embassies, 222n40
Israel Military Industries, 7
Israel national master plan, 74–76
Israel Prize in Architecture, 27
Italy, 11, 76–77, 178
*It Is Not Africa Here* (*Kan lo Africa*) (Yacobi), 15
Ivory Coast, 205–10

Jerusalem, 20, 33–38, 40–41
Jewish architects, 41, 224n74
Jewish body, 143–46
Jewish emancipation, 143–44, 153
Jewish settlement, in Palestine, 12–13, 29–30, 46, 74, 224n74, 225n12, 250n36
Jewish workforce, 46, 48–49, 56–57, 179
Jews: anti-Semitism and, 131–34; assimilation of, 29; border crossings and, 12; in Ethiopia, 167–69, 188; Holocaust and, 9; immigration and, 48–49, 77–78, 250n36; Krio and, 30; Moroccan, 77–78, 215; postcolonial development and, 29, 225n4; Settlement Department of the Jewish Agency and, 20, 77. *See also* Labor Zionism
*Journal of the Association of Architects, Engineers, and Town Planning*, 25
Judaism, 143

Kahn, Louis, 42, 160, 171, 227n44
Kandeh, Jimmy D., 229n77
*Kan lo Africa* (*It Is Not Africa Here*) (Yacobi), 15
Karefa-Smart, John, 49
Karmis (Dov and Ram), 20, 22, 106, 197–98; Histadrut Headquarters and, 226n24; Israel Prize in Architecture and, 27; Knesset and, 33, 37, 40; photos of, 33, 45; Sierra Leone parliament building and, 25, 27, 31, 33–45, 66; Solel Boneh and, 33; Wright, F. L. and, 228n55
Kelfa-Caulker, Richard, 32–33
Kemp, Adriana, 12
*Kibbutz + Bauhaus* (Sharon), 135–36, 160–61, 254n90
*kibbutzim* (Zionist agricultural collectives), 21, 74–75, 82, 119–24, 136
kibush ha'avoda (conquest of labor), 13–14, 46
kibush hashmama (conquest of wasteland), 14
"Kibush HaShmama" (*The Conquest of Wasteland* exhibition), 60–63
Kiewiet, Cornelius de, 98
Klarwein, Joseph, 27, 36–37, 59
Klein, Naomi, 212
Knesset, 20, 228n46, 233n141; construction of, 38, 60; influences of, 36, 227n44, 228n56; Karmis and, 33, 37, 40; Klarwein and, 36–37; materials in, 40, 227n42; neoclassicism and, 36; Sierra Leone parliament building and, 27–28, 40–41; sunken library of, 228n56
know-how, 8–9, 18, 85
knowledge: colonialism and, 50–53, 84–85; "imperial scientific knowledge,"

84–85; science and, 50–53, 84–85, 126–27, 238n72
Koenigsberger, Otto, 79–80, 237n50
Kovačević, Zdravko, 172
"kova tembel," 55
Kozlovsky, Roy, 230n85
Krio (creole), 29–30, 55–56, 198–99, 225n6, 225n9, 227n34; British colonialism and, 30, 73, 225n12

labor: aesthetics and, 197–202; affective, 232n107; agricultural, 78–79, 200–201, 214–16; conquest of, 13–14, 46; construction and, 42, 48–49, 178–81, 192; by foreigners, 178; Hebrew, 46, 48–49; identity and, 57; immigration, construction, and, 48–49, 230n85; productivity and, 56–58, 78, 232n107, 232n124; race and, 54–55; strikes, 231n100; trade and, 47
labor force: decolonization and, 48; in Ethiopia, 178–81, 185, 201–2; Jewish, 46, 48–49, 56–57, 179; job creation and, 123; manual labor and, 50–57, 178; manufacturing and, 48–49; nation building and, 46–58, 197–202; in Sierra Leone, 229n76; Sierra Leone parliament building and, 26–27, 65–67; of Solel Boneh, 55, 58–59, 65–66; stereotypes of, 51–55; technology and, 50–53, 65; trade unions and, 10, 55–56; training and, 47–50
Labor Party (Mapai), 43, 84–85
Labor Zionism, 20; agricultural settlement and, 74–75, 78–82; constructive socialism of, 10; development aid and, 197–200, 213–17; in Ethiopia, 179–80; Histadrut and, 7–8, 219n2; human material and, 126–28; ideology of, 55–59, 126–28, 250n36; Israeli-African relations and, 7–15, 22–23; "pioneering" in, 11–14, 74–76; regeneration and, 145–46, 153; in Sierra Leone, 26–27; trade unions and, 10, 56; urban planning and, 74–75, 200
Lagos, 109–10
Lakhish: Lakhish Region settlement project, 76–82, 92–93; Sierra Leone national urbanization plan and, 71, 76–82, 92–93, 238n97
Lamptey, G. Odartey, 5–6

land: grants, 21, 112–15; rights, 225n7; tenure, 73–74, 93, 113, 245n89
Land Grant University, 21, 100, 111–15, 118
"land of milk and honey," 135–36
Larkin, Brian, 50, 230n84
laterite, 41–42, 51, 197, 199, 228n58
Latin America, 113–14, 147–48, 159–60
Lavon, Pinhas, 56
law, customary, 73–74, 93
Le Corbusier, 42, 142, 228n56, 251n47
Leitersdorf, Tommy, 206, 209–10, 239n115
Lemma, Menasse, 174
Lévi-Strauss, Claude, 71, 84, 87, 89
liberalism, European, 29
liberated slaves, 10, 29–30
Liberia, 9, 30, 40, 205
Liberia Construction Corporation, 203–4
Lightfoot Boston, Henry Josiah, 65–66
Lindahl, J. Bernhard, 182
loans: in Ethiopia, 258n49; in Ghana, 6; land grants and, 112–13; in Nigeria, 103–5, 240n11; for Sierra Leone parliament building, 33, 48, 63, 226n22
Lombroso, Cesare, 142
Loos, Adolf, 142–43, 163, 251n49, 252n55
Lorch, Netanel, 222n40
louvers, 147–48
Lutyens, Edwin Landseer, 36, 145

Mabogunje, Akin L., 236n35
malaria, 12–13, 137–38
*mamlakhtiut*, 11–12, 221n34
Mansfeld, Alfred, 105–6, 243n48
manual labor, 50–57, 178. See also construction
manufacturing, 47–48, 229n71
Mapai (Labor Party), 84–85
Margai, Milton, 45
Marmorek, Alexander, 222n41
Martello tower, Freetown, 36
Mashav (Department of International Cooperation), 69, 231n100
masonry, 178
Massad, Joseph, 25
master plan, 70–74, 82, 86–87, 106, 240n2
materials: concrete, 42, 139, 146–47, 149–50, 160, 182, 188; in Jerusalem, 41; in Knesset, 40, 227n42; laterite, 41–42, 51, 197, 199, 228n58; in Sierra Leone, 40–41, 228n57; in Sierra Leone parliament building, 41–43, 51

Mayer brothers, 23, 202–10
Mbembe, Achille, 224n66
Mboya, Tom, 4–5
Mead, Margaret, 88
Meir, Golda, 6, 9, 33, 136–37, 226n21
Mellanby, Kenneth, 111
Meltzer, Zvi, 1–2, 25, 41–45, 57, 106
Menelik II (Emperor), 178, 257n25
Meridor, Yaacov, 255n7
"metis," 71, 83–84
Mexico, 113–14, 159–60, 254n90
Meyer, Hannes, 121, 135
Mezzedimi, Arturo, 172, 175
military, 7, 75, 174–75, 193; coup, 96, 99, 167, 186–87; tourism and, 202–3; Zionist, 59, 169
Mitchell, J. C., 48
mobility, 18
modernism. *See* architectural modernism
modernity, Ethiopian, 186–92, 201–2
modernization theory: agricultural labor and, 78–79; development and, 5, 195–96; high modernism and, 71, 83–86, 94–95, 137; postcolonialism and, 17–18; on urbanization, 72, 92–96
Monuments and Relics Commission, Sierra Leone, 36
morality, 11–12, 211
Moroccan Jews, 77–78, 215
Mufti, Aamir, 225n4
Mumford, Lewis, 224n3
Muriel, Shlomo, 203
muscular Judaism, 143
Muslims, 10, 11, 57, 226n18
mythical thinking, 84

Nahal, 78–79, 233n132
Nahum, Gabi, 214–15
Nasser, Gamal Abdel, 11, 168
National Autonomous University of Mexico, 159–60
national belonging, 37–43
national identity, 10, 30–32, 57, 171
National Military Organization in the Land of Israel (Irgun Zvai Leumi Be'Eretz Yisrael), 169
nation building: construction and, 50–52, 57–58, 230n85; in Israel, 28; labor force and, 46–58, 197–202; national becoming and, 197–202; regions and, 91–94; representation and, 28–32; in Sierra Leone, 28–29, 91–94
Nation Buildings (Binyanei Ha'Uma), 60–63
nativism, 68–69, 158, 161, 198–99
nativist modernism, 38–42
naturalization, 12
Nazi Germany, 144
Ne'eman, Yuval, 75
Nehru, Jawaharlal, 53
neoclassicism, 28, 32, 36
neocolonialism, 2, 48
neoliberalism, 214–16
Neumann, Boaz, 127
"new monumentality," 28
new towns, 21, 28, 75–76, 85–86
Niemann, Bernard J., 133
Nigeria, 234n2; agriculture in, 101–2, 106–7, 114–23, 247n118; civil war in, 10, 247n109; construction in, 100–106; decolonization of, 98–99; development of, 98–99; economy in, 103–5; education in, 99, 109–16; geopolitics in, 99–101; governance in, 10–11; independence of, 10, 98–103, 156–57; infrastructure in, 117; Israeli-African relations in, 10–11, 102–6, 113–14; loans in, 103–5, 240n11; military coup in, 99; Muslims in, 10, 226n18; politics in, 99–106; US and, 112–15, 134–35, 153, 247n109. *See also* University of Ife
*Nigerian Daily Sketch* (newspaper), 116–17
Nigersol, 100–106, 242n36, 242n43
Nitzan-Shiftan, Alona, 38, 144, 146–47
Nkrumah, Kwame, 9
Non-Aligned Movement, 3
Nordau, Max, 127, 142–43
Nye, David, 51
Nyerere, Julius, 53

Obafemi Awolowo University. *See* University of Ife
Oduduwa Hall, 118, 120, 160–64, *p17*
Oelsner, Ursula, 70, 89–91, 235n8, *p4*
O'Gorman, Juan, 160
oil, 115, 124
Okotie-Eboh, Festus Samuel, 105
Olgyay, Victor, 132, 134–35
Oluwasanmi, Hezekiah, 116–17, 123–26, 241n17
Omosini, Olufemi, 98, 110

Onabamiro, Sanya Dojo, 102, 107, 241n17
Opa Oranmiyan, 158–59, 253n84
Order of the Queen of Sheba, 188
Organization of African Unity, 187–88
Orientalism, 129–30, 134
"Ornament and Crime" (Loos), 142–43
ornamentation, 127–28, 142–44, 158–61, 208–9
Overseas and Harbour Works, 221n25
Oxbridge, 111–12

Padmore, George, 9
Palestine: Jewish settlement in, 12–13, 29–30, 46, 74, 224n74, 225n12, 250n36; Partition Plan for, 75; riots in, 250n36; Settlement Department of the Jewish Agency and, 20, 77; urban planning of, 74; Zionism, environment, and, 135–39
Palestinian refugees, 75
Palestinian vernacular, 39–40
Pan-African movement intellectuals, 8–9, 29–30
paramount chiefs, 21, 69, 93
Partition Plan for Palestine, 75
*Patterns of Culture* (Benedict), 188
Pearl, D. F., 48, 62
Pereira, William, 206
performing expertise, 19–23
Peter, Yehuda, 183
Peters, Joel, 222n38
philanthropy, 6, 225n17
Philip, Prince, 1
physics, 143
pilgrimage, 69
"pioneering," 4, 11–15, 27, 74–76, 211
Point Four aid program, 13–14, 171, 231n95
policy making, 89–91
political tourism, 184, 262n102
politics: Cold War, 3; development aid and, 3, 5–6, 11–13, 210–12; entrepreneurship and, 210–12; ethnic favoritism and, 93; land tenure and, 93; *mamlakhtiut* and, 11–12, 221n34; in Nigeria, 99–106; settlement patterns and, 77–78; in Sierra Leone, 28–33, 62–67, 93–96; tourism and, 203–5; University of Ife and, 99–106; urbanization and, 72–73, 93–96. *See also* geopolitics
Polónyi, Charles, 249n9
population distribution: immigration and, 69; settlement patterns, urban planning, and, 73–76; Sierra Leone national urbanization plan and, 69–79, 91–96
population movement, 88–91
"Population Movements" (Doudai and Oelsner), 89, 90
Portugal, 213
Posener, Julius, 144–45, 252n58
"postcolonial colony," 25–26
postcolonial development, 213–17; construction and, 46–54; development aid and, 54–55; engineering and, 53; Enlightenment colony and, 28–32; of Freetown, 29–32; Israeli-African relations and, 5, 25–26; Jews and, 29, 225n4; trade and, 46–47; urbanization and, 72–74
postcolonialism, 2, 17–18
postcolonial leaders, 52–54
postwar international order, 28–30
pragmatic socialism, 103
Prakash, Vikramaditya, 19
prefabrication, 20, 51, 59–60, 111, 192, 198–201, 216
Premier Hotel, Ibadan, 208–9
"primitives," 142–43
Prince, Neal, p20–p21
private interests, 22–23, 65, 173–75; entrepreneurship and, 210–13
productivity: labor and, 56–58, 78, 232n107, 232n124; resource mobilization and, 134–35; Sierra Leone parliament building and, 57–58
"Province of Freedom," 29

race: Black skin and, 157–58, 253n82; colonialism and, 153–58; "cultured skin" and, 158–64; degeneration and, 128–34; Enlightenment and, 225n4; geopolitics and, 9, 26, 225n4; labor and, 54–55; Zionism and, 156–58
racial discrimination, 171, 173
racial oppression, 8–9
racial segregation, 35
Rahman, Abdul Fattah, 226n18
Ratner, Yohanan, 59
refugees, 75, 78
regeneration: architectural modernism and, 142–47; University of Ife and architecture of, 139–58; Zionism and, 142–46, 153

"Regional Pattern" (Doudai and Oelsner), 89, 91
regions, 71, 91–94
"Rehovot Approach," 94
religion, 135–37, 188, 225n4. *See also specific religions*
René Larémont, Ricardo, 229n77
repatriation, 8–9
representation, 18, 28–32, 50, 95, 154–59
resource management, 134–35
resource mobilization, 18, 124, 134–35
Reynolds (firm), 175, 258n45
road building, 61, 233n141
Roberts, George, 54
Rockefeller Foundation, 9, 245n90
"rootedness," 72–79
Roskam, Cole, 18
Rosoff, Shmuel, 105, 208
Rostow, Walt Whitman, 85
Rotbard, Sharon, 232n124
Rothschild, Baron de, 236n28
Rubin, Harold, 118, 149–50, 159–60
Rubinow, Isaac M., 139
rural rebranding, 116–18
rural-urban migration, 100–101, 116–22

"Sabra" architects, 39
Said, Edward, 129–30
Schreiber, Eliezer, 148–53, *p5*
Schwartz, Moshe, 84
science: colonialism and, 13; education and, 246n108; knowledge and, 50–53, 84–85, 126–27, 238n72; physics and, 143; social, 88
Scott, James, 71, 83–84, 137, 238n72
screens, 147, 169–70
sculptural objects, 159–64
Section for Technical Cooperation, 6
security-trade-diplomacy complex, 167–70
*Seeing Like a State* (Scott), 83–84
Selassie, Haile, 23, 166–68, 173–74, 177, 186–87, 201, 256n18
self-help approach, 182–85, 202
"self-protecting" building, 139–42, 158
separatism, 30
Sert, José Luis, 113
Settlement Department of the Jewish Agency, 20, 77
settlement patterns: immigration and, 76–80, 236n28; in Lakhish Region settlement project, 76–82, 92–93; politics and, 77–78; urban planning and, 73–83
settler colonialism, 4, 11–15, 21–22, 30, 197, 221n36. *See also* Labor Zionism
settler primitivism, 39
Shalom Meir Tower, 209
Shalom Shelemay Apartment building, 169–70, *p18*
Sharett, Moshe, 7
Sharon, Arieh, 20–22, 250n30; balconies and, 146–47; "cultured skin" and, 159–64; Israel national master plan and, 74–76; *Kibbutz + Bauhaus* by, 135–36, 160–61, 254n90; *kibbutzim* and, 119–22, 136; tropical architecture and, 128–29, 135–39; University of Ife and, 106–9, 112–22, 127–29, 135–42, 146–64, 243nn55–56, *p5*, *p9*, *p11*; urban planning by, 74–76, 85–86, 238n97
Sharon, Ariel, 193, 264n135
Sharp, Granville, 28–29
Shelemay, Shalom, 169–70
Shenhav, Yehouda, 232nn107–8
shipping, 46–47
Sierra Leone: All People's Congress in, 96; Black Star and, 229n68; civil war in, 66, 96; development of, 32–33; Enlightenment and, 28–29, 225n4; from Enlightenment colony to nation-state, 28–32; *Five-Year Plan of Economic and Social Development* in, 70; governance in, 10, 229n77; housing in, 49, 70; independence of, 10, 43, 229n77; indirect rule in, 29; Israel and, 2, 226n18; Israeli-African relations in, 10, 25–33, 66–67; Jerusalem and, 33; Krio and, 29–30, 55–56, 73, 198–99, 225n6, 225n9, 227n34; labor force in, 229n76; Labor Zionism in, 26–27; manufacturing in, 47–48; materials in, 40–41, 228n57; military coup in, 96; national identity of, 30–32; nation building in, 28–29, 91–94; paramount chiefs, 21, 69, 93; politics in, 28–33, 62–67, 93–96; separatism in, 30; Sierra Leone People's Party, 30–32; slavery and, 10, 29–30; Solel Boneh and, 229n68; taxes in, 72–73, 229n77, 230n87; *Ten-Year Plan of Economic and Social Development* in, 70; tourism in, 203; "traditional" houses in, 41–42, 228n57

Sierra Leone Company, 29
*Sierra Leone Interim Town Planning Committee Report*, 227n34
Sierra Leone National Construction Company (SLNCC), 51, 58, 60–65, 106
*Sierra Leone National Urbanisation Plan* (Doudai and Oelsner), 68–69
Sierra Leone national urbanization plan, 4, 20–21; agricultural projects and, 79; data and, 87–92; Doudai and, 68–74, 79–96, 239n98, *p4*; experimentation and, 79–85; as feedback mechanism, 85–91; immigration and, 79; IPD and, 68–70, 95–96; for Lakhish regions, 71, 76–82, 92–93, 238n97; nativism and, 68–69; Oelsner and, 70, 89–91, *p4*; politics and, 93–96; population distribution and, 69–79, 91–96; population movement and, 88–91; postscript on, 94–96; regions and, 71, 91–94; rhetorical structure of, 71; "rootedness" and, 72–79; surveying for, 70, 80–81
Sierra Leone parliament building, 1–2, 4, 20; architectural design of, 33–43, 58–66; architectural modernism and, 27–28; assembly hall, interior of, 43–44; building, without a plan, 58–66; completion of, 66–67; construction of, 43–67; cost of, 33, 61–63, 226n22; *Daily Mail* coverage of, 31–32, 49–51, 66; Fallingwater and, 40–41; as "growing from the ground," 32–43; Israeli-African relations and, 25–32; Karmis and, 25, 27, 31, 33–45, 66; Knesset and, 27–28, 40–41; labor force and, 26–27, 65–67; loans for, 33, 48, 63, 226n22; materials in, 41–43, 51; Meltzer and, 25, 41–45, 57; nativity and, 41–42; Palestinian vernacular and, 39–40; photos of, 26, 31, 41, 44–45, 62–64, *p1, p2, p3*; politics and, 28–33, 62–67; productivity and, 57–58; representation and, 28–32; Solel Boneh and, 27, 33, 43–51, 55–67; symbolism of, 27–28, 51; three phases of, 46; Tower Hill site and surveying for, 33–40
Simonovitch, Simon, 203, 264n5
Sirkin, S., 83
skin, human, 157–58, 197–202, 253n82
slavery, 10, 29–30, 178

SLNCC (Sierra Leone National Construction Company), 51, 58, 60–65, 106
social capital, 126–27
socialism, 10, 76, 103, 214–15
social science, 88
social welfare, 18
Solel Boneh, 2, 18, 22, 96, 198, 242n47; criticism of, 58–59; in Ethiopia, 173–75, 179, 193, 258n42, 258n48; governance of, 33; "He tells *me* this" cartoon by, 61, 64; Histadrut and, 7–8, 46, 173–74; Israeli-African relations and, 7–8, 12; Jewish workforce and, 46; Karmis and, 33; labor force of, 55, 58–59, 65–66; manager work relations and, 231n100; Nigersol and, 100–106, 242n36, 242n43; operation and success of, 48; promotional films for, 231n100; Sierra Leone and, 229n68; Sierra Leone parliament building and, 27, 33, 43–51, 55–67; "The specification never leaves the manager's desk!" cartoon by, 61, 64; subdivisions of, 8; "supervision" cartoon and, 8; University of Ife and, 99–106, 240n2; urban planning and, 69
Soviet Union, 9, 72, 166, 255n2
"The specification never leaves the manager's desk!" cartoon, 61, 64
Spira, Ephraim, 179–80
Spitz, Amos, 26, 140, 150–51, 161, 208
Spitz, Mordechai, 33
Stanek, Łukasz, 18
stereotypes, 51–55
Stevens, Siaka, 96
Štraus, Ivan, 172
structuralism, 227n44
Suez Crisis, 8
sun-shading devices: balconies and, 145–50, 153, 252n66; brise-soleil, 142, 147–48, 160, 199, 251n47; in Israel, 147–48; louvers, 147–48; screens and, 147, 169–70; verandas, 147–48, 253n76
"supervision" cartoon, 8
surveying: for Sierra Leone national urbanization plan, 70, 80–81; for Sierra Leone parliament building, 33–40; University of Ife site selection and, 98, 106–9
Sweden, 23, 177–86, 202
symbolism, 145, 163–64; colonial, 36;

national identity and, 30–32; of Sierra Leone parliament building, 27–28, 51

Tahal Group, 213
Tanzania, 193–94
taxes, 49, 72–73, 229n77, 230n87
Taylor Woodrow, 2
Team X, 38–39
Technical College, Addis Ababa, 170–79
Technion, 179–81; design for, 106
technology, 2, 50–53, 65, 84
Tedros, Michael, 22–23, 167–74, 184, 187–94, 201, 257n21, *p18–p19*
Teferra, Alemayehu, 260n76
Tel Aviv, 144, 145–47, 203, 209, 226n24
Tel Aviv Engineering Club, 82–83
temporality, 27, 68–69, 216–17, 228n54
Tennessee Valley Authority, 86
Tettegah, John, 4
theater of development, 4, 142, 177; architectural modernism and, 15–18; term usage, 16, 223n59
Tishler, William H., 133
"to build and be built," 46, 81–82, 164
totalitarianism, 28
tourism, 202–10, 265n22; political, 184, 262n102
Tower and Stockade operation, 59–60, 75, 78
Tower Hill, 33–40, 226n27
trade: in Ethiopia, 167–70; Israeli-African relations and, 10, 102, 105, 220n14, 241n19; labor and, 47; manufacturing and, 47–48; postcolonial development and, 46–47; unions, 10, 55–56
training, 47–50
transportation, 61, 117
tropical abundance, 135–37
tropical architecture, 165–66; architectural design and, 126–37, 142; British colonial architecture and, 128–35, 200; Department of Tropical Architecture at the Architectural Association (AA), 130, 165–66, 172–73, 190–92; Enav and, 172–73; Sharon and, 128–29, 135–39
*Tropical Architecture in the Humid Zone* (Fry and Drew), 129–35, 153–58, 253n81
tropical climate, 125–36
"tropical people," 130
"tropical Zionism," 135–39, 199–200

Tubman, William, 203
"turn to locality," 38–41
Tzur, A., 104
Tzur, Dan, 136

United Nations (UN), 6, 70, 219n5, 224n3; Economic Commission for Africa, 165
United States (US): American Embassy, Athens, Greece, 227n42; Department of Interior, 13–14; development aid and, 9, 13–14, 21; education in, 115, 121; Ethiopia and, 175, 176, 231n95; Ford Foundation and, 9, 245n90; Indigenous Americans and, 13–14; Israel and, 14–15, 78, 239n114; Israeli-African relations and, 6, 9; modernization theory and, 5; Nigeria and, 112–15, 134–35, 153, 247n109; Point Four aid program and, 13–14, 171, 231n95; Rockefeller Foundation and, 9, 245n90; settler colonialism and, 13–14; tourism and, 203
United States Agency for International Development (USAID), 113, 122, 134
University College Ibadan, 21–22, 98, 101, 109–15
University of Ife (Obafemi Awolowo University), 4, 21–22; agriculture and, 118–24, 200–201; architectural design for, 125–64; campus plan for, 118–22; climate and, 108–9, 125–36; coda, 158–64; construction of, 99–100; development aid and, 100–106; environment and, 107–9, 121–22, 128–36; faculty buildings at, 149–52, 154, 159, *p10–p16*; goal of, 98; housing at, 98, 117, *p5–p9*; humanities buildings at, 139–42, 148–50, 154, 159; impressions of, 97–98; *kibbutzim* and, 119–24, 136; land grant and, 112–15; model for, 109–15; Oduduwa Hall, 118, 120, 160–64, *p17*; planning, 97–124; politics and, 99–106; population of, 112; postscript on, 122–24; regeneration and, 139–58; rural rebranding and, 116–18; rural-urban migration and, 100–101, 118–22; Sharon and, 106–9, 112–22, 127–29, 135–42, 146–64, 243nn55–56, *p5, p9, p11*; site selection and surveying, 98, 106–9; Solel Boneh and, 99–106, 240n2; tropical climate, 125–36; Zionism and, 135–39, 199–200
University of Wisconsin, 134–35, 149, 153

INDEX     307

"Urban Framework" (Doudai and Oelsner), 89, 91, *p4*
urbanization, 69; agricultural settlement and, 74–75, 78–82; colonialism and, 72–74; cultural preservation and, 72, 92–93; economy and, 72–73; geopolitics and, 73–78; modernization theory on, 72, 92–96; politics and, 72–73, 93–96; postcolonial development and, 72–74; rural-urban migration and, 100–101, 116–22
urban planning: data and, 87–92; "developing world" and, 72–73; European, 74–75, 236n27; flow maps and, 89–92; in France, 82; in Freetown, 35, 92; of German "folk" communities, 76; housing and, 70; immigration and, 69; in Israel, 69, 74, 76–78; Israeli architecture and, 14; *kibbutzim* and, 21, 74–75, 82, 119–22; Labor Zionism and, 74–75, 200; in Lakhish Region settlement project, 76–82, 92–93; "pioneering" and, 74–76; policy making and, 89–91; settlement patterns and, 73–83; by Sharon, Arieh, 20–22, 74–76, 85–86, 238n97; in Sierra Leone national urbanization plan, 68–96; Solel Boneh and, 69; transportation and, 117; UN and, 70; Western, 86–88; in Zambia, 95
USAID (United States Agency for International Development), 113, 122, 134

van Eyck, Aldo, 227n44
Veracini, Lorenzo, 221n36
verandas, 147–48, 253n76
Viipuri Library, 228n56
villagization, 95, 117
visualization techniques, 89
Volkish movement, 76

Warburg, Otto, 222n41
wattle and daub construction, 228n57
weathering stone, 42
Weitz, Raanan, 76–78, 80–82, 94, 236n41, 237n64

Weitz, Yosef, 78
wells, 84
Wesley Girls' Secondary School, Cape Coast, 153–58, 253n81
Westad, Odd Arne, 14
Western modernity, 5, 19, 223n62, 224n67
Western urban planning, 86–88
Wollamo Soddo, 184
Woodrow-Taylor, 48
working class, 55–56
World Bank, 100, 184, 193, 263n133
*The Wretched of the Earth* (Fanon), 52–53
Wright, Frank Lloyd, 40–41, 228n55
Wright, Reuben Johnson Oluwole, 70
Wright, Richard, 53
Wright, Stephen, 190

Yacobi, Haim, 14–15, 264n135
Yahalom, Lipa, 136
Yavetz, Zvi, 187
Yavor, Hannan, 243nn48–49
Yemen, 22, 256n15; Yemenite Jews, 49
Yoruba, 158–64, 253n84, 254n97
Young, Crawford, 103
youth, rural, 78–79, 231nn98–100

Zambia, 84, 95
*Zede* journal, 172, 188, 263n128
Zim shipping company, 46–47, 205, 229n68
Zionism, 7–8; birth of, 12–13; body and, 127–28, 131–34, 145; degeneration and, 142–44; environment and, 135–39, 199–200; Israeli architecture and, 15, 19, 21–22, 37, 40; race and, 156–58; regeneration and, 142–46, 153; settler colonialism and, 12–15, 21–22, 30, 221n36; University of Ife and, 135–39, 199–200. *See also* Labor Zionism
Zionist agricultural collectives (*kibbutzim*), 21, 74–75, 82, 119–22, 136
Zionist Congress, 60
Zionist new man, 13
Zionist pioneer (*halutz*), 55, 57, 139

www.ingramcontent.com/pod-product-compliance
Lightning Source LLC
Chambersburg PA
CBHW080838290525
27270CB00020B/319